BUILDING MEMORIES

THE RENTERIA GUTIEREZ FAMILY

ISBN
978-1-960861-37-5 (Paperback)
978-1-960861-38-2 (eBook)

BUILDING MEMORIES

Prologue

The following is a history of my family and me, Salvador Renteria Gutierrez. It is a historical account written from personal knowledge. The information in this historical account is taken from stories that I heard while growing up on a farm near the town of Fabens, Texas but also while I lived in Fabens, Texas as an adolescent.

The remainder of the history transpired while living in Horizon City, Texas. The history is presented in biographical form.

My father's and mother's migration to the United States started when my father signed up for the "bracero" program which was a U.S. government sponsored program designed to recruit farm workers from Mexico to work in the United States. This memoir features various written articles that described the hard life that those farms workers experienced while in the United States. By means of these articles, I was able to trace my father's footsteps as he was processed at the migrant facilities operated by the United States.

My life started when I lived as a child with my family in the original adobe/stucco building on the Ryan farm adjacent to the railroad tracks. Today, the cotton farm that used to belong to the Ryan family is still there although it is now a pecan nut farm and is owned by other people. A sign near one of the entrances to the farm shows the words "Oro Farm Inc." I dug into the web to find the name of the owner of the farm and I found that the farm belongs to a person by the name of Javier Santos.

My first spoken language was Spanish. I didn't start to learn English until I was 6 years old when I entered school in Fabens, Texas in 1957.

The adobe/stucco building where we lived is no longer present. However, even today, when I happen to be driving down Texas State Highway 20 near where that adobe/stucco building used to stand, I'll glance toward the location where the building used to stand years ago in the 1950s and smile. That building structure is well ingrained in my mind with good memories of my family.

The location where Beto Muñoz and his family used to live is also dear and near to me. Beto and his family lived about a mile to the east toward the small town of Tornillo. His family was related to my family by way of a family relationship between his mother and my father sharing the Renteria surname. I still remember Beto as a young boy. I spoke with him on the phone sometime in 2018 and we relived the old times when we both lived on the respective farms. He was 83 years old and I was 67 years old at the time when we first made contact with each other again.

The small town of Fabens, Texas was central in my upbringing. Fabens was the subject of a 1969 sociological study developed by the Sociology Department of Notre Dame. The results of that study were again reviewed in the year 2008 by Dr. R.R. Verdugo. The study established a link between socio-economic dependency and the education system. Parity is the state or condition of being equal, especially regarding social status and economic condition. The subject of parity is important to me because I came from that educational school system.

Today, Mexican Americans represent 82 percent of the population in the El Paso area. I recently spoke with Lorenzo Renteria who is an uncle of mine. He works in the construction industry. For many years he lived and worked in the local El Paso area and worked as a concrete worker. He recently moved away to gain employment in Carlsbad, New Mexico; again working as a concrete worker. He now earns double the wage that he was earning in the local El Paso area doing the same type of work. Based on that fact, there is still work to be done in enabling true economic success in the local area.

A review of the Fabens High School yearbooks shows that a very small minority of teachers in the school district were of Hispanic descent in the 1960s. This leads to the realization that few Hispanics were pursuing college degrees in those days. In comparison, today's representation of teachers in the yearbooks shows that a majority of Hispanics now have college degrees.

This memoir presents my life experiences starting from the days when I lived as a child in the adobe/stucco building adjacent to the railroad tracks along what was known as highway 80 to today when I am nearing 70 years of age living in Horizon City, Texas.

A Memoir to Preserve the Past

A memoir is simply a document written to preserve important events of the past. It is an informational resource. This specific memoir provides a glimpse of my ancestors' history as well as my own history. It describes the origins and the life of my father. The initial part of this memoir describes the important events that led to the formation of my family while the latter part is a biographical account of my past.

The Importance of the Family History

The origin of our ancestors is important. The history of my family is important as well. All of my children and especially my grandchildren should know where they came from. It is important that they know the history so that in their future years, they too can add their history to the rich history of their ancestors.

The Most Important Persons

I originated from the Renteria Gutierrez family. The most important persons in my family were my parents. My father was my mentor during my life. My mother provided the foundation that enabled my development.

I am now a mature man and still remember the lessons my parents taught me. My father taught me by example to persevere even in the most difficult of circumstances. My mother took great care to teach me right from wrong. I will always love and respect them.

All in all, I see my father as a builder of monuments in relation to my family. My father was not an educated man; he was a working man. He was a man that commanded respect. Placed among equals, he would eventually assume the lead role. The men he supervised, which will be described later in this memoir, looked to him for direction. When I was growing up, from time to time, people would comment that I looked like my father. Looking like my father was a positive attribute to me. I see him as the man that formed and shaped me into becoming the complete person that I am now.

I see my mother as a builder of memories. She remained in the background while my father took the lead; at the same time lending support to my father. The nurturing that she provided enabled a development of an inner confidence in me. I grew to be very close to my mother. She provided the refuge that I many times needed. In the end, she is the person that I gravitated to for warmth and comfort.

Pivotal Events in Our History

There were pivotal events that occurred which pointed me toward specific directions. These pivotal events are part of our family's vibrant history. I have this history of my family to share. I have written this memoir so that my children and grandchildren can appreciate the rich traditions of my family. In conclusion, this memoir is a history of my family and how we came to be.

The Origins of the Renteria and Gutierrez Surnames

The Renteria surname is documented in an internet document titled *"Some Renteria History and Coat of Arms"*. It was authored by Joseph Renteria on August 20, 2004; there is no relation between Joseph and our family except for the Renteria name. The internet document can be found using the following link: http://www.genealogy.com/forum/surnames/topics/renteria/148/

The following is an excerpt taken from that document:

> *"The Renteria family of Spain and Portugal originated in the villa of Bermeo in Vizcaya and later branches of the family were established in Baqui, Ajanguiz, Guernica, Ondarroa and in Aldeola. The Renteria warriors were members of the hidalgo (the noble warrior class of Spain and Portugal) and don Francisco RamÓn [sic] de la Renteria was named Procurador General of the Señorio of Vizcaya on 9 March, 1582 A.D. by the King of Spain and by the Basque lords assembled.*

> *For valor in combat against the enemies of Spain, the Renteria warriors were elevated to the military knighthoods. Don José Manuel do la Renteria, don Carlos Miguel de Renteria and don Felipe Juan do la Renteria were created Knights of the most noble Order of Santiago (founded 1160 A.D. by King Don Fernando II to guard the Holy Sepulchre of the Apostol Santiago in Compostela from the ravaging Arabs).*
>
> *Don Luis Pedro de la Renteria and don Antonio Miguel de la Renteria were created Knights of the most noble Order of Calatrava (founded 1158 A.D. by King Don Sancho III and confirmed by Pope Alejandro III in 1164A.D. to make Holy war upon the invading Arab armies with fire and sword and, hasta la muerte).*
>
> *The Renteria caballeros were Conquistadores del Nuevo Mundo and their descendants reside throughout the Americas."*

The Gutierrez surname is documented in a copyrighted document titled "The Most Distinguished Surname Gutierrez". Copyright 1998-2017 Swyrich Corporation. All Rights Reserved.

The following are three excerpts taken from that document:

1. *"The prestigious surname Gutierrez originated in Spain, a country which has figured prominently in world affairs for hundreds of years."*
2. *"From the diverse traditions and regions of Spain come distinguished family names which have carried the pride and heritage of Hispanic culture around the world. The name Gutierrez was traced to its source in Castile, where the name originated in Visigothic times."*
3. *"This [sic] name originally derived from the baptismal name Gutierre."*

Paternal/Maternal Naming Method

The names of my relatives shown in this memoir are configured in a method known as "paternal/maternal" naming method. This naming method is typically used in Mexico.

Using the "paternal/maternal" naming method, my name is Salvador Renteria Gutierrez. My name is composed of a given name and two surnames. My given name is Salvador. My paternal surname, Renteria, is the surname of my father, Jesus Jose Renteria Tarango. My maternal surname, Gutierrez, is the surname of my mother, Maria Gutierrez Gonzalez. That said, the first surname is my paternal surname and my second surname is my maternal surname. The "paternal/maternal" naming method allows easy identification of the origin of a particular person.

In contrast to the "paternal/maternal" naming method used in Mexico, many in the United States might consider my name to be Salvador G. Renteria. The problem with this naming method is that the middle initial "G" could be mistaken for a second given name and not the first letter of my maternal surname.

Sources of Information on Ancestors

Most of the information on the Gutierrez side of my family contained in this memoir was provided by a relative of ours, Arturo Gonzalez. His name is Arturo Gonzalez but his maternal name is Mediano so therefore, his name is Arturo Gonzalez Mediano. He is the son of Jesus Gonzalez Valles and Josefina Mediano Aguilar who used to live in Eloy, Arizona. Arturo currently lives in Phoenix, Arizona. Arturo is my mother's cousin because his father is Jesus Gonzalez Valles who was my maternal grandmother's brother.

Some of the information was also provided by Consuelo Zapata Martinez who is the wife of my uncle Fernando Renteria Tarango. She provided most of the information on the Renteria side of the family.

The stories I heard during my early years were fragments that my father and mother would tell from time to time. They would sometimes remember stories about their families and would converse about their parents and grandparents.

Many of my recollections are from stories that I heard when my father would speak of his ancestors. This is also the case with my mother. This is why I will sometimes say phrases such as "during story times with my father" or "during story times with my mother". I will always remember their stories because they were memorable.

I should have asked more questions and should have recorded the history more completely so that the stories could have been more illustrative.

The Ancestral Origins of My Family

I have often wondered where my ancestors came from. I personally knew my grandfather Jose Renteria. He was my grandfather on my father's side. He was a tall, slender man with a "güero" complexion. The word "güero" in Mexico is used to denote a person of fair complexion with blonde or light brown hair. In addition to my grandfather Jose being of "güero" complexion, my father Jesus was also of "güero" complexion. I am of "güero" complexion as well.

As a result of this fair skin characteristic in my family, I sensed that my ancestors might have originated from Spain. In early 2016 I had an ethnicity study performed by AncestryDNA. AncestryDNA sent me a prepackaged test kit. The placed some of my saliva into a vial and then capped the vial. I then sent the saliva sample to AncestryDNA.

The results of the ethnicity test are shown below.

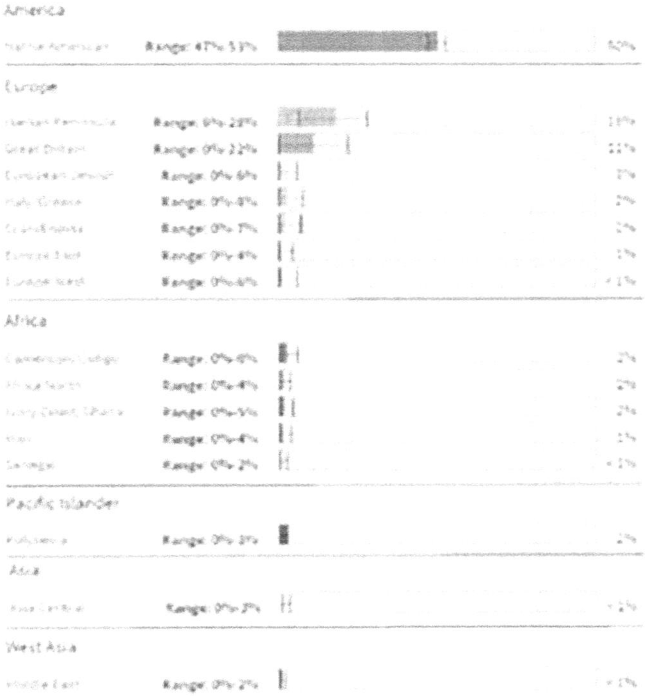

The majority of my ethnicity comes from what Ancestry DNA refers to as Native America. The genetic ethnicity study indicates that 50

% of my ancestry is from the region that is home to the indigenous people of the Americas. The statistical certainty ranges from 47 % to 53 %. Native America as defined by AncestryDNA is the vast region stretching over two continents that includes the rugged territory of Alaska and Canada, mountains and plains of the United States, dry valleys of Mexico, tropical jungles of Central America and South America, and the Patagonian steppes of southern Argentina and Chile.

My ethnicity also comes from a region which AncestryDNA refers to as the Iberian Peninsula. The Iberian Peninsula is that land mass that is occupied by Spain and Portugal. My ethnicity was therefore likely introduced by Spanish and/or Portuguese inhabitants. The genetic ethnicity study estimates that 18 % of my ancestry is from the Iberian Peninsula region. The statistical certainty ranges from 6 % to 28 %.

Additionally, my ethnicity also comes from a region which is referred to as the Great Britain region. The Great Britain region primarily includes England, Scotland and Wales but also secondarily includes Ireland, France, Germany, Denmark, Belgium, Netherlands, Switzerland. The genetic ethnicity study estimates that 11% of my ancestry is from the Great Britain region. The statistical certainty ranges from 0 % to 22 %.

Finally, the rest of the ethnic contribution in the ethnicity study is from other miscellaneous areas. The contribution to my ethnicity from these various miscellaneous areas ranges from less than 1% to 3%.

In summary, the following is my AncestryDNA ethnicity estimate determined from the saliva sample I sent AncestryDNA:

Native American	50%
Iberian Peninsula	18%
Great Britain	11%

As a result of the AncestryDNA ethnicity study, my father telling me that my great grandfather Pedro Renteria was from Spain was probably true. This may be the reason why my grandfather Jose, my father Jesus, I and most of my siblings are fair skinned.

During April of 2015, my wife, Socorro, made contact with a person by the name of Beto Muñoz through the social media service known as Facebook. It turns out that he is related to our family. More about Beto

Muñoz will be presented in later chapters. Anyway, the following is an excerpt from that internet communication from him:

"The name "Renteria" is Basque, a race of people from the North of Spain, from the area of the Spanish city of Bilbao. The name is actually "Erenteria"". In his communication, Beto Muñoz believes that the name "Renteria" originated from the name "Erenteria" which is a surname in Spain.

My Father, Jesus Jose Renteria Tarango

My father's name was Jesus Jose Renteria Tarango. My father's birth certificate shows he was born on January 19, 1928 in San Lucas, Chihuahua. I am in possession of my father's birth certificate. My cousin Lorenza Renteria who lives in Delicias, Chihuahua assisted me in obtaining a copy of his birth certificate from the town of Rosales, Chihuahua.

It seems that the population records were transferred to Rosales, Chihuahua when San Lucas was flooded by a dam known as "Presa de las Virgenes". The construction of the "Presa de las Virgenes" was a very significant event in the life of father, Jesus. More about the subject of the village of San Lucas and the dam known as "Presa de las Virgenes" will be presented in the coming chapters.

My Ancestor s Ages

My great grandfather was Pedro Renteria. The following is an attempt to determine the approximate date of my great grandfather's date of birth. My father's birth certificate shows that my grandfather Jose Renteria was 23 years of age when my father was born. That would make my grandfather Jose's birth year to be 1905. Assuming that my grandfather Jose was born when my great grandfather Pedro Renteria was 20 years of age, then my great grandfather Pedro would have been born on or about 1885.

My father told me that my great grandfather Pedro was an immigrant from Spain. I never asked my father about the reason my great grandfather Pedro traveled to Mexico. I can only guess that he traveled to Mexico in search of a better life. By the way, my father's birth certificate shows that my great grandfather, Pedro, was married to Anita Rivera.

In the previous section, I mentioned a person by the name of Beto Muñoz. In that section, he states that his grandfather, Justo Renteria, was my great grandfather's brother. Justo Renteria was born on May 5, 1896. The reason I know his birth date is because I researched the internet and found Justo Renteria's birth date along with his date of passing.

First Generation and Second Generation Names

My aunt, Consuelo Zapata Martinez told me that Pedro Renteria and Anita Rivera bore the following Renteria Rivera children:

- Jose Renteria Rivera (my grandfather)
- Bonifacio Renteria Rivera
- Inocente Renteria Rivera

My aunt, Consuelo Zapata Martinez, also said that Anita Rivera passed away and that Pedro Rivera married his second wife, Ines Portillo. She indicated that to her knowledge they had only one son. The son's name was Manuel Renteria Portillo.

On my grandmother Espedita's side, I know that her parents were Ciriaco Tarango and Gorgonia Ortiz. This information is present in my father's birth certificate that Lorenza Renteria obtained for me. My aunt, Consuelo Zapata Martinez, filled in the gaps and told me that their children were Espedita, Manuel, Bonifacio and Margarita.

The following graphic shows my father's ancestors:

Jesus Jose Renteria Tarango Ancestors

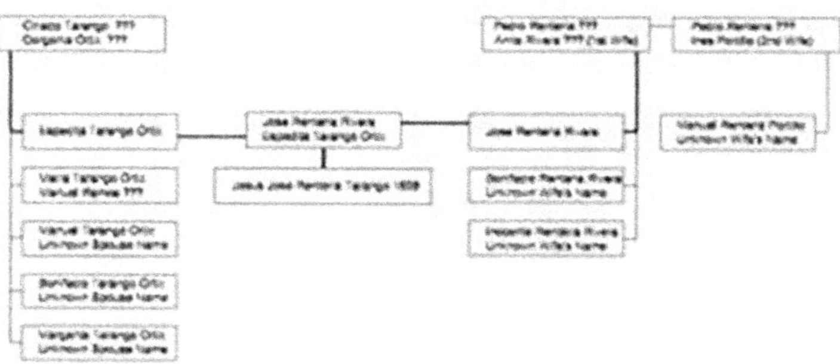

Espedita Tarango Ortiz

Espedita Tarango Ortiz was my grandmother. She was married to my grandfather Jose Renteria Rivera. I knew of Espedita because my father spoke of her during story times. I also now know the complete name of Espedita because she also appears on my father's birth certificate. Her name is Espedita Tarango Ortiz.

During story times with my father, he would sometimes mention his mother's name. He described Espedita as being of diminutive stature and had an Indian-like appearance. He used the following words to describe his mother: "tenía el parecer de una Indíta". The words are paraphrased into Spanish as follows: "she had the appearance of a diminutive Indian woman".

Although I never asked my father, I assume she was of "Tarahumares tepehuanes" Indian origin, sometimes referred to as "Tarahumaras". The reason for this assumption is that the internet literature mentions Indian tribes such as Conchos, Toboscos, Chizos, Coahuileños, Sisimbles, Tarahumares tepehuanes and other Indian tribes being present in Northern Chihuahua. A search using an internet search engine such as Google can be performed by entering "San Francisco de Conchos" and the name Tarahumares tepehuanes appears as the name of one of the Indian tribes. By the way, Espedita passed away when my father was approximately 2 years old).

Another interesting tidbit about my grandmother Espedita is that I believe she was a faithful Catholic. My father's formal name was Jesus Jose Renteria Tarango. It is interesting to me that his given names are the biblical names of Jesus and Jose. Because of these given names, I assume that Espedita, his mother, was a devoted Catholic.

My Aunt Anita and Uncle Fernando

My father's siblings were Anita Renteria Tarango and Fernando Renteria Tarango. Anita was born in September of 1929 and Fernando was born in May of 1930.

My uncle Fernando was one of two children born as twins. However, one of the twins passed away shortly after being born; possibly about 1 to 2 weeks after their birth. My aunt Consuelo, my uncle's wife, told me that the twin's name that passed away was Antonio. My father and his two live siblings, Anita and Fernando were orphaned when their mother passed away soon after my uncle Fernando and Antonio were born.

My Mother, Maria Encarnacion Gutierrez Gonzalez

My mother's name was Maria Encarnacion Gutierrez Gonzalez. She was born on March 25, 1929 in Hatch, New Mexico. My mother's maiden name consists of her paternal surname, Gutierrez, and then her maternal surname, Gonzalez. As before, the paternal surname followed by the maternal surname is the common method used in Mexico to designate the lineage of a person, be it male or female. My mother's given name was Maria Encarnacion.

My Grandfather Gregorio Gutierrez Salas

My grandfather on my mother's side was Gregorio Gutierrez. His parents were Lino Gutierrez and Valeria Salas. I learned of Lino Gutierrez and Valeria Salas from Arturo Gonzalez Mediano who as indicated before, is my mother's cousin and lives in Phoenix, Arizona. As a result, the complete name of my grandfather on my mother's side is Gregorio Gutierrez Salas.

The following are the names of the Gutierrez Salas siblings as provided by Arturo Gonzalez Mediano:

- Gregorio Gutierrez Salas (passed approx. 1953)
- Margarita Gutierrez Salas
- Guadalupe Villareal (maternal name is unknown) (half brother)

My Grandmother Maria Gonzalez Valles

My grandmother on my mother's side was Maria Gonzalez Valles. I have some loving stories to tell about her in the following sections. That is why she is so dear to me. Her siblings were Antonia, Jesus, Alejandra, Roberto and Ester. The reason I know of the entire list of siblings is because I confirmed the list of her siblings with my aunt Consuelo Zapata Martinez, who again is my uncle Fernando's wife. My grandmother Maria would visit us on the farm and then in Fabens when we were children and then adolescents. I wish I had asked her questions about our family but somehow I didn't think of it. Our objectives as children were different than now when it is important to record my family's history. I remember some stories that I will share about my grandmother Maria. One of those stories that I will relate later, had to do with my grandmother Maria asking me to travel with her to Delicias to live with her. My mother feared that my grandmother might not bring me back and so she refused my grandmother's request.

My Great Grandparents on My Mother's Side

My great grandparents on my mother's side were Jose Maria Gonzalez Arras and Maria Valles Baeza. The parents of Jose Maria Gonzalez were Jorge Gonzalez & Veviana Arras. The parents of Maria Valles Baeza were Placido Valles and Maccedonia Baeza. This information was provided again by Arthur Gonzalez who lives in Phoenix, Arizona.

The following graphic shows my mother's ancestors:

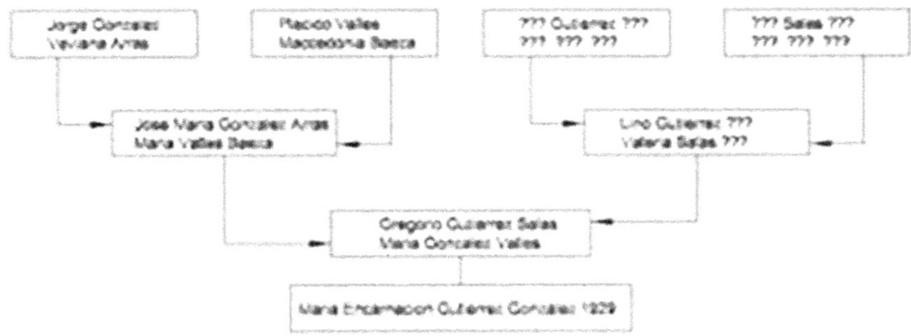

The Gonzalez Valles Siblings

The following are my grandmother, Maria's siblings. They are the Gonzalez Valles siblings:

- Antonia Gonzalez Valles
- Maria Gonzalez Valles (my grandmother)

- Jesus Gonzalez Valles (passed 1994)
- Alejandra Gonzalez Valles
- Roberto Gonzalez Valles
- Ester Gonzalez Valles (born 1920)(died 2002)

The Gutierrez Gonzalez Siblings

My mother was the second of seven children. The following are the names of all the Gutierrez Gonzalez siblings:

- Manuela Gutierrez Gonzalez
- Maria Encarnacion Gutierrez Gonzalez (my mother)
- Esteban Gutierrez Gonzalez
- Patricio Gutierrez Gonzalez
- Adrian Gutierrez Gonzalez

A Former Governor

A former Governor of the State of Chihuahua was a relative of my great grandmother, Maria Valles Baeza. His name was the same as my great grandmother's maternal surname, Baeza. I know this because my aunt Manuela Gutierrez Gonzalez mentioned to me that he was a relative. I came to know of this information when I was involved in a law suit against a former employee of my Mexican company in Cd. Juarez, Mexico in 1990.

My Grandfather Gregorio Gutierrez Salas

My mother passed away in 2002; however, during story times with her much prior to her passing, I remember her telling me that her father, Gregorio Gutierrez Salas, was from or lived in the State of Colorado in the United States. Socorro, my wife, remembers a conversation she had with my mother about my grandfather Gregorio. She remembers my mother telling her that my grandfather Gregorio spoke English. Socorro also recalls that my mother told her that my grandfather Gregorio was born in Denver, Colorado and that he was a United States citizen.

My mother told me that as a child, she found it interesting that from time to time, her father would say words that she didn't understand. The word "beeldin" was one of those words. He would say that word when calling attention to a building structure. My mother told me that it wasn't until we began to attend school in Fabens and then we began to speak a little bit of English at home, that she realized that her father was actually saying the word "building" and not "beeldin".

Another interesting tidbit about my grandfather Gregorio had to do with my mother's name "Méri". As I indicated before, my mother's given name was Maria but everyone called her by the name of "Méri", not "Merí"; the accent being on the letter "e" instead of the accent on the letter "i". Anyway, it never occurred to me until now that I am writing this piece that the name "Méri" is not a typical Méxican name. "Méri" sounds like the name "Mary". I'll never know for sure but I think my grandfather Gregorio probably referred to my mother as "Mary"; however, everyone else in Delicias, México understood her name to be "Méri" instead of "Mary".

My grandfather Gregorio passed away in 1955. I remember having seen him; however, I must have been when I was about 4 years because the image of him in my mind is hazy. I do remember seeing a photograph of my grandfather Gregorio sometime during my high school years but I don't know what happened to it. Very little was said of my grandfather Gregorio. Family members would tell us that grandfather Gregorio passed away and that he lost his life in a railroad train accident.

My Grandfather Jose Renteria Rivera's Second Marriage to Ester Gonzalez Valles

As indicated previously, my grandfather on my father's side was Jose Renteria Rivera. My grandfather's first marriage was with Espedita Tarango Ortiz.

Sometime after the death of Espedita, my grandfather Jose married Ester Gonzalez Valles. Prior to my grandfather Jose marrying Ester, Ester had formerly been married to another person. She and her former husband had a son named Socorro. I don't know the name of Socorro's father and therefore I don't know Socorro's paternal surname. For now I will assume that his surnames are the same as his mother Ester's surnames and therefore his name for purposes of this family history will be Socorro Gonzalez Valles.

The following are the Renteria Gonzalez siblings which are half brothers and sisters of my father, Jesus Jose Renteria Tarango:

- Socorro Gonzalez Valles (male; this given name is used for males and females in Mexico)
- Esteban Renteria Gonzalez
- Sara Renteria Gonzalez
- Marcos Renteria Gonzalez
- Reyes Renteria Gonzalez
- Manuel Renteria Gonzalez
- Maria Renteria Gonzalez
- Velia Renteria Gonzalez
- Lorenzo Renteria Gonzalez
- Guadalupe Renteria Gonzalez (female; this given name is used for males and females in Mexico)
- Angelica Renteria Gonzalez

It is interesting to note that Ester Gonzalez Valles was the sister of my grandmother on my mother's side; Maria Gonzalez Valles. Therefore, the children of my grandfather Jose and Ester are my mother's cousins. This includes Socorro, Ester's son.

My Core Family

Our family was a relatively large family of 10 members including my parents. The following is the list of the children born of my parents, Jesus Jose and Maria Encarnacion:

Jesus	May 6, 1949
Salvador	January 23, 1951
Irma	May 30, 1954
Gloria	February 16, 1956
Mario	February 17, 1958
Graciela	July 30, 1959
Norma	January 18, 1963
Martin	April 25, 1965

The Significance of the "Presa de las Virgenes"

When we were growing up on the farm in Fabens, my parents would frequently take us to visit relatives in Delicias, Chihuahua. I remember some of these family trips. We would visit my grandmother Maria and other family members who lived there.

On one occasion, while visiting in Delicias, an uncle of ours took my older brother, Jesus, and I to visit a dam called "Presa de las Virgenes". I remember having seen a large expanse of water which is the lake that the dam had created soon after it was built. At the time, I didn't realize the significance of that place. I also didn't realize that the nearby town of San Lucas was also key in my father's up-bringing. Later in life, I would find out that the village of San Lucas, where my father was born, was flooded by the "Presa de las Virgenes" dam.

For the "techie" readers that use Google Maps, the approximate coordinates where San Lucas used to be located is at the coordinates: latitude 28.115401, longitude -105.699941. The location of the "Presa de las Virgenes" dam is located at the coordinates: latitude 28.165645, longitude: -105.628812. The dam was about 4.5 miles from Rosales and about 10 miles from Delicias as the crow flies.

The village of Nuevo San Lucas is another village that is significant in my father's history. Nuevo San Lucas is located in the area between the towns of Pedro Meoqui and Lazaro Cardenas. The Google Maps coordinates for the village of Nuevo San Lucas are latitude 28.355688, longitude -105.568836.

Nuevo San Lucas is significant because it is part of my father's history. Nuevo San Lucas was created when the original village of San Lucas was flooded by the lake that the "Presa de la Virgenes" dam created. I don't remember my father ever taking us to visit the town of "Nuevo San Lucas" even though it appears to be only about 15 miles from Delicias. I suppose he didn't feel drawn to visit there.

Ultimately the dam referred to as the "Presa de las Virgenes" was placed in operation and the lake formed in the year of 1949.

Later in life, I grew more and more inquisitive about where my father came from. At the time of our visit to the "Presa de las Virgenes", my father had not yet told me about his days as a youth in that region. I didn't know that this dam created the lake that ultimately flooded the village of "San Lucas" where my father was born and raised.

Later on in life, my curiosity led me to ask my father and mother questions about where they came from. Sometimes I would listen to their conversations and I would glean information from simply listening closely. Little by little I began to form a sequence of events that helped me ask more specific questions about their experiences growing up in the Delicias area.

I am fortunate in a way because I remember many facts about their history. Unfortunately, I didn't ask my mother as many questions and that's why this family history contains more information about my father than about my mother.

The following is the regional map of the Delicias area where my mother and father grew up:

A Glimpse of San Lucas

My father told me that San Lucas was an agricultural village. During the time when my father was growing up, San Lucas was destroyed when the Mexican government built a dam downstream to capture the waters from the nearby San Pedro River. More detail will be presented about the dam which is known as the "Presa de las Virgenes". The mainstay of San Lucas was agriculture. I don't know for sure but judging from the way my father spoke about San Lucas, I am guessing that the population of the town was probably around 300 people. The majority of the families in San Lucas were very poor.

There were only a handful of property owners that owned the local farm lands. My father's family was one of those very poor families.

In those days, there was no running water available for the poor families in San Lucas. There was no water distribution piping system that is typical of water distribution systems in modern townships. The water for the poor families was obtained from open wells.

During story times, my father described the water wells that were typical in the small village of San Lucas. The typical well was dug such that the diameter of the well was about 3 to 4 feet in diameter all the way to the water level below. Since the San Pedro River was about 2 miles east of the township, the water level from the surface of the well to the bottom was fairly shallow. The part of the well that protruded from the ground level upward was constructed with an upright rock wall structure that was approximately 3 feet tall. The protruding rock structure served as a barrier to keep the surrounding dirt from falling into the well hole.

To obtain water from the well, a pail was tied to a rope and the pail would then be lowered manually until the pail fell to the water level down hole in the well. Once the pail filled and sank below the water level, the person would then manually begin to slowly pull the pail filled with water up to the top. The water was obtained in this manner and it was used for drinking, cooking, as well as for bathing.

The water would have to be carried from the location of the well back into the living quarters using pails. In order to bathe, the family members would use large circular tubs measuring about 36" inches in diameter and 18" deep. I imagine it was quite a chore walking back and forth from the living quarters to the location of the well to fetch water when bath time rolled around. After a bath, the used bath water still had to be carried outdoors in a pail and then dumped on the ground. If the person wanted a warm bath then some of the water had to be heated up on the wood burning stove and then mixed-in with the colder water in the tub.

Pitcher Pump

Only a handful of well-to-do families had small manual pumps that were used to pump water from their own wells to the ground level. The small manual pumps were fitted with a cantilever type handle and were constructed of cast iron. My father described the same type of pump that we used when we lived on the Ryan farm up until I was about 4 years of age.

I clearly remember the type of pump we used when we lived on the Ryan farm. When I was writing this piece, I searched the internet to determine the name of this type of pump. It turns out that the pump is known as a "pitcher pump". The photograph on the left shows the pitcher pump.

To operate the pump, the person would grasp the cantilever handle and then press the handle downward. Once it reached the bottom-most position, the person would then pull the cantilever handle back up until it reached the top-most position. This action was performed in cyclical fashion up and down, up and down until water started pouring out of the built-in spout. The water poured out of the spout into a collection pail. When the pail was full of water, the person operating the cantilever handle would stop the cyclical up and down motion and the water flow from the pump would then stop as well.

My father described the types of homes that were typical of the building structures in the village of San Lucas. All of the homes in San Lucas were built with adobe block. Adobe blocks were made by first mixing earthen clay with water. Sand was not suitable for constructing adobe blocks. The mud mixture was then poured onto a wooden rectangular form that measured about 10 inches in width by about 18 inches in length and about 4 inches in height.

Once poured into the wooden form, the mud mixture was then left to dry for about 10 days. During those 10 days, the mud mixture would dry and harden inside the wooden form. At the end of the 10 days, the form would be removed leaving the adobe block ready to be used to construct a house or some other building structure. The photograph on the left shows the adobe blocks.

The adobe house would be constructed in much the same manner as that used when constructing a house using concrete cinder blocks. However, instead of using concrete mortar when laying the concrete block, mud was used as the mortar material.

I asked my father if the floors were constructed of concrete and he replied that the floors were not constructed of wood or concrete. He indicated that the floors were constructed of an earthen clay material that was compacted to form a level floor. This type of floor was common in the homes built during those times.

All of the men that lived in San Lucas worked the fields that belonged to a handful of land owners. Corn, wheat and beans were grown on the farm lands. In the early days, very few farmers had tractors to work the farm lands. The majority of the farmers would farm the lands with mule drawn farm implements. As time progressed, several of the farm owners began to acquire tractors to farm the land. My father told me that the tractors were brought-in from the United States.

In summary, life in San Lucas was not easy for the average person. With the exception of the few land owners, all of the inhabitants were poor and the small population that comprised the small village worked the farm fields. Life in San Lucas was indeed was very difficult.

My Grandfather Gave His Children Away

When my father's mother, Espedita, passed away, my grandfather was left having to care for my father who was about 2 years of age at the time. Anita was a 1 year and Fernando was a newborn. The photograph on the left shows my grandfather Jose Renteria.

After her passing, my father, Anita and Fernando were passed around from one family to another. He told me that the families they stayed with were very poor. My father, Anita and Fernando weren't well treated, after all, they weren't natural born children of the families that took them in.

My father never told me the details regarding the families that they stayed with and somehow I failed to ask him for those details. In retrospect, I should have asked. All I can surmise is that it must have been hard on my father and his siblings having to get accustomed with new persons every time they were passed around from one family to the next.

My father remembered that they eventually wound up with a family that was related to my grandfather Jose. As a young child, my father didn't initially know for sure how my grandfather Jose was related to that family. In time, he found out that the head of the family was my grandfather Jose's brother, Bonifacio. Bonifacio was married and they had several children themselves.

My father was only 2 years of age when all of this occurred. My father told me that my grandfather Jose passed them on to those other families because he had to work the fields and could not care for Anita, Fernando and my father.

My father, Anita and Fernando were very, very young. Remember, Fernando was a newborn and Anita was a 1 year old when this happened. My father told me that he faintly remembered that he and Anita would cry whenever my grandfather Jose would leave them with a strange family here and there.

My father told me that they stayed with Bonifacio's family believing that my grandfather Jose would come back for them sometime in the future. The days, weeks and months passed. My grandfather Jose didn't come for them. As the months wore on, they began to forget the trauma of being without their real father and mother. Everything had changed so quickly for them.

Slowly but surely, they became used to living with Bonifacio's family. Remember that Fernando was a new born when my grandfather Jose left them with Bonifacio and his family. My father told me that because Fernando was a baby, he didn't think Fernando felt the same sense of abandonment that he and Anita felt.

My father told me that when he was about 4 years of age, Bonifacio and his family members began to direct them to do the light household chores. They didn't mind doing the chores; however, the chores did become more numerous as time wore on. More and more, the parents would direct my father and Anita to do more of the chores.

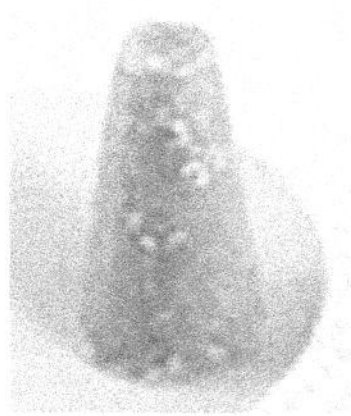

Christmas for my father and his siblings was something that normally occurred without gifts. My father told me he remembered during one specific Christmas having received a gift consisting of a "flour" tortilla and a piece of "piloncillo". The "flour" tortilla was very special to him because they normally ate their meals with corn tortillas; not tortillas made of real wheat flour.

By the way, "piloncillo" is a Spanish word that is used to describe unrefined brown sugar that is formed by pressing sugar granules into the form of a hard, solid cone. The photograph shown here shows a "piloncillo" cone. I am familiar with "piloncillo" cones. The height of the cone is usually about 5 or 6 inches. The taste is a very sweet, sugary taste. There is nothing elegant about "piloncillo". In my father's case, "piloncillo" was the poor people's candy in those days. It saddens me to think that as a little boy, my father thought "piloncillo" was something special when in fact it really wasn't.

At that early age, my father tended the large garden where melons, watermelon, chile, corn, beans and squash were grown. He would assist with the planting. He was responsible for cutting the weeds and irrigating the garden. Anita would be directed to do the household chores like washing the dishes, making the beds and sweeping the floors, even at that early age. In fact, Anita and my father were doing more work than the rest of the family's own children. My father used to tell me that it just seemed that the parent's children weren't directed to do any of the work. To my father, it seemed that Anita and he were being mistreated. My father continued to live with his uncle Bonifacio until about 13 years of age.

The Longing to Reunite With My Grandfather Jose

My father was now 13 years of age. My father was angry. He longed to have his sister, brother and himself reunited with my grandfather Jose. My father felt a need to go and find my grandfather Jose. My father never forgot that my grandfather Jose had told them that he would be back for them. My father felt a sense of betrayal toward my grandfather.

My father told me that he kept asking his uncle Bonifacio and his family members for the whereabouts of my grandfather Jose. Bonifacio somehow always managed to avoid having to answer my father's questions about the whereabouts of my grandfather Jose. My father never found out where my grandfather Jose went.

My father told me that he wanted to live with my grandfather Jose instead of his father's relatives. My father actually left Bonifacio's family in search of my grandfather at the age of 13 years of age. He told me that he had no intention of returning back to Bonifacio's family. He told me that he didn't remember if he had asked Anita to go with him. In the end, my father went searching for my grandfather alone.

My father was finally able to locate my grandfather Jose. As indicated before, my father was 13 years old at the time. My father told me that he found that my grandfather didn't actually live far from Bonifacio's home. My grandfather Jose lived about 10 miles away. Five miles doesn't seem to be very far to a grown up but to a 13 year old, 5 miles is a great distance. My father never told me exactly how he happened to find my grandfather Jose and so I am not aware of that part of his life.

When he found my grandfather Jose, my father found that my grandfather had already married another woman. My grandfather Jose had married a woman by the name of Ester Gonzalez Valles. He also found that Ester Gonzalez Valles had a son from a previous marriage. The son's name was Socorro. Socorro was about 10 years of age compared to my father being 13 years of age.

My father told me that at that point, he now knew why my grandfather Jose had not returned for Anita, Fernando and himself. While away, my grandfather Jose had started a new life with Ester and her son, Socorro. I asked him if he had forgiven my grandfather Jose for having abandoned them. He told me that indeed he had forgiven him. In the end, my grandfather Jose did allow my father to live with him and his new family.

My Father Reunited With My Grandfather

My father told me that when he rejoined my grandfather Jose's new family, he would help out with the chores. In addition, he would help my grandfather on the farm where he worked. Wheat, corn and beans were the crops that were grown on the farm.

My father as a boy didn't actually get paid by the farm owner. My grandfather Jose did have daily farm work quotas. My father helped my grandfather Jose do the work that the foreman directed my grandfather to do. This went on until my father was 16 years of age in 1944.

I asked my father if he visited Anita and Fernando during the time that he lived with my grandfather Jose's new family and he told me that he did. In fact, he told me that Anita and Fernando continued to live with his uncle Bonifacio because Bonifacio was better able to care for them economically. My grandfather Jose was very poor and could not afford to care for Anita and Fernando.

Previously, my father started school at about 8 years of age in San Lucas. This was during 1936. He continued to live with his uncle Bonifacio during the 3 years that he attended school. He continued his schooling until he was about 11 years of age. He told me that he didn't really like school. He was just not interested in attending school.

All through his school years he continued to help his uncle Bonifacio on the farm where they lived. Again, this included the tending to the crops in the field. The work included irrigating the fields and hoeing the crops.

Sometime during my father's 3rd year in school, my father made a decision to discontinue going to school. He just didn't show up to school anymore. He told me that he never retrieved any of his notebooks and books that he used in school. He just quit going to school.

In 1944, my father was 16 years of age. At that time, he began to sense that Anita and Fernando should rejoin my grandfather Jose's family. He told me a visit to Bonifacio's home during the time when he was 16 years of age.

My father told me that he felt that both of them were being mistreated. Anita was now 15 years of age and Fernando was 14 years old. Anita would do all the house work such as washing the dishes, making the beds and so forth while Fernando would tend to the chores outdoors. My father told me in no uncertain terms that "they were being treated as slaves".

The Final Attempt to Reunite The Family

The following sequence of events is what I surmise happened based on the story that my father told me about reuniting my grandfather Jose's new family with my aunt Anita and my uncle Fernando. If the story sounds too explicit, it's because that's how I imagine the events might have transpired.

Anyway, my father returned to his uncle Bonifacio's home where Anita and Fernando had been staying for the past 13 years. My father went there with the intention of meeting with Anita and Fernando in private.

My father first waited some distance away from the home. He saw both Anita and Fernando exit from the house. They were seated just outside the house. He continued to wait from a distance because my father's intent was to approach Anita and Fernando without being detected by his uncle Bonifacio or a member of his family.

After a while my father saw Bonifacio and his wife leave the house. I suppose they left to visit friends or possibly left to run errands, one or the other. In short my father saw that they left the house. When they disappeared from sight, my father was still concerned that some of Bonifacio's children might still be present inside the home. He continued to wait a while longer until he finally decided to risk it. He approached Anita and Fernando while they were outdoors at Bonifacio's home.

During their conversation, my father told Anita that he hated to see Fernando and her live with his uncle Bonifacio and his wife. He told Anita that he felt they were treated not as family but as simple slaves.

He told Anita that he had observed that she was always kept busy in the kitchen doing house work while his uncle Bonifacio's wife did nothing. He told her that he had observed Fernando being mistreated. He told her that in a previous trip to his uncle Bonifacio's house, he had stayed a distance away to observe them. He told her that he had observed Fernando doing the busy work outdoors. He had seen Fernando tending the chickens and tending the milk cows. He told Anita that he felt that Fernando was doing that too much of the work.

When he visited Anita and Fernando clandestinely that one time, he told them of a plan he had. His plan was to have them leave and rejoin my grandfather Jose's family that was located some distance away. He told them that this would occur during the following week but that it would be during the night. My father informed them of the specific day in which the plan would come to pass. He also told them the specific hour during which he would wait for them to join him. He told them that he would wait for them in a near-by arroyo at a specific hour during the night. He told Anita and Fernando not to tell his uncle Bonifacio, his wife or Bonifacio's children about him coming for them during the following week. Everything needed to be kept a secret.

My father told me that during the following week, he began to prepare a wagon equipped with wooden sidings. It was an old style horse-drawn wagon supported by wooden wheels. He also made sure that a mule would be available to pull the wagon. My grandfather Jose didn't own a mule and so my father borrowed a mule from one of his friends. He also began to collect wood and then loaded it onto the wagon. The wood would enable Anita and Fernando to hide so as not to be seen by others after being picked up.

As planned, my father told me that he waited for Anita and Fernando to show up at the designated place and time. Sure enough, Anita and Fernando showed up holding hands. My father told me that he immediately helped them board the wagon.

My father was in a hurry to get away. He wanted to avoid being detected. Once they were on the wagon, my father told them to lie down and hide as best they could. He then worked feverishly to place the wood already on the wagon around them to hide their presence. My father boarded the wagon and he then began to drive the mule drawn wagon slowly forward. They drove along an alternate wagon trail different from the well traveled trail that ultimately passed by my grandfather Jose's home.

My father was nervous about secretly transporting Anita and Fernando and therefore he drove the wagon very carefully along the trail. He told me that the last thing he wanted was to be discovered by a person who knew Anita or Fernando.

The plan worked. About 4 hours later, they all arrived at my grandfather Jose's home. It was about midnight and my father began to help Anita step off the wagon. Fernando was asleep and my father shook him gently in order to wake him. Shortly thereafter, Fernando awoke and my father also helped him step off the wagon.

After having gotten off the wagon, my father told Anita and Fernando to wait until he was able to remove the harness from the mule. As an aside, a mule is a horse-like animal that is the offspring of a horse and a burro. Anyway, my father then led the mule to the pen where my grandfather Jose kept his cows. He then let the mule roam into the pen.

When my father returned to where Anita and Fernando were waiting, he led them to the house's entrance door. The door was locked and so my father knocked on the door. My father told me that my grandfather's wife, Ester, opened the door.

When Ester opened the door, she was holding an old style kerosene lamp that in those days was used for lighting. The light from the kerosene lamp was somewhat dim; she therefore was unable to distinguish who the two persons.

Ester asked my father why he was out so late. My father quickly responded that the persons were Anita and Fernando. Ester asked again, "Who are they?" My father then pulled Anita and Fernando closer so that the light from the kerosene lamp could shine on them. He then repeated that the persons were his sister Anita and his brother Fernando. Ester took a closer look and it finally dawned on Ester who they were.

She then asked, "Why did you bring them here?" and my father quickly responded "I brought them here to live with us." Ester was confused. It took her a while to understand the meaning of my father's words.

Without inviting them into the house, she immediately stepped back into the house and then awoke my grandfather Jose. My father told me that he overheard Ester tell my grandfather Jose "Jesus is at the door with two persons." I suppose that Ester was so surprised that she failed to say that the persons were Anita and Fernando.

My grandfather Jose awoke and walked to the door. My grandfather Jose was surprised to see my father Jesus at the door; accompanied by Anita and Fernando. Anita held on to my father's hand while Fernando stood beside them. My father flatly told my grandfather Jose; "I brought Anita and Fernando to live with us." My grandfather stood there for a few seconds without saying a word. My father told me that Anita and Fernando didn't really know who my grandfather Jose was. Remember, Anita was a 1 year old and Fernando had just been born when my grandfather Jose left them at his brother's home. My grandfather Jose never did visit his brother Bonfacio and that's the reason that Anita and Fernando really didn't sense that my grandfather Jose was their father.

After my grandfather Jose became fully aware of what my father had done, he then quickly told my father to bring them inside. My father told me that Anita clung to him tightly because she was unfamiliar with this new environment. They really didn't know my grandfather Jose or his wife, Ester. They remained standing close to my father while my father explained to my grandfather Jose how he had managed to bring them with him.

Shortly thereafter, my grandfather Jose extended his arms as if to embrace them and Anita and Fernando both immediately hid behind my father in fear. My grandfather attempted to gain their trust by speaking gently to them and Anita and Fernando little by little began to feel more at ease; however, they still hid behind my father as if embarrassed.

It became apparent to my grandfather Jose that Ester knew what was about to happen. It seems that Ester already knew about the existence of my grandfather Jose's children and that he had given them away to his brother Bonifacio a long time ago.

Ester was not so eager to accept Anita and Fernando. Although Ester knew about Anita and Fernando, she had never laid eyes on them. My grandfather Jose told Ester that Anita and Fernando would now be staying in his home. My father told me that he could tell that Ester didn't seem to accept the fact that Anita and Fernando would now be staying in my grandfather Jose's home.

After everything was said and done, my grandfather Jose told my father to arrange the sleeping quarters for Anita and Fernando. Ester was somewhat hesitant about the idea of having Anita and Fernando come to live with them; however, she did assist in setting up the sleeping arrangements.

My grandfather Jose's family was so poor that everyone slept on the floor. There was no money to purchase beds and so everyone grew accustomed to sleeping on the floor.

My father told me that early the next morning, my grandfather Jose awoke very early and proceeded to travel to Bonifacio's home to inform him of the whereabouts of Anita and Fernando. My father never told me the extent of the conversation my grandfather Jose had with his brother Bonifacio and I failed to ask him about it.

Life With the Reunited Family

As the days wore on, both Anita and Fernando slowly began to accept their new life with my grandfather Jose and Ester. They began to interrelate with Socorro, Ester's son. The photograph on the left shows a portrait of Ester.

All six persons lived out of the one room house. My father told me that a few months thereafter, my grandfather Jose built an additional room. Everyone pitched in to help my grandfather build the additional room. That room offered more living space. The house now seemed less cramped.

As the family grew to include Anita and Fernando, a new problem began to develop. Ester, my grandfather's wife, would favor Socorro, her son, more than my father, Anita and Fernando. For example, Socorro would receive the better clothing as compared to my father and his siblings. My father told me that even the amount of food on their plates was less for them as compared to Socorro. Socorro was given more blankets for sleeping compared to the number of blankets my father and his siblings received.

When Esteban, Sara and Marcos were born into the family, the problem became worse. The food portions were smaller for everyone. Almost everyone had outdoor gardens where melons, watermelons, squash and the like were grown. The work outside was constantly doled out to my father and his siblings and not so much to the rest of the children.

All in all, life in San Lucas with my grandfather Jose was a meager existence.

The Dream

My father told me that back when he was around 10 years of age, he would think about traveling to other far-away places. He told me that he would sometimes listen to men talking about their travels to the United States and that he would ask questions about their visits there. He'd wonder what it might be to travel and visit the United States.

One of those men was an older man by the name of Guadalupe Amaro. He was about 19 years of age and therefore he was older than my father. Guadalupe Amaro had been to the United States once before as a farm worker. Guadalupe had crossed into the United States illegally. My father asked him if he could go with him to the United States the next time he went there again. Guadalupe replied that one had to be at least 16 years of age because the farm owners wouldn't employ anyone less than 16 years of age.

I remember my father telling me that a man that had been to the United States once told him that one could actually pick up dollars right off the street in the United States. He initially thought the man was kidding but as he thought about it more and more, he started to think that it might actually be true. He started to think that perhaps it might be that easy. Picking dollars off the street seemed real to him.

He asked that man if he could go along with him during his next trip to the United States and the man responded to him that it was impossible. As with Guadalupe Amaro before, the man told him that he would have to wait until he was at least 16 years of age.

Unbeknownst to my father his dream would become a reality later on in his life.

San Lucas Visited By Survey Teams - 1940

My father told me that sometime during 1940 when he was 12 years old, groups of men dressed in khaki uniforms began coming to the area. They could be seen inspecting the areas along the San Pedro River valley. San Lucas was located about 2 miles west of the San Pedro River. Each group would consist of 4 to 5 men. Each group of men would move from location to location and at times, would even come close in proximity to the village of San Lucas.

It was obvious that these men were not from the local area because they were dressed differently. They were not the local people that worked in the local farm fields. These men were well dressed in khaki pants and shirts and wore rugged boots. It turned out that they actually worked for the Mexican Federal government.

Some of the men in the groups carried notebooks while others managed a device that appeared to be a type of telescope mounted on a tripod apparatus. Still others carried long poles. The poles were marked with numbers along the length of the poles. The men that carried the long poles would walk some distance away from the location of the men manning the tripod apparatus. The people in the towns called these men "ingenieros" which means engineers in English.

My father referred to the the tripod apparatus as a "teodolito". Using a Spanish to English translator on my laptop computer, I found that the Spanish word "teodolito" translates to the English word "theodolite". Upon reviewing several internet articles containing that specific word, I found that a "theodolite" is a surveying instrument with a rotating telescope mounted on a tripod base. The instrument is used to measure horizontal and vertical angles. Judging from my father's account of the "ingenieros" and "teodolitos", I think they were groups of survey teams that were responsible for developing topography maps that are used to record elevations and contours of the land.

Later on, a dam would be built that would eventually create a lake along the path of the San Pedro River. It stands to reason that the survey teams were in fact those men that were seen in the area. They performed the preparatory work for what was to be the construction of a man-made dam. That dam was to be known as the "Presa de las Virgenes".

The Building of the Dam Known as "Presa de Las Virgenes"

The village of San Lucas, which later became known as San Lucas Viejo, is where my father, Jesus Renteria Tarango, was born and raised. The town no longer exists because it was flooded by a lake that resulted from the construction of a huge dam. This little now non-existent town is important in the history of the Renteria family. The following internet article was published in the website publication known as "La Crónica de Chihuahua" in October 2010. The title of the article is "La Epopeya Del Pueblo Anegado" which translates to "The Epic of a Flooded Town". The article was authored by Froilián Meza Rivera. The article describes the origins of San Lucas, Chihuahua. It also describes how the town of San Lucas, Chihuahua was flooded by the formation of a lake when the dam known as the "Presa de la Virgenes" was built. "Presa" is the Spanish word for dam.

Based on information in several other internet articles, I found that construction of the dam started in the year 1941 and it was inaugurated in May of 1949. It took 8 years to build the dam. The article "La Epopeya Del Pueblo Anegado" was written in Spanish; however, I translated the article into English. By the way the title of the article in English is "The Epic of the Waterlogged Town". The article is written in Spanish poetic form and therefore, I paraphrased the article to make it easier to be read in English. The text in parenthesis was inserted to provide context and is annotated by the text "SR note". The original internet article "La Epopeya Del Pueblo Anegado" can be viewed using the following link: http://www.cronicadechihuahua.com/La-epopeya-del-pueblo-anegado.html

NUEVO SAN LUCAS, MEOQUI. - The fact that the people of Nuevo San Lucas are heirs to a village that was flooded and sunk to the bottom of the Presa Francisco I. Madero (SR note – Commonly known as Presa de las Virgenes), *is remembered only by a few. This story has already been lost. Lost in the mists of time; or better said lost in the waters of the dam.*

That original village was called San Lucas and was located on the banks of the Rio San Pedro. (SR note - Rio is the Spanish word for river.)

San Lucas was evicted by technicians from the National Irrigation Commission when they decided to build a giant dam in the canyon between Charco del Gallo and Villalba. The objective was to take advantage of the waters of the river for planting crops in the area known as Irrigation District 05. The people who were evicted from San Lucas were sent to establish Nuevo San Lucas near the neighboring municipality of Meoqui. These people were given land in compensation for those lands left behind. Others stayed there to work the land left over from the ejido San Lucas, and now live scattered in Rosales and Delicias, Chihuahua.

Interviewed as an inhabitant of Nuevo San Lucas, Arturo Hernandez Magallanes recalled that he left the flooded village when he was just 5 years of age. His father, Guadalupe Hernandez Hernandez, acquired a small Ford truck from his brother, and brought all the family's properties in one sole trip. They loaded a wood-fired stove and an oil-fired stove, table, chairs, a small wooden tableware vanity and beds, which were unassembled.

FIRST, A PROVISIONAL DAM

In the area of San Lucas, government technicians first built a temporary dam made of earth and stones, to plug the water flow of the river, which in those

years, between 1948 and 1950, they say had little water. (SR note - This phraseology seems to imply that the dam was built after the years of 1948 and 1950. On the contrary, I found several other documented references indicating that the dam construction was started in 1941. Those same references indicate that the dam was filled during the year of 1949 and that it was inaugurated in May of 1949. See Internet Reference "San Lucas 1", Internet Reference "San Lucas 2" and Internet Reference "San Lucas 3".) *This small dam, which was where today is the location of the Rebalse de las Virgenes, was necessary to keep the downstream area dry so that the construction of the large structures of steel and concrete at the dam site could occur. In other words, San Lucas was flooded before the larger dam filled.*

"But don't believe that the people came to the new town in one fell swoop. (SR note - The reference to the "new town" is Nuevo San Lucas.) *No. Many remained for months in the encampment on top of the Rebalse placed by the National Irrigation Commission, who we also knew as 'Las Carpas'... and there were the people, peering towards the town that was gradually being flooded"*, Arturo relates.

The adobe houses were soaked. All the loose things that the inhabitants had left in the courtyards and on the streets were floating. And as the water rose, the anxiety of the local San Lucas citizens increased. They were witnessing the water eating their beloved town.

The last thing they saw was the only church steeple constructed of adobe. It was just like the one erected in the new town. It was consecrated to the original San Lucas.

SAN LUCAS, PUEBLO OF THE CONCHOS INDIANS

But how long has San Lucas been in these canyons? The town and Hacienda San Lucas originate from the time of the Spanish colonization of the territory.

After the discovery of the mines in Parral in 1631, the Spaniards went beyond the border of the Conchos River, and moved north more consistently. In 1640, these Europeans began to regularly use the waters of the San Pedro River. In that year, next to one of its tributaries, the Jesuits founded the mission of Satevó. Shortly thereafter, the Franciscans of the Province of Zacatecas founded the mission of San Pedro de Conchos. It was located south of the waters from Satevó and on the left bank of the river, about 40 kilometers north of San Francisco de Conchos, and about 110 from Parral. In 1665, the same Franciscans founded the mission of the Concho Indians of Babonoyaba, also in the vicinity of the tributary of the San Pedro. At this point, the westernmost location of the river, almost at its beginning, came to an end of the territory of the Conchos, and then began that of the Tarahumaras.

In a letter of 1736, the chronicler Arlegui said of the San Pedro that the conversion of San Pedro de Conchos regularly had eleven very distant Indian towns from its beginning location, and one of those towns mentioned was San Lucas.

San Lucas was later recognized as an hacienda (farm/ranch) with the same name, and was owned by Carmen Salas at a time when this prominent woman landowner hosted at her Rosales home Don Benito Juarez. In times of war against the French and the empire of Maximilian, the Hacienda San Lucas had an area of 372 hectares. The channel or ditch on the right bank irrigated 139 hectares of wheat, corn and beans and a garden of six hectares; the left margin served to give irrigation to 217 hectares of wheat, corn and beans, and 10 hectares of orchards.

THE HACIENDA, DONATED TO BENEFIT THE POOR

The Hacienda San Lucas was one of many properties of Salas. She ceded it to sustain the sanatorium she supported with her own money in the capital city of Chihuahua. Doña Carmen lived in the region which today is the municipality of Rosales. She was of good character. The wealthy Doña Carmen Salas founded with her resources, a hospital to care for homeless people and poor people. It opened in March 1905 at 310 Avenue Ocampo in the capital of Chihuahua. In April 1905, Doña Carmen died and left her fortune to sustain this center of charity, declaring that it be named "Sanatorium Miguel Salas" in memory of her father.

"I SAW THE RUINS OF THE TOWN"

*When Don Manuel Corral came here to El Rebalse (*SR note - see rebalse note 1 below for the definition of "rebalse"*) in 1958 (*SR note - see rebalse note 2 below*), the town of San Lucas which now had been flooded for five* *years by the waters of the presa Francisco I. Madero, was the great technological innovation that would transform the entire region.*

(SR note – Rebalse Note 1: The Spanish word "rebalse" signifies water in a river that has been slowed down and brought to a stand- still by a dam-like structure that is typically made of dirt and rock. The "rebalse" in this story was a dam-like structure that was constructed to retain the waters of the San Pedro river from flowing downstream. Once the river water was contained at the location of the "rebalse", the area downstream of the "rebalse" could be kept dry so that the construction of the Francisco I. Madero dam could then proceed. It was the waters retained by the "rebalse" that ultimately flooded the small village of San Lucas Viejo.)

(SR note - Rebalse Note 2: Another item that needs clarification is the date of 1958 indicated in this paragraph. The wording in this paragraph seems to imply that the "rebalse" was constructed 5 years prior to 1958. This wording implies that the "rebalse" was constructed in 1953. This does not make sense since other literature and video sources show that the Francisco I. Madero dam was completed in 1949. As a result, the town of San Lucas would have to have been flooded at the location of the "rebalse" much earlier than 1949. I believe the year given of 1958 was provided in error.")

Sacrificing the town of San Lucas was inevitable.

"I saw the ruins of the village which still protruded from the water. The church was still there, but little by little the water gradually completely engulfed all that. The dam reached the water level that it now has; that now are the floodgates".

Today, the little town called El Rebalse, which currently is almost completely uninhabited, was known in the fifties as "the camp". The inhabitants of San Lucas temporarily lived there when their homes were flooded. Many know El Rebalse as the "The Little School", because in the midst of such desolation, many felt that a school for the children of the fishermen should be built in this location.

*Although ghostly, this is a settlement. A total of 10 houses are located here. There is a school and church. There's even a restaurant that serves fried fish and bear soup on the weekends. (**SR note – The phrase "bear soup" appears in the article, however, there are no bears in that arid region. In the video titled "PRESA LAS VIRGENES.-SU HISTORIA, 22" the narrator*** *speaks of a "caldo odioso" which was the name given to fish soup. The narrator then goes on to say that the local people slowly converted the phrase "caldo odioso" to "caldo de oso". In English "caldo de oso" is "bear soup".)*

OLD SAN LUCAS AND FISHING

Fishing has an importance, because besides the fact that these fishermen live from this type of work, hundreds of fishermen per week come to El Rebalse for sport.

Fishing as a business, "is not that good, look: during a good season, starting from Easter, with the warm weather, one can earn up to 150 and 200 pesos per day. But right now, for example, many tilapia died from the cold," explained Don Manuel.

Fish are taken from here to Delicias to fisheries or Rosales to picnic areas. There is no need to use coolers or ice to preserve the product, because it is immediately brought to market. "Only when kept during the night, then yes, we place them on ice, but it is rare. We try to transport them as soon as possible, so that our work is rewarded".

In this town, the houses are inhabited by fishermen only because their families are in the cities of the region. "There's nothing here for them, no school, no amenities, nothing," said Manuel Corral, who is sure that, sooner or later, these ruins should be abandoned as well.

The future of El Rebalse is the same as Viejo San Lucas who, like the legendary Atlantis, lies under water.

(SR note: This story stirs up in me a sense of sadness. The village where my father was raised was engulfed by the waters created by the dam known as "Presa de las Virgenes.)

The References Relating to the Presa de la Virgenes

The following is a list of internet links to written articles and maps that relate to the construction and location of the dam known as presa Francisco I. Madero which is now known as "Presa de las Virgenes". I invite you to view the videos and internet articles relating to the "Presa de la Virgenes".

Internet Reference "San Lucas 1"

The following is a reference to two videos on the internet that depict the construction of the "Presa de Las Virgenes" (also known as "La Presa Francisco I. Madero"). The videos are important because the lake that resulted from the construction work of the dam wound up flooding the town of San Lucas. San Lucas was where my father, Jesus Renteria Tarango, was born and raised. The narration indicates that the dam was built during the years of 1941 through 1949.

Name of Video 1: PRESA LAS VIRGENES.-SU HISTORIA

1/2 - Video 1 of 2, Reference: https://www.youtube.com/watch?v= LAT7cfPQUF8

Name of Video 2: PRESA LAS VIRGENES.-SU HISTORIA

2/2 - Video 2 of 2, Reference: https://www.youtube.com/watch?v= ZZ6ZziT8Uus

Internet Reference "San Lucas 2"

This internet article provides information relating to the construction of the "Presa de las Virgenes", also known as "La Presa Francisco I. Madero", which was built during the years of 1941 through 1949.

Reference:

https://books.google.com/books?id=SEU0IIobJCcC&pg=PA369 &lpg=PA369&dq=when+was+las+virgenes+dam+in+Chihuahua+constructed&source=bl&ots=Dz3H5wannv&sig=ACmyYWJLQWl NIKj0nAM5ak7UyAk&hl=en&sa=X&ved=0ahUKEwi06pjXyL7OA hXHKyYKHbw2C1wQ6AEIJjAC#v=onepage&q=when%20was%20 las%20virgenes%20dam%20in%20Chihuahua%20constructed& f=false

Internet Reference "San Lucas 3"

This internet article indicates that construction of the Presa de las Virgenes, also known as La Presa Francisco I. Madero, started in 1941.

Reference:

https://www.clubensayos.com/Historia/Presa-Francisco-I- Madero/1600414.html

The following internet article was originally written in Spanish. I translated and loosely paraphrased part of the article into English as follows:

"It was then that the construction of one of the largest hydraulic works of the State began. It was the Francisco I. Madero dam which had its seat in the municipality of Rosales, the house of Benémerito of the Americas. Ingenuity and inventiveness always timely and accurate, would result in changing the official name from that of the father of Mexican democracy to that of presa "Las Virgenes". This was in memory of the ranch that previously existed and which was buried together with the town of San Lucas. The new seat was established near the municipality of Meoqui.

In the year 1941, a group of engineers and workers under the direction of the engineer Enrique Rubio Castañeda were given the task of initiating this monumental work. They broke down hills, pulverized huge rocks, overcame the elusive and reluctant nature while also obeying the project direction of the engineer Ignacio Cobo. His main objective was to regulate the flow of the San Pedro River to take advantage of its waters. This was done so that crop irrigation of the land north of this stream could be developed in the area known as Irrigation District 05."

Internet Reference "San Lucas 4"

This internet link presents another reference to the destruction of San Lucas prior to building the dam.

http://www.cronicadechihuahua.com/La-epopeya-del-pueblo- anegado.html

The article was originally written in Spanish. The following is a part of that article that I translated and loosely paraphrased to English:

"The people of San Lucas were evicted by technicians from the National Irrigation Commission when they decided to build a giant dam in the canyon between Charco del Gallo and Villalba. The objective was to take advantage of the waters of the river for planting crops in the area known

as Irrigation District 05. The people who were evicted from San Lucas were sent to establish Nuevo San Lucas near the neighboring municipality of Meoqui. These people were given land in compensation for those lands left behind. The persons who stayed to work the land vacated in San Lucas, now live scattered in Rosales and Delicias, Chihuahua."

Internet Reference "San Lucas 5"

The following link can be used to determine the location of the lake formed by the dam known as the "Presa Francisco I. Madero" near Rosales, Chihuahua.

https://www.google.com/maps/place/
Nuevo+San+Lucas,+ Chihuahua,+Mexico/@28.1080115,-
105.7515803,11.48z/data=!4m5!3
m4!1s0x86eb0fc095284a9f:0xa23dfdbd0043be64!8m2!3d28.3572222
!4d-105.5686111

Internet Reference "San Lucas 6"

The following internet article shows that the lake area created by the Presa Francisco I. Madero, also known as Presa de las Virgenes, was filled in 1949. It also indicates that the dam was inaugurated on May 25, 1949.

http://elsentido.com/noticias/mxm/cumple-64-
anos-presa-las- virgenes/

The following is a part of the article that I translated and loosely paraphrased to English:

"It was on May 25, 1949, when the then President of the Republic, Miguel Alemán Valdez, the Secretary of Hydraulic Resources, Adolfo Orive Alba and the Governor Fernando Foglio Miramontes, officially inaugurated the operation of the dam, at which time the dam was filled during that same year."

Internet Reference "San Lucas 7"

The following link provides the longitudinal location of the original San Lucas and which is now known as San Lucas Viejo.

http://www.weatheravenue.com/en/america/ mx/chihuahua/san- lucas-viejo-pictures.html

The approximate lat-long coordinates are as follows:

Latitude:28° 6›38.31»N, Longitude: 105°42'28.12"W

Internet Reference "San Lucas 8"

The following link provides the location of the "Presa Francisco I. Madero" which is now known as "Presa de las Virgenes".

http://www.dices.net/mapas/mexico/mapa.php? nombre=Presa- Francisco-I-Madero&id=25985

Witnessing The Flooding of San Lucas

In a previous section, the presence of surveying teams in the village of San Lucas was described. My father told me that groups of men with "teodolitos" were seen in the area of San Lucas. As indicated before, this occurred during the year 1940 when my father was 12 years of age. As a result of the story he told me, I now know that these men were part of surveying teams that were combing the San Pedro river valley where San Lucas was located. They were probably preparing topography maps to prepare for the construction of the "Presa de las Virgenes" which was to be constructed.

My father told me that about a year after having observed what I now know were teams of surveyors near San Lucas, my grandfather Jose seemed to be acting restlessly. My father was now 13 years of age in 1941. He told me that one day during those restless days, he overheard my grandfather Jose speaking with Ester about having to move from San Lucas. They were speaking about something having to do with the waters of the San Pedro River. Sometime later after that, my father asked my grandfather Jose about the discussion he had overheard about the waters from the San Lucas River.

My grandfather Jose spoke about a town meeting that he had attended in which representatives from the Mexican government had informed them that a new dam was going to be constructed in the area close to Rosales, Chihuahua. My grandfather went on to tell my father that sooner or later the town of San Lucas was going to be flooded with waters from a lake that would be created by the new dam.

My grandfather Jose indicated that the Mexican government representatives had told them that landowners in San Lucas would be provided new lands in a new town that was to be called Nuevo San Lucas. This means "New San Lucas" in English. Nuevo San Lucas was planned to be built northeast from the town of Meoqui. I never asked my father whether land was given to my grandfather Jose in exchange for the land where his house was built in San Lucas. The subject of them moving to what was now called Nuevo San Lucas was never broached so therefore I truly don't know if my grandfather Jose's family moved there.

My grandfather continued to tell my father that a provisional earthen dam would be constructed somewhere between the location of the town of San Lucas and the location of the new dam. The provisional earthen dam would be used to hold back the water flow of the San Pedro River. The provisional dam would then block the water flow from reaching the area where the new dam was going to be constructed. My grandfather told my father that sooner or later they would have to move from San Lucas. My father finally understood why my grandfather Jose seemed so fidgety. It was a time of uncertainty.

My father told me that about a year later, which I believe to be sometime in 1942, the construction of the earthen dam began. The provisional dam located in the San Pedro River valley was built with earth and large stones from the nearby mountains. Just as my grandfather Jose had predicted earlier, the dam was placed at a location between the town of San Lucas and the area where the new large concrete dam was going to be constructed. The Spanish phrase "El Rebalse" is used to describe a dam usually constructed of earthen material that is used to block the flow of running water.

Shortly before the earthen dam was constructed, representatives from the Mexican government notified the residents of San Lucas that they would now be required to leave. Some of the inhabitants moved to Nuevo San Lucas but some refused to go. In the meantime, the earthen dam had begun to accumulate water from the San Pedro River. The waters had not yet reached the area of San Lucas and there were still residents that hadn't moved out. The government representatives continued to pressure those locals to move.

As the water continued to be held back by the earthen dam known as "el rebalse", the water kept slowly creeping toward the town of San Lucas. This continued for about 2 years. More people began to leave. The more militant citizens that had previously refused to move finally had no choice. My grandfather Jose and his family were those people that had refused to go. Those that did not move as originally planned finally decided to leave.

Some of those remaining people settled in an elevated area opposite and across the small lake from the town of San Lucas. The new settlement began to take on the look and feel of a small town in itself. Tents were built for protection from the elements; the wind, the sun, the rain, etc. In fact, the internet article titled "La Epopeya Del Pueblo Anegado" which translates to "The Epic of a Flooded Town" that was earlier described, tells about a ghostly settlement where a total of 10 houses stood along with a school and a church. That was the settlement that is now known as "El Rebalse".

The days wore on. From the elevated vantage point of this new settlement, the people could now see the waters slowly creeping toward San Lucas. A feeling of doom and sadness prevailed. Months passed and the on-lookers could see the water slowly begin to gobble up the small town. The people's sense of loss increased when at last wooden furniture and wooden roof beams began to float away from the location of the once thriving village. The town of San Lucas was disappearing as the accumulating water rose higher and higher.

The days continued to wear on. The church building which rose above the rest of the home structures in San Lucas was now beginning to disappear underneath the rising water. Eventually, the only structure that could be discerned from a distance was the upper part of the church and the church steeple. Months passed and finally even the church steeple was lost. Finally the people felt a deep sense of loss.

The retained water had gobbled up the town of San Lucas but the earthen dam still had enough capacity to hold back the water for another 5 years. These additional years were necessary to allow the major dam construction downstream. From the time of the completion of the earthen retaining dam which was known as the "rebalse" in 1942 to the time when the church steeple finally disappeared, 2 years had gone by. In that year 1944, my father was 16 years of age.

What happened to the remaining people that persisted in the small settlement known as "El Rebalse"? My grandfather Jose and his family finally did proceed to move to a location near Nuevo San Lucas. As for the rest of the people remaining, my father didn't tell me; I wish I had asked.

The Portillo Ranch – Tending Horses

My father told me that in 1944 when he was 16 years of age, he decided to strike out on his own. Somehow he managed to find employment on a ranch located some distance away from San Lucas. The ranch was owned by a man by the name of Juan Portillo. He wound up working there until August of 1947.

By the way, the Spanish surname "Portillo" is pronounced similarly to pronouncing "Portiyo". In later years after having married, my father would wind up working on a farm in Fabens. The farm belonged to James Ryan. My father would refer to the Ryan farm as a "rancho" which in English means "ranch". In reality Mr. Ryan owned a "farm" and not a "ranch". The English word "farm" means "granja" in Spanish but is pronounced similarly to the word "granha". As a result, although the Portillo ranch did have horses and cattle and therefore was a "ranch", I don't really know if it also had elements of being a farm or again in Spanish, a "granja" where crops could be grown.

As indicated before, my father told me that cattle and horses were raised on the ranch. When he began working at the Portillo ranch, his job was that of tending the horses. Several men in addition to him tended the horses. He never specifically told me, but by the manner in which he spoke about the ranch, I imagine the ranch must have had numerous horses.

The tamed horses and the wild horses were kept in separate corrals. A separate corral was used to break the horses. The phrase "breaking the horses" means "taming the horses".

The horses were primarily used to herd cattle that roamed throughout the large expanse of arid land. The Portillo ranch and other neighboring ranches were confined to specific land areas. Unlike barb wire fences that are used today to delineate land areas belonging to specific ranchers, the delineations in those days were marked stone walls that stood about 4 feet high and about 2 feet wide. The stone walls were constructed of stones that were loosely laid on top of each other without the use of mortar. The terrain was mountainous and the stone walls ran along the hilly elevations of the terrain. The stone fences therefore confined the horses and the cattle to specific grazing areas belonging to the specific ranches.

My father continued his job on the ranch tending the horses for about a year. My father told me that during that year, he remained on the ranch and didn't visit my grandfather Jose and his family. Remember that the family included Anita and Fernando with whom he felt a deep attachment. After that year he began to visit his family frequently.

The Portillo Ranch – The Problem With Genovevo

Back at the Portillo ranch, my father tended the horses. It was the type of job that most young men did. Remember, he was 17 years of age at the time. It was now 1945.

He told me that the name of the ranch foreman was a person by the name of Genovevo. Out of several young men, Genovevo would pick my father more often to break the horses. Remember, breaking horses meant taming the horses. My father told me that breaking the horses was a dangerous task. In spite of him asking Genovevo to spread the wealth, so to speak, Genovevo would insist that most of the horses be broken by my father. As a result, the task fell almost entirely to my father.

My father didn't anticipate that he would wind up being the person that would now be breaking the majority of the horses. It was an unintended consequence that resulted from my father's exceptional ability to manage horses.

My father felt that this was unfair to him. After all, breaking horses was indeed a dangerous task and Genovevo knew it. My father couldn't understand why it was that he was the ranch hand that had to perform that dangerous task more frequently than the others. My father insisted to Genovevo that each man should break his own horse. In that way, the horse would be able to better respond to the man that broke the horse in the first place. He felt that each ranch hand could better control their horse when herding the cattle and the other wild horses on the ranch.

All this occurred when my father was about 18 years of age in 1947. My father's objection to Genovevo's decision remained unresolved. Eventually, my father was able to convince Juan Portillo, the owner of the ranch, that each man should break the same equal number of horses that he broke or better yet that each man should break his own horse. Genovevo found out about my father having spoken with Juan Portillo and from then on, Genovevo purposefully selected my father to break only the wildest of the horses. Yes, no longer did my father have to break most of the horses; he now had to break the meanest of the horses, unbeknownst to Juan Portillo, the owner. I suppose Genovevo did it as revenge for my father having spoken with Juan Portillo. As a result, my father made it a point to make no further comment to the owner, Juan Portillo.

Because of the manner in which my father spoke about Genovevo, it seemed to me that my father continued to hold a grudge toward Genovevo, even as a grown man. He never outright told me that he did; it just seemed that he did. My father never told me Genovevo's full name, so as a result, I am unable to share it.

The Portillo Ranch - Breaking Horses

As indicated previously, breaking a horse is required to transform a wild horse into a tamed horse. Once tamed, the trained horse can be ridden safely to herd cattle on a ranch.

I've never broken a horse; but I have ridden several. I consider myself an above average horse rider; Chuy, my older brother, was even more an expert. The reason, that I can ride a horse well is because we owned horses during my adolescent years. My father bought our first horse when I was about 11 years of age. A few years later my father traded that horse in for another horse. I remember that second horse well because it was an all white color. We could even prompt it to walk backwards. That is how Chuy and I learned how to care and ride horses.

Horses seemed important to my father. My father used to tell me about his experiences breaking horses as a young man. As I said before, I have never broken a horse; however, I know how it is done.

I know how it is done because I heard my father's many stories about having broken horses during the time he worked on the Juan Portillo ranch as a young man. That's the reason that I now find it necessary to tell what I learned from my father in relation to breaking horses.

The first step in breaking a horse is to "bridle" the horse. A "bridle" is a piece of equipment used to control a horse. The "bridle" includes the headstall that is fitted with a metal bit that is placed inside the mouth of the horse. The reins are long, narrow leather straps attached to each end of the horse's bit. They are used to guide or direct a horse while it is being ridden.

It's no easy task to "bridle" a wild horse since the horse is not accustomed to wearing the headstall on its head. The wild horse won't easily accept having the metal bit placed in its mouth. Bridling a wild horse is at least a two man job; the horse won't stand still during the first few times it is bridled. Once the horse is bridled, one of the cowboys holds on to the bridle while another cowboy slowly places a cloth shroud on the horse's head. This is done to keep the horse from observing the next step, which is placing the saddle on the horse's back.

A saddle gives the rider the necessary support, security, and control over the horse. In essence, the saddle is a supportive structure for the rider to sit on. The saddle is fastened to the horse's back with a strong woven flat girth, sometimes called a cinch. It passes horizontally underneath the horse's belly and ultimately each end of the girth is attached to the sides of the saddle. The girth is manually pulled to tighten the saddle in-place on the horse's back.

Stirrups hang on both sides of the saddle by way of straps that are often called stirrup leathers. A stirrup is a light frame or ring that holds the foot of a rider. The stirrups are used to aid in mounting the horse and they provide the rider foot support while the horse is being ridden.

While one person holds the bridled horse still, the other person then slowly begins to place the saddle onto the horse's back making sure to avoid jerky movements that might spook the horse. Remember, we're talking about a wild horse. Anyway, placing the saddle on a wild horse is a challenge because the wild horse is not really used to having a saddle on its back. Once the saddle is placed on the horses back, the cinch is tightened underneath the horse's belly to insure that the saddle stays on the horse's back.

Once saddled, the person, fully expecting that the horse is going to attempt to throw him off its back, slowly mounts the horse. Since this is the first time that the horse is being mounted, the horse is initially confused and initially remains motionless. Just after the horse is mounted, the person still holding the horse by the bridle then slowly removes the cloth shroud from the horses head . . . now the fun begins.

In some cases, after realizing that the rider is on its back, the horse will begin to run without prompting. In other cases, the horse begins to buck up and down trying to rid itself of the rider and the saddle. The rider reacts to the horse's every move to make sure that he remains mounted on top of the horse as the horse runs or bucks up and down. The objective is to keep the horse running until it tires itself out. Ultimately, the horse continues to run or buck up and down until he eventually begins to tire. When the horse begins to tire, it typically then begins to run at a slower more controlled gait or it might even come to a complete stop. By the way, having a horse buck up and down is only done in rodeos for show.

At this point, the horse has accepted the fact that the rider is going to remain seated on the horse's back no matter what the horse does. That is when the rider then begins to prompt the horse to run at a slow gait around the corral. Running at a slow gait is known as a "trotting" gait. This is done to get the horse used to accepting the rider's commands.

This is how breaking a horse should normally occur; however, many times the horse does manage to throw the rider off its back. When this happens the process of breaking the horse continues all over again, starting with one person holding the horse's head by the bridle and the other person slowly mounting the horse. The horse may continue to buck even after being re-mounted or may just continue to trot around inside the fence.

Re-mounting the horse as soon as possible is of utmost importance. If the horse is not immediately re-mounted after it throws off the rider, the horse regains its confidence and it will revert back to its original inclination of not allowing a rider to mount it. The key is to break the horse's will and to force it to accept being ridden.

My father told me that successfully breaking a wild horse that first time was not enough. The horse had to endure the same breaking process several more times during the following days. After several more episodes, the cowboy can reliably mount the horse without the horse running off or bucking up and down uncontrollably.

My father told me that the tamed horse often remembers the person who "broke" it; in other words, the person who tamed it. He felt that the broken horse forms strong bonds with the rider that broke or tamed it and as a result, the horse tends to obey that rider much more.

By the way, since my father broke most of the horses on the Portillo ranch, most of the horses felt more at ease with my father when he mounted them. The men that worked on the ranch took notice and as a result, they would tease my father. The men would sometimes insinuate that the horses were somehow enamored with my father. Obviously, that wasn't true. But it did seem to my father that a horse did seem to remember the person that managed to "break" it.

The Portillo Ranch - How My Father Met My Mother

The Portillo ranch was in itself a small village consisting mostly of men and a few women. Some of the men and women were married couples. Everyone lived in the main central ranch compound.

During the time when my father worked on the Portillo ranch, it was sometimes necessary for equipment to be brought in from the nearby city of Delicias and sometimes Rosales. Men would be dispatched to the city of Delicias or Rosales to transport equipment and food stuffs back to the ranch. Some of the men, and at times my father, would be assigned to transport those items to the ranch.

Somehow my father and mother met in Delicias during one of those trips that he made to Delicias. I never asked my father or mother about their courtship and so I don't know how long my father courted my mother before they eloped later on.

I remember either my father or my mother telling me that they did get together at festivals. They are called "fiestas" in Spanish. They mentioned that dances were held at the festivals. These festivals were sometimes even held at the Portillo ranch.

From time to time, the ranch owner, Juan Portillo, would arrange parties for the workers on the ranch property. Some of the men knew how to play the guitar and others the double bass instrument. The double bass instrument looks like a cello instrument but is much larger. In Mexico the double bass instrument is known as a "tololoche". These men would form rudimentary musical bands that would play Mexican country music that was typical of those days.

As an aside, I remember my mother telling me that her sister Manuela always had to accompany my mother during outings with my father at the "fiesta" dances. In olden times in Mexico, unmarried women were never allowed to be courted by a man unless accompanied by a "chaperone".

Anyway, my father met my mother in Delicias during one of his visits from the Portillo ranch. And as stated before, their courtship occurred during meetings at dance festivals both in Delicias and at the Portillo ranch. That courtship would later bear fruit in the form of my family.

The Portillo Ranch - My Father's Eureka Moment

One day while riding a horse that he had broken previously, my father happened to place the stirrups against the horse's sides in a somewhat unique manner while at the same time gently pulling back on the reins. All of a sudden the horse began to slowly walk backwards. My father didn't expect this to happen. He tried it again and found that the horse again repeated slowly walking backwards. To confirm that the technique worked on other horses, he tried the same leg movement on the horse's sides while also pulling gently on the reins and again the other horse walked backwards. He tried it on several other horses that he had broken and again he achieved the same result on those horses. From the way he described this discovery, I knew this was exciting to him.

He now knew how to make every horse he broke move in that manner. It worked every time the horse sensed the stirrups placed in that very unique manner while at the same time pulling back gently on the reins. At the time when he told me about this discovery, it didn't dawn on me to ask him to show me how he placed the stirrups on the horse's side to make it walk backwards. It was a significant discovery that he didn't share with the others.

He began to show off his ability to make the horses walk backwards and eventually the ranch foreman, Genovevo, noticed him doing this with several horses. Genovevo never asked my father how he managed to get the horses to obey him in that manner; he was too proud to do that. It did seem evident to my father that Genovevo was somewhat envious of him because of his mastery with horses. I suppose it turned out to be my father's dig at Genovevo.

The Portillo Ranch – The Leg Injury

One day, when my father was breaking one of the wildest of the horses, he was thrown off the horse. As a result of the fall, he wound up hurting his leg. He was not able to work breaking horses anymore. He was about 19 years of age at the time.

For a while, he continued working at the ranch. He was now placed back in his old job which was that of tending the horses. The fall and subsequent injury from the horse was a pivotal moment for him. He now knew that his future would no longer include the dangerous task of breaking horses. In the end, he decided to leave the Portillo ranch.

Discovery of the Past and Researching the Later Years

I am fortunate that I remember the stories that my father, little by little, told about his years growing up in the little village of San Lucas as well as stories of his later years as a young man working at the Juan Portillo ranch. Those little tidbits that he remembered about his youth are what I used in describing the history up to this point in natural progression. I am sure there is much more to the story of his formative years that I will never know.

There are many things that I never got to fully know about his life after he left the Juan Portillo ranch. Those details weren't as important to me when he was living; however, now they are. In order to piece together the history of his life after he left the Juan Portillo ranch, I now had to resort to other resources. One such resource was his military documentation, which I possess. Another resource was the labor time booklets that he prepared later on when he entered the United States. The subsequent stories, for the most part, are still based on my recollection of his verbal stories but because I failed to ask sufficient questions of him, I have had to assume the role of researcher in order to be able to understand that part of his history. The next chapters in this memoir are presented in a format more akin to that of an investigation; in other words, using documentation and recollection to arrive at historical conclusions.

As a result, the following chapters are written not in normal story manner but more in a manner where historical segments are pieced together to form a historical conclusion.

Rodrigo Molina Ranch – Final Employment In The Delicias Area

As indicated previously, my father injured his leg while breaking horses at the Portillo Ranch. He resigned from the Portillo Ranch and went to work at the Rodrigo Molina Ranch.

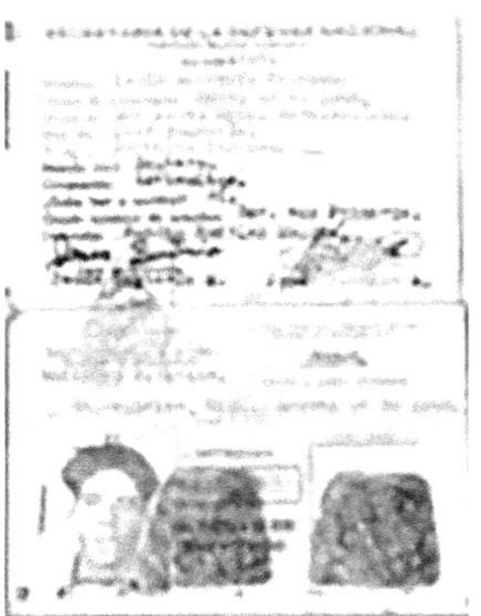

My father never spoke about working at the Rodrigo Molina Ranch. I found out about this fact while reviewing information that was contained in his military documentation. His military documentation from the "Secretaria de la Defensa Nacional" shows that on the date of August 14, 1948, my father was single and that he resided at the "Rodrigo Molina" ranch.

I never knew of my father having worked anywhere else in the Delicias area other than at the Juan Portillo ranch. Having discovered that he worked on the Rodrigo Molina Ranch was a surprise to me now while I was writing this chapter of his life.

The Marriage

In a previous section, I indicated that my father met my mother in Delicias and that the courtship included meetings at festival dances both in Delicias and at the Portillo Ranch. I have never been able to pinpoint the date of my father's and mother's elopement. I know they eloped because my father told me so. When he was describing their elopement, he used the phrase in a playful way "me robé a tu mama" which in English: "I stole your mother".

I never got around to asking my parents why they eloped instead of simply getting married. When my time came to get married, I did ask

Socorro's mother for her daughter's hand in marriage. For all I know, he may have asked my grandmother Maria for her daughter's hand in marriage and it's possible that my grandmother Maria turned him down. I should have asked more questions.

My Father's Entry Into The United States

My preoccupation with the date of my parent's elopement date is not merely to know the date but it is was more because I wanted to accurately pinpoint the date of my father's entry into the United States as a bracero. More information on the details as to the meaning of the word "bracero" is presented in subsequent chapters. For now, suffice it to be mean "legal immigrant farm worker". When my father entered the United States, I know that he and my mother were already together as husband and wife.

On one hand, I know that on August 14, 1948 my father was a bachelor. The date of August 14, 1948 is contained in the military service document issued by the "Secretaria de la Defensa Nacional" which in English translates to "Secretary of National Defense". This document shows that he was single at the time. The documentation also indicates that his residence was at the Rodrigo Molina Ranch in Mexico. On the other hand, I know that my father entered the United States as a bracero when he was already together with my mother. Finally, I know that my older brother, Jesus, was born on May 6, 1949 while in the United States.

By removing nine months from my older brother's date of birth, I wind up with a date of August 6, 1948 as the conception date. As a result of this date, it appears that my father crossed into the United States as a bracero approximately 2 or 3 weeks prior to my older brother being born. This would be sometime during the middle of April 1949.

My Father's Military Service – "Bola Negra" and "Bola Blanca"

When I was a young boy, we interacted quite a bit with my grandfather Jose's family when they lived in Caseta, Distrito Bravo, Chihuahua. Caseta is a small Mexican village across the border from Tornillo, Texas on the United States side. From time

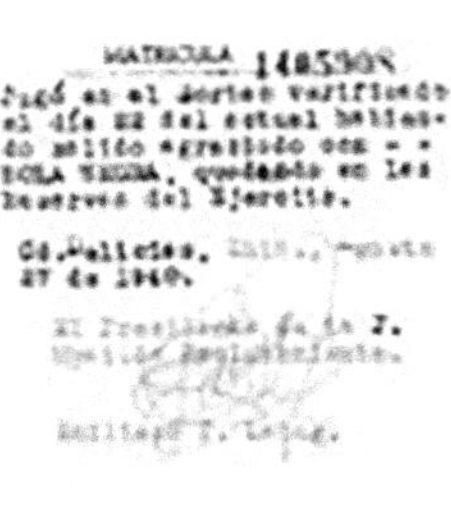

to time, I would hear the words "bola negra" and "bola blanca" when someone was referring to the subject having to do with the Mexican military service. "Bola negra" translates to English as "black ball" while "bola blanca" translates to English as "white ball".

As indicated previously, I happened upon my father's military records in the form of a 5 page booklet. The title of the booklet is "Cartilla de Identidad, Servicio Militar Nacional" issued by the "Secretaria de la Defensa Nacional". All this translates in English as "Identity Card, National Military Service" issued by the "Secretary of National Defense".

I read the contents of the booklet and noticed that page 5 of the booklet contains a reference to "sorteo" and "bola negra". That page 5 of my father's military booklet contains the record that shows that my father participated in a "sorteo" which means "military lottery drawing" in English on August 27, 1948. As a result of the booklet, I now know that during the "military lottery drawing", my father officially drew a black marble from a jar having black and white marbles. This occurred in Delicias, Chihuahua on August 27, 1948 when he was 19 years of age.

My understanding is that those that drew the "bola negra" or the "black marble" were exempt from regular duty in the military service. Instead of the extended 3 years of regular continuous military duty, those that drew "bola negra" or the "black marble" would only have to participate in reserve training lasting 1 or 2 weeks every year for 3 years.

Further, I found that the succeeding 3 pages in my father's military booklet shows that he attended reserve military training on the following dates: March 20, 1950; March 20, 1951 and March 20, 1952. The military booklet shows that he attended reserve training in Guadalupe, Distrito Bravo, Chihuahua, which is just across the U.S./Mexico border close to Caseta where my grandfather Jose's family lived.

I finally understand the significance of the phrase "bola negra".

The Start of my Father's Family

My parents eloped sometime around August of 1948. My father, Jesus Renteria Tarango, was 20 years of age and my mother, Maria Encarnacion Gutierrez Gonzalez was 19 years old.

Everyone called him by the Mexican nickname of "Chuy" and we called him "Apá". My mother was the exception; she would always call my father by his true name of "Jesus". People would call my mother by the nickname of "Méri" and we called her "Amá". Remember, accents in the Spanish language are important.

Shortly after they eloped, they migrated from Delicias, Chihuahua, Mexico to the Cd. Juarez, Chihuahua area. As indicated previously, Delicias, Chihuahua, Mexico is a small city located about 294 miles south of Cd. Juarez.

My father was a Mexican citizen and my mother was a U.S. citizen. My mother was born in Hatch, New Mexico but since her entire family moved to Delicias, Chihuahua when she was a baby, she grew up in Mexico and as a result, she spoke Spanish and no English.

Why "Apá" and "Amá" and Not "Papá" and "Mamá"

Sometime later as a grown-up when I owned and managed a business known as Fluid Process Systems, Inc., a trusted employee asked me why it was that my family addressed our father as "Apá" and not "Papá". Note the use of the accent symbol on the letter "a". Many words in the Spanish language contain accent symbols atop some of the letters. The accent symbol, for example, on the fourth letter "a" in the word Papá makes the word sound different from the word Papa when spoken in English. In the English language, the word Papa is normally spoken as if the accent symbol is on the second letter "a" as in Pápa. The word Apá that we used to address our father was therefore the short version of Papá.

Anyway, after my employee asked the question as to why we called my father by the word Apá, I was initially surprised that he had noticed and so I asked him the reason for the question. He told me that the word Apá sounded funny to him and that he had never heard anyone address their father in that manner. I simply told him that this was the manner we learned as children and left it at that.

Thinking about it further later, I felt that he asked the question because it seemed to him a sort of backward, unsophisticated way of addressing my father. I hadn't thought about the origins of "Apá" and "Amá" until now. It's apparent to me now that the reason we use "Apá" and "Amá" is because my mother would use the words "Apá" and "Amá" when addressing her parents. My father, on the other hand, always used the word "Papá" to address his father, Jose. Now as a grown up, I've found that accent symbols used in the Spanish language are important because they indicate where emphasis is placed on a word when it is pronounced.

My Father the Bracero

Soon after my father and mother eloped in August of 1948, my father somehow became aware of a program known as the "Bracero" program in the United States. I read that the Bracero program originated as a result of a series of laws and diplomatic agreements initiated in 1942, when the United States signed the Mexican Farm Labor Agreement with Mexico. The Spanish term "bracero" means "manual laborer" or "one who works using his arms".

Although my father's knowledge of the Bracero program was limited, he and my mother decided to travel to Cd. Juarez, Chihuahua. Cd. Juarez is located across the U.S./Mexico border from El Paso, Texas. His intention was to find out how to become a "bracero" and work in the United States. The letters "Cd." is short for "Ciudad" and translates to the word "City" in English. Cd. Juarez therefore can be termed as "City of Juarez".

My mother told me that when they arrived at Cd. Juarez, my father and mother stayed with family relatives. I never asked her for the names of the persons or families that that they stayed with. Later on when I was a child, my family would frequently visit a family in Cd. Juarez with the surname of Valdiviezo. The heads of the household were Domitila Villarreal and Jesus Valdiviezo. She was called by the nickname of "Tila" as in the word "Teela" and was my mother's distant cousin. Although I don't know it for certain, it is very probable that my father and mother stayed with the Valdiviezo's when they first arrived in Cd. Juarez from Delicias.

On one occasion, my mother told me that during their stay in Cd. Juarez, a family relative made them aware of an immigration attorney whose surname was "Anchondo". Somehow they managed to meet with the attorney. During their meeting with the attorney, the attorney asked to review my father's and mother's documents.

After finishing the review of my mother's documents, the attorney looked up at my mother, stared at her for a few seconds and then told her: *"What are you doing in Mexico! You are free to travel to the United States anytime you want. Your documents indicate that you are a United States citizen.".* Of course, the previous remark was spoken in Spanish but I paraphrased it into English.

Looking back today, I am astonished that as a young woman, my mother didn't understand or was never told of the significance of her having been born in Hatch, New Mexico. Remember that she was born in Hatch but her family moved to Delicias when she was a baby. As far as she was concerned, she was from Mexico. In the end, Mr. Anchondo provided them guidance in getting my father enrolled into the Bracero program.

I never questioned my mother about the course of events after their meeting with Mr. Anchondo. I only know that shortly thereafter, my father was contracted as a bracero and ended up at the Ryan farm near Fabens, Texas. I won't ever know the course of events that occurred between the meeting with Mr. Anchondo and their arrival at the Ryan farm. However, I did come across a very interesting article on the internet that provides a clue as to what my father might have gone through to become a bracero. The internet article can be found at the following link:

http://braceroarchive.org/items/show/37

The internet article consists of an interview of a person named Carlos Corella who at the age of 22 worked for the United States Department

of Labor at a bracero reception center in Socorro, Texas. The name of the reception center was Rio Vista. Today, the Rio Vista reception facility still stands although it is no longer used as a bracero reception center. Anyway, the Carlos Corella interview took place in 2003 when he was 70 years of age. Carlos Corella managed the braceros through the Rio Vista reception center for a 3 year period starting in 1955. In his interview, Carlos Corella describes the processing of the braceros through the Rio Vista reception facility.

I recently visited the site of the Rio Vista reception center and I observed an official plaque located in front of the facility that shows it was in use as a bracero reception center from 1951 to 1964. Although the plaque indicates that the Rio Vista reception center began operating a bracero processing center in 1951, my father told me that he entered the United States as a bracero through the Rio Vista reception center sometime in April of 1949. So therefore, the 1951 Rio Vista start date is probably presented in error on the plaque.

Based on the information I read in relation to the bracero program, the El Paso Coliseum was the first facility used as the bracero reception center much prior to the opening of the Rio Vista reception center.

I have visited the Rio Vista reception center several times. During one of those visits, I took my time taking in the sight of the buildings that formed the complex. The buildings are constructed of adobe and are in disrepair.

During that specific visit I began to realize the real significance of the buildings that are still erect. The building architecture is similar to the architecture of the old Camp School buildings in Fabens where I started school as a very young child. My father was processed through this facility initially in 1949 and then again about 2 years later. My father walked through this site. It was as if I was walking the steps that my father walked.

I remember my father telling me about having entered the United States through the Rio Vista facility but at the time, I didn't grasp the importance or the significance of these buildings. I highly recommend that the reader of this memoir visit the site just to feel the sense that I felt. I took several photographs of the facility. The photographs on the left show the Rio Vista reception center as it exists today.

The two excerpts from Carlos Corella's interview shown below describe what my father probably went through after the orientation he received from the attorney, Mr. Anchondo.

During his interview, Carlos Corella spoke about want-to-be braceros having to start their sign-up process in the city of Chihuahua, approximately 300 miles south of El Paso. The city of Chihuahua was one of three bracero reception centers that processed braceros for entry into the United States. The other two were located in El Centro, California and Eagle Pass, Texas.

Even those men that lived in Cd. Juarez had to travel to the city of Chihuahua to start the bracero sign-up process. By the way, after reading an internet article, I found that Chihuahua was one of several cities in Mexico that were designated as an "estación migratoria" or in English "migratory station". The city of Empalme in the state of Sonora was another "migratory station". These "migratory stations" served as the first stepping stone for Mexican nationals to become braceros. If they passed the qualification tests at the "mirgratory stations", then they would be transported to the bracero reception centers in the United Sates. There were probably other "migratory stations" in Mexico; however, I am only familiar with those two cities as having been designated "migratory stations".

My father was in Cd. Juarez at the time and probably had to return to the "migratory station" in Chihuahua to start his bracero sign-up process. The following is Carlos Corella's statement regarding the start of the sign-up process in the city of Chihuahua:

> *"Even the Mexican Nationals that lived around Juárez*
> *that wanted to become braceros would have to make the trip*
> *to Chihuahua where they were processed by the Mexican*
> *government and then sent back to Juárez."*

I know from his stories that my father was processed at the Rio Vista reception center twice. Therefore, he probably made the trip from Cd. Juarez to Chihuahua twice; the first in April of 1949 and the other about 2 years later.

In that same interview, Carlos Corella spoke about the new enrollee's trip from the city of Chihuahua to Cd. Juarez. The following is his statement that describes that trip:

> *"The trip, incidentally, going back from Chihuahua to Juárez was a horrendous trip for 'em [sic]. It was by rail, and they were brought over from Chihuahua in cattle cars. I don't know how many stops they made, but it was about a seven-hour trip. If you can imagine, packed in rail cars, and as I said before, I don't know whether they made any stops to allow them to relieve themselves."*

Those that have a keen interest in the Bracero program should read Mr. Corella's interview presented below in its entirety. The interview is important because it comes from the perspective of a person fully versed with the bracero sign-up process. He was employed with the United States Department of Labor which is the agency that managed the Bracero program.

The Treatment of the Braceros In The Words of Carlos Corella

This section further expands on Carlos Corellas first-hand knowledge of the process of becoming a bracero. Carlos Corella's words are relevant to me because they show what my father probably endured during the process of becoming a bracero himself. As I indicated before, I know from personal knowledge that my father was processed through the Rio Vista facility a total of 2 times.

Carlos Corella's complete interview provides an in-depth view of what the want-to-be bracero had to endure to legally cross into the United States. Mr. Carlos Corella was interviewed by Patricia Craver on February 5, 2003 when he was 70 years old. The interview is copyrighted as follows: © 2016, Center for History and New Media. The document copyright

Rights Holder is shown as the Institute of Oral History, The University of Texas at El Paso.

There are some discrepancies that are present in the interview text. The following are the discrepancies and some corresponding clarifications:

Carlos Corella indicates that to the best of his knowledge, the bracero program began in 1949 or 1950. In reality, the Bracero program originated as a result of a series of laws and diplomatic agreements initiated in 1942, when the United States signed the Mexican Farm Labor Agreement with Mexico.

- Carlos Corella indicates that he worked for a total of three years at the Rio Vista reception facility and that to the best of his knowledge, the Bracero Program began sometime in 1949 or 1950. He further stated that it was not until two or three years later that the Rio Vista reception center was moved to Rio Vista from the original location of the El Paso Coliseum. This would infer that the Rio Vista facility began operating as a bracero reception center in the year 1951 or 1952. However, from personal knowledge, I know that my father was processed during his first crossing as a bracero at the Rio Vista reception center sometime in April of 1949. Therefore, I believe that the Carlos Corella statement regarding the date of the opening of the Rio Vista reception center is in error.

- In the introduction part of the interview, a reference is made to a piece of paper referred to as Form 414, which showed the name, the address, height, weight, and a very brief physical description of the bracero. However, in the body of the interview, Carlos Corella twice refers to the same form as Form 14. Although I don't know for sure, judging from the two times that he refers to that specific form, it appears to me that the correct designation of the form is Form 14.

In the introduction part of the interview, the birth date of Carlos Corella is indicated as October 2, 1933. In addition, a reference is made that he started his employment at the bracero reception center in 1955. Therefore, his age at the start of his employment was 22 years of age. This information is offered only to clarify his young age as an official at the bracero reception center.

The Carlos Corella interview text contains several grammatical errors. However, these grammatical errors were not corrected in order to preserve the originality of the interview and text as well as to respect the copyright of the Rights Holder which in this case is the Institute of Oral History, The University of Texas at El Paso.

For clarifications sake, Carlos Corella was interviewed by Patricia Craver. The entire interview was taken from the following web link: http://braceroarchive.org/items/show/37

The following is the entire script of the Carlos Corella interview.

It is presented in italics text for clarity.

Description
Biographical Synopsis of Interviewee on Feb. 5, 2003 (70 years old):
Carlos Corella was born on October 2, 1933, in Clint, Texas, where he grew up; he graduated from high school and was drafted into the Army; he served from 1953 to 1955; after being discharged, he went to work for the United States Department of Labor, at Rio Vista, a processing center for braceros in Socorro, Texas.

Summary of Interview:
Mr. Corella briefly recalls his time in the Army and the various places he traveled; upon being discharged in 1955, he went to work for the United States Department of Labor, at Rio Vista, a processing center for braceros in Socorro, Texas; while there, he was put in charge of escorting the braceros through immigration on both sides of the border; he remembers a particular form for the braceros called a 414, which they needed to have when going through immigration; it included their name, address, height, weight, and a brief physical description; the U.S. Department of Labor, U.S. Immigration, and U.S. Public Health were the three

governmental agencies present at the reception center; he describes their first order of business, which was to disinfect or delouse the braceros, and he goes on to explain what each agency was responsible for; later, he became part of the on-site crew at the reception center; he worked for a total of three years at Rio Vista; to the best of his knowledge, the Bracero Program began sometime in 1949 or 1950 and one of the original reception centers was at the El Paso County Coliseum; it was not until two or three years later that the reception/processing center was moved to Rio Vista.

Name of Interviewee: Carlos Corella
Date of Interview: February 5, 2003
Name of Interviewer: Rebecca Craver.

Today is February 5, 2003, and this is an interview with Carlos Corella, and I am Rebecca Craver, and this interview will be part of the Bracero Project.

RC: Okay, let's just start kind of with some biographical information, that's usually the way we start. So, tell me where you were born and when.

CC: I was born and raised in Clint; it's a little town about six miles east of El Paso. I was born on October 2, 1933, which means that I'm going to be seventy here, in three or four months. I graduated from Clint High School. Shortly after my graduation, I was drafted for the Korean War. The Korean War ended two weeks before I finished my infantry training, so we were scattered all over. Fortunately, I was sent to Europe. I spent eighteen months in Germany, and I traveled all over Germany, France, Italy, Spain, Austria, and Switzerland. After my discharge, I went to work for the U.S. Department of Labor, at the bracero reception center, also known as Rio Vista.

RC: Okay, so let's get some of these dates, years, down for me. When did you start service in the Army? Was it '50?

CC: From June of '53 to April of '55.

RC: Okay. And how did you hear about this job at the Department of Labor? Why did you go to work for them?

CC: I don't really remember. The only thing I can remember is that there were a lot of young men and women working there. I was a mechanic in the Army, and I didn't want to do anymore mechanic work, so I decided to try Rio Vista, even though I was making probably a third of the money that I would have been making as a mechanic working at Fort Bliss. (interviewer laughs) And that's how I got started. I started there probably in June of 1955, April or June of 1955, April or May of 1955. Shortly thereafter, I was placed in charge of the importation of the braceros.

I had two helpers under me, in addition to two other nongovernmental employees that worked for a contractor that were responsible for feeding the braceros. You want me to follow the progression?

RC: Yeah, but let me back up a little bit. What qualified you for the job?

CC: There were no specific qualifications. It was not considered a job that required a lot of education or talent, I suppose. The grades were very low, I started as a GS3, if you can imagine, and I think the lowest grade way back then in government services was GS2. Fortunately, I had just gotten out of the service, and I was husky and aggressive, disciplined, and I suppose my supervisors noticed that, and they placed me in charge of the importation of braceros. So, there were no special requirements.

RC: And what particular instructions did you have?

CC: Absolutely none. (interviewer laughs) My supervisor just said, "Look Carlos, I'm gonna take you over there, and you can watch me, what it is that I'm doing, me and these other two young men." My supervisor at the time was Teodoro Alejandro, who was the chief of transportation, and he was only a GS7. I say only because I retired as a [GS]13, so you know, to me a [GS]5 was a huge number. But anyway, looking at it retrospectively, he was only a GS5, GS7, and I went over there. We went to the train station in Juárez, and we talked to some Mexican personnel at the train station, and we picked up the list of the braceros, from there, we marched them to downtown Juárez, through the Mexican officials at the Santa Fe Bridge.

RC: And how many would be in this group?

CC: Anywhere from eight hundred to sixteen hundred, at a time, so getting them from the train station, through the city, and to the bridge was a big problem.

RC: Describe what it looked like.

CC: Well, fortunately, I was in excellent shape. The train station is about a mile and a half, two miles from the bridge, so I would run that trek three or four times so as to keep order and make sure that the Mexican police in Juárez would assist me in stopping the traffic to let two or three hundred braceros cross the streets, and then they'd open the street back to traffic, and then they'd close it back out, let another two or three hundred braceros cross that particular street, we're talking about ten, fifteen streets that braceros had to cross, so needless to say, Mexican city police were very occupied (interviewer laughs) in helping me. I'm very, very appreciative that they did that, I don't think that they did that to assist me, but they did that to assist their own people, because they knew that if someone did not control the traffic, some of the braceros would get hurt, nonetheless, I'm very appreciative that they were helping at the bridge. I would very, very cursorily process them through Mexican immigration, hand them the manifest, which was the list of the braceros, their names and addresses, and I would help Mexican immigration identify them, I said, "Well, these are my people," you know, "these are the braceros."

RC: At this point they had no ID on them?

CC: They had a piece of paper, which we called Form 14, which showed their name, the address, and other information, height, weight, a very brief physical description, that's about all I remember that was on that sheet of paper, which was about four and a half inches by about seven inches. I would process them through Mexican workers, and then I'd do the same thing, very cursorily, through American immigration. The Mexican and American officials knew me, so they assumed that everybody that was in line crossing the bridge under the guise of a bracero was a bracero. I don't recall that they ever questioned any individual or me for that matter, "Are you sure that all these people are braceros?" They just had to assume, because otherwise it would have taken us two days to process these people. After the processing went through American immigration, then they were on the U.S. side of the border, and below there is a huge levee where I would congregate 'em, and I would feed 'em individually a sack lunch, which consisted of an apple and two gringo bologna sandwiches in a brown paper bag. They would look at it, some of them were surprised, they didn't know what it was. Some of 'em that had come before knew that they were bologna sandwiches, and they ate 'em anyway, they were hungry. The trip, incidentally, going back from Chihuahua to Juárez was a horrendous trip for 'em. It was by rail, and they were brought over from Chihuahua in cattle cars. I don't know how many stops they made, but it was about a seven-hour trip. If you can imagine, packed in rail cars, and as I said before, I don't know whether they made any stops to allow them to relieve themselves. That part of the story I don't know. I'm sure that the braceros would be able to fill in that portion of it. So, to get back to where we were on the U.S. side of the border, then I would feed 'em, and they would eat anything, poor devils. Then I would order the buses, I would call the bracero reception center, "I'm ready for the buses," and the buses were yellow buses that were owned by Orville Story. He was a private contractor with the government. He had about fifty buses, and we would load 'em onto the buses. The buses would carry them to the bracero reception center, also known as Rio Vista. Until the last bracero left, then I would get on the last bus, and go up to the bracero reception center. Incidentally, most of the braceros would arrive about nine or ten or eleven o'clock in the morning, which means that they were traveling at night, although on occasion, they would come in at three or four or five o'clock in the afternoon, which tells me that they left Chihuahua in the morning. Even the Mexican Nationals that lived around Juárez that wanted to become braceros would have to make the trip to Chihuahua where they were processed by the Mexican government and then sent back to Juárez. So we would process 'em. They were fed by another private contractor for the U.S. Department of Labor, and way back then, it was Amen Wardy.

He was the person in charge of, well the person that fed 'em, not only there at the levee, but also at the bracero reception center. At the bracero reception center there were hot lunches, and they would consist of several items, some consisted of beans, naturally the Mexican staple, and mashed potatoes, and sometimes ham, and sometimes bologna sandwiches, and sometimes fried pieces of meat. It would vary.

RC: How long would the bracero stay at Rio Vista before he was transported out to a job?

CC: It would depend. The bracero reception center was always crowded with what we called contractors. Some of the contractors were private contractors that had been hired by farmers. Some of the farmers were local farmers, and some of 'em were from Dell City and Pecos, and even from out of El Paso, even from out of state. After they would be processed, the first order of business for the braceros when they got to the bracero reception center was that they had to be disinfected, so they would go through U.S. Public Health, one of the governmental agencies there. There were three governmental agencies at the bracero reception center, which were U.S. Public Health, U.S. Department of Labor, for whom I worked, and U.S. Immigration, which also processed them. So, first order of business was to disinfect them. They would go through, they were formed in about four or five lines, they were placed through a Quonset hut, and they were asked to strip, and they were sprayed with a white powder all over their body, including their hair, facial hair, the hair on their head, and even around the low area. Some of the braceros that experienced that for the first time were embarrassed, and some thought it was kind of cute, it was a laughing matter. When they would come out of the Quonset hut, they would look at each other, and they were all white, and they'd say, "Well, I guess we're gringos now." (both laugh) Humor was always part of the way that they tolerated the adventure. After they were processed through public health, then we feed them, after we would feed them, then we would send them to a selection line. We called it a selection line, and there the contractors or farmers, whichever would happen to be the case, would speak to them, and based on a very, very short interview, three, four questions: "Do you know how to pick cotton? Do you know how to pick cantaloupe? Do you know how to pick corn? Do know how to pick strawberries? Do you know how to pick watermelons? Do you know how to pick cantaloupe?" Depending on their response, they would choose the braceros. They would select them, and they were considered then the property of that contractor or that farmer. They were placed aside and processed individually under that contractor, under that farmer, and eventually transported to their final destination, either the farm of the individual farmer or wherever the contractor would choose to send them, because the contractors would contract for several farmers. Some of the braceros would leave that afternoon, but most of them would not. I would say about 20 percent would leave that afternoon, which means that 80 percent would have to be housed there. We had four or five barracks, the army type, [with] cots. We would issue blankets at night, whether they needed them or not, if they didn't need them, they could use them as pillows. The next morning, we would feed them breakfast, and the contractors would be there at seven o'clock in the morning at the selection line to contract more. Well, I need to back up. After they were processed through public health, then they were sent through contracting, no, they were selected and then they were sent through contracting. Contracting wrote up all the contracts, and the contract was very, very extensive. I don't know whether anybody ever read it, I never read one. They consisted of about three or four pages of small print and in English, mind you. I don't know that even the contractors read them; I don't know that even the farmers read them, but it was all legalese. Then they were processed. There were about twenty young pretty ladies, just out of high school, that would type all the documents, insert the names on documents that had already been prepared, and they would then type the name and address of the individual bracero onto the document. A U.S. government official would sign it, the braceros would sign it (coughs) and then they were processed through U.S. Immigration. (coughs) After they were processed through U.S. Immigration, then they were clear to be contracted, and that's when they were moved to the selection line. Once they were selected, then they would go through the transportation department of the Department of Labor, which is the department for whom I worked, and there at the bracero reception center, they were loaded onto buses or trucks, some of them were cattle trucks, some of them were sixteen-wheelers, eighteen-wheelers, buses, pick-ups. A farmer would come in, and he'd want four or five; he'd take them in the back of his pickup. Some farmer would bring his own bus, he wanted fifty or sixty, and then we wouldn't see them until four, five, six, seven, eight, nine, ten months later. But getting back to the 80 percent that remained at the bracero reception center, the next morning, another 20 or 30 percent would leave, they were selected and contracted and processed. Normally, within three and a half days all one thousand or sixteen hundred braceros would be gone, which means that by that time another load of braceros would be coming in [the others would be gone], which was my job to go pick 'em up and send 'em to the bracero reception center.

RC: Did you ever have trouble, like, doubling up where there would be sixteen hundred at Rio Vista and then here came another shipment?

CC: No, no, the timing was practically perfect. The flow of braceros was controlled at Chihuahua, and when my supervisor, the senior manager, Mr. Rhodes, would see that the bracero reception center could accommodate X number of braceros, he would call Chihuahua and say, "Well okay, we're practically vacant now so you can send another load." That's how the population at the bracero reception center was controlled.

RC: I see, okay. Now when you talked about feeding them, was there a mess hall at Rio Vista?

CC: There was a humongous mess hall that would seat about two hundred at a time. Of course, the braceros got used to the idea of the Army, that you hurry up and wait and stand in line, you stand in line to be fed, you stand in line to be contracted, you stand in line to be processed through immigration, you stand in line to be processed through public health, you stand in line to get blankets, you stand in line to do this and that and the other. That's where some of the problem would arise for some of the employees, because some of the braceros were not used to discipline. Some of them were so humble, coming from remote villages, that they really didn't know what an order was. They thought it was easy enough if they would see a friend or a relative at the head of the line, that it was easy enough for him to run, he or three or four of them from the same little town, to run and get in line with his friends. It was up to us to let them know that they had to form the line at the rear. That was the main problem that we had, keeping order, keeping people from bucking the line, as we used call it in the service, forming the line at the end of the line, but other than that, I don't recall having any major problems. There were a few that were experienced, that had come over as braceros five, six, seven, perhaps even eight or ten times before, so they were not as shy, and they were more daring, and they would try things that the other braceros would not try to do, of course, buck the line, and this and that and the other, cheat as to where they wanted to go. I don't blame them. Some of them, many of them, had a choice where to go depending on their experience; a lot of them did not. They would try to go to a place where all of their friends and or relatives would be sent to, which is understandable. Sometimes the little groups had to be broken up. I'm gonna get a little ahead of myself, because this remark needs to be made here. After I was no longer in charge of the importation of braceros, I was part of the crew at the bracero reception center. I would overhear some of the braceros wanting to make some kind of a (?), some kind of a plan so that they would go to the same farm, and I would tell them, "Well, the best way to do that is when the contractor asks you, 'Do you know how to pick cotton?' Tell him, 'yes,' even if you've never picked it before, you can learn how to pick cotton in fifteen minutes. So, if all of you say yes to just about everything the contractor is asking you, it's very likely that all of us will go to the same farm. If two or three of you have experience picking cotton and then four or five of you don't, well you know they're not going to send you to the same place, because the contractor wants people with experience, because they're the braceros that pick cotton the quickest and the fastest and who become the most profitable. So, just tell them, no matter what kind of a job you're gonna do, whether it's melon picking, watermelon, cherries, strawberries, cotton, corn, whatever, just tell them yeah, you can learn it in five minutes." I felt kinda obligated to keep some of these humble people together (coughs) although I suppose that I felt kinda guilty, because I used to mistreat them in order to keep order. Even though I was a U.S. government official, I had no time for courtesies. I would look into their bewildered faces and bark orders at them, "Go over there. Run over here. Stand over there," and they'd wanna ask me questions, "I don't have time for you, just get in line," and this and that and the other. I was young and aggressive, and sometimes when they would buck the line, I'd just grab them by the shoulders and just kick them out of the line, throw them out. It seemed that some of the braceros would see that we were so harsh with them that they would make fewer attempts to do the things that they were not supposed to do, and since we didn't carry weapons, the only thing that we had to keep order was our harsh manner of speaking and hollering at them.

RC: Oh gee. Did you have a bullhorn or—

CC: Yes, we had bullhorns, and the bracero reception center had a PA system. When we wanted to give orders to the general populous at the center, then of course that was done through the PA system. When we wanted to localize the order to a certain corner of the center, we would use bullhorns. I must also say that at the bracero reception center there was another federal office, and there was the Mexican Consulate. A Mexican consul with two assistants was at the center to, I suppose, keep us from being excessively abusive. When they were coming back after they had completed the contract or when the job had been finished, whichever would come first, they would come back to the bracero reception center, and they would go back home. The Mexican consul would invariably get together with them, every single load, and ask them if they had any complaints, if they had been mistreated, if they had been abused, if they had been exploited, if they had been paid properly. He would prod 'em, because most of them would not want to complain, understandably, because they anticipated coming back next year, and they got used to the idea that certain exploitation, certain abuse was expected, it was part of being a bracero, so they tolerated it. There were some braceros that were promised X number of dollars, and they were not paid the correct amount. Some of the farmers would have their commissaries, stores on site at the farm, to provide whatever the bracero needed, so that they wouldn't have to go to town, so that they could work them sometimes seven days a week. The braceros would tell me, and sometimes the Mexican consul, that the prices that they would have to pay at the commissary, at the store at the farm, was inflated 30, 40, 50 percent, sometimes 100 percent, and they would discern that when they would go to town on a weekend, and they would check the prices in the grocery stores in town. (interviewer laughs) They'd say, "Wow, we're paying too much for our food," and sometimes they would go back and tell the farmer, "You've been charging us too much," those that had a little more nerve. Some of the farmers would bring down the price. The idea was the farmers to accommodate the braceros, and the braceros to accommodate the farmer in the work. Nonetheless, the farmer had the knife and the cheese, and he would slice it anyway he pleased, so the braceros, was many times victimized. Getting back to my friend who was a Mexican consul, he and I became friends when I was assigned to the bracero reception center and no longer in charge of the importation of the braceros. He saw that I was so harsh with the braceros in my barking orders at them and the way I would handle them, that he gave me the title of Sargento Mal Pagado, which translated literally means the poorly paid sergeant, but what it really connotes, idiomatically, is a sergeant with a bad attitude, because he's so poorly paid. Sometimes, I would be going by when he was querying them, after their return from the farms, and he would point at me, and he would ask them, in Spanish of course, "¿Cómo los trato el Sargento Mal Pagado?". "How were you treated by this badass sergeant?" They would look at me and grin, and they didn't know what to say, and then of course I'd just keep walking, and they were free to speak their mind. I'm sure that there were a lot of complaints that were made to my supervisor about me and about other employees. They were legitimate, but there was no other way to keep order, and finally my supervisors knew that, and finally, I have to assume, the Mexican consul and his assistants discerned the same thing. There's just no other way but to be very, very harsh with these people, and everything was permissible, other than hitting them, but jerking them out of lines and pushing them, all that was permissible. It was overlooked. I don't know whether that would be true today, but that way back then, it was permissible.

RC: Did everybody at Rio Vista speak Spanish?

CC: Yes, well, um— RC: Most of them?

CC: Well, I said yes immediately, because every single employee was bilingual. The only non-bilingual personnel was the center manager, Mr. Rhodes, the assistant to the manager, Mr. Rucker, the chief of reception, Mr. Schaeffer, and the chief of contracting, Mr. McDonald, but their assistants were all Mexican American, all bilingual.

RC: Okay, for the record, could you give me those people's first names along with their title?

CC: Well, Mr. Rhodes, no, I don't remember his first name. Mr. Rucker, H.L. Rucker, I don't remember his first name, was the center assistant. Mr. Schaeffer, chief of reception, I don't remember his first name, all of us knew him as Mr. Schaeffer, chief of contracting, McDonald, everybody called him. You have to realize that the managers at the bracero reception center were not only older than us, but they were college graduates. Some of them had been officers in the Army. I think McDonald had been a captain in the Army during the Second World War, and Mr. Rucker had been an officer in the Navy. Since they dealt with their assistants who were bilingual, they were not required to be bilingual, because they did not have to deal with the braceros, and that's why everybody under the managers were required definitely to be bilingual. If you were not bilingual, you could not work there.

RC: Okay. That's good to know. Do any particular incidents stand out in your mind where there was unrest or the braceros disobeyed or caused trouble?

CC: There were several instances. Let me go back when I was in charge of the importation of the braceros. Invariably, every single time that I received a load from Chihuahua, there were some people who were trying to buck the line. I got used to that, and invariably, I would have to go to where they would run on to the line, and grab them by the shoulders and pull them out, and stand right in front of their face and yell at them and tell them, "Go back to the end of the line or I'm going to send you back to Mexico, so take your choice." They knew that I had that authority. We were given the authority that if we found people that would not accept the discipline, that would not take orders, that we could pick up their Form 14, which was their identification. Without that form they couldn't be processed, and we would isolate them on the manifest, on the list of the braceros, and send them back. I don't remember ever having to do that more than once or twice, because in spite of the fact that I was very harsh, I was not a cruel man. I knew that they needed the jobs. The only reason for my harshness was that that was the only tool that I had to keep discipline. I remember very distinctly, one time that I was close to the front of the line, and there were three black men coming up to pick up lunch, they were getting up close to the lunch area. (coughs) I went to talk to them, and I asked them, "Are you guys that hungry that you are willing to eat one of these lunches?" They looked at me and did not respond, and I asked them again, "Are you guys after a free lunch?" Then finally, one of them looked at the other one, and he said, "¿Qué dice?" Then I asked them, "Are you braceros, then? You don't speak English, no?" They told me in Spanish, "No, we don't speak English. We're braceros," and they were black men, black men with all the features. So, needless to say, I was very curious, and I asked them where they were from. They told me that they were from (?) which is a port in the Gulf of Mexico, the name escapes me, it'll come back to me, which is where the Portuguese would drop off a lot of black slaves, and also some of the Spaniards. Way back then, in the mid-1800s, some of the black slaves remained in that area, and some of them intermarried with the indigenous people, and they became Mexican citizens, and on that occasion those three black men became braceros. (interviewer laughs) I was in charge of the importation of braceros for three years, and then I got a letter from the Army telling me that I had six months to enroll in a university or I would lose my GI bill of rights. All this time, for two and a half years, almost three years, I had plans to go to college, I wanted to go to college, get a degree, and get a super job, and I had kept postponing it. I ended up getting married. I was married, and I had two kids when I received the letter from the VA. Immediately I called UTEP, it was Texas Western College at the time, I asked them when I could enroll, and they told me, "You can enroll in February, which is about three months away," and I said, "I'll be there." I asked (coughs) my immediate supervisor if I could transfer to the night crew, because I wanted to go to college during the day, and he wouldn't allow me. He said, "No, I need you. I need you over there. You're doing a super job, and I need you over there." Finally, after proddin' him about two weeks, and he would not relent, I spoke to his supervisor, and I informed him, who was the assistant center manager, who was a college graduate. My supervisor was not a college graduate; he was Mexican American. Then I spoke to the assistant center manager, and I told him exactly what I wanted to do, that I wanted to transfer to the night crew, because I wanted to go to college and get a degree. He had a degree, and he could understand. He said, "Carlos, don't worry about it. I'll talk to your supervisor. Just tell me when it is, when you want to start." And that's how I was transferred to the night crew, which means that I worked from 3:30 in the afternoon to midnight. There was another guard that would relieve me at midnight, who worked from midnight to six in the morning. My job then was to feed them, keep order in the chow line, and make sure that each one of them were fed properly. Sometimes the contractor would fudge on the lunches. It got to the point where we were weighing every single plate to make sure that they got the ounces that the government was paying for.

RC: And these people that made the food for 'em, did they set up kitchens at Rio Vista?

CC: They had a humongous kitchen there at the center. The mess hall had a large kitchen, you can imagine, it was large enough to prepare food for fifteen, sixteen hundred braceros.

RC: And you mentioned Amen Wardy.

CC: Amen Wardy was the private contractor who contracted with the Department of Labor to feed the braceros.

RC: And he did that the whole three years?

CC: I think he did that for about eight or ten years.

RC: Is that right?

CC: He did that for the seven years that I was there. (coughs) So, when I was transferred to the night crew, I would make sure that they would be fed. After they were fed, I would issue blankets, and I would make sure that they were in bed by nine o'clock, lights were out by nine o'clock. I would have to patrol the area, make sure that nobody was fighting. On occasion, I'd see some fights, and I'd manage to diffuse them just by sheer intimidation. They knew that I had the authority to call the police officers, and once the police officers were there, they knew that they were going back to Mexico, and maybe even to jail locally. They didn't know what would happen to them.

RC: And these were just fistfights? CC: Yes.

RC: Were there ever knives, knife—

CC: No, never did I see anybody pull a knife, I not saying that they didn't carry one, but never did I see anyone pull a knife on another bracero. There was a lot of pushing, a lot of shoving, once and a while fist fights. I could normally tell from my office, because I had a clear view of the center, because the lights would go on, and I would hear a lot of ruckus and yelling and on and on, so I would head in that direction, and I had no weapon. They knew my reputation already, that I was a very harsh man, and I was five eleven, almost six feet tall, and I weighed a hundred and ninety, so I was a good sized man, bigger than most of the braceros, and they knew that I was in good shape. So they not only had to tangle with me, but actually, what they were fearful of was the unknown, "What is going to happen to me if I don't stop? Are they going to take me to jail here? Are they going to send me back to Mexico?" And it was the fear of the unknown, a tool that I utilized very well. After they were in bed, I would patrol the area, and I had some paperwork to do. I'd have about an hour and a half of free time to study. I was relieved at midnight. I would study from midnight till about three o'clock in the morning there at the bracero reception center, and then I would go home. I would sleep for about three hours, get up, take a shower, eat breakfast, and go to college. And when I had lab in the afternoon, because I was taking accounting and invariably would have labs, so I would get out of class at 2:30 or three o'clock in the afternoon. I'd go to my house, pick up my lunch, to be at the bracero reception center at 3:30, and I did that for four years. Finally, I got my accounting degree.

RC: And what year did you get your degree? CC: In 1962 is when I graduated.

RC: Okay. Were you in uniform?

CC: Well, yes and no. I was in uniform, we were not required to wear uniforms, but those of us that had been in the military would wear our military uniform, which means khaki. We would wear our combat boots, we would wear our khaki pants, we would wear our khaki shirts, but no insignias and no stripes, but by looking at us, anybody could tell that there was a military uniform. And one of the young men that assisted me had been in the Marines, so he would like to wear his Marine uniform with, as I said, no insignias, no stripes, no rank, nothing. We were required to take all that off.

RC: Oh. What did the braceros bring with them?

CC: They would bring practically nothing. They carried what I would call a gym bag, which means, in my gym bag, to this day, I carry shorts, bathing suits, a solar belt, sweat pants, a sweatshirt, a change of underwear, change of socks, and soap in this. I don't think they carried soap, but maybe they did, but they carried probably a change of clothing, and maybe a change of underwear, and a change of socks, and a jacket in case it was needed, and that was it. It was a very small bag. They were told in Chihuahua that they had to travel light.

RC: Did they search those bags?

CC: None of us ever searched them. Nowadays, I can imagine that would be terrible, but way back then, nobody ever searched them. Mexican immigration didn't search them, American immigration didn't search them, I didn't search them, nobody at the bracero reception center searched them. We had had no experience of any need to search them, so until we discerned that there was an absolute need to do something, we would refrain from it. During the seven years that I was there, I don't recall that any braceros were searched, because we never saw the need for it.

RC: When you were working there, how long had the Rio Vista been open?

CC: I really don't know, but I received the impression that it started sometime in 1949 or 1950, way back then. It's my understanding that the bracero reception center was at the Coliseum, the El Paso Coliseum, which still exists, and as two or three years later, it was transferred to the Rio Vista location. I think it had been there for about three or four years, in 1955, when I started working there. And needless to say, there was a lot of turnover, because the jobs didn't pay very well. As I said before, that I started as GS3, and then when I transferred to the night crew, I was demoted to a GS2, but I made up for that with a humongous amount that I got from the VA for my going to college, which was one hundred and twenty dollars a month.

RC: (laughs) Well, it all adds up, doesn't it? What did the braceros do when you were on the night shift, after dinner?

CC: They would play cards, they had a lot of conversations, they would get together in groups, planning strategies, you know, what's available? "You guys have been here before, tell us," you know, "what is it we need to do? What is it we need to learn from you guys to go and do what we want to do?" So the experienced bracero was invaluable to the inexperienced bracero. And it was at night that they would exchange information and educate each other.

RC: Um-hm. You remember any music?

CC: Oh, yes. Some of them carried a little radio. I had a radio, and once in a while I'd play music for them over the PA system, Mexican music, which I still love, and of course they loved. Now I did that till about nine o'clock, 9:30 max, because most of them were tired, and they wanted to get some rest. That is not to say that they could not sleep with nice music in the air.

RC: After they completed their work contract, and they came back through, tell me about when they would come back. What kind of processing did they have to go through to go back home?

CC: It was very minor. They would go through contracting, and the contract would be terminated, nullified, or whatever, I don't recall the terminology. And as far as the feeding was concerned, it was the same. As far as the housing was concerned, it was the same. And the en masse interviews by the Mexican Consul was the same, because the Mexican Consul would speak to them before they left, keep track of all the injustices that you received, the exploitation, because we need to know, and the only way that we're gonna correct that is by getting information from your people. And they were debriefed, as we would say in the Army, when they were returning. They would bring, by the thousands, old Singer sewing machines. They would have problems carrying them, and problems loading them onto the buses that would bring them to the center, and the buses that would take them from the center to the bridge to be processed through American immigration again at the bridge, which is very minor. The American immigration knew that just by looking at them, they knew that they were braceros. Mexican immigration knew that they were braceros, and of course they would try to shake them down for money. I guess so, a lot of them were, "What it is that you bring? Well, you can't bring that. If you do, you need to give me some pesos," and this and that and the other." They had to face that from the time they left their homes in Mexico, and in the United States, they were victims, they, they were, there's no other way to put it. They were victims even in their own country. The Mexican government was callous, didn't care very much about them. They were the poor, still the poor. In this country, again they were the poorest of the poor. The only people that could related to them were people like me, and I didn't have time to relate to them. The gringo farmers, and some of them were Mexican Americans, most of the them were gringo farmers, could relate to them only to the extent that they needed them, and they would try to accommodate them to extent that they would do the job, because they needed them. That is not to say that they wouldn't fudge here and there the things that they would do for them.

RC: What is your sense of what percentage of braceros actually returned to Mexico?

CC: Wow, uh, that's very, very difficult to say. When I was working there, my guess is that only 1 or 2 percent remained behind, and a lot of them remained behind, because their contracts were extended, which was legal. The farmer, or the rancher, or the contractor would contact the bracero reception center and provide the information that was needed to the Department of Labor, detailing who needed whom for what, for what extended period of time. Some braceros had their contracts extended time and time and time again, for years, and the farmers would allow them, in between contracts, to go back home and visit family. And also it was rumored, and I don't know this first hand, that some of the braceros would leave the farms when the contract was up, and they'd go to another farmer and work illegally as undocumented Mexican. What percentage did that, I don't have the foggiest.

RC: When they would go home, and then they'd want to work as a bracero again, did they have to go through the entire process with you?

CC: The entire process. RC: And then to Rio Vista?

CC: The whole process had to be repeated every single time, every single time. Now, I must mention that there were several, there were three bracero reception centers that I know of in the country. One of them was in Eagle Pass, one of them was in El Paso, and the other one was in El Centro, California, and from those three bracero reception centers, the braceros were sent all over the nation. Some would even go to Colorado and Nebraska and Wyoming and do ranch work, Colorado to do beets and Arkansas and Louisiana. Well, I don't know that any state was exempt. If they could show need for the bracero, the bracero was sent there.

RC: Do you recall a favorite location for the braceros?

CC: Well, sure. The braceros that were from Juárez would prefer to stay in the El Paso area, because on weekends they could go visit family, and particularly the experienced ones.

RC: So all they'd need to cross, to see the family and come back, would be the ID card that was issued?

CC: Right, at the bracero reception center. So it was not a major problem. And then some of them that were expertly in picking cotton or picking cantaloupe would want to go to Pecos, because you earn a lot more money over there. So they would sacrifice seeing relatives, weekly or monthly, so as to receive higher wages and make more money.

RC: Did you ever witness any results of accidents on the job or did you ever hear [of any]?

CC: Yes, we would hear of them, and on occasion we would hear some braceros returning home on crutches or with canes. I never saw anybody return home or return to the bracero center by ambulance, obviously because then that was not our job. If somebody was seriously hurt at the farms, then medical personnel would take over. They had precedence, and they were treated at hospitals until they were recuperated. And then from there, they were either sent home or they were sent to the bracero reception center to be processed back home. If the accident was severe, their contracts were cancelled there at the hospital, and they were sent back home.

RC: Did they receive any inoculations at Rio Vista?

CC: You know, I don't remember that they received any, but it wouldn't surprise me if they did [or] if they did not. I'm hoping that you get to speak to (coughs) some personnel. I have a friend, Lopez, who I'm gonna contact, if you haven't contacted him, and he worked for U.S. Public Health, and he can give you all the details.

RC: All right. What is your personal opinion of the Bracero Program?

CC: I think it was needed. (clears throat) Based on my observations now in society, and I'm a writer now, so I'm very observative, I'm very conscious of people all around me. I write about philosophy, psychology, sociology. I don't think that they're in the dire need now that they were back then. Way back then they were needed, because they were not sufficient or at least it was proven to the satisfaction of the government they were not sufficient, the laborers in the United States to do the job. Some of them had been drafted for the Second World War, a lot of them had been drafted for the Korean War, as I was drafted for the Korean War. Right now, getting back to the future, there's no draft. There are a lot of people, a lot of men on welfare. There are a lot of women that could do work, that would do the work in lieu of the bracero. I'm not going to be so presumptuous to say that there're some areas within the United States that have need for them. Now in the El Paso area, I have not discerned a need. To begin with, way back then, they, the braceros, were chopping cotton, picking cotton. Way back then, a farmer would require, depending on the size of his farm, anywhere between twenty-five to a hundred and fifty, two hundred braceros to pick the cotton. Limón farms, which had about fifteen hundred acres, which I measured later on in life as an employee of the Agriculture Extension Service and Conservation Service, had about fourteen, fifteen acres in cultivation in alfalfa and cotton, milo. They would utilize two or three hundred braceros to pick that cotton. Right now, they use four or five cotton- picking machines. So, as far as picking cotton, the braceros, there's no need for 'em, picking onions, there's no need for 'em, it's all done by machinery, bailing hay, there's no need for them. I used to help my father in the bailing of hay when I was nine years old. I was the block man, block boy. Imagine this, there was a tractor driver, two pitchfork men, one on each side of the bailer, the two men sittin' on the bailer, one was the wire passer, the other one was a wire tire, and me, the block boy. So there was one, two, three, four, five, six persons. Now, one person, the tractor driver, does all the work. So, the modern inventions have eliminated millions and millions of menial jobs, of labor jobs. Even pickin' chile there's machines. I don't know that there's not a machine to pick anything anymore.

RC: So you don't think the program should be revived?

CC: I am not going to be so presumptive as to say no. I will say this, I don't see any need for them locally.

RC: Okay. Well, I think that will put an end to this interview now, and I'll thank you formally on the tape, and I'll say this is the end. Bracero History Archive is a project of the Roy Rosenzweig Center for History and New Media, George Mason University, the Smithsonian National Museum of American History, Brown University, and The Institute of Oral History at the University of Texas at El Paso. Funding provided by the National Endowment for the Humanities.

© 2016, Center for History and New Media

The Carlos Corella interview presented above is vitally important to me because of his first-hand knowledge of the process of becoming a bracero. At the risk of being repetitive, Carlos Corella's words are relevant to me because they show what my father probably endured during the process of becoming a bracero himself.

The Significance Of The El Paso Valley Area

My formative years were spent on the Ryan farm and in the town of Fabens, Texas. The following is the regional map of the area where my mother and father ultimately ended up and where I was raised. The red arrow at the bottom right of the regional map shows the location of the Ryan farm:

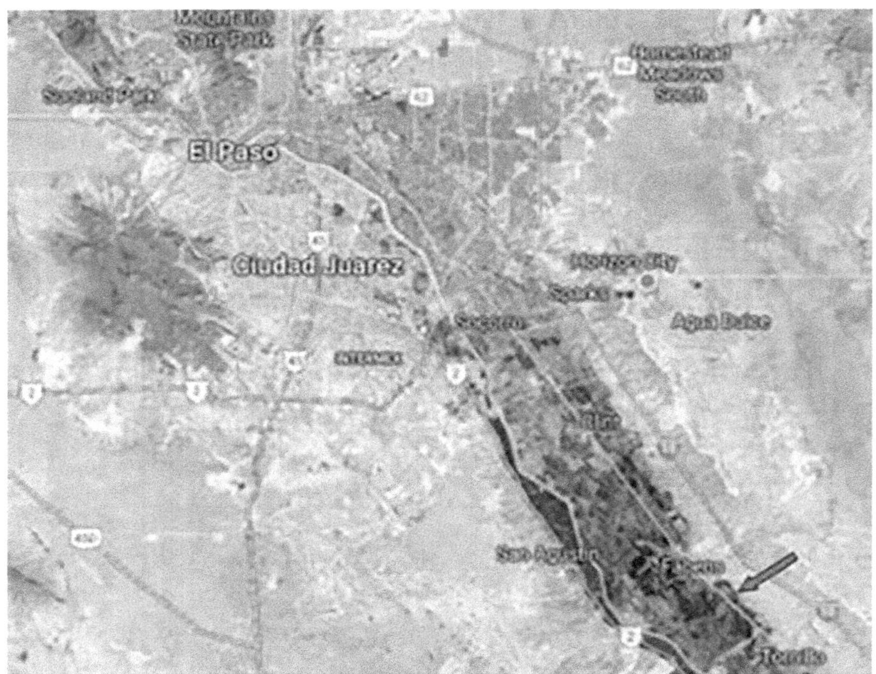

Working at the Ryan Farm

Ultimately, my father was contracted to work at a cotton farm owned by Joe Ryan and his son James Ryan. My father traveled to the city of Chihuahua for processing into the bracero program a total of 2 times during a 2 year period of time. My mother probably remained in Cd. Juarez when my father left for Chihuahua during the first time that he was processed into the Bracero program. As indicated before, during April of 1949, when he began his journey to become a bracero, the Rio Vista reception center was being used as the bracero reception center. After his train trip from Chihuahua to Cd. Juarez, along with numerous other braceros, he was transported to the Rio Vista reception facility. It was at that location that James Ryan or possibly a representative of his, questioned my father about his ability to work on a cotton farm.

James Ryan spoke Spanish sufficiently well to make himself understood. Based on internet bracero stories that I've read, the questioning probably took place with both parties separated by a wire mesh fence. It is at that time that James Ryan selected my father to work on his farm. Also, based on those internet stories, it is probable that on the same day of the interview and after having been selected, my father signed the bracero labor contract and again on that same day, my father was transported to the Ryan farm.

During those days when my father first arrived at the Ryan farm, a boy by the name of Roberto Muñoz Renteria lived on a nearby farm owned by a person named Al Crider. In a strange twist of fate, Roberto would later turn out to be a family member of my father's. At that time, my father was 19 years of age and Roberto Muñoz Renteria was about 13 years of age in 1948. The details as to how they confirmed this family relationship are described elsewhere in this memoir.

During September of 2016, I had the great fortune of discussing our family history with Roberto who is now 81 years of age. He told me that my mother arrived at the Ryan farm two weeks after my father arrived. I can only guess that my mother remained in Cd. Juarez when my father left for Chihuahua for inscription into the Bracero program. I surmise that after he initially arrived at the Ryan farm, it probably took my father several weeks before he could travel to Cd. Juarez to then travel with my mother back to the Ryan farm. In that same conversation with Roberto, he told me that both my father and my father's brother, Fernando, arrived at the Ryan farm at the same time. My uncle Fernando passed away in 2013, so now it is important to communicate with my uncle's family to determine if he ever told them the story of his arrival at the Ryan farm at the same time as my father's arrival.

The Ryan cotton farm was located between the towns of Fabens and Tornillo about 30 miles southeast of El Paso, Texas. With all due respect, their names were actually Joseph Ryan and James Lawrence Ryan but everyone seemed to refer to them as Joe and Jimmy. My parents used to address them by their informal names as well without knowing they were doing so. In fact, I remember that my parents would refer to James Lawrence Ryan as "el Jimmy".

James Ryan supervised the operation of the cotton farm while his father, Joseph Ryan, managed a lumber company in Fabens, Texas. The lumber company was called the Ryan Lumber Company. I always felt that Mr. James Ryan was about the same age as my father. I recently reviewed Mr. James Ryan's obituary and found that he was born in 1924 whereas my father was born in 1928. The Ryan family was a Catholic family just like our family. We went to the same Catholic Church in Fabens as they did. The Ryan kids were also about the same age as we were.

The Consolidation of the Family

Little by little my family began to become stronger and more solidified. The consolidation of my family began with the migration into the area of one of my forebear's and then my parent's migration to the El Paso valley area.

When my father and mother both moved to live in the United States they both left behind their nuclear families. I believe that their migration to the El Paso valley area created a hole in my parent's psyche; especially my father's. My father's actions, which will be

described later, leads me to believe that he felt badly about having left his family members behind in the Delicias area. Those family members left behind would not have the same opportunity to prosper as him. The process or sequence of that migration is important to me because I feel that my forbear's and my parent's migration ultimately pulled our extended family together into the El Paso valley area from the Delicias area. Many factors contributed to make that happen.

As indicated before, my father's first entry into the United States as a bracero occurred sometime in April of 1949. At the time, his nuclear family consisted solely of my mother and himself. When he and my mother left Delicias to seek a better life in Cd. Juarez, my father left his extended family behind in the Delicias area. My father's extended family consisted of my grandfather Jose and his family.

The first known presence of a family member with the name of Renteria in the El Paso valley area was the family of Jesusita Renteria Alcoset. Her parents were Justo Renteria and Cleotilde Alcoset. This occurred in the year of 1918. She later married a person by the name of Gregorio Muñoz. More about their marriage and their impact on our lives will be told later in this memoir but suffice it to say that Jesusita was my father's cousin twice removed.

The new presence of my father and Fernando, his brother, to the area was the next step in the start of the migration of my relatives to the area. Based on a conversation with Roberto Muñoz that will also be described later, Fernando Renteria Tarango, my uncle, arrived at the Ryan farm together with my father. Later on in 1952 or 1953, my aunt Anita and her husband Tomas Bejarano would enter the United States and join my father on the Ryan farm. Next, my uncle Esteban Gutierrez who was married to Rosa, my aunt, would appear at the Ryan farm although I don't know the approximate date of their arrival. Eventually, Patricio Gutierrez and Adrian Gutierrez who were also my mother's brothers would also begin to work on the Ryan farm. Patricio's and Adrian's approximate arrival date to the area was when I was about 5 or 6 years of age which would be 1956 or 1957. Yes, my family's migration started with Jesusita Renteria Alcoset. As indicated before, her parents were Justo Renteria and Cleotilde Alcoset

The final entry to the El Paso Valley area was my grandfather Jose's family which was my father's extended family. I believe this is the component that was missing in my father's life.

It concerns me that I don't know the date of my father's extended family's arrival into the area; after all, they played an important role in my father's life. However it seems that the most effective way to establish their arrival date to the area is knowing which of my grandfather Jose's children was first to be born in Caseta. This assumes that Caseta was the place they first inhabited after leaving the Delicias area. I had an opportunity recently to speak with some of my father's half-siblings during a family get-together. We got- together at a local restaurant on May 13, 2018. They confirmed that Manuel was the last Renteria Gonzalez sibling that was born in the Delicias area and he was born in 1952. Maria was the next sibling that was born after having left the Delicias area and that was in 1954. Based on this information, the arrival date of my father's extended family from the Delicias area to the El Paso valley area is somewhere between 1952 and 1954.

As far back as I can remember, my father's extended family lived in Caseta. Caseta is a small village located adjacent to the Rio Grande River which forms the border between the United States and Mexico. Caseta was the closest accessible town to the location of the Ryan farm and that's why I think my father had much to do with pulling his extended family to Caseta. In fact, my father owned property in Caseta. That is where his extended family lived in as far back as I can remember. My father purchased the property on November 6, 1959. So from 1954 to 1959, the property was probably rented by my father and that's where his extended family lived during that period of time. Anyway, according to the property documents, the lot measured

15 meters (49.2 feet) by 30 meters (98.4 feet). The street name where the lot was located was "Calle Aldama". The property was purchased from a Rafael Aguilera Gallegos.

In the end, my father succeeded in pulling his extended family from the Delicias area to live in Caseta. Yes, it was Caseta on the Mexico side but it was the closest and the most accessible place to the Ryan farm short of being in the United States. It is my opinion that he needed his extended family close to him. It is supposition based on what I believe comes close to being fact. All his actions, which will come to light later in this memoir, point to the fact that he continually tried to make his extended family prosper. At least for the time being, consolidation of the extended families was achieved.

Our First Home - The Bracero Living Quarters

I was born on January 23, 1951 while my parents were living on the Ryan farm. The earliest I remember was when I crawled around the floor chasing after my mother.

As a very young child of 3 or 4 years of age, I still remember the location of the building structure that served as the housing quarters for the farm workers and our family. We lived in those housing quarters. The building structure was located adjacent to the railroad tracks.

The building structure length ran parallel to the railroad tracks. The exact location of the building structure can be found using the Google Maps software by entering the following latitude and longitude coordinates: 31.468948 latitude and -106.117275 longitude.

The approximate distance between the housing quarters and the railroad tracks was about 105 feet. Beyond the railroad tracks was a two lane highway that also ran parallel to the railroad tracks. That highway is today known as Texas State Highway 20. Back in those days, the highway was known as U.S. Highway 80. Because U.S. Interstate 10 had not yet been built, U.S. Highway 80 was a very busy traffic conduit. Cotton trailers, automobiles and even heavy haul tractor/trailer rigs would travel along that highway.

The building that we lived in was a building structure constructed of adobe blocks. The exterior and interior walls were covered with a plaster material known as stucco. The exterior stucco protected the adobe blocks from disintegrating from the rain water. I even remember the whitewashed exterior color of the building. Whitewashing consisted of mixing lime with water and then applying the liquid mixture with a brush onto the stuccoed surface. It was probably a cheaper alternative to using real paint.

Although I don't remember the exact dimensions, the narrow width of the building was about 20 feet but the length had to be at least 200 feet. The building structure was subdivided into apartments that housed the "bracero" farm workers, several other families as well as my family. All down the length of the building structure were screen doors that each corresponded to an individual apartment. The screen doors along the length of the building structures all faced toward the railroad tracks and the highway.

At the far left end of the building structure that served as the living quarters, was another structure constructed of numerous wooden vertical support columns that was fitted with only a corrugated tin metal roof. This structure served as a storage area for alfalfa hay bales. It also served as a parking space for tractors and farm implements that were used on the farm. About 20 to 30 feet along the front length of the building structure toward the railroad tracks was a row of huge cottonwood trees that provided shade from the sun.

There was no running water available for the residents of the housing quarters. A single cast iron hand pump located outdoors served to provide water for all the residents. I don't remember the Spanish term my parents used to refer to the hand pump. Anyway, when I was writing this piece, I searched the internet to determine the name of this type of pump. It turns out that the pump is known as a "pitcher pump". A picture of a "pitcher" pump is provided here.

The hand pump was positioned over a hole in the ground. I do remember that my father would sometimes remove the hand pump from its location and would then pull out long lengths of pipe from the hole. At the very end of the pipe was a type of device that he referred to as a "cedazo". The Spanish word "cedazo" is pronounced similar to "sedaso". The Spanish word "cedazo" signifies a device that serves as a sieve to keep dirt, sand or gravel solids from flowing into the vertical pipe. It is likely that the sieve device was also combined with a foot valve that acted like a check valve. I now know from experience that foot valves are used to keep water from flowing backward from the well pipe back into the water table.

Anyway, if a resident was in need of water for drinking, cooking or bathing, the resident would have to carry an empty pail to the location of the pump. The resident would then hang the handle of the pail onto the pump discharge spout and then the person would begin to manipulate the pump to fill the water pail.

To operate the hand pump, the person would first grasp the cantilever handle and then press the handle down and then subsequently pull the handle back up again. After a few more up and down strokes of the cantilever handle, water would then begin to flow outward from the discharge spout to fill the pail. As long as the person continued the up and down stroking motion, water would continue to flow out the discharge spout and into the pail.

The water would then have to be carried in the pail from the location of the pitcher pump back into the living quarters. I remember that my mother and my grandmother would bathe my older brother and I in large circular galvanized tubs measuring about 36" inches in diameter and about 18" deep. It must have been quite a chore walking back and forth from the location of our apartment to the location of the pitcher pump to fetch water when bath time rolled around. After the bath, the bath water still had to be carried outdoors in a pail and then dumped onto the ground. One other thing about baths, if the person wanted a warm bath then some of the water had to be heated up on the stove and then mixed with the colder water already in the tub.

Toilets of the Day

As for bathrooms or toilets of today; there weren't any. Outdoor toilets called "escusados" were used as toilets. The Spanish word "escusados" is a term used to denote "outhouses" in the English language.

These outhouses consisted of small wooden structures which were used as a cover for pit latrines. The interior of the "outhouse" was configured so as to provide a seating area equipped with a hole that measured about 12 inches in diameter. The wooden structure itself was about 4 feet wide by 4 feet long and about 7 feet tall. The pit latrine consisted of a 4 foot by 4 foot square pit with a depth of 6 to 10 feet. The latrine pit was dug at a location some distance away from the main living quarters.

The Potential for Potable Water Contamination

When I was writing these memoirs, it dawn on me that outhouses were indeed things that posed danger to our health. Everyone today takes for granted bathrooms equipped with water tanks that flush the human excrement away to septic tanks or to waste water treatment plants. In those days, we were not so lucky.

It's a miracle we didn't die from fecal matter contaminated drinking and cooking water. We were using "pitcher pumps" to obtain drinking, cooking and bathing water from the water table that was about 18 feet below the ground level. At the same time, we were using "outhouses" equipped with pit latrines to dispose of fecal matter 6 to10 feet below the ground level.

I now realize that we were extracting our potable water from the same approximate location in which we were disposing of fecal matter. I don't remember anybody ever mentioning the need to chlorinate the drinking water. And I don't remember anyone ever expressing concern about the possibility of fecal matter migrating downward to the water table and then contaminating the water that we ultimately used to drink, cook and bathe. Borrowing a phrase frequently used to describe the animal pecking order; "we as bracero families were at the bottom of the food chain".

As indicated above, a pitcher pump was used for pumping water from the water table below the soil subsurface on the Ryan farm. At the same time, the nearby outhouse was used to deposit human excrement in a 4 foot by 4 foot hole that was perhaps as much as 10 feet deep.

While writing this section of the memoir, I sensed that a problem existed that I hadn't thought about before. A possibility existed that the excrement from the nearby outhouse could migrate downward to the water table. The result would be that the fecal matter would end up contaminating the water in the underground aquifer.

To determine the degree of pollution potential, I needed to get an idea of the vertical separation distance between the depth of the excrement and the depth of the aquifer, which is to say, the water table. Obviously there was no way to reverse time to actually go and measure the depth of the water table at the farm. However, I could estimate the depth of the water table by knowing the depth that a pitcher pump could reasonably draw water. Clearly, this was an indirect method but it was the only method I could use to obtain an estimate of the depth of the water table in those days on the farm. I felt that once the approximate depth of the water table was determined, then a conclusion could be drawn as to the extent of the probability of pollution of the water table by the excrement.

An internet article I read contained the following in regard to the water lift capability of a pitcher pump: *"Pitcher Pumps [sic] are great for shallow wells with a water level of less than 20 feet from the bottom of the pump"*. The article can be viewed by using the following link: www.simmonsmfg.com/downloads/pdf/ppump_instructions.pdf

One thing is for sure; we did use a pitcher pump to pump water up from the shallow underground aquifer on the farm. And now knowing that the pitcher pump could only have operated successfully at water levels less than 20 feet of depth, I could unequivocally confirm that the water table in those days had to be no deeper than 18 feet from ground level. This is because 2 feet is subtracted from the value of 20 feet to account for the distance above the ground level that was necessary to mount the pitcher pump. Mounting the pitcher pump about 2 feet above the ground level was necessary so that the person using the pitcher pump wouldn't have to stoop over too much to use the pump. As a result, the actual water table could not have been deeper than 18 feet from the ground level.

Optimally, if the bottom of the latrine pit underneath the "outhouse" was 10 feet below the ground surface, and the water table was 18 feet below the ground surface, then an 8 foot vertical earth barrier existed between the bottom of the "outhouse" latrine and the top of the water table. However, the water table depth had to have been less than 18 feet since 18 feet is the deepest possible depth that the hand pump could operate.

A more realistic depth to the water table would be a value less than 18 feet because the foot valve/strainer device at the bottom of the well had to have been immersed in the water. I assumed that the foot valve/strainer device would be immersed by at least 2 feet of water depth. The depth to the water table would now be 16 feet instead of 18 feet. The result would then have been only 6 feet of distance between the bottom of the earthen latrine to the top of the water table. Only a 6 foot vertical earth barrier stood in the way of the excrement migrating to the underground aquifer.

One can propose that the contamination danger could have been avoided by locating the "outhouse" some distance away from the location of the "pitcher pump". In fact, I remember that the "outhouse" was indeed placed some distance away from the well and I would guess that the distance might have been 70 to 100 feet away. However, I am sure that this was done more for privacy concerns rather than because of contamination concerns.

One might think that the lateral distance between the location of the "pitcher pump" and the "outhouse" was perhaps the only saving grace that prevented contamination of the drinking water by the fecal matter in the earthen hole underneath the "outhouse". In hindsight, however, it really didn't matter that the "outhouse" was placed 70 to 100 feet away from the well. The depth of the water table 70 to 100 feet away from the well was probably still 16 feet. Just like rain water, the fecal matter would have migrated to the underground aquifer. And sooner or later, the contaminated water from the location of the "outhouse" would have migrated laterally to the location where the water was being withdrawn from the aquifer; namely, the location of the "pitcher pump".

The vertical distance of the water table in relation to the depth of the outhouse latrine hole was an insidious problem. In a way, ignorance was bliss. Everyone went about their business while in the presence of a potentially horrific outcome.

The following drawing shows two scenarios for the vertical distance between the bottom of the "outhouse" latrine pit to the top of the underground aquifer:

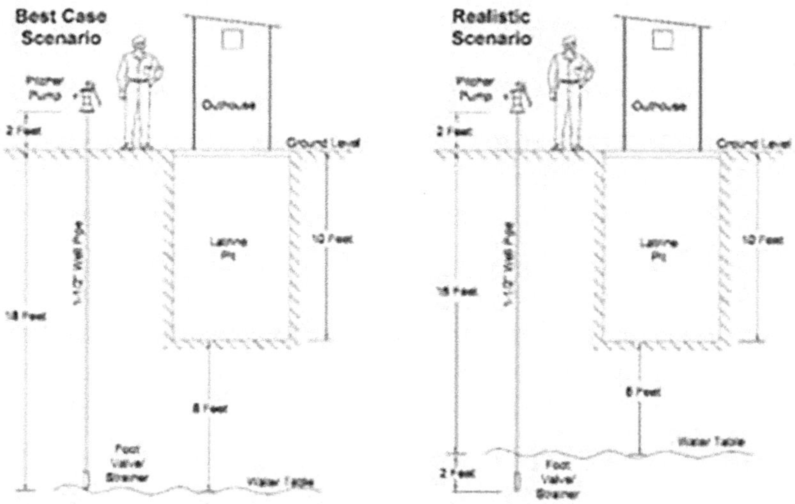

The medical literature that one finds on the internet is replete with information that states tuberculosis can be caused by fecal contaminated food or water. Some sources state that the fecal contaminated water can cause gastroenteritis, ear infections, typhoid, dysentery, hepatitis A, and cholera.

I recently found out that a family member that lived during those times indeed passed away from complications due to tuberculosis. Although contaminated groundwater could have been to blame for the death, I will never truly know the cause that led to that incidence of tuberculosis. The fecal contaminated water is important to me because my father too contracted tuberculosis. However, his illness occurred later in life when "outhouses" were not in use.

One internet article published by the Centers for Disease Control titled "TB Incidence in the United States, 1953-2014" states that 84,304 cases of TB occurred in 1953 compared to only 9,421 occurrences in 2014. That same reference states 52.6 TB occurrences per 100,000 inhabitants in 1953 and 3 occurrences per 100,000 inhabitants in 2014. That's a whopping 94 percent reduction. I firmly believe that tuberculosis occurrences decreased as a result of the implementation of modern day waste water treatment systems.

Again, from my perspective, the bracero farm workers and my family members who lived in those housing quarters were at the bottom of the food chain.

Life in The Bracero Housing Quarters

As indicated previously, my family lived in the bracero housing quarters on the Ryan farm. The bracero housing quarters were located adjacent to the railroad tracks.

I can only remember the presence of two other families occupying the housing quarters at the Ryan farm. The rest of the apartments were occupied by individual "bracero" farm workers. Remember, I was 3 or 4 years of age when we lived in the bracero housing quarters. I presume that those same quarters were where my father and mother came to live soon after him having entered the United States.

One of the families that lived in the bracero housing quarters was the Bejarano family. My aunt Anita, was married to Tomas Bejarano and they

had two children at the time. Our cousin's names were Ramona and Jose. My uncle Tomas was one of the laborers on the farm. I remember they lived a few doors down from us in the bracero living quarters.

During a recent discussion with Ramona, she told me that they entered the United States when she was 3 or 4 years of age. Based on her age at the time I spoke with her, I determined that they entered into the United States in 1952 or 1953. They later moved to California. During the conversation with Ramona recently, I confirmed that they moved to California in 1956. When we first visited them as a young man, they lived in Huntington Beach, California.

The composite photograph on the left shows my uncle Tomas picking cotton and my aunt Anita sitting on one of the tractors on the Ryan farm. I labeled both photographs with the date of Dec. 1955 because the original pictures had that date imprinted on them.

During story times, my mother would tell me that my aunt Anita and she were always at odds with each other because Ramona and Chuy, my brother, would constantly fight. Chuy always seemed to wind up on the losing side. As a result, my father would have to intercede to keep the peace between my mother and his sister and to quell the fights between the children.

The other family that lived in the bracero housing quarters was the Bowles family. John Bowles and his wife, Hortencia, were the heads of that family. I faintly remember a family living there but I didn't know it was specifically the Bowles family that lived there. I learned it was the Bowles family because of a conversation I overheard between Hortencia and my mother later on during my high school years. By the way, somehow I also learned that they moved away to Watsonville, California after leaving the Ryan farm. It wasn't until I was older when we now lived in the home adjacent to the sand hills on the Ryan farm, that they returned to the Fabens area. They lived with their kids on the adjacent farm to the north of the Ryan farm.

One of the bracero workers that also lived in the bracero housing quarters was a man by the name of Guadalupe Amaro. He was my "padrino" by virtue of the fact that he was my baptism sponsor. The Spanish word "padrino" means "godfather" in English. I remember he was older than my parents. He was of short stature and somewhat fair complected. I remember Guadalupe Amaro was a kind and gentle man. I don't remember what became of him.

Another name that comes to mind in relation to my baptism is a woman by the name of Julianita. My mother would refer to her as "tu madrina" which translated to English means "your godmother". I believe that Julianita was my mother's cousin. It's interesting; I do remember Guadalupe Amaro's face but I don't remember Julianita's face. I knew of Julianita because she visited us on the farm several times; unlike Guadalupe Amaro, she didn't live in the bracero housing quarters at the Ryan farm. I think she lived in Cd. Juarez, Mexico at the time.

As far as I can remember, Mr. Ryan trusted my father. My father managed many of the day to day operations on the farm. Mr. Ryan spoke Spanish and therefore, there was no language barrier between my father and Mr. Ryan. My father was assigned the role of foreman early on and directed several other bracero laborers on the Ryan farm. The reason I know he was the foreman is because of two booklets that show labor hour entries for the farm workers during the time period from May 2, 1952 to July 4, 1952. The booklets show that my father's hourly rate was higher than the other men listed in the booklets. More information on these labor hour booklets will be presented in a later chapter.

My older brother, Chuy, and I were fortunate to have been born on the United States side of the border during the time that my father's "bracero" labor contract was in effect. My older brother was born on May 6, 1949. His formal name was Jesus but we called him by his Spanish nickname of "Chuy". I was born on January 23, 1951 and was named Salvador; however, everyone called me by my Spanish nickname of "Chava". Both my parents were non-English speaking and so the Spanish language was our primary language during our pre-school years as children. It wasn't until my brother and I started elementary school later on that we began to learn the English language.

My Father's Inadvertent Bracero Assignment

My mother once told me a story about my father having been inadvertently assigned to work at a farm in Pecos, Texas. This memory was clear in her mind because it involved our family being left alone for a period of time without my father's presence.

The duration of the bracero farm labor contracts was for fixed periods of time. With a little help from the internet, I found one source that referenced bracero contract durations of 9 to 12 months. I found another document that referenced bracero contract durations on the internet titled "Harvest of Loneliness: The Bracero Program (A Teacher's Guide)". The document references contracts as short as 45 days and contract renewals as long as "a year and a half or more".

The document can be found at the following internet link: http://fod.infobase.com/HTTP/43700/43712_guide.pdf

That document serves as "A Teacher's Guide" for an hour long video that chronicled the story of how bracero men were treated starting from their origins in Mexico to the farms in the United States. The video also describes the subject of labor contract durations.

The video can be found at the following internet link: https://www.youtube.com/watch?v=PcV2EOo-Xdc

The video can also be found by performing a Google search using the following text: "Harvest of Loneliness: The Bracero Program".

The following excerpt is taken from that document:

> *"The men were then transported in overcrowded trucks, trains or buses to the work site to become the charge of an employer under contract for a specified time, generally 45 days or six weeks. Often men renewed for longer periods sometimes reaching a year and a half or more. The short contract period served as a protection for the growers who preferred the renewable shorter contract in order to weed out 'incompetents' and re-contract the efficient workers."*

I never did discuss the subject of bracero labor contract durations with my father or mother. But, based on specific events involving my family's move to Arizona, that will be described later in this memoir, I know my father worked for Mr. Ryan for at least two bracero labor contract periods starting in 1949 through approximately 1955. Thereafter, our family moved to Arizona sometime during 1955 and then returned back to the Ryan farm shortly thereafter; possibly within a year's period of time.

My mother once told me a story having to do with my father's bracero labor contract nearing its conclusion. She told me that when my father's bracero labor contract neared its conclusion date, Mr. Ryan informed my father that he would have to return to Chihuahua, Mexico. Mr. Ryan further told my father that once in Chihuahua, my father was to proceed to re-apply for another bracero contract so that he could again return to work on Mr. Ryan's farm.

A review of the internet literature shows that contract renewals were common. However, based on my mother's story having to do with my father returning back to Chihuahua, Mexico, I can only surmise that his existing bracero labor contract could only be renewed a set number of times. Having reached that set number of contract renewals, I suppose the only alternative was to return to Chihuahua to start the contracting process all over again from scratch.

According to my mother, Mr. Ryan assured my father that he would personally contact the bracero reception center and arrange it so that upon my father's arrival at the reception center, my father would be assigned to work on the Ryan farm. When the day came to return to Chihuahua, my father traveled to Mexico leaving my mother, my brother and I at the Ryan farm. In later life, I never asked my mother if my father traveled to Cd. Juarez to reapply for a new bracero labor contract or whether he had to return all the way back to the city of Chihuahua to reapply. Now knowing more about the bracero sign-up process, I now know that he did return to the "migratory station" in Chihuahua to start all over again.

I can only assume that Mr. Ryan did contact the bracero reception center and specifically requested my father by name as the laborer of choice for the Ryan farm. Anyway, during the assignment process of the Mexican laborers at the bracero facilities, an error occurred and my father wound up being assigned to a farm in Pecos, Texas and not to the Ryan farm. Pecos, Texas was about 209 miles east of El Paso. Without giving him the opportunity to return to the Ryan farm to say goodbye to my mother or to inform Mr. Ryan of the pending assignment to Pecos, Texas, my father was transported to Pecos, Texas. He was taken to a farm in Pecos.

When all was said and done at the bracero reception center in El Paso, Mr. Ryan returned to the farm and reported the bad news to my mother. Mr. Ryan spoke Spanish well and told my mother about the unfortunate occurrence. Mr. Ryan also told her that he was familiar with the owner of the farm in Pecos, Texas where my father had been assigned. He told my mother that he would be speaking with the farm owner in Pecos and that somehow he would arrange to have my father reassigned to the Ryan farm.

My mother told me that we continued to live on the farm for some time during my father's absence. True to his word, somehow Mr. Ryan was able to arrange the reassignment of my father to his farm for another bracero labor contract period. My mother didn't know the specifics of what actually occurred to reassign my father to the Ryan farm. All she knew was that Mr. Ryan kept his word.

Oh, and one more thing about Pecos, Texas. Never have I driven through Pecos on my way to or from Midland or Dallas on Interstate Highway 20 without thinking; "this is where my father worked as a bracero way back in the 1950s".

Bracero Wages – A Trip Back in Time to 1952

As a young boy, I never really paid much attention to the amount of money my father was paid when he worked on the Ryan farm. I do remember; however, having seen one of his weekly paychecks but alas I am not able to recall the amount. Now while writing this memoir, I became very interested in the amount of money my father earned during his early years at the Ryan farm. The reason I became interested in his salary was because I wanted to see how he fared in comparison to others.

I do remember that during summer school breaks when I was 10 through 13 years of age, I worked "chopping cotton" on the Ryan farm as well as in several other surrounding farms. We were paid $.50 per hour for "chopping cotton" during the years from about 1961 to about 1965.

Sometime during the time when I was writing this piece, my brother, Martin, invited the Renteria clan to a 4th of July 2016 family get-together at his home. During the get-together, I began to tell Irma, my sister, the story of my father taking Chuy and I to see him load crop duster airplanes with fumigation powder when we were children. My sister, Graciela, overheard our conversation and she mentioned that she was in possession of my father's log books that showed the wages he earned when he worked on the farm. We refer to Graciela by the name "Gracie".

As a result of Gracie telling me that she had my father's log books that showed the wages he earned, I became interested in digging into the issue of bracero wages and the issue of wage fairness. I found that the internet contains many stories about braceros and the wages they were paid. This was interesting to me because along the way I had previously read a reference to bracero wage rates being as low as $.30 per hour.

The wage reference can be found in the book titled *"Race and Ethnicity in Arkansas: New Perspectives" edited by John A. Kirk*. The specific passage in the book is as follows:

"In Arkansas, however, prevailing hourly wages were 30 to 40 cents. Only in Arkansas was the prevailing hourly wage substantially below the Bracero Program's 50-cent floor."

Sometime later, Gracie provided me with two hard bound booklets measuring 4 inches wide by 6 inches high. The text "Perfection Time Book Weekly No 657" is printed on the front cover of the booklets. The two booklets contain handwritten date entries from May 2, 1952 to July 4, 1952. The following is a photograph of the front cover of the labor hour booklet and two pages that were contained inside the booklet:

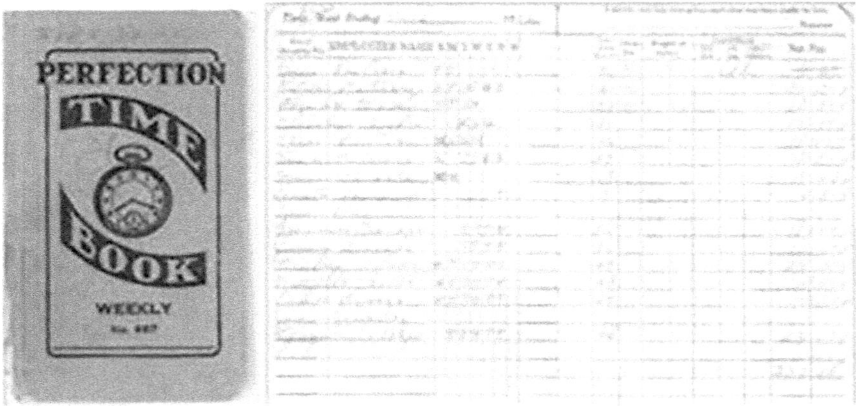

The labor hour booklets contain the handwritten names of my father and several farm workers. In addition to the names of the farm workers, the labor hour booklets contain English cursive handwriting that annotates loans, repayments and hours worked for the farm workers. Examples of annotations are "Elias Beltran short 12.5 hrs last week that was not on book" and "deduct 20.00 on Jesus Renteria loan". Only one page contains farm worker names entered in my father's handwriting.

I recognized several of the farm worker's names. One name was Esteban Gutierrez who was my uncle on my mother's side. Another name was Tomas Bejarano who was married to my aunt Anita, my father's sister. Still another name was Guadalupe Amaro who was my godfather. During the period of time represented in the two labor hour booklets the number of workers on the farm varied from 11 to 16 workers.

The two labor hour booklets contain handwritten worker's names, hours worked, wage rates and total amounts earned for the date entries from May 2, 1952 to July 4, 1952. Both labor hour booklets show the wage rate of $.50 per hour paid to the bracero farm workers and $.60 per hour paid to my father as the foreman.

I grew interested in determining where the wage rates originated and whether the wage rates were fair. With a little help from the internet, I found that according to the U.S. Census Bureau, the minimum wage rate in 1952 was $.75 per hour. The "Fair Labor Standards Act" (FLSA) that set the minimum wage requirement was enacted in 1938. Until 1966, the FLSA excluded farm workers from the minimum wage requirements. It became pretty obvious that if the U.S. farm worker wasn't protected by the FLSA in 1952 then the Mexican bracero farm worker wasn't either.

In a previous section above, I made a reference to the book titled *"Race and Ethnicity in Arkansas: New Perspectives" edited by John A. Kirk*. A specific passage in the book describes how the bracero farm worker wage rate was established as well as the amount of the wage rate. The following is that specific passage in the book:

> *"The role Mexican workers and consulates played in undermining the farmers' fight against New Deal worker protection in agriculture became apparent by 1952-53, when Mexicans became the first workers in Arkansas's fields to earn*

a minimum wage. Bracero agreements stated that braceros should be paid the local prevailing wage or an amount "necessary to cover their living needs," whichever was higher. During the early 1950s, consulates set a floor of 50 cents per hour or $2.50 per hundred pounds of cotton. During the 1953-54 picking season, farm jobs in other bracer-receiving [sic] areas had prevailing wages as low as 45 to 60 cents per hour in Texas and as high as $1.00 to

$1.25 per hour in Oregon. In Arkansas, however, prevailing hourly wages were 30 to 40 cents. Only in Arkansas was the prevailing hourly wage substantially below the Bracero Program's 50-cent floor."

It appears from the content of the above referenced book that the Bracero program along with the Mexican Consulate's offices established what the book refers to as the "50-cent floor", i.e. the $.50 per hour wage rate. The "50-cent floor" mentioned in the book is probably the reason for the presence of the $.50 per hour wage rate on the two labor hour booklets that Gracie provided me.

Now that the issue of who set the "50-cent floor" was resolved, I was now interested in determining how my father's wage rate of $.60 per hour compared to the rest of the wages in the United States. The reason that my father's wage rate was $.60 per hour and not $.50 per hour was that my father was the "mayordomo" at the Ryan farm. The English translation of the Spanish word "mayordomo" is "foreman". I then reviewed the two labor hour booklets in more detail.

I found that the front cover of one booklet was marked with the word "Jim". On the upper left of each page containing worker's names and hours worked, the letters "Jimmy" or "J.R." were present. The other booklet's front cover was marked with the words "Ryan Farms". On the upper left of each page containing worker's names and hours worked were the letters "RF". The page dated 5/23/1952 in the booklet marked "Jim" contains the words "Rancho Verde" followed by a listing of worker's names and hours worked. The "Rancho Verde" worker's names appear only on this one page and not on any other page.

I remember the term "Rancho Verde" because I would sometimes overhear my father referring to that farm in his conversations with other men. For those that are interested, the "Rancho Verde" farm can be found using Google Earth or Google Maps by entering the following address: 938 Hole in The Wall Road, San Elizario, TX 79849. I originally thought that the two labor hour booklets contained worker's names and wages in sequentially date order such that the ending date of one booklet would be the starting date of the next booklet. As I continued reviewing the booklets, I discovered that the booklets both had dates encompassing about the same time period. The booklet marked "Jim" had date entries from 5/2/1952 to 7/4/1952 while the booklet marked "Ryan Farms" had date entries from 5/16/1952 to 7/4/1952. The overlapping date ranges on the two booklets puzzled me. Even more puzzling was that in some cases, the worker's names appeared on both booklets for the same week but with different number of hours worked. In order to provide an example, I constructed a data table to show my father's work hours that were present in the two booklets for the week ending on Friday, June 6, 1952. The following is the data table showing my father's work hours:

Data Table 1: Jesus Renteria, Hours Worked

Booklet	Week Ending	S	M	T	W	T	F	S	Total
"Ryan Farm"	06/06/1952	9	8.5	5	5	4	0	0	31.5
"Jim"	06/06/1952	0	0	0	5	0	10	0	15

During the days that I was writing this piece, I kept wondering why were two labor hour booklets kept; one marked "Ryan Farm" and the other marked "Jim"? Why did the booklet marked with the letters "Jim" contain the names and work hours for a list of "Rancho Verde" workers for the date of May 23, 1952? I can only surmise that there must have been times when the owners of the "Rancho Verde" farm needed additional workers and Mr. Ryan provided them a helping hand with some of his workers. If this is correct, then the booklet marked "Jim" contains the worker's names and hours of those workers who worked on-loan on the "Rancho Verde" farm.

As indicated before, the two booklets provide a small window into my family's history. I was a little more than a year old during the days from May 2, 1952 to July 4, 1952 which are the dates represented in the two booklets.

The information showing the hours worked in the booklets show that his daily work hours varied greatly. That is, the hours were not what we today know as normal working hours from 8:00 am to 5:00 pm with an hour off for lunch. The daily working hours seemed too erratic to me. I noticed that during one week, he showed no working hours whereas on the week where the most hours were annotated, he worked 63.5 hours.

It didn't make sense to me that my father's weekly working hours were so variable. As I indicated before, his hours were just too erratic. I remember that later on when I was an adolescent, he always seemed to work more consistent hours. This might have been because during those later years there weren't any bracero men working on the farm and there might have been more work left for him to do on the farm. At any rate, it seems to me that it was unfair that the bracero men were not occupied during the entire 40 or 48 hour week.

I reviewed the time booklets more thoroughly in an attempt to determine the average weekly wage he earned during the dates contained in the booklets. My objective was to attempt to determine his yearly bracero income and compare that amount to the normal average income that is earned by a typical United States citizen. The following table identified as Data Table 2 shows his income as recorded in the 2 labor hour booklets during the time period from May 2, 1952 to July 4, 1952.

Data Table 2: Jesus Renteria, Hours Worked and Weekly Wage

Week Ending Date	"Jim" Booklet	"Ryan Farm" Booklet	Total Hours	Wage Per Hr	Weekly Total	
5/2/1952	18	0	18	$ 60	$10 80	(See Note 1)
5/9/1952	8	0	8	$ 60	$ 4 80	(See Note 1)
5/16/1952	0	16	16	$ 60	$ 9 60	
5/23/1952	0	0	0	$ 60	$ 0 00	(See Note 2)
5/30/1952	4	27	31	$ 60	$18 60	
6/6/1952	15	31 5	46 5	$ 60	$27 90	
6/13/1952	0	39	39	$ 60	$23 40	
6/20/1952	20 5	40	60 5	$ 60	$36 30	
6/27/1952	6 5	57	63 5	$ 60	$38 10	
7/4/1952	6	21	27	$ 60	$16 20	
				Weekly Average	$18 57	

Note 1 The "Ryan Farm" booklet has no entries for this week

Note 2 The "Ryan Farm" and "Jim" booklets have no entries for the week of 5/23/1952

The content in Data Table 2 shows that my father's weekly income, at least for the period covered between the dates of May 2, 1952 to July 4, 1952, was $18.57 per week. Obviously, the data set was very small but that's all I had available to me.

I searched for articles on the web in an attempt to determine the going wage rate for United States citizens. I was lucky enough to find information published by the United States Department of Commerce that contained average yearly incomes in the United States. The following is an excerpt from one of those publications. The following prefaces the publication:

> ***"Data showing income received in 1952 by persons 14 years old and over appear in the report, "Income of Persons in the United States: 1952," Series P-60, No. 14"***

The following is the title of the publication:

> ***"Current Population Reports, Consumer Income, April 27, 1954"***

The following shows the average income in the United States in 1952:

> ***"The median (average) family income in the United States was estimated at $3,900 in 1952 or $200 higher than in 1951, according to figures released by Robert W. Burgess, Director, Bureau of the Census, Department of Commerce."***

In the end, my father's yearly income in 1952 was estimated to be about $965.64 compared to an average yearly wage of a United States citizen of $3,900.00. Therefore, my father earned roughly 74 percent less than the average wage in the United States in 1952 as a bracero.

By the way, I located an inflation calculator on the web. Using the inflation calculator, the amount of $965.64 annually in 1952 had the same buying power as $8,983.15 in 2018. That's pretty low. Again, using the inflation calculator, the amount of $3,900 annually in 1952 had the same buying power as $36,280.89 in 2018. The inflation calculator can be found using the following web link:

https://www.dollartimes.com/inflation/inflat ion.php?amount=4000&year=1970

Another piece of information relative to my father's income is a check stub that Gracie, my sister, provided me when she also lent me my father's labor hour booklets that originated from his work on the Ryan farm and possibly the Rancho Verde farm. The check stub was not attached to the actual check therefore I don't know the total check amount. The check stub was issued by Vowell Construction Company and it did show the hourly amount of $2.45. I remember my father having worked for a company by the name of Vowell Construction Company. I remember that Vowell Construction Company operated a fleet of concrete trucks and therefore my father probably worked on a concrete crew. By the way, Vowell Construction Company ultimately became a company by the name of El Paso Sand.

I was again interested in determining how his earnings compared to the average income in 1974. I found a web article that showed that the average yearly income in 1974 was $12,893.00. The web article was titled ***"Household Money Income In 1874 And Selected Social and Economic Characteristics of Households, Issued 1975"*** and can be found on the web using the following web link: https://www2.census.gov/prod2/popscan/p60-100.pdf

In the end, based on a 40 hour work week in 1974, my father earned an amount of $5,096.00 when the average income in the United States was $12,840.00. He earned 60.3 percent less than the average income in the United States. Chuy and I had already started our own families and lived apart from my parents and our siblings. Now the family members that depended on his income were my mother and 6 children. That's the reason my family needed welfare assistance at the time.

As an aside, when he was working with the concrete company, I remember that one of the projects that the construction company was involved with was at a bridge located at a location on highway route 62. The location where the bridge is located is known as Cornudas. This road is the same road that is used to travel to Dell City, Texas. The distance between Fabens, Texas and the Cornudas location is about 75 miles. That's how far my father traveled in his own vehicle to work. That's surprising but that is what it took to care for our family.

United States Permanent Resident

I never asked my parents how my father became a United States "permanent resident alien". The term "green card holder" is commonly used to denote a person who is a United States permanent resident alien. With the "green card", my father was allowed to permanently live and work anywhere in the United States. No longer did he have to be concerned with bracero labor contracts and contract renewals. As far back as I can remember as a child, my father's immigration status had always been that of United States permanent resident alien. But of course prior to that, he entered the United States as a bracero. It wasn't until 1999 that he was naturalized as a United States citizen.

Sometime during one of my father's subsequent bracero labor contracts, my father applied to the United States Immigration Department for permanent resident alien status. It is possible that he was granted a "green card" because my mother was a U.S. citizen and further because my brother and I had already been born in the United States and were United States citizens as well. This is what most people today refer to as an "anchor baby" or an "anchor wife". My wife, Socorro, once commented to me that my mother had told her that Mr. Ryan encouraged my father to formally marry my mother. I suspect that Mr. Ryan knew that my father's chances in obtaining permanent resident status would increase if he was married to a United States citizen, in this case, my mother. Although I never asked, I suppose that Mr. Ryan knew that my mother was a United States citizen because of the ease with which she was able to follow my father to the Ryan farm when he was first contracted as a bracero to work on the Ryan farm.

My father and mother were formally married on August 6, 1949 by Mr. W.A. Yarbro, Justice of the Peace in El Paso County, Texas.

The pictorial on the left shows the marriage certificate issued by the County of El Paso.

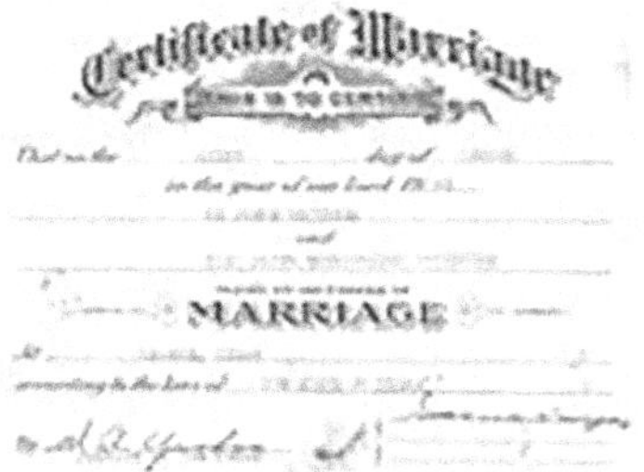

By the way, I remember that sometime when I was about 8 years old in 1959, my father and mother participated in a wedding ceremony at the Fabens Catholic Church. In those days and on a yearly basis, a traveling "missionary" priest would visit the parish. During the week of his stay at the parish, the missionary priest would speak to the parishioners in the church every evening about subjects relating to Catholic comportment. The sessions were attended by people that were devoted to the Catholic faith. It was during those missionary visits that the missionary priest would marry multiple couples that had previously not taken their vows of marriage in the Catholic Church.

In olden times, the Catholic Church didn't recognize civil marriages or cohabitating unions (couples that elope) between men and women. This is probably the reason that in spite of having been married civilly on August 6, 1949, my parents felt it necessary to also exchange marriage vows in the Catholic Church in 1959.

As his employer, Mr. Ryan probably sponsored my father and that action helped him obtain permanent resident alien status. During story times with my mother she often said "el Jimmie nos ayudó mucho"; in English "Jimmie helped us a lot". Today, I am certain that had Mr. Ryan not sponsored my father in his application for permanent resident alien status, my father would have continued in the Bracero program and ultimately our family would have had to return back to Delicias, Chihuahua. For all of those reasons, my family is deeply indebted to Mr. James Ryan.

From personal experience, sponsoring a Mexican citizen in obtaining United States permanent resident alien status is a two edged sword. After reading Mr. Ryan's obituary, I found that Mr. Ryan was an educated man. I am almost positive that it crossed his mind that my father might seek employment with some other competing farms once he obtained U.S. permanent resident alien status. After all, with a "green card", my father would be free to work anywhere and for anyone in the United States. After leaving his employment at the Ryan farm, my father worked for other companies with only his immigration "green card".

I think that my father was granted United States permanent resident alien status prior to or my being 4 years of age, which would correspond to the year 1955. The reason I believe that this occurred prior to 1955 is because I remember that our family migrated to Arizona when I was about 4 years of age. He wouldn't have been able to leave his employment as a bracero without a "green card". More on the details of this move to Arizona is yet to come.

In the end, Mr. Ryan chose the high ground because only through his sponsorship could my father have received the "permanent resident alien" status. After returning back from Arizona, my father continued to work for him for another ten years thereafter as a United States permanent resident alien.

My Family's Fond Memories of Mr. James Ryan

Mr. James Ryan passed away on Feb. 12, 2003 in Fabens, Texas at the age of 78 years. He died of prostate problems and emphysema.

I attended his viewing on Feb. 17, 2003 at Hampton Funeral Home. Socorro, my wife, and I attended the Mass at Our Lady of Guadalupe Church in Fabens on Feb. 18, 2003. We then proceeded to the funeral site at Ft. Bliss National Cemetery.

I met all the Ryan brothers; Joseph, Patrick, Mark, Paul and Michael. With the exception of Paul and Mark, the rest of the Ryan brothers had moved away from Fabens years ago. Joe and Pat moved away sometime around 1967. I was glad to see them and converse with them.

Mrs. Jane Ryan was in good spirits. She told me that Mr. Ryan had died in her arms. They had been expecting his death. When I spoke with her immediately after the funeral service I hugged her and told her "you are my life-long friend and fourth grade teacher". She looked around and responded so everyone could hear and she then said "and I take credit for Chava's success". She then proceeded to say "and I take credit for the success of everyone that came through my class room".

Joe asked that I say hello to Chuy. He told me that he had been keeping tabs on Chuy through his dad, Mr. Ryan.

Many members of my family were positively affected by Mr. Ryan. Our family, the Renterias, lived, worked and grew up on the Ryan farm. My uncle Tomas and aunt Anita worked and lived at the Ryan farm. My uncle Esteban and aunt Rosa lived and worked at the Ryan farm as well.

From his obituary, I found out that Mr. Ryan was in the Marine Corps and fought in World War II. That's where I found out that he was a college graduate. By the way, he also attended the Fabens Independent School District in his younger days.

I was saddened by his death. He touched our family in a meaningful way.

The following is the text of the obituary dated Feb. 16, 2003 taken from the El Paso Times newspaper website:

"JAMES LAWRENCE RYAN 5/30/24 - 2/12/03 Born the first of three children to Joseph and Mary Adams Ryan in Des Moines, New Mexico, "Jim" moved to Fabens at the age of one. He was a graduate of Fabens High School and attended Texas A&M University. Jim served in the Marine Corps in WWII and was an entrepreneur with interests in agriculture and the hardware industry. An avid sportsman, Jim enjoyed hunting, fishing and golfing with family and friends. Jim is survived by his wife of 54 years, Mary Jane and their six sons and daughters-in-law, Joe and Denise, Seth and Pam, Mark and Sherry, Paul and Kit, Michael and Patti and David as well as 13 grandchildren, 3 great-grandchildren and his sisters Mary King of Marble Falls, Texas and Helen Drake of Dallas, Texas. Visitation - Monday 3:00 - 7:00 p.m. at Hampton Valley Mortuary in Fabens. Mass - Tuesday at 11:00 a.m. at Our Lady of Guadalupe in Fabens. Burial - Ft. Bliss National Cemetery. In lieu of flowers, please make a donation to your favorite charity."

As I indicated before, I've found numerous interesting articles about the bracero program on the internet. I also found several articles that revealed horror stories about bracero farm workers having been mistreated by farm owners. My father and mother never told me or implied that Jimmy Ryan, as they called him, mistreated them or any other bracero workers.

Soon after learning of his passing, I emailed my brother, Chuy, to inform him of Mr. Ryan's passing. The following is Chuy's email in response to my email to him.

Subj: RE: Mr. Ryan's Death

Date: 2/19/2003 9:07:09 AM Mountain Standard Time From: RENTEJE@mail.northgrum.com (Renteria, Jesse) To: SaRenteria@aol.com ('SaRenteria@aol.com')

Hello Chava,

Hey......................
Thank you for the heads-up on Mr. Ryan passing. I really felt this one. It really set me back a bit.
When we lived on the farm. We lived down hill from the Martinez [sic].
Behind the house we had alot of sand (soft sand) in which to play. We were always playing on our knees with little toys.
Well around Christmas time, Mr. Ryan would come and deliver plastic bags of fruits, and nuts and candy to us.
But best of all ....for us as kids he would give us bags of little green soldiers, tanks and little toy military jeeps.
That was big for me................................
Thanks..

Chuy

That was Chuy's last tribute to Mr. Ryan. Like Chuy, I also remember him as a kind man.

When I think of Mr. Ryan, I remember his gentle smile. I'll never forget the time when my father put us to work cutting tree trunks to supply Mr. Ryan and his family with wood for their fireplace. My father provided us with a "two-man crosscut saw" that is typically used by lumberjacks to cut trees. To use the two-handled saw, the person at one end of the saw pulls while the person at the opposite end of the saw pushes the saw forward. The two persons push and pull the saw back and forth until the tree trunk is completely cut into smaller stumps.

I remember one specific day while Chuy and I were cutting a tree trunk with the saw that Mr. Ryan happened to be slowly driving by in his car. When we heard the noise of the vehicle, we both stopped and looked up to see who was driving it. It was Mr. Ryan slowly driving past. I could see his face. He looked at us and smiled as he drove by. I don't remember ever having conversed with Mr. Ryan when I was a young boy; I only remember his kind smiles.

Mr. James Ryan was every bit of a gentle man. Again, my family is deeply indebted to Mr. James Ryan.

But For My Mother, I Would Have Been Raised In Mexico

As I indicated before, my grandmother's maiden name on my mother's side was "Maria Gonzalez Valles". Her married name was "Maria Gutierrez Gonzalez". She was a widow when we were growing up. We were told that my grandfather Gregorio passed away in a railroad train accident when Chuy and I were very young.

I remember that when we were children, our family would travel to Delicias, Mexico to visit my parent's relatives and my grandmother Maria. The Spanish translation for grandmother is "abuela" and the more loving term is "abuelita". The word "abuelita" somehow turned into "agüelita" (with the umlaut mark over the letter u) because as children, we found it easier to pronounce. As I indicated before, Delicias is a small city located in Mexico about 300 miles south of El Paso, Texas.

I remember that during our visits to Delicias, we would be taken to see horses and donkeys. The Spanish word for donkey is "burro".

The burros were small enough in height that with a little help, I was able to ride them. It was fun going to Delicias.

I also remember that from time to time my "agüelita" would travel from Delicias to visit us at the farm. We loved our "agüelita" dearly. During one of my "agüelita's" trips to our home at the Ryan farm, she asked me if I would like to go with her to Delicias to live with her for awhile. I remember that this occurred when I was very young. It could have been when I was 3 or 4 years of age.

Although I don't remember her exact words, I remember her telling me that if I went to live with her in Delicias, I would be able to ride the "burritos". "Burrito" is the slang word for "burro". The word "burrito" in those days was used in context with the horse-like animal known as a donkey and not in context to the tortilla wrap that nowadays is also called a "burrito". By the way, the word used to describe the traditional tortilla wrap in Mexico is "taco" and not "burrito".

Anyway, I remember that my "agüelita" even promised to buy me a burro of my own. I was excited at the prospect of going to Delicias to live with my "agüelita" and ride the burritos. I must have responded to my "agüelita" in the affirmative because shortly thereafter my mother interceded and halted any thoughts that my "agüelita" might have had about taking me to live with her in Delicias.

In an effort to convince my mother to let me go with her, my "agüelita" told my mother that it would only be for awhile and that she would bring me back soon. My mother would have none of that. The day came when my "agüelita" was to leave to return back to Delicias and my mother told me that I was not going to Delicias with my "agüelita". I remember crying while begging my mother to let me go with my "agüelita". I cried and cried when she left.

In the end, my "agüelita" left without me. But for my mother's resistence, I probably would have grown up in Mexico with my "agüelita". It was not uncommon in those days in Mexico to have children raised by the grandparents. It was sometimes an economic necessity for a family, especially families with a large number of children. We weren't a large family at the time, but the tradition of the grandparents taking and raising grandchildren nonetheless was prevalent in those times.

I'll never forget my agüelita Maria and the effort she made in those days to take me with her. Later on when I was a little older we would visit her in Delicias and we always looked forward to visiting with her. She was always very kind to us.

Family Member's Life Spans

I have always been interested in the life spans of my ancestors because I feel that to some degree, their life spans determine my own life span. Granted, life in olden times was physically harder than life now in modern times. Our forebears tended to work outdoors in extreme hot days and extreme cold days; that had to have contributed to some shortening of their life spans. Based on the fact that their work was physically harder, my life span in comparison to theirs will probably be slightly more.

I am not certain of the exact year when my "agüelita" Maria passed away. While I was writing this memoir, I struggled to remember the date of my "agüelita's" passing. Fortunately, my wife, Socorro, remembered that we went to my "agüelita's" funeral in Delicias sometime after my wife and I married in February of 1971 but before I graduated from college in December of 1974.

As I indicated before, I never thought to ask about my "agüelita's" age when she passed away. However, for the following reasons, I believe she was 66 years of age when she passed. My mother was born in 1929. Manuela, my mother's sister, was the oldest. I don't know my aunt Manuela's year of birth but for purposes of this subject, I am guessing it might have been about 2 years prior to my mother's birth. Manuela's birth year would therefore be 1927.

Although my "agüelita" might have married at a very young age, as was common in olden days, let's provide the benefit of the doubt and say that she married and had her first child when she was 20 years of age. As a result, it is likely that she was born on or about the year 1907. Assuming my "agüelita" passed away in the year 1973, her age would have been 66 years at the time of her passing.

My own mother passed away in the year 2002 at the age of 73 years and my father passed away at the age of 72 years in the year 2000. Further, my older brother, Chuy, passed away when he was 65 years of age.

This information kind of provides a forecast as to when I will be kicking the bucket (chuckle).

A "Charro" in the Outhouse And Other Superstitions

Living on the farm was living with limited lighting during the night time; it got really dark during the nights on the farm. To a child blessed with a huge imagination, living life without outdoor lighting during the night time was very frightening. There seemed to be no shortage of scary stories that could scare the living daylights out of a child like me. The following are a few examples of scary stories that I used to hear when I was a child as well as later on when I was an adolescent.

As indicated before, during the time when we lived in the "adobe/stucco building" near the railroad tracks, we used an "outhouse" for toilet purposes. I remember my mother making a big to do about something that happened when she went outside during one night to use the "outhouse". During that one night, she returned back from the "outhouse" very startled. I remember her saying to my father "Jesus, está un charro en el escusado. Andale ve a ver.". That occurred during the time in my life prior to attending school. In the translation to English this meant "Jesus, there is a charro at the toilet. Hurry, go see.". "Charro" is a word that is used to refer to a traditional horseman from México, who wears a type of wide-brimmed hat that is broad enough to cast a shadow over his head, neck and shoulders. Today, we know these hats to be "charro hats".

Anyway, upon hearing my mother begging him to go see for himself, my father quickly proceeded to walk to the outhouse while my mother, my siblings and I waited inside the apartment. A few minutes later, my father returned and told my mother that he had not seen anyone inside or near the outhouse. Unconvinced, my mother forced my father to accompany her to the outhouse; she felt that he hadn't really looked thoroughly enough. We waited inside the apartment while they left to see. When they returned, it was apparent that they found nothing. For some time thereafter, when a family member needed to go to use the outhouse during the night, my father would have to accompany that family member to the outhouse. Needless to say, the matter was never really resolved.

That night of the incident, my father accused my mother of exaggerating. I remember my mother and my father discussing the matter. He was telling her that she had seen something that was not really there. This seemed spooky to me because I took it to mean that my mother had seen some sort of apparition such as a ghost.

The "charro" episode would not be the last when my father would have to come to my mother's aid. There would be several times when my mother would see things and my father would have to investigate to see if what she claimed she saw was real.

Another strange episode occurred when we lived in that same "adobe/ stucco building" near the railroad tracks. The apartment window was located facing toward the farm fields opposite the direction of the railroad tracks. The apartment window to the rear was constructed such that the bottom part of the window was only about 2 feet high from the ground. One night she awoke my father and told him that there was a little boy standing outside the window and that he should go out to see what he needed. My father quickly walked out the door and around the building to where the window was located and found nothing.

Upon returning back into the apartment, he asked my mother to describe what she had seen. My mother claimed to have seen a little boy standing outside the window looking directly at her through the window. He had stood there staring at my mother for a few minutes. She told my father that she had asked the little boy where his parents were and if he needed anything. The little boy remained motionless and just kept looking at her without answering her questions. That is when she decided to wake my father.

During my father's questioning, my mother indicated to him that she thought the little boy might have been Ruly Ochoa. The name Ruly is pronounced as "Rulee". Ruly was the son of Jose and Maria Elena Ochoa who lived on a separate farm about a half mile walking distance toward the direction of Tornillo. I was 3 or 4 years of age when this occurred and so Ruly would have had to have been 5 or 6 years of age. I don't remember if my mother followed up with the Ochoa's about the possibility that it might have been Ruly whom she saw in the window that night. Clearly, my mother was spooked by the presence of the little boy at the window. Again, this matter was never fully resolved.

Once more during the time that we lived in the same "adobe/ stucco building" near the railroad tracks, my parents befriended the Salvador Muñoz family that lived on a nearby farm known as the Stahmann farm. For some reason the bracero men would refer to that farm as "el rancho Estorman". Later in life I found out that the name of the farm was really "Stahmann farms". I guess that to the bracero men, the word "Stahmann" sounded the same as the word "Estorman".

The Stahmann farm was located on the opposite side of what was then Highway 80 from the location where we lived on the Ryan farm. The house where the Muñoz's lived was offset away from the highway even further by about a quarter of a mile. The heads of their household were Salvador and Margarita Muñoz. They were my parent's "compadres". The word "compadre" means that that they were present as sponsors during the baptism of one of our siblings. I don't remember which one of our family members was their baptismal godchild.

Anyway, Chuy and I became friends with their two eldest sons named Antonio and Salvador Muñoz. We used to call them "Toño" and "Salva". The name "Toño" is pronounced as "Tonyo". I remember that I was the runt of the foursome. Chuy and Salva were about the same age and Toño was about 1 or 2 years older than Chuy and Salva. On one occasion, Chuy and I walked to the Muñoz's house to play with "Toño" and "Salva" but we overstayed and before we knew it, daylight had turned into darkness. Toño and Salva decided to accompany us to the midway point along the quarter mile distance so that we could get back to our house across the highway as well as across the railroad tracks.

I remember it was very dark but Toño was carrying a flashlight so we all could see as we walked along the dirt road. They accompanied us up to the highway which was farther than the midway point between their house and our house. As we were about to cross the highway, "Toño" pointed the flashlight toward the direction of the tracks and toward our house so as to show us the path to take to our house. Before we had time to look toward where he was directing the flashlight, we noticed that he became startled. He turned to us and told us to look toward the direction he was pointing the flashlight and we all saw someone walking along the railroad tracks as if walking in the direction toward Fabens. The odd thing was that the outline of the person walking along the length of the tracks seemed to be in the form of a white silhouette.

During those startling moments, Toño had somehow moved the flashlight away from the direction of the white silhouette form and when he redirected the flashlight to where the white silhouette form had been, nothing was visible. He moved the flashlight so as to point it to the right and then to the left along the railroad tracks but what we had seen earlier was no longer there. Needless to say, we all felt the "heebee jeebies". Toño and Salva wound up having to walk us the entire way to our house. After telling my father about what we had seen, my father decided to drive Toño and Salva in his truck back to their house at the Stahmann farm.

Later on as a grown up in the late 1980s, I traveled to Chihuahua, Mexico on a business trip. Chihuahua is about 235 miles south from El Paso, Texas. At the time, I owned a company known as "Fluid Process Systems" and I went on the trip to visit several clients we had in Chihuahua.

During the trip, I visited with a cousin of my mother's whose name was Ramon Gonzalez. He was interested in my purchasing a vacant lot in Chihuahua that he owned. He had previously written me a letter asking me if I was interested in a property that he owned. He indicated that it might be suitable for a building structure where I could locate my business office in Chihuahua, Mexico. The property was located in an area very close to the downtown section of the city. A high adobe wall surrounded the property. When he opened a large wooden door to gain access into the property, I saw numerous large holes in the ground and various dirt mounds all over the property. I asked him why the holes had been dug. He responded that apparitions had occurred on the property and that led him to believe that there was buried treasure on the property.

During a subsequent visit with my mother, I told her about Ramon Gonzalez's property having holes and dirt mounds. She confirmed that apparitions occur in locations where someone has buried money or treasure in the ground. She went on to say that in olden times there were few banks in México and that people frequently buried their money to protect it from thieves. She said that some people even buried gold and silver. When the person that buried the money passed away, the money would remain undisturbed in the ground. She continued by saying that wherever people see apparitions, treasure is nearby. I used to think that this folklore was strictly a Mexican one. However, with a little help from the internet, I've found that this folklore is more universal than I thought.

From time to time, my father would accuse my mother of exaggerating about things. He would say to her "no seas tan soflamera". As a child, I noticed that my father would use the word "soflamera" or "soflamero" whenever a particular person was lying, being disingenuous or would exaggerate about things. I always wondered about the true meaning of the word "soflamera". With a little help from the internet I found that the word "soflamera" has the following meaning: "exaggerates the truth to the extent of sounding ridiculous or makes a big deal out of nothing". So in the end, I called it somewhat correctly as a child. In our case, the phrase "no seas tan soflamera" translates to "don't exaggerate so much".

Another spooky story was that of "La Llorona" or in English; "the weeping woman". In Spanish, the word "La" is the feminine form and therefore infers that the weeping person is a woman. Parents often used the story of "La Llorona" to keep their children from wandering out at night. My parents never threatened us with the "Llorona" story but I do remember the grown up kids scaring us simply by saying "wait, wait, wait, be still, be still . . . can you hear the Llorona?".

The following excerpts taken from Wikipedia describe the myth of "La Llorona":

> ***"The most basic story tells of a beautiful woman by the name of Maria who drowns her children in a river as a means of revenge because her husband left her for a younger woman. She soon realizes that her children are dead, so she drowns herself in the river. Challenged at the gates of Heaven as to the whereabouts of her children, she is not permitted to enter the afterlife until she has found them. Maria is forced to wander the Earth for all eternity, searching in vain for her drowned offspring, with her constant weeping giving her the name "La Llorona". She is trapped in between the living world and the spirit world.".***

Another spooky subject had to do with the word "alechusa". The word "alechusa" used to strike fear in me as a child. I once heard my mother say to my father; "Jesus, está una alechusa en el poste de la luz". In English, the phrase translates to "Jesus, there is an alechusa on top of the light post". I remember her saying those words in a manner that implied worry that the "alechusa" was on the light post. I don't remember how my father responded to her words but from that day on, my hearing the word "alechusa" would frighten me. Thereafter, to me, the word "alechusa" meant "witch". In my mind, my mother had said "Jesus, there is a witch sitting on top of the light post". To a child with a huge imagination, that phrase was frightening. In reality, she actually said "Jesus, there is an owl on top of the light post".

The apparitions that presented themselves seemed to occur when we lived in the "adobe/stucco building" near the railroad tracks but not at the house near the sand hills where we later moved into. I've often wondered if my father as well saw strange things on the farm. I always had the sense that he did and if he did, perhaps he chose not to disclose them to my mother or ourselves. Yes, I was superstitious and so was my mother. My father wasn't as expressive about things as much as my mother. To this day, I have a sense that even if he had seen strange things he wouldn't have told us so as not to "stir the pot" any more than needed.

Today I wonder if I should proceed to the place where the old "adobe/stucco building" used to stand. Metal detector in hand, perhaps I can find the buried treasure or buried money (chuckle).

My father bought our family a black and white television set. I think I was about 8 years of age in 1959 when that happened. Although we didn't know it at the time, the movie "The Wizard of Oz" was released in 1956 when I was 5 years of age. When I first saw the movie on our television set, I knew the "Wicked Witch of the West" was an "alechusa". Later in life, our family would move from the farm to live in our own house in Fabens. I remember that at times I would walk home in the dark from a boy scout meeting or perhaps from a friend's house while all the time keeping my eyes focused toward the ground immediately in front of me. I did not want my eyes wandering up the top of the electric light poles or telephone poles for fear of seeing an "alechusa". It wouldn't be until I would graduate from high school as a grown up that I would learn that the word "alechusa" simply meant "owl" in English. Who knew (chuckle).

As a side note, Irma, my sister, was 5 years of age when we first watched the "The Wizard of Oz" movie. I was 8 years old and Chuy was 10 years old. I remember she was terrified of the Wicked Witch of the West and the flying monkeys. In the spirit of fun, Chuy and I would adjust the channel knob on the television set so as to move to the channel showing the movie when Irma wasn't expecting it. As soon as she realized that the movie was showing, she would rush off to another room in fright (chuckle).

The Family Cures

When we were growing up as kids on the farm near the housing structure near the railroad tracks, like any other normal child, we would sometimes get sick or suffer some physical malady. Money always seemed to be scarce because we were a poor family. When we got sick, it was up to my mother to decide what was causing the sickness. In that respect, my mother was the in-house family doctor. Not really being trained in how to deal with sick kids, I think "doctoring" was a hit or miss proposition. Don't get me wrong, there were times when we actually were taken to the doctor in Fabens but those visits were few and far between. My mother had to exhaust her efforts before the decision was made to take us to be attended by a doctor.

The methods my mother used to deal with our sicknesses seemed normal to me at the time. Now as a grown up, I look back and wonder how we made it without dying from illnesses caused by bacteria or viruses. In a previous section, I described the potential of groundwater contamination due to the proximity of the human waste in the outhouse latrine relative to the underground water aquifer. It may be that those childhood sicknesses were caused by contaminated ground water . . . I will never know if some of those ailments were brought on by that fact. Anyway, it seemed that there was always a cure for our ailments. I suppose in some respects a mother's love is all it took to make us well.

Swept With An Egg

One of those "hit or miss" cures was what was known as "el barrido con el huevo". Translated to English, this means "swept with an egg". I remember that my grandmother Maria would from time to time perform that cure for a variety of our ailments. One of those ailments was fever or an ailment she referred to as "empacho".

I grew up knowing that the word "empacho" had something to do with a problem with the stomach when someone might have eaten an inappropriate food. Anyway, the condition known as "empacho" always seemed to be accompanied by pain in the abdomen or vomiting. Another ailment that was treated with "el barrido con huevo" was what was known as "mal de ojo" which in English is translated to "the evil eye". This ailment typically occurred in cute babies being cradled or carried in public by the mother. Supposedly, the baby's ailment occurred as a result of some passerby staring at the baby; especially if the baby was a pretty or cute baby. If the passerby then happened to touch the baby after having stared at it, then the "mal de ojo" ailment would disappear. However, if the passerby just continued walking past after having stared at the child without touching it, then the belief was that the ailment would indeed present itself in the baby. The cure known as "el barrido con el huevo" or "being swept with an egg" was one of those supposed cures that my grandmother administered for "empacho" and "mal de ojo". This cure was administered to babies but it was also administered on my older brother and I when we were young children. In my case, the first step was that my grandmother would first place me on the bed in the supine position; that is, in the position where my body was lying face up. My grandmother would then hold a chicken egg still in its shell with her hand. With the egg grasped in her hand, she would then move the egg over the entire length of my body making sure to move the egg over my extremities as well. I don't remember whether the movement of the egg with her hand was done with the egg touching my body or whether the egg was just held above a few inches above my body. Anyway, she would perform this movement repeatedly sometimes up to three times.

After having swept the egg over my body, she would then fill a glass half-full with water. She would break the egg and then drop the yolk along with the egg white into the water inside the glass. Depending on whether the egg remained floating on the top or dropped to the bottom of the half-filled glass, then a conclusion would be made as to whether the curative "egg sweeping" process was successful or not. Sometimes, the interpretation of the results was done by observing whether the egg white grew to become a heavy dense white color or whether the egg white just remained clear in the water. I really didn't understand the interpretation of the results. But leave it to my grandmother; somehow she always seemed to be able to drum up some conclusion, one way or the other.

Anyway, it seemed to me to be a very complex process. Today, at the risk of seeming disrespectful to my grandmother and her efforts, it now seems a little like hocus pocus to me. However, it also seems to me that her kindness and her positive energy was what really cured us . . . she had good intentions.

"El Lavado"

Another family cure was a procedure known as "el lavado". The literal translation of the phrase "el lavado" to English is "the wash". It seems humorous to me now but this procedure struck terror in us as children. The phrase seems innocent enough but the mere mention of the word from my mother sent us quickly to want to exit the house in a hurry. Later on as a grownup I learned that the correct English translation is "enema".

The first step in the "el lavado" procedure was to remove our pants and then our underwear. Since I was the younger of the two, I would be the first one to go. Chuy, my brother, would make such a fuss that my mother would start with me to spare Chuy for the moment. However, Chuy would eventually have to endure the same process.

Anyway, my mother would instruct me to lie down on the bed in the prone position; that is, I would lie horizontally on the bed with my chest downward. My mother would then heat up water in a deep pan. Once the water warmed up to a relatively high temperature, she would pour the contents into a flat, red rubber bag that was fitted with a long rubber tube. The end of the tube was fitted with a rigid, slender plastic nozzle that had a hole in it. Before she poured the water into the rubber bag, she would bend the rubber tube so that the water in the rubber bag would not drain out from the rubber bag.

My mother would then perform her magic. Mind you, I was usually the first to go through the treatment while Chuy, my brother, snickered as he peeked from behind the door in the next room. The magic would begin.

She first inserted the slender plastic nozzle into my behind. This was not a happy event for me but she kept insisting that I remain still. As soon as the nozzle was inserted, she released the bend in the rubber tube so that the water was free to enter into my behind. She then elevated the liquid-filled rubber bag so that gravity would push the water inward. As soon as she lifted the bag to a higher elevation, I could feel the water entering my behind and I then began to feel the sensation of going to the bathroom. The water pressure resulting from the elevated bag was enough for me to sense a bloated sensation in my abdomen. The pressure in my abdomen was such that the sensation of having to go the bathroom to do "number 2" increased more and more.

After laying there with the water inside me, my mother would then inform me that she was about to remove the nozzle. She would further instruct me that once she removed the nozzle, I was to go immediately to the bathroom as soon as possible. When she actually removed the nozzle, I felt the immediate urge to go and I would then run to the bathroom, sit on the toilet and wah-lah

. . . all the water inside me would exit along with excrement. What a relief that was. Chuy was next and now it was my time to enjoy the sight.

Pomada De La Campana

Another cure involved a product that was referred to as "Pomada de la Campana". To hear my mother and my grandmother speak about the product one would conclude that the product could be used to cure cancer . . . ha, ha. "Pomada de la Campana" literally translates to English as "Cream from the Bell". I remember that "Pomada del la Campana" was a white, thick cream product that came packaged in a round, white metal container about 4 or 5 inches in diameter. My mother and my grandmother used it for skin ailments such as burns, mosquito bites, scrapes and skin tears or for any skin condition. They even used it for ankle sprains and wrist sprains even though this had nothing to do with skin conditions.

I decided to find out once and for all whether this cream that in a humorous way "could cure cancer" was really an effective medication. When I searched the internet, I found that the cream was actually first introduced in the United States and was marketed as "Dr. Bell's Pomade". Mind you, my mother always purchased it in Mexico.

I further found out that indeed the product does have curative effects because of the zinc component it contained. One of those internet references is as follows: ***Zinc oxide cream can be applied directly on acne outbreaks. Its antibacterial properties kill the acne causing bacteria and the anti-inflammatory properties bring down the skin inflammation This cream is highly effective for curing diaper rash.***

Another internet reference contained the following: ***"Zinc is used for treatment and prevention of zinc deficiency and its consequences, including stunted growth and acute diarrhea in children, and slow wound healing Zinc is also applied to the skin for treating acne, aging skin, herpes simplex infections, and to speed wound healing."***

So in the end, this doubting Thomas was in fact in error about the product known as the "Pomada de la Campana". This product didn't really cure cancer but it sure came close ha, ha.

So these are the funny stories about the cures we had to endure when we were growing up. Yes, they might seem backward but somehow we were able to survive our childhood without serious injuries. Bless my grandmother Maria because she taught my mother how to keep us healthy. These memories are near and dear to me.

The Goyo Muñoz Family

During our growing up years on the Ryan farm, my father and mother became very good friends with various families who also lived on the farms surrounding the farm where we lived. I remember that one such family was the Muñoz family.

By the way, the pronunciation of the surname "Muñoz" with the letter "ñ" is different than the word "Munoz" with the letter "n". The letter "ñ" is pronounced in almost the same manner as the pronunciation of the letters "ny" in the English word "canyon". There's one other item about the pronunciation of the surname "Muñoz". Although the Spanish surname "Muñoz" does not normally contain an accent symbol, the name is pronounced with the emphasis on the letter "o" and not the letter "u" as in "Muñóz". In Spanish, accents matter.

Anyway, the Muñoz family lived toward the direction of Tornillo, about 1 mile east from where we lived. The Muñoz's home was located away from the railroad tracks about a quarter mile and inward toward where the desert begins. Using "Google Maps" in "satellite" mode on the computer, the location where the Muñoz home used to be located can be viewed using the following latitude-longitude coordinates: 31.464604, -106.107139.

The home is no longer present at that location. A new Freeway access road was constructed in that general area where their home used to be located. By the way, I remember that the farm road leading from the railroad tracks to the Muñoz's house was lined with huge shade trees along an irrigation ditch parallel to the dirt road.

The head of the household was a man that my father used to call Goyo Muñoz. My mother used to refer to his wife as Jesusita. I don't remember Jesusita's face but I do remember Goyo's. Goyo Muñoz was much older than my father. I remember that now and again while driving down the farm dirt roads, my father would at times meet up with Goyo as he was driving in the opposite direction. Chuy, my older brother, and I would sometimes ride along with my father inside the cab of the farm pickup truck.

When they happened to meet on a farm road, Goyo and my father would both step off their pickup trucks and proceed to shake hands. They always greeted each other as if they very glad to see each other. I remember that Goyo would always have a big smile on his face. By the way, at that time, I didn't know that his true name was Gregorio because my father always called him Goyo. Their children were much older than we were and therefore, we didn't get together with them to play. I remember that the oldest son's name was Roberto and one of his sister's names was Polly.

Many years later, Roberto Muñoz visited my parents in Fabens. I recently asked my wife Socorro whether she remembered a Roberto Muñoz visiting my parents in Fabens. She indeed remembered that my father had told us about an impending visit by a Roberto Muñoz and she and I had made it a point to be present when Roberto visited. Socorro remembers that I was in college at the time so I think the visit occurred sometime during 1971 to 1974 after I was married and was attending college. When we met during that visit, I recognized him as the Roberto that used to live on the farm near the Ryan farm. He was all grown up now and I think he was employed by the U.S. Foreign Service at an Embassy. In subsequent conversations with him now as a grownup, he indicated that he worked at the U.S. Embassy in Spain. He was well spoken and was a very impressive person. In my mind, he was a local boy that made good.

Later in life, my sister Graciela, who is 8 years younger than I, married a young man by the name of Rodolfo Rodriguez. Everyone called him Rudy. His father's name was Esteban and his mother's name was Polly. My mother and father knew Polly very well. I never interacted with Polly when we lived on the farm because she was much older than I; however, I did remember Polly during the Rudy's and Gracie's wedding ceremony as the Polly that was Goyo's daughter. In the ensuing years, Rudy and Gracie had two beautiful daughters; Carla and then Claudia. Sometime after that, unfortunately, Rudy and Gracie divorced.

Some years later during one of our family get-togethers, I overheard one of my younger sisters joking around with Gracie and saying to her that Rudy was her cousin. I can't remember which family member it was that spoke about the subject of cousins. At the time, I just felt that the family member was playfully trying to embarrass Gracie. I didn't pay much attention to the reasons why that family member was saying that Rudy and Gracie were cousins. During family get-togethers, I used to hear Claudia talk about an Uncle Bob that lived in Virginia. I had a feeling they were talking about the Roberto that I knew when I was growing up on the Ryan farm.

In the year 2015, I began constructing a graphical family tree on my computer. At about the same time, Socorro, my wife, was interchanging messages with Carla or Claudia on Facebook. A Mr. Roberto Muñoz, Sr. took notice of my wife's surname "Renteria" on Facebook and a Facebook dialog ensued between Roberto and my wife. It turned out that Roberto Muñoz, Sr. was Carla's and Claudia's uncle. He was the same Roberto that used to live on the farm near where we used to live.

In the ensuing communications via Facebook, my wife posted a picture of one of my granddaughters whose name is Araceli Renteria. The following is the message Roberto wrote to my wife, Socorro, on April 20, 2015; exactly as he sent it:

> ***"Thanks for the info. As you know, I'm very interested in the Renteria family because until Don Jesus and Fernando, my Grandfather Justo Renteria knew of no relatives. He had joined the revolution in Mexiico [sic] and lost track of his family. He did***

remember his brother Pedro and confirmed to be his brother by Jesus and Fernando. They never saw each other. Don Pedro died in Juarez before I could arrange for them to meet. The name "Renteria" is Basque, a race of people from the North of Spain, from the area of the Spanish city of Bilbao. The name is actually "Erenteria". The name ""Aracely" [sic] as that of your Granddaughter is very much a derivatively [sic] Basque. When these people immigrated to Mexico and to what is now USA they kept to themselves and married within the same Baque [sic] people communities; for example - San Eli, Clint, Socorro. My mother came from the same group of people "Alcoset Renteria". If you have any questions, let me know. Take care and may you and your family be blessed."

My wife, Socorro, showed me the text that Roberto sent. It was exciting to read Roberto's message. All of a sudden I began to understand the relationship between the Goyo Muñoz family and my family. His reference to "Don Jesus" is a reference to my father Jesus Renteria. His reference to "Don Pedro" is a reference to Pedro Renteria who was my father's grandfather. In Mexico, the prefix "Don" before the given name is used to denote respect.

After reading his message, I felt an urge to contact him to start firing questions at him. On April 30, 2015, I wrote Claudia, Gracie's daughter, asking her for Roberto Muñoz's contact information and that same day she wrote me back providing his telephone number, email address and his home address. I backed off from contacting Roberto. I felt I needed to wrap my head around more family information before contacting him. I continued working on the graphical family tree and forgot about contacting Roberto. It was now early August of 2016 and now, when I was writing this memoir, I remembered this chapter of our history.

It gets a little confusing from here on but here is my attempt to unravel a family mystery based on Roberto's April 20, 2015 email. My father had always told me that his grandfather's name was Pedro Renteria. Pedro Renteria's and Anita Rivera's family included a son whose name was Jose

Renteria Rivera. Jose Renteria Rivera and Espedita Tarango Ortiz were my father's parents; my grandparents. In addition, during story times with my mother, I would hear her mention a man by the name of Justo Renteria that according to her even lived in Fabens. I often wondered how Justo Renteria fit into our family tree but I never took the time to investigate the name further.

As a result of Roberto's April 20, 2015 email, I was now learning that Justo Renteria, whose name my mother used to mention, was indeed Pedro Renteria's brother. This was big to me because at last someone had confirmed that both Pedro and Justo were brothers. I dug into the internet and found Justo Renteria's birth date and date of passing. The information I found is as follows: Justo Renteria, Born: May 5, 1896, Deceased: Oct, 1978, 82 years.

The following is that internet reference:

http://www. legacy.com/obituaries/elpasotimes/obituary-search.aspx?daterange=99999&firstname=Justo&lastname=Renteria&countryid=1&stateid=57&affiliateid=2220

The following is a clip of the information found using that link:

Justo Renteria

Although Roberto had mentioned his mother by both paternal and maternal surnames in the April 20, 2015 email, he had not stated that her given name was Jesusita. Now all that remained was to confirm that Roberto's mother whose surnames he mentioned in his message as "Alcoset Renteria" was indeed Jesusita, the daughter of Justo Renteria. If so, then following the Mexican naming method, her true name would be "Jesusita Renteria Alcoset" and her married name would now be "Jesusita Muñoz Renteria". The photograph of Roberto's mother, Jesusita, is shown here. I cropped the picture of "Jesusita" from a Facebook picture provided by Roberto Muñoz.

I found a reference to Jesusita Muñoz Renteria at this link

http://www.legacy.com/obituaries/elpasotimes/obituary-search.aspx?daterange=99999&

firstname=Jesusita &lastname=Munoz&countryid=1&stateid=57&affiliateid=2220

Jesusita Munoz

Cleotilde Alcoset | Justo Renteria | 18 Sep 1918 - Mexico (villa Ahumada, Chih)"

The following is a clip of the information found in that link:

Jesusita Munoz

On August 10, 2016, with some trepidation, I decided to contact Roberto myself via email. For all I knew Roberto Muñoz probably wouldn't know who Salvador Renteria was or worse, he could have thought I was some wacko trying to harvest personal information from him. My thought was that if I sent him pictures of my father, he might immediately know that I wasn't someone with ulterior motives.

I decided to take a gamble and email him. After I completed the email text and then loaded the attachment along with the pictures, for several long minutes I wondered whether I should "click" the "send" button or just forget about disturbing Roberto. I finally did it. The following is the email message I sent him on August 10, 2016:

"Subject: The Renteria Family
From: sarenteria <sarenteria@aol.com>
To: renteriamunoz <renteriamunoz@gmail.com>
Date: Wed, Aug 10, 2016 11:44 am

Roberto,

My name is Salvador Renteria. I am Jesus Renteria's son that used to live on the Ryan Farm back in the day.

By the way, Claudia, Gracie's daughter, provided me your contact information. She calls you Uncle Bob.

I am attaching a PDF file that describes the history of the Muñoz family with the Renteria family.

> ***At the bottom of the document are several questions.
> Hope you may be able to fill in some of the gaps in
> our history.
> God bless you and your family.***
>
> ***Sal Renteria"***

This is the list of questions contained in the email attachment:

1. ***Did Justo Renteria have two children: Jesusita and Jesus?***
2. ***What was Justo Renteria's wife's name?***
3. ***Was Jesusita the name of Roberto's mother?***
4. ***Does Roberto have pictures of Goyo and Jesusita?***
5. ***Does Roberto have pictures of Pedro Renteria or Justo Renteria***
6. ***What are the names of Roberto's siblings?***
7. ***What was the farm owner's name where the Muñoz's lived?***

The following day after sending Roberto my email message I checked my email browser to see if there was a reply. Nope; no reply. Every day thereafter I checked for an email from Roberto and after a few days, I began to think that either I hadn't used the correct email address or Roberto just wasn't interested in the subject matter or worse he may have thought I was some sort of a "wacko".

The following is the message Roberto wrote me 5 days later on August 15, 2016; exactly as he sent it:

"Dear Chava, I hope you and your family are all well with the Grace of God. I was very surprised and extremely happy with your letter and its attachments. I read the info in your letter with keen interest, being that for a long time now, I too, have been trying to connect family both from a maternity and paternity relations. My mother, Jesusita (Chita) was the instigator that led to the initial introduction of my Muñoz and your Renteria family. She was very interested and adamant to finding Renteria relatives, since she, nor we, knew of none. All that was known is that Abuelo Justo had joined the Mexican revolution with Pancho Villa when very young which caused the separation from his parents and siblings. I remember my mother trying to get information from him to no avail.

All the info she had managed to get from him during her interrogations indicated that he remembered a brother named Pedro! I believe my Abuelo blocked his memory about his family on purpose because he might have felt guilty that he had abandoned or lost them at one time or another during the turmoil caused by the revolution. My mom suffered from poor health most of her life and died young at 36 years of age in 1955. My siblings were very young and all of us were in search of our destinies under the shadow of poverty and ignorance that came with our inherent environment. We had no interest, even though now I wished I had, to followup on acquiring family ptiz. At this time, however, we were aware of our relationship between your family and mine. I always inquired over the welfare and whereabouts of your dad and mom and I also knew about the marriage between Rudy and Gracie.

In the latter part of the 1940's and early 1950's there was an influx of Mexican workers coming to the El Paso lower valley to work some under a bracero program or not. I remember my mom asking dad to check through his contacts for anyone with a "Renteria" surname; I too remember the time dad told mom he had been told there were two young men working on the adjoining farm with the "Renteria" name. I remember because it made my mom so very happy with the instructions to dad that he go see about them right away and invite them to come to the house so that she would meet with them and find out if they might relatives [sic] or not. A few days later, I remember, two men coming to meet with mom. They were brothers named Jesus and Fernando Renteria. Your mom was not yet in the U.S. She came later. Anyway, after the meeting which took quite a long time, mom proclaimed that Jesus and Fernando were indeed relatives and from that date on they were, in fact, considered that they and their children were family. Mom and I baptized Chuy at the church in Fabens. Incidentally, Chuy and I were in contact for a couple of years before he died. I would like to talk to you about Chuy at another time. I also spoke with Fernando a few years ago before he died in Delicias. When we first made telephone contact he remembered me immediately. He did asked [sic] me if I knew about the whereabouts of Chuy. I gave him Chuy's address and telephone number and told him Chuy was ok at that time.

I guess it's been a couple of years now that I learned that Fernando had died and I think it was Chuy who told me. Claudia, her husband and two children, were in Virginia visiting with Miguel's sister and they came to visit with me for a few hours. I showed Carla a portrait of my Mom and told her that she was her great grandmother. She was so happy that she cried.

My Abuelo Justo Renteria and his wife Cleotilde Alcoset came to the U.S., when my mom was one month old in October 1918. He never returned to Mexico. Not even to meet with his brother Pedro. Likewise, Pedro would not come to the U.S. Their children were: Jose, Jesusita, Maria and Francisco.

Jesusita (Chita) Renteria and Gregorio (Gollo) Munoz were the parents of Roberto (Beto/Bob), Theodora (Dora), Apolonia (Polly), Cleotilde (Cleo), Alfredo (Freddy) and Maria Teresa. All living!

Dad worked for Al and Sis Crider for many, many years as their farm foreman and manager. No photos of Pedro. You could view photos of my mom, dad and, I think my Abuelo in Face Book [sic]. I'm FB of Socorro and she would probably allow you to view photos therein.

If you have FB account we could be connected. I warn you, however, I'm a very liberal democrat!

Regards to your family. Have a wonderful joyous day. BetoMunoz! Let me know what you think about this matter."

Beto Muñoz filled-in the gaps for me. Now in April of 2018, I have had two long telephone discussions with him. During the first discussion, he remembered and spoke about the town of Rosales, Mexico. As indicated before, the town of Rosales is near the city of Delicias, Mexico which is in the area where my parents originated. During that first conversation, he mentioned that he was going to visit our area soon and he invited me to travel with him to Rosales to reminisce old times.

He called recently for the second time and this time he indicated that again he would shortly be visiting us here in El Paso and had plans to travel to Los Angeles to visit with friends there. During the April 2018 telephone call, I asked Beto for his age and he indicated that he was 83 years of age. That would make 1935 as his birth year. Every time I speak with him he fills-in more gaps for me. He is a true friend of mine.

Arizona, 1955

I faintly remember that our family moved to Arizona. I can't remember all of the events relating to that move to Arizona; I only remember bits and pieces of that event. I don't know the exact location where we lived in Arizona but for reasons which I will describe later, it must have been in the Phoenix or the Tucson area. Later in this section, I'll explain why I think this event took place in 1955 when I was 4 years old.

As a bracero, my father could only have moved from one employer to another by repeating the bracero indoctrination process all over again. I believe my family moved to Arizona after my father's second bracero contract expired. My family could only have moved away from the Ryan farm if my father had obtained U.S. permanent resident alien status. With a "green card", my father would have had the freedom to choose where he wanted to work anywhere in the U.S., whereas under a bracero labor contract, he had no choice.

I faintly remember a story my mother told me about us moving to Arizona. She told me something having to do with wages in Arizona being much better than at the Ryan farm. She indicated that the higher wages in Arizona sparked their interest in my father seeking employment there. I also faintly remember the trip to Arizona because somewhere along the way to Arizona, our car broke down. I remember the incident because it seemed that it took a while for our car to get repaired. At least I remember the long wait time waiting beside the road. At the same time, I don't remember the return trip back to Fabens; I am drawing a blank there. I do; however, remember some key items related to having lived there for a brief period of time which will be described later in this section.

I remember that during our stay in this new place, our family lived in living quarters similar to those quarters that I previously described as the "adobe/stucco building" on the Ryan cotton farm near Fabens, Texas. Unlike the living quarters on the Ryan farm, the living quarters where we now lived in was situated somewhere within a populated area and not on a farm. The reason this is so is because I remember streets and other homes in the general vicinity of our family's living quarters.

I remember my family having visited my mother's uncle, Jesus Gonzalez, and his family. It is possible that Jesus Gonzalez was the person that told my parents about the higher wages in Arizona. My mother's uncle, Jesus, was married to Delfina. We called her "Fina". I remember that their two children were much older than my brother, Chuy, and I. Their names were Alfredo and Romelia. Alfredo was the oldest.

I remember the house they lived in. They lived in a real house and not in housing quarters like we did on the farm near Fabens and now in Arizona. Their back yard was huge and was planted with watermelons, squash and many other vegetables. They must have lived on the outskirts of a city or on a farm because of the presence of their huge garden.

The reason I know that these events took place in Arizona is because I overheard my father or mother say that Jesus Gonzalez and his family lived nearby in a town by the name of Chandler. The only town I've ever known to be named in that manner is Chandler, Arizona.

During the stay in Arizona, my father and mother worked picking cotton. I remember spending entire days in the cotton fields while both my father and mother worked in the fields picking cotton. The reason why I believe I was 4 or 5 years of age at the time when we lived in Arizona is because I had not yet started attending school. I actually started school later on in Fabens when I was 6 years of age. Cotton picking was done by both men and women. During that time, tractor driven automatic cotton picking equipment had not yet been developed, at least I don't remember seeing that kind of equipment during that time. The objective was simple; as quickly as possible, pick the cotton from the cotton boll and place it in a cotton pick sack. The farm workers were paid a set amount for each pound of cotton picked. I don't remember the amount that was paid for each pound of cotton picked. Farm workers who were ambidextrous and could use their right and left hand simultaneously could pick cotton at a faster rate and therefore could make more money.

Nowadays, only a few of us from the baby boomer generation know what picking cotton was like so I'll describe the process of picking cotton. Note that my knowledge of the process of picking cotton comes from what little I can remember about the cotton fields in Arizona but in addition, because I did pick cotton on the Ryan farm when we later returned to live on the Ryan farm after the move back from Arizona.

Picking cotton was the type of work that didn't require muscle strength and therefore women and even children could also pick cotton. The farm workers that picked the cotton were each assigned a long, tubular cloth sack that was closed on one end but open at the other. The top horizontal part of the cotton pick sacks were constructed of heavy duty duck cloth horizontally sewn to a type of brown colored plastic material that lay underneath. The brown colored plastic material was the rugged part of the cotton pick sack that made contact with the ground as it was dragged along by the worker picking the cotton. The cotton pick sacks were about 8 or 10 feet in length and about 30 inches in diameter.

The cotton pick sacks were fitted with cloth tie straps on the open side of the sack that the worker could use to tie around his or her waist. After tying the straps around the waist, the worker would then spread his or her feet apart and then push the main body of the sack between his or her legs. With the sack tie straps secured to the worker's waist, the worker would walk along the cotton row picking cotton while dragging the sack behind him. As the worker slowly walked along the cotton furrow, the worker would grasp the cotton with his or her hands and then place the cotton into the sack through the opening of the sack that was located down between his or her legs.

While writing this part of the memoir, I looked for pictures that demonstrated the manner in which the cotton pick sacks were used by persons picking cotton; specifically the type of cotton pick sack that was used way back then in the Fabens area. The picture on the left demonstrates how the cotton sack was tied around the worker's waist with what I call "waist tie straps". Note the opening of the cotton pick sack located between the person's legs. This was the way we strapped on the cotton pick sack later on when I too worked picking cotton on the Ryan farm.

By the way, the fluffy cotton grew inside in what was called a cotton boll. When the cotton bolls opened and exposed the cotton inside, the exterior hard petals of the boll slowly dried up. This occurred in the fall season. That's when the cotton was picked. The exposed cotton was cradled inside the dried boll. However, the boll itself now had hard, sharp pointy petals that could prick the worker's fingers when the cotton was picked away from the boll. The hard, sharp pointy tips were hard on the hands.

The picture on the left shows the cotton along with the sharp pointy petals. As a result of the sharp pointy petals, many of the women that worked picking cotton would wear cloth gloves for protection. The gloves protected their hands and fingers from being pricked.

I remember that both my father and my mother picked cotton while in Arizona. I even remember riding on top of the cotton sack as my father pulled the sack forward while at the same time picking the cotton. He and my mother would take turns pulling me along on top of the sack. I must have been too young to pick cotton.

Anyway, ultimately the weight of the cotton would become too heavy or the sack would become full. At that point, the worker would un-tie the cloth straps from his or her waist. The cloth straps would then be tied in a knot so that the cotton would not spill out of the open end of the cotton pick sack. The worker would then throw the cotton pick sack over his shoulder and carry it to be weighed by the foreman. If the sack was too heavy, the worker  would just drag the cotton pick sack to the location where the weighing of the cotton sacks was performed. The weigh scale was located adjacent to the cotton trailer where all the picked cotton was temporarily stored.

After the cotton sack was weighed, the person weighing the sack would record the weight of the cotton in a section of the log book corresponding to the name of the worker. Recording the weight of the cotton was important because the workers were paid based on the weight of the cotton that the worker picked.

The worker would then remove the sack from the weigh scale and again toss the sack over his shoulder and then with the sack on his shoulder, the worker would climb an inclined ladder that was situated on the side of the cotton trailer. Once at the top of the ladder, the worker would dump the sack full of cotton into the trailer. He would then jump into the trailer and then would begin to empty the contents of the sack inside the trailer.

Climbing the ladder and emptying the contents of the sack into the trailer was sometimes very difficult for the women and in some instances; the weigh scale foreman would assist the women and climb the ladder with the sack over his shoulder himself. He would then empty the contents of the sack into the trailer as a favor to the women.

As indicated before, the person performing the weighing would write the number of pounds of cotton picked by each respective worker in a log book. At the end of the week, each worker would receive his or her pay consistent with the number of pounds of cotton picked.

In Arizona, however, I remember that the person that performed the weighing of the cotton pick sacks would pay the worker in cash right on the spot. Because the worker was paid immediately after dumping the cotton into the trailer, the workers were always flush with cash. I remember my parents would buy grape soft drinks for me when they worked on the cotton fields in Arizona. To this day, if I happen to open a bottle of grape soda, the initial scent of the grape soda will remind me of the days in Arizona. Grape soda is my favorite; however, I've yet to find a sugar-free grape soda . . . old age of course.

I am pretty certain that all this occurred when I was 4 years of age in the year 1955 because Chuy was already in school. He would have been 6 years old and in school at the time. It may be that he had just started first grade in elementary school and perhaps that's the reason why he didn't accompany us to the cotton fields during the work days. My sister Irma was born in May of 1954 so she was probably only a year old during our move to Arizona. Although she had to have been there, I just don't remember Irma in Arizona.

The cotton fields must have been located near an Air Force base because I remember jet-like noisy airplanes landing and taking off from a location in relative close proximity to the cotton fields. I couldn't actually see the place where the landings and take offs were occurring because I was too short but I could see the airplanes when they were in the air flying around the area.

I remember that the airplanes were very loud. Seeing them flying around, they appeared to have what I now know as aerodynamically formed tanks mounted on the wing tips. I don't know why but the image of those airplanes is ingrained in my memory. When writing this section of the memoir, I decided to determine the type of airplane that was equipped with streamlined tanks on its  wing tips. I found that the "noisy airplanes" that I saw as a child were those known as the Republic F-84 turbojet. According to a Wikipedia article, that type of airplane was indeed in service in the U.S. Air Force from 1947 to 1958. When it is all said and done, the cotton field where my parents picked cotton was located nearby some Air Force base in Arizona. It could have been the Davis-Monthan Air Force base in Tucson or Luke Air Force base in Phoenix.

Another important event that is engrained in my memory is my first encounter with the African American race during our stay in Arizona. As I previously indicated, I remember we lived in an apartment on the farm worker housing quarters during our stay in Arizona. The front yard was covered with green lawn grass all down the length of the building that housed the workers and their families. Each apartment had its entry door down the length of the building. The green lawn grass was especially noteworthy to me because prior to this, I don't remember ever having seen this type of lawn grass in front of a home. I remember playing outside on the front yard of the housing quarters.

One day while playing outside, a neighbor boy walked out from one of the apartments. To my surprise, his face and all of his skin were black. This was surprising to me because although it was common to see other Hispanic people with darker skin, I had never seen a boy with completely black skin.

My skin color is light and fair. It's the type of skin color that most Hispanics refer to as "güero". Chuy's skin color, however, was a darker brown color and was the type of skin color that most Hispanics call a "moreno". I am "güero" complected because my father was "güero" complected as well; however Chuy was "moreno" because my mother was of a "moreno" complexion. By the way, during story times with my mother, she would tell us a story about my grandmother Maria. She would jokingly say that when my grandmother Maria would bathe us in the circular galvanized tub, she would routinely comment that I would clean up almost immediately however, Chuy almost always seemed to need additional scrubbing . . . get it? Ha, ha.

Now in Arizona, seeing a boy with an entirely black face and skin for the first time was startling to me. The problem with the boy was that he didn't seem to like me. As soon as he'd see me after exiting from his apartment door, he would run toward me waving his arms in the air as if to want to cause me harm. Upon seeing him waving his arms, I would immediately start running towards the door of our apartment. I would open the door and quickly enter our apartment to escape from the little black boy.

It didn't matter that he was about my size or maybe a little bigger; he still seemed threatening to me. He would never bother me if my older brother, Chuy, was outside on the front yard with me. But if I was alone outside, the little boy would repeat his menacing ways. I remember living in terror of that little black boy. I don't remember him actually hitting me or causing me harm but his actions sure were scary to me.

That was my first introduction to the African American race. In later years, my father and mother would smile and even snicker every time I told the story of the little black boy that didn't like me. It's possible that he didn't like me because I too was new to him or possibly because I was fair complected and the rest of the kids were "moreno" complected like Chuy, my brother.

I believe my father too had his first experience with the African American race during that trip to Arizona. I remember overhearing a specific conversation my father was having with someone in our family. It could have been my mother or my mother's uncle, Jesus Gonzalez, that he was talking with; I just don't remember. However, my father was telling that person that he had met some "negro" men and that he noticed that they liked to be called by the name of "parna". That seemed reasonable to me at the time. Who knew different?

A few years later now as a grown up, I began to wonder why it was that my dad thought that "negro" men prefer to be called by the name of "parna". I now think that my father must have witnessed two African American men greeting each other possibly with the words "hello partner" and that's how my father came to believe that "negro" men address each other as "parna". Based on this recollection, I am almost certain that this was the first time my father too was introduced to the African American race. As a grown up, I never told my father of that very specific recollection. I didn't want to seem disrespectful to him.

Although I don't know for sure because I was only 4 years old at the time, moving to Arizona in search of higher paying work didn't turn out for the best. Ultimately, our family ended up back at the Ryan farm near Fabens, Texas. I never asked my parents what prompted their return back to the Ryan farm near Fabens. I will never know for sure but I am glad they did.

By the way, my uncle Jesus Gonzalez and my aunt Fina who I indicated previously lived in Chandler, Arizona and later on in Eloy, they passed away. The Gonzalez clan still lives in the Eloy and Phoenix area of Arizona. I remember attending both my uncle's and aunt's funerals.

The Return to the Ryan Farm

Somehow our family ended up back at the Ryan farm after returning from the move to Arizona. As I indicated before, I don't remember the trip back from Arizona. However, I vividly remember now living in a house close to the sand hills on the Ryan farm property. The living quarters were no longer the original white stuccoed building that was located adjacent to the railroad tracks and Highway 80.

I am not certain, but the move back to the Ryan farm probably occurred when I was 5 years old. I say "probably" because I don't remember having moved into that house near the sand hills but we did. I suppose I don't remember because I was too young.

By the way, the exact location of the building structure near the sand hills can be found using the Google Maps and entering the following latitude and longitude coordinates: 31.475696, -106.116831.

No longer did we live in the same housing structure as the rest of the "bracero" farm workers. The new living quarters for our family consisted of a standalone home. It was our private home.

The housing for the farm bracero workers now consisted of three wooden barracks set apart toward the right from our family's home. Each wooden barrack was set atop concrete cinder blocks that served to keep the barrack floor elevated from the ground. I remember that a number of "bracero" farm workers lived in the three wooden barracks. Each barrack was equipped with several cots on which the bracero farm workers slept. The cots were single person metal beds that were light, simple and foldable. The cots were constructed of a metal frame with lateral springs that kept the internal wire netting taut within the rectangular metal frame. After laying a 3" thick mattress on the wire netting, the bed was ready to be used.

Those were the days when cotton was hand-picked. Bracero farm workers were recruited to pick the cotton in the fields. I remember that two of the "braceros" living in the barracks were my mother's two younger brothers. Their names were Patricio Gutierrez and Adrian Gutierrez.

My uncle Adrian knew how to play the guitar and I remember him playing his guitar while singing Mexican songs. Nowadays, once in a while driving down

the road as I am changing the channels on the car radio, just by chance I'll somehow end up on a Mexican music channel that plays Mexican songs. A few times I've ended up on a channel that is playing one of the songs that my uncle Adrian used to sing and play on his guitar. I'm sure most of the bracero men were lonely and home sick. I'm almost sure my uncle Adrian played those ballads because he was home sick for Delicias, his home. Later in life when I married my wife Socorro, I named my first child after my uncle Adrian.

By the way, I remember that my uncle Adrian liked to sing and play songs that were originally authored by a popular Mexican artist by the name of Pedro Infante. In those days, the name Pedro Infante in our home was a household name. A search on the internet shows that he authored about 350 songs. My parents loved his songs. He passed away in an airplane crash in 1957 at the age of 39. I remember that my parents were grief stricken when they heard the news that Pedro Infante had passed. It was as if they had lost a family relative. Anyway, at that time when my uncle Patricio and uncle Adrian lived in the barracks as braceros, I was about 6 years of age and my uncle Patricio was about 25 years of age. My uncle Adrian was about 22 years of age. Fast forward into the future in 1988, I founded a water treatment business in Cd. Juarez, Mexico and the name of the company would be Procesos de Fluidos, S.A. de C.V. Both my uncles worked for my company for many years.

Unlike the original white stuccoed building by the railroad tracks, the standalone home we were now living in had a singular pressurized water faucet. It was located about 20 feet in front of the house. No longer did we have to use a pitcher pump as we had back when we lived on the stuccoed building beside the railroad tracks. If water was needed inside the house for dishwashing or bathing, it would be carried indoors in pails. As for bathrooms; there still weren't any. Outhouses were still used for toilet purposes. The aquifer contamination potential that I described before was probably still there but as the saying goes "ignorance is bliss".

Sometime during the time when we lived in the home near the sand hills, I remember that we had a chicken coup full of chickens.

I don't remember my father having initially built the chicken coup. It was Chuy and I who had to tend the chicken coup. Chickens don't really care where they go to do the bathroom; they just spread doo- doo anywhere they want. It was our job to clean the chicken coup from time to time and of course to feed them on a daily basis.

The reason I remember the chicken coup is because I played a trick on Irma that involved the chicken coup. As I said before, the chicken doo-doo was on the floor inside the coup. One day, when Irma was watching us tending the chicken coup, without Irma seeing, I placed a piece of gum in my hand. I acted as if I picked up a piece of chicken doo-doo from the floor with that hand. I then quickly placed the gum in that hand in my mouth. When I began to chew the gum; Irma began to gag. She thought that I had actually placed the chicken doo-doo in my mouth. She probably doesn't remember that joke . . . ha-ha.

The House on the Hill Top

I remember that behind the standalone home by the desert that we lived in was a high sand hill. A farm road was located in front of our house. The house was situated such that the length of the house was at a 45 degree angle with respect to the road. As one followed the farm road to the right facing the home, the road would follow a track up the sandy hill and then come to the top of the hill where another housing structure was located. This house structure was constructed of adobe block but without a stucco covering. The rains had partially eaten away at the adobe bricks so much so that the masonry mortar holding the adobe blocks in place protruded from the main building walls.

Two families lived in that adobe structure located on the hill top. I remember my uncle Esteban Gutierrez and his wife, Rosa, lived on the far side of the building structure while the Roberto Martinez family lived on the near side. My uncle Esteban was my mother's younger brother. My uncle and Rosa did not have children. On the other hand, Roberto Martinez and his wife, Celia, had several children. Their names were Roberto Jr., Apolonio, Dora, Felipe and Cano. Both my uncle Esteban and Roberto, Sr. worked on the Ryan farm and reported to my father, their supervisor.

Roberto Jr. was a few years older than Chuy, my brother. I don't remember Roberto Jr. playing with us when the Martinez family lived on the farm. I do remember Chuy, Irma and I playing with the rest of the Martinez kids.

I remember one day while we were playing with the Martinez kids at their house, one of the Martinez kids, Felipe, asked his mother for a cup of coffee. I overheard his mother telling him that children should not drink coffee because it makes them "burros". Again, the Spanish word "burro" means "donkey" in English. In context, however, his mother really meant to say that coffee makes young children dumb or illiterate. Felipe responded to his mother "but the Renterias are allowed to have coffee, why can't we?" His mother responded something like "well that's up to their parents". My sister, Irma, and I still chuckle about the coffee episode with the Martinez's. I don't think that drinking coffee made us dumb or illiterate . . . well, who knows . . . ha-ha.

I also remember an episode that occurred that involved Felipe. It was an accident that happened in which he wound up with a large gash on his chin. We weren't present when the accident happened. The gash was pronounced and it was curved in similar fashion to the curvature of his mouth. Later on when the wound healed, his siblings began to call him by the name "el dos bocas" which in English means "a person with two mouths". When we heard his siblings refer to him as "dos bocas", we too began to tease him. He didn't like that very much.

A year ago in 2017 when I was 66 years of age, I happened to meet up with Felipe Martinez. I think he is about 2 years younger than I was. We became reacquainted because I had previously attended the funeral of one of his younger brothers. I don't recall his brother's name. Anyway, I ran into to him at a restaurant at a local truck stop. We reminisced about our families when we all lived on the Ryan farm. During that conversation, we began talking about how accident prone we all were when his family and my family lived on the Ryan farm. We happened to hit upon the subject of the "dos bocas" stories. He described how the accident happened.

It seems that he fell into a deep hole that his father had dug on the farm. The hole was used by his father to work on the underside of his car. At the bottom of the hole was a 5 gallon, metal container. When he accidentally fell into the hole, his chin hit the edge of the 5 gallon container and that's how he ended up with the gash on his chin. He told me that when the accident happened, they took him to a medical doctor in Caseta which is located just across from the United States/ Mexico border bridge. Somehow nobody thought about suturing the wound. As a result, the wound just healed by itself. So this was the "dos bocas" saga . . . ha, ha.

That injury would not be the last to occur on the Ryan farm. The old saying "boys will be boys" was very applicable to us. It never failed that we would get into wars with them. Sometimes the wars would consist of throwing "terremotes" at each other. The word "terremotes" means "dirt clods" in English. These wars were often between the Martinez boys and us, the Renteria boys. At other times, we would mix and match; Martinez and Renteria boys on one side and another group of Martinez and Renteria boys on the other. Yes, it hurt to get hit by a "dirt clod" but things really got serious when the projectiles became stones and rocks. There is a term used in Spanish that describes getting hit by a stone on the head that then results in bleeding. The word is "descalabrado" which in English literally means "broken". In context, "descalabrado" really means a "gash in the head". Yep, it happened when the projectiles became stones or rocks. Luckily nobody got severely hurt . . . well, maybe that's the reason I'm not so bright today . . . ha, ha.

About 300 feet from the house where my uncle Esteban Gutierrez and the Martinez's lived and toward the direction of Highway 80, was a clump of large mulberry trees. A dirt road sloped downward from their house to the location of the mulberry trees. We called them "the moras" which in English means "blackberries" but no, in reality they were mulberries.

The trees were huge. The mulberry tree trunks dwarfed any other tree trunk that I had ever seen. When summer time came, we could always count on picking a bunch of large, plump mulberries to eat. A mulberry is a small fruit about 1/2 to 1 inch in size that turns purple or black and has a sweet flavor when fully ripe. The branches of the trees were huge. I remember that we would climb on the branches and then race to see who could climb the highest. The trees were easily 75 to 100 feet in height. The shaded area under the trees was enormous. It was a fun place to play.

The Martinez family would later move to Fabens while our family would remain living on the farm. I don't remember when the Martinez's moved from the farm to Fabens.

My uncle Esteban continued to work at the Ryan farm for quite some time. Ultimately, he and my aunt Rosa moved away. The next time I would see them again would be in the year 1965 when they were living in California. I don't remember anything having to do with my uncle and aunt's move to California.

The Gophers

In a previous section of this memoir I spoke about the fact that my father and mother befriended the Salvador Muñoz family that lived on the nearby Stahmann farm. I don't exactly know how it happened but later on, the name of the Stahmann farm changed to the R.T. Hoover farm. The farm was probably purchased by some other owner. . . I really don't know.

Anyway, Toño and Salva were the sons of Salvador and Margarita Muñoz. As I indicated before, we would sometimes walk to where they lived on the Stahmann farm to play with them. One day, Chuy and I accompanied them to one of the Stahmann farm fields. Toño and Salva were carrying several small metal traps. Chuy and I followed them to an area on one of the fields that seemed to have several dirt mounds. Toño and Salva began to remove the loose soil from a dirt mound to uncover a hole in the ground. They told us that the holes were dug by "ardillas". The word "ardillas" means "gophers" in English. A gopher is a burrowing rodent.

Anyway, when they removed the soil to expose the gopher hole, they then carefully placed the trap partway into the hole. They then pounded a small stake or stick into the ground and then tied a string from the stick to the metal trap. Mind you this was all done very carefully and silently so as not to make too much commotion for fear of scaring the gopher inside the hole. They repeated the same process at the location of other nearby dirt mounds. So this may sound strange to the reader but there was a business objective involved . . . bear with me.

It turns out that the owners of the Stahmann farm would pay a bounty of 25 cents for each gopher tail that Toño and Salva as well as neighboring kids could produce. It turns out that the gopher tail was evidence of having killed a gopher. The gophers tended to eat the roots of the cotton plants and therefore this bounty was the owner's way of ridding the farm fields of gophers. The Stahmann farm had a store that was called the "commissary". Presenting gopher tails to the manager of the "commissary" was better than presenting the dead gophers that were trapped in the metal traps.

Well, since Toño and Salva were doing it, Chuy and I decided to do the same thing. There was money to be made. My father purchased several gopher traps for us and we began to do the same. Initially we began to place our traps on the Stahmann farm field and yes we too would present the gopher tails to the manager of the Stahmann commissary and yes we would be paid the 25 cent bounty for each tail. Business was good but it got even better when we decided to trap gophers on the Ryan farm fields. We trapped the gophers on the Ryan farm and continued to take them to the Stahmann commissary. We were no fools . . . we didn't tell them that the gopher tails came from gophers caught on the Ryan farm fields and not the Stahmann farm fields.

That's all I remember. I don't remember how long we kept that up. In the end, the intent of the Stahmann 25 cent bounty was to rid itself of the pesky gophers on the Stahmann farm fields not on the Ryan farm fields. The good thing is that nobody was ever the wiser.

"El Arabe"

Life on the farm was a life of isolation especially in the 50s when most people didn't own automobiles. The braceros were isolated. The closest town was Fabens. The bracero men worked long hours and they were only allowed to leave the farm during Saturday afternoons and on Sundays. To me at the age of 6 years of age, it seemed that Fabens was far away but it was actually only about 3 or 4 miles away.

By the way, in those days, Fabens had 2 movie theaters and at one time it even had a drive-in movie theater. The main street used to be lined with clothing stores. It even had a pharmacy and a large, well-stocked grocery store.

I remember a man that my father used to refer to as "el arabe". I knew that wasn't the name of the man and I really didn't understand what the words "el arabe" meant. By the way, the word "arabe" means "Arab" in English as in a person from Arabia.

The man drove a station wagon full of clothes for sale. Once a week he would drive to the location where the barracks were situated and park his station wagon there. At other times he would proceed on to the farm dirt roads toward where the bracero men would be working. His business was that of selling what is known as "dry goods" or better said; clothing. His business was a clothing business on wheels.

When he parked his station wagon, the bracero men would come to the parked station wagon. The man known as "el arabe" would then take clothing out from his station wagon so that the men could view the clothes. The men would purchase denim pants and shirts. My mother too would purchase clothing. It was fairly easy to purchase the clothing because "el arabe" would offer the products for sale on an installment basis. So that's how the bracero men and even my mother sometimes purchased clothing.

I've always remembered the man that drove the station wagon filled with clothing articles. I remember he was a heavy set, short man. While I was working with Garratt-Callahan Company, the company rented office space at a location on Texas Street in El Paso. During that time, the owner of the office space decided to place the property up for sale. He hired a realtor to assist with the sale. The realtor's name was Bryan. I didn't make note of his surname at the time. He would, from time to time, bring in potential purchasers to the property and that's how I got to know Bryan.

Socorro, my wife, was a realtor and sold homes in the El Paso area. Without me knowing, she somehow met up with Bryan. She told me about a conversation she had with Bryan. It turns out that during their conversation, the subject of Socorro living on the Grijalva farm, when she was a young girl, came up. Bryan somehow remembered the Grijalva farm and told Socorro that his dad used to sell dry goods to the people on the farms. That is when Socorro put two and two together and concluded that Bryan was the son of the person that everybody knew as "el arabe". In fact he told Socorro that as a young boy, he would ride along with his father on the sales trips to the farms. His name turned out to be Bryan Haddad. Needless to say, the name Haddad has its origins in the Middle East and that's why Bryan's dad was known locally as "el arabe". How coincidental . . . the past meets the present.

The Ryan Boys

As I indicated before, the owner of the cotton farm where we lived was Mr. James Ryan. He was married to Mrs. Mary Jane Ryan. At the time, they seemed to be about the same age as my father and mother. However, based on the information that I found in Mr. Jim Ryan's obituary, he was 4 years older than my father. By the way, Mrs. Mary Jane Ryan was 3 years older than my father. Their two children, Joe and Pat, seemed to be the same age as my older brother, Chuy, and I.

So the eldest Ryan boy was Joseph but we called him "Joe" and the second son was Seth but we called him "Pat". Because we always called him "Pat", I always thought that his formal name was Patrick. It wasn't until recently when I carefully read Mr. and Mrs. Ryan's obituaries that I found out that the second child's name was Seth. It could be that Patrick was Pat's middle name and Chuy and I just didn't know it at the time. As far as I can remember, he was always known as Pat in school.

Later on when we were all enrolled in elementary school, Joe was in Chuy's grade and Pat was in my grade. The Ryan family would later grow to have four more children. Their names were Mark, Paul, Michael and David. When our family lived in the adobe/stucco building adjacent to the railroad tracks, the Ryan home was less than a quarter mile away. Later on, when we lived in the home adjacent to the sand hills, the Ryan house was now farther away; about three quarters of a mile from us. I don't remember having known of Joe or Pat when I was younger and lived in the adobe/stucco building adjacent to the railroad tracks. But I do remember interacting with them when we lived in the home adjacent to the sand hills.

My brother, Chuy, and I grew up with Joe and Pat. I can't remember the first time I met Joe or Pat. Joe and Pat seemed so different than Chuy and I. Their skin seemed so white in comparison to ours and they didn't speak the same language that Chuy and I spoke. I sometimes would hear Mr. James Ryan speaking with my father but he always spoke to my father in Spanish. My older brother, Chuy, was 2 years older than I and so Chuy probably knew of them before I did. Because Chuy was 2 years ahead of me in school, there was a time when he knew a little bit of English and I didn't. What I can remember is that I used to struggle to understand the words that Joe and Pat would utter because they weren't speaking Spanish.

I remember having to constantly ask Chuy "qué dicen?" or in English "what are they saying?".

I previously mentioned that the Ryan house was about three quarters of a mile away from us. The two Ryan boys would hike across the farm fields the entire distance from their house to our house to play with us. This is noteworthy because they were only 6 or 7 years old. They were a hardy pair. Mr. Ryan would sometimes come to drive them back to their house but in many instances they would hike back to their home themselves. In contrast, I don't ever remember us having played with the Ryan boys at their house. I remember that my father was always surprised that the Ryan boys walked that far to our home. My father would ask them "para qué caminan tan lejos?". In English, this meant "why do you walk so far?". The Ryan boys didn't understand him and so they would just shrug their shoulders as if to signal that they didn't understand him.

I am not sure how we managed early on because they didn't speak Spanish and we didn't speak English but somehow we did manage to communicate. Chuy must have been the interpreter. We shared our toys with them and we all enjoyed playing together. Later on, they would bring toys themselves and they too shared them with us. Needless to say, their large metal Tonka Truck toys were much nicer than our small, plastic toy trucks and cars.

The Ryan Boys Were A Rough Pair

I remember that Joe and Pat were a "rough and tumble" pair. They played roughly; Pat even more so than Joe. On occasions when we weren't playing with toy cars and trucks, we would play war games with them. The ammunition consisted of soil dirt clods. Dirt clods were compacted soil fragments that were formed from irrigated farm soil that was subsequently plowed by a farm implement known as a "cultivator". The "cultivator" was pulled by a farm tractor. The "cultivator" was used to break up the surface of the soil in the furrows. The result was that hand-size dirt clods were formed.

Chuy and I would team-up against Joe and Pat and the dirt clod wars would begin. The wars would start out innocently enough. Each team would gently lob dirt clods with an underhand motion at each other.

Eventually, Pat would begin to escalate by throwing harder dirt clods with an overhand motion with more force and we would respond in kind. Ultimately, the war would end when Pat would get hit with a hard dirt clod and then he would begin to cry. I remember that my father would scold us after noticing that Pat was crying. Pat was always the "cry-baby". My father would accuse Chuy and I of having played roughly and as a result, we would always be the ones to get scolded. He never scolded Joe and Pat; that seemed unfair to me. I suppose we received the scoldings because Joe and Pat were the boss's children and my father really didn't have any choice.

During one Christmas morning, Chuy and I opened the gifts that Santa Claus left for us under the Christmas tree. To our surprise, we found two brand new BB gun rifles under the Christmas tree. Each rifle was packaged on a printed cardboard backing with the rifle and the cardboard backing all covered in cellophane. They were beautiful rifles. They were fitted with a gold colored, textured plastic trim. I clearly remember the plastic trim and to this day, I've never seen a BB gun rifle as nice as those were. During the Ryan boy's subsequent visit to our house, we showed them the BB gun rifles. We let them use the rifles; they were awed at the sight of the nice looking rifles. The next time they showed up at our house, they were both now sporting BB gun rifles. I remember that their rifles weren't as nice as ours. We all played target shooting with the BB guns. We shot at empty cans and competed to see who had a better aim.

One of the secrets that Chuy and I never told my parents is that like dirt clod wars, we played war with the Ryan boys but now with BB guns. I don't remember whether we actually hit each with a BB but I do remember hiding behind tin roofing sheets and shooting at them while they shot back. I could hear the BBs bounce off the tin metal that protected me. It's a wonder we didn't shoot our eyes out with those things. As a result, I never bought my children BB guns when they were growing up. I knew firsthand what kids could do with BB guns. When my kids were growing up, a friend of my son, Andy, was playing BB gun wars with some friends of his and Andy's friend actually got his eye shot out . . . no BB gun rifles for my kids.

Learning to Swim

Living on the farm was great fun. There was always something to do. We learned how to swim in the farm's irrigation ditches. Normally, the Rio Grande River supplied and still supplies the irrigation water for the farmers. From time to time a large engine driven pump was used to irrigate the cotton fields on the Ryan farm. When the pump was operating, the large pump outlet pipe would spill huge amounts of water into a large round earthen pit adjacent to the pump. The pit was later reconstructed with concrete. The water would flow out of the pit to the irrigation ditches. The engine driven pump was located on a part of the farm that was elevated higher than the farm fields. It was situated in the sand hill area. A small concrete ditch would carry the water from the concrete pit to the downstream irrigation ditches. It was amazing to watch the clear water as it cascaded at high velocity down the small ditch on its way to the concrete ditches downstream. Now as a grown up, am I understand the science of fluid dynamics. I have a feeling that those early water flow observations influenced me in my studies later on in college. I did very well in my college fluid dynamics course.

Anyway, I remember that the well water was crystal clean. We played in the concrete pit whenever my father began irrigating the fields with well water. That's how we learned to swim.

My father would always warn us to watch out for snakes in the water. Rattle snakes were very common then and still are now in the desert southwest. I remember that we didn't pay much attention to my father's warnings because in our mind, snakes just didn't swim. One of the side streams from the concrete pit was a ditch that ended up at another large round earthen pit. One day while we were all swimming in that pit, I remember seeing a snake swimming in the water crossing the pit from one side to the other. From there on, we would take turns watching out for snakes from outside the pit.

Real Cowboys and Interstate 10 Freeway

During the time that we lived in the house adjacent to the sand hills, I remember that my father would now and then remind us to keep an eye out to make sure that the "canoa" would always have water. Although the true English translation for "canoa" is canoe, my father used the word "canoa" to signify the watering trough from which cattle or horses drank water. The "canoa" was a long galvanized tub with rounded ends that measured about 10 feet long, 4 feet wide and about 3 feet in depth.

The "canoa" was located adjacent to the bracero barracks and was separated from the barracks with a barb wire fence. The barb wire fence separating the barracks from the "canoa" was about 50 feet in length. At each end of that length, the barb wire fence turned 90 degrees at both ends upwards and towards the desert, away from the barracks. The barb wire fence created a 50 foot wide corridor leading from the location of the "canoa" towards the desert. I remember that the "canoa" was equipped with a float valve that served to keep a constant water level in the tank. The pressurized water was provided by a well pump that was located near our home.

At any rate, for some reason my father never told us the reason the "canoa" had to be constantly filled with water and I don't remember having asked. I do remember following my father's orders and therefore we would indeed check the "canoa" on a daily basis to make sure it had water in it. In retrospect, I believe my father was concerned that the float valve that allowed water flow into the trough would malfunction. This would result in stopping the inlet water flow into the "canoa". Chuy and I followed my father's instruction without question for a long time.

One day, we saw a cloud of dust far away towards the desert. The cloud seemed to be moving towards the bracero barracks. After a while, we saw a multitude of cows trotting toward the location of the barracks. We never took a count of the number of cows but it must have been every bit of 100 cows. When they reached the barracks, the cows congregated around the "canoa" and began to drink the water. Shortly thereafter, we saw two men mounted on horseback coming down from the desert following the cows. At long last we realized why it was that we had been ordered to tend the "canoa". It was so that the cattle herd could drink water. Although I am not certain, Mr. Ryan probably had some agreement with the cattle owner to maintain the tank full of water so that the cattle herd could periodically come down from the desert to drink the water.

We got to see real cowboys mounted on horses. The men on the horses wore sweat stained hats and chaps. Chaps were leather leg coverings used to protect the cowboy's legs from the thorns in the mesquite bushes. They also wore spurs on the back of their boots. A spur is a small spiked wheel that is worn on a rider's boot heel and used for urging a horse forward. Coiled ropes were strapped to their saddles. 

The men were "Americanos" and they seemed way too skinny. We referred to them as "Americanos" because that's what my father called them. We could see that their skin was very sun burned and they seemed tired. Their shoulders drooped and their backs curved as they sat on the saddles waiting for the cows to get their fill of water. I remember seeing one of them roll a cigarette out of a piece of paper and a small can of tobacco. After rolling the cigarette, he began to smoke it. I don't remember having seen them wear pistols or gun holsters. After what seemed an hour, the cowboys began to herd the cattle so as to make their way back to the desert.

It was an exciting time for us living on the farm. I feel fortunate that as kids, we actually got to see real cowboys mounted on horses. It was one more exciting thing that we experienced on the farm. It just seemed like there was always something to do when we lived on the farm. There seemed to be no boundaries.

From the very first time that we saw the cowboys herding the cattle from the desert to the location of the "canoa", Chuy and I would wonder where the cattle came from. This curiosity was so great that one day Chuy decided that we were going to find out. I still remember Chuy's typical phrase "no le digas a mi Amá" which in English means "don't tell my mother". After those words, he would then tell me the plan that "we" were about to execute. This was one more mission we were about to embark on. Chuy felt certain that we were going to find the location where the cattle came from.

One thing for sure about Chuy's "no le digas a mi Amá" phrase; if for some reason Chuy's plan went awry after the fact, we were in for a spanking from my mother. But even worse, if she were to utter the phrase "le voy a decir a tu Papa", then we knew we were in really deep trouble. The words "le voy a decir a tu Papa" translates to "I'm going to tell your father". Those words meant that we were in for a belt spanking when my father returned from work.

One day, without telling my mother, we began to hike toward the desert along the route of the two parallel barb wire fences. We followed the fenced corridor up the same path that we had observed the cattle follow. After what seemed an eternity of walking along the cattle corridor route, we came to the end of the fenced corridor. We found that at the end of the corridor, the fence to the right of the corridor turned 90 degrees to the right and continued onward while the fence to the left of the corridor turned 90 degrees to the left and continued onward. It was as if the mouth of the fenced-in corridor opened up to the entire desolate desert.

I don't remember us having continued our search once we reached the mouth of the fenced-in corridor but I do remember walking back down to the farm. For some reason, our walk back to the house is ingrained in my memory. Even as a grownup in my mind's eye, I can still see the "greasewood" bushes that are typical of the desert landscape as well as the small arroyos that were formed by the rains. I'll even go so far as to say that as a grown up, while asleep, I have had dreams of walking down the path of the cattle corridor back to the house. Those were exciting days at the farm.

We tended the cattle watering trough for some time until the cattle and cowboys stopped coming. I remember that was when I was 5 or 7 years of age when we tended the "canoa". At the rear of our house was a very high sand hill that dwarfed all of the surrounding sand hills. I remember that one day, while playing at the top of that sand hill; we noticed what seemed to be equipment far, far away toward the north. It was difficult to discern what type of equipment it was because of the distance. We could see the black exhaust smoke probably produced by construction equipment. The equipment seemed to be moving back and forth as if constructing something.

When I first began writing this piece, I didn't remember Chuy and I ever having hiked to that location to explore what was going on. I recently had the opportunity to reminisce with Felipe Martinez who also grew up on the Ryan farm with us. In a previous section of this memoir, I mentioned that we got reacquainted after the death of his brother. Anyway, he remembers that he and his brothers as well as Chuy and I did indeed take a hike to see all the commotion that was happening toward the direction we had seen the construction equipment moving back and forth. He clearly remembers the heavy equipment being used to construct a highway.

As a grownup, I now know that in about 1959, Interstate 10 highway was constructed approximately 1.6 miles east of the farm. It was constructed toward the direction where we had observed the construction equipment when we were very young. I imagine that the construction of Interstate 10 highway did away with the cattle and the cowboys.

As kids, we were lucky that my father purchased a black and white television set for our home when we lived on the farm. In contrast to today's f lat screen sets, the television set at that time was a bulky monster. The depth dimension alone was almost 3 feet in length. There was no such thing as a hand-held remote control. It was a television set that showed programs and commercials only in black and white. This was before the time of color television sets.

I remember watching cowboy and Indian shows on the television set. I specifically remember watching television shows like Gunsmoke, Have Gun Will Travel and Rawhide. The television show, Rawhide, portrayed cowboys and cattle drives. It was exciting to have seen real cowboys mounted on horses herding cattle when we lived on the farm. It was just like we had seen on the television shows.

Picking Cotton on the Ryan Farm

My older brother and I started working on the farm at an early age. I was 6 years of age when I began to work on the farm. I don't remember when Chuy began. Anyway, at the time, Chuy was 8 years old when I was 6 years of age.

Harvesting cotton occurred during the fall, starting with the month of September. I remember that I worked picking cotton during Saturdays. I was in school during the weekdays. I was part of a crew of about 15 to 20 persons that picked cotton.

In a previous section, I indicated that my family moved to Arizona when I was about 4 years of age. In that part of the memoir, I described the details of picking cotton. Cotton picking on the Ryan farm was not much different than picking cotton in Arizona. The same pick sacks were used and the cotton was weighed in the same manner as in Arizona. The only difference was that in Arizona, the workers were paid in cash right after the cotton sack was weighed on the weigh scale. Now on the Ryan farm, the cotton was still weighed as in Arizona but the workers were paid at the end of the week.

Anyway, no longer did I ride on my father's or mother's cotton sack like I did when I was 4 years of age in Arizona. Now, Chuy and I had to work to contribute to our family's well being.

I was very good at picking cotton. As I indicated before, having the ability to pick cotton simultaneously with both hands was an advantage. I was one of those persons who was ambidextrous. Because of that ability, I was able to keep up with the other workers as they slowly inched forward picking cotton. With the exception of my aunt Rosa and my mother, the other workers were bracero men from Mexico. I would listen to the men's conversations as they picked cotton. It was obvious they were lonely. They spoke about their homes in Mexico and their wives. The unmarried men spoke about their girlfriends. In some instances, I heard conversations that only grownups should hear. I just kept quiet and continued picking cotton as if minding my own business.

I especially remember an episode involving my aunt Rosa when I was a little older; possibly 7 years of age. As I indicated previously, she was married to my uncle Esteban Gutierrez who was my mother's brother. At the time, she was probably 20 or 24 years old. For some reason, she and I wound up alone picking cotton at one of the fields on the farm. Anyway, we finished picking the last few rows of cotton on that particular field and we then waited for my father to come for us. We waited and waited, perhaps for about an hour.

I don't exactly remember how it happened but my father's pickup truck was parked nearby. Anyway, I told my aunt Rosa that I could drive both of us to the next field in my father's pickup truck. She was hesitant. She insisted that we stay and wait. She didn't want me driving the pickup truck for fear of running off the road or having an accident. I insisted that I could drive the pickup truck safely although in reality, at 7 years of age, I wasn't very tall and I would have had to struggle to reach the brake pedals and the clutch and even the accelerator pedal. After some additional discussion, she finally agreed to my plan. We boarded the pickup truck; I sat as erect as possible to be able to see forward through the front windshield and still be able to reach the pedals on the floorboard. Little by little I maneuvered the pickup truck around on the dirt road and then began to drive forward.

I drove slowly to make sure that my aunt Rosa wouldn't get nervous. Remember, I was short and I had to really sit erect on the seat to see the road ahead. I finally turned onto the dirt road that led to the location where the rest of the workers were picking cotton. It was now a straight shot to our destination. Without thinking, I sped up and a few minutes later we were now approaching a large horizontal hump that protruded up from the surface of the road. The hump was constructed of a large diameter concrete tube, half-way buried in the dirt. The tube protruding from the dirt road connected the two concrete ditches on either side of the dirt road. It was like a small bridge that allowed vehicles to slowly pass over the concrete tube.

Anyway, I was speeding along too rapidly and I was already too close to the hump; it was too late to slow down. My aunt alerted me to slow down but by that time, it was too late. We approached the hump and the pickup truck suddenly pitched upward at an angle and for a second or two the pickup truck with us inside the cab became airborne. A second later, the pickup truck slammed down onto the dirt road shaking every item inside the cab of the truck including ourselves. I immediately pressed on the brakes and brought the pickup truck to a complete stop. Firmly holding on to the steering wheel, I turned to look at my aunt and she too looked at me . . . a second later, we both burst out laughing. We had achieved zero gravity for a second. It was a ha-ha moment.

My aunt never forgot that experience. Later on as a grown up, Socorro and I would sometimes visit my aunt Rosa and she would tell the story of how we both had the surprise of our lives that day. She thought it was unusual that such a little boy felt so sure about driving the pickup truck. She would say "you looked very cute driving the truck when you were a child". I'll never forget that episode with my aunt Rosa.

Later on when I was 10 or 12 years of age, cotton picking was no longer done by hand. I remember that my father began to drive an automated cotton picker that could pick cotton very rapidly. A photograph of the automated cotton picking machine is shown on the left.

The machine was mounted on what looked like a reverse moving tractor with the two large wheels to the front and the one single wheel on the rear. The front of the machine consisted of two sets of forks that were used to align the cotton plants toward the part of the machine that stripped the cotton from the cotton bolls. A large wire mesh bin that served to store the cotton that was just removed by the machine was located on top of the tractor. When the wire mesh bin was full, my father would drive the machine towards the cotton trailer. He would then position the tractor so that the bin was as close as possible to the side of the cotton trailer. He would then activate a control on the machine to tilt the wire mesh bin so that the cotton inside the bin would then be transferred to the cotton trailer. It was now that easy to pick the cotton in the fields.

The introduction of the automated cotton picker on the Ryan farm meant that workers were no longer necessary to pick cotton. When this happened, the need for bracero men lessened. Although the automated cotton picker did do away with the large number of men formerly required to pick the cotton, there was one flaw in the design of the machine. When the machine completed picking the two rows of cotton, it would then need to completely around to resume picking the next set of rows. The process of turning the large machine ended up trampling the cotton plants at the ends of the cotton rows where the machine turned. As a result, the cotton that was trampled couldn't be harvested.

The solution to this problem was to have workers pick the cotton at the ends of the rows before the automated cotton pickers were used on that cotton field. The workers would pick the cotton on the cotton plants that were located about 10 to 15 feet from either end of the cotton rows. Once the cotton at the end of the rows was manually picked, the automated cotton pickers could turn around and proceed to trample the plants that no longer had cotton on them. At that point, trampling the bare cotton plants was no longer a problem.

Today, picking the ends of the cotton rows isn't done. I don't really know why, but I think that the reason for not manually picking the ends of the cotton rows is because as a percentage of the overall cotton yield, the amount of trampled cotton is considered miniscule.

Automated robotics controlled equipment of today are taking over many manufacturing functions that skilled workers used to perform. Automobile manufacturing is an example. Automated cotton pickers were the robots of yesteryear that began to put many people out of work.

Irrigating the Cotton Fields

One of the most important parts in growing cotton is the irrigation of the cotton plants. I worked irrigating the cotton fields on the Ryan farm. This occurred when I was about 7 years of age.

The irrigation of the cotton fields on the Ryan farm began whenever the "irrigation canal supervisor" informed my father or Mr. Ryan that the irrigation water was now available for use on the Ryan farm. That prompted my father to prepare for the irrigation of the fields.

The irrigation canal supervisor was a key component in the management of the irrigation of the farm. The irrigation canal supervisor's responsibility was to keep an eye on the irrigation water that flowed into the canals from the Rio Grande. It was his job to manage the distribution of the irrigation water to each individual farm including the Ryan farm. His responsibility included informing the farm owners when their turn came up to use the irrigation water. The irrigation canal supervisor frequently drove up and down along the dirt roadways adjacent to the water distribution canals. He kept an eye out for problems with the integrity of the canal network. His most important function, as far as my father and Mr. Ryan was concerned, was to inform them that the canal water was now available for use.

By the way, the word "canal" translates to English as "channel" which in context means "artificial conduit through which water is conducted to distribute it for irrigation or other purposes". The person controlling the volume of flow from the irrigation canal to the distribution ditches on the farm was the "canalero". That's the term my father used when referring to that person. The word "canalero" is a derivative of the word "canal" in Spanish. The word "canalero" is loosely translated to mean "irrigation canal supervisor".

Anyway, when word came from the irrigation canal supervisor that the canal water was available for use, my father would quickly activate the troops, so to speak. The troops consisted of my uncle Esteban, a man by the name of Agustin Lazalde, Chuy and myself. We took it for granted that the water would be available to irrigate all of the fields at one time on the Ryan farm. The water would be available non-stop, 24 hours a day until all the fields were irrigated. At that time, Chuy was paired with Agustin Lazalde while I was paired with my uncle Esteban Gutierrez. Agustin Lazalde lived in nearby Tornillo and not on the farm. Agustin Lazalde and Chuy would manage the irrigation of the cotton fields starting at 6:00 a.m. in the morning and then proceeding 24 hours all the way to 6:00 a.m. the next morning. At the conclusion of their 24 hour shift irrigating the fields, my uncle Esteban and I would take over and begin to manage the irrigation process starting right after the conclusion of Agustin's and Chuy's shift. We would take over from 6:00 a.m. that morning to the next morning at 6:00 a.m. This went on in alternating fashion until the entire farm was irrigated.

During that time, almost the entire Ryan farm was planted in cotton. The remaining land was planted in alfalfa. Alfalfa was and is still used as fodder to feed cattle and horses.

Irrigating the fields meant that the incoming water from the canals had to be distributed evenly throughout the fields. Our responsibility was to route the incoming water from the canal outside the farm property to specific individual ditches that then distributed the water to each of the separate fields. The drawing on left shows  three distribution ditches in red color that were used to irrigate the total of 6 fields. The first field to be irrigated was the left-most field shown on the diagram to the left. After that field was completely irrigated then the next field to its right was irrigated. This was done until all of the 6 fields were irrigated.

The water from the distribution ditches had to be transferred to the fields using what were called "aluminum siphon tubes". We used to call them "pipas". The word "pipas" in Spanish sounds similarly to "peepas".

The word "pipas" simply meant "pipes" in English. Anyway, being constructed of aluminum, these siphon tubes were very light weight and one could easily carry several in one's arms. The photograph on the left shows the siphon tubes.

There was a trick to initiating the water flow through the siphon tubes so that the water could then travel from the ditch to the cotton field. After reviewing some internet articles describing these tubes, I found out that "tube setting" is the correct phrase used to denote placing the tubes into operation.

In order to "set the siphon tube", I would grasp an individual tube with both hands so that the end of the tube to my left was immersed in the water in the ditch. I would then push the left side of the tube as far as possible into the water. I would position my right hand on the other end of the tube so as to cover the opening of the tube. It was important to create as tight a seal as possible on the tube opening with my right hand. Short of that, flow wouldn't subsequently occur. Anyway, I would "pump" the tube forward and backward from one side to the other reciprocally while at the same time making sure that the tube opening already immersed in the ditch water remained immersed. Now when I felt the presence of water on the covered opening of the tube, with one motion, I would then swing the tube onto the ground toward the direction of the field and wah-lah, water flow would begin. Water would then continuously flow from the ditch to furrows in the field. There was a trick to it and I learned it when I was 7 years old.

As indicated before, the number of siphon tubes that had to be activated in this manner depended on how fast the ditch was filling up with water from the larger irrigation canal. If the ditch was in danger of overflowing its banks, then it was necessary to set more siphon tubes in operation to balance out the water flowing into the ditch with the water flowing in from the irrigation canal. That's the reason we had to remain very vigilant throughout the 24 hour period.

At the same time that we had to balance the water flow with sufficient siphon tubes transferring water into the furrows, we also had to keep an eye on the opposite end of the field that was being irrigated. This was necessary to insure that each furrow was covered with water from end to end. My recollection is kind of fuzzy as to how my uncle Esteban and I managed the work. This is because one of us had to have been responsible for setting the siphon tubes while the other had to have been stationed on the other end of the field to monitor the water as the flow reached the ends of the furrows. How we communicated back and forth, I don't remember. Logic indicates that we probably communicated by signaling back and forth with our arms and hands and probably even yelling back and forth at one another. The approximate distance from the ditch to the end of the furrows was about 500 feet. Anyway; somehow we managed.

As the furrows being irrigated filled up with water, we would then move the siphon tubes forward along the ditch in order to begin irrigating the next set of furrows. This went on until the entire section of the field was irrigated.

That was during the day; now came the night. It was more difficult during the night because now we had to battle more obstacles. We had to manage the irrigation process while at the same time fighting sleeplessness.

By the way, during the night time hours we used portable kerosene lanterns. We used to refer to kerosene as "petroleo" and lanterns as "linternas". Anyway, the portable kerosene lamps were vital in enabling us to continue the irrigation work during the night.

We had limited visibility in the dark so communications between us waving our hands and arms was impossible. As I indicated before, we carried portable lanterns to provide sufficient lighting for us to detect the constantly changing level of the water in the ditch as well as the coverage of water in each furrow in the field. Somehow we managed. From time to time during the morning hours when work conditions were stable, my uncle would take a nap in his car. When he woke up, it was my turn to take a nap, again in his car.

Working during the night was scary for me. I had a vivid imagination. In a previous section of this memoir I described the topic of "alechusas" and that of "la llorona". From time to time, I would hear the howl of coyotes off in the distance in the desert. I never actually saw a coyote during my

24 hours shifts but they were always there in the desert. Snakes were also a problem. The irrigations were done during the summer months when snakes seemed to be more numerous. Thank God I never encountered a snake in the cotton fields. I remember being very tired during the wee hours of the morning.

My eyes were bloodshot and I remember being very sleepy. As the sun was about to rise over the horizon, we could now see without having to use our lanterns. Little by little the sun began to rise. It was a welcomed sight. Soon Agustin Lazalde and Chuy would be coming to take over and assume their next 24 hour shift. I was beat.

My father showed up about half an hour before 6:00 a.m. along with Chuy. My father began catching up with the goings-on primarily with my uncle Esteban while I looked on. Soon Agustin Lazalde showed up and it was time for Chuy and Agustin to take over. My father would drive me home and that was that. I don't exactly remember how many 24 hour shifts I worked every time that the fields were irrigated but I do remember that it wasn't just one shift.

I never knew how much Chuy and I were paid for the work we did irrigating the fields; my father handled those matters. Looking back and reflecting upon the fact that my family was poor; it was probably helpful that Chuy and I worked to help augment the family finances. And yes, I learned how to work at an early age. My son, Adrian, didn't work at that early age because I chose not to push him into it. My father didn't have that choice. In the end, perhaps it was a blessing that I had to work at that early age because that was probably one of the reasons why later on, I would decide to better myself and go on to college.

Fast Food, Cholesterol and Fat

Nowadays, a hamburger and fries is the staple food for kids. It's easy to make a hamburger. If you make it at home, you just slap a piece of lettuce on a bread bun. Slap on a slice of tomato, some mustard, a slice of cheese and finally a cooked ground meat paddy and wah-lah; you have a hamburger. Oh and let's not forget to deep fry a handful of sliced potatoes in a bath of vegetable oil and again wah-lah; you have golden crisp French fries. If you can't make these items yourself, just go to the local fast food eatery and order a hamburger with fries. Wait 3 minutes after you pay for your order and again wah-lah; you have a hamburger and French fries. The result is 25 to 35 grams of cholesterol and about 7 grams of saturated fat!

Oh and let's not forget pizza. You can purchase flour, then make the flour into dough and then shape the dough into a large circular shape. Throw some grated mozzarella cheese on top of the dough and then a few slices of pepperoni on top. Place it in a large oven and wait maybe 15 or 20 minutes and there; you have homemade pizza. But this is too time consuming; so the alternative is to go to a pizza eatery or restaurant. Order the pizza, wait 10 minutes after you pay for your order and there again; you have a pizza. The result is 20 to 30 grams of cholesterol and 6 grams of saturated fat!

Would you believe that during our childhood we had neither tasted hamburgers or pizza? It wouldn't be until I was 14 or 15 years of age when Chuy and I traveled to California that we would get our first taste of a hamburger and a pizza. I guess the reason we didn't know about hamburgers and pizza is because when we lived on the farm and later when we moved to Fabens, we never knew of the their existence. Although our teachers were mostly Anglo, we weren't really integrated into the Anglo culture during those growing up years. It took that long for us to catch up because we just didn't know of the existence of hamburgers and pizza. And now knowing what I know about cholesterol and saturated fats in modern fast foods, I suppose it was a blessing in disguise.

When we lived on the farm, we were a poor family but my mother saw to it that we had sufficient nourishment. Our diet consisted primarily of Mexican food. The main staple was pinto beans and rice. Of course, we also ate meat products and a soup known as "caldo de res" which is a soup mixture of meat, potatoes and other assorted vegetables.

But beans and rice was a staple and that's what we ate when we were growing up. Some will say that beans and rice aren't nutritious. I used to think the same; however, here are a few quotes I obtained from several internet articles regarding pinto beans that show otherwise:

"Pinto beans are a very good source of cholesterol-lowering fiber, as are most other beans Pinto beans are also an excellent source of molybdenum, a very good source of folate, and a good source of protein, vitamin B1, and vitamin B6 as well as the minerals copper, phosphorus, iron, magnesium, manganese, and potassium."

Another article describes the benefits of eating beans as it relates to cholesterol and fat. The quote from the article is as follows:

"Beans are also full of fiber, potassium, folate, iron, manganese and magnesium, and they are cholesterol- [sic] and fat-free."

Fast forward to the year 2006 when I competed in a body building contest which I will later describe. During the preparation for the contest, my trainer stressed repeatedly to me that a good diet was very important. He placed more importance on chicken products rather than red meat products as a source of protein. As a result of his insistence of a good diet, I become interested in knowing more about combining foods to gain greater nutrition.

I remember having seen several articles related to the synergistic effect when beans and rice are eaten together. Synergy has to do with combining substances together to produce a combined effect that is greater than the sum of their separate effects. As a result of that recollection related to synergy, I recently dug into that topic again. I found the following two quotes related to beans and rice on a web site:

"We often hear that many foods are best combined to provide better nutrition. Probably the most common is beans and rice. Served together they form a complete amino acid, especially important in vegetarian diets. That is what is called ' food synergy.' Foods that go together for health benefits. The vitamins and minerals each contains work best with another food to maximize the benefits. The pairing of specific foods can play an important part in risk reduction for some diseases."

The information was obtained from the following web link: http://jaquo.com/what-is-food-synergy/

So in the end, eating pinto beans provided nourishment and in addition, they were cholesterol-free as well as fat-free. Along with rice as a carbohydrate, the beans with meat provided all the nourishment we needed when we were growing up. It's possible that my mother knew that these products provided us sufficient nutrition but I didn't. Yes, we didn't have hamburgers and pizza but we had sometime better; foods that were low in cholesterol and fat. Yes, I suppose that being oblivious to hamburgers and pizza was indeed a blessing in disguise.

Quelites and Verdolagas

In those days, we ate vegetables; but not the vegetables that we now eat today. My mother would prepare a stew-like dish that contained pieces of meat, potatoes and spices. In addition, the stew sometimes contained wild vegetables that we found growing along the irrigation ditches on the farm.

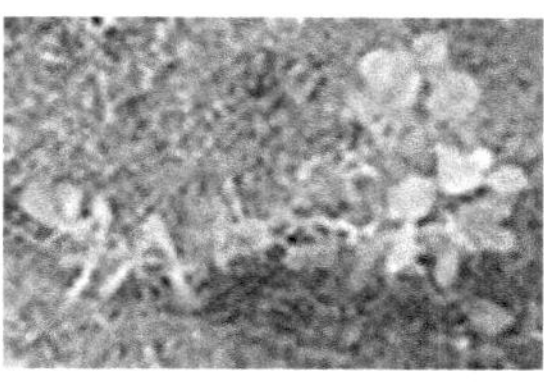

One of those plants that my mother used as a vegetable was what she called "verdolagas". Verdolagas could easily be found growing along the irrigation ditches. I suppose they grew there because of the presence of residual moisture that remained along the irrigation ditches.

Until recently, I didn't know that the plant was referred to in English as "purslane". The small leaves were the part of the plant that were removed from the stems and then cooked in the stew. Purslane is a plant that has fleshy succulent leaves. The stems of the plant lie flat on the ground and radiate from a single root sometimes forming large mats of leaves.

I found the following article on the web. It describes the nutrient value of purslane or "verdolagas".

"Soft, succulent purslane leaves have more omega-3 fatty acids than in some of the fish oils. If you are a vegetarian and pledge to avoid all forms of animal products, then here is the answer! Go for this healthy dark-green leafy vegetable and soon you will forget fish!"

The quote can be viewed using the following web link: https://www.nutrition-and-you.com/purslane.html

Another web article contained the following quote; however, I failed to copy the web link:

"Health Benefits of Purslane. This wonderful green leafy vegetable is very low in calories and fats; nonetheless, it is rich in dietary fiber, vitamins, and minerals. Fresh leaves contain surprisingly more omega-3 fatty acids (a-linolenic acid) than any other leafy vegetable plant."

Another plant that my mother used in our food was what my parents called "quelites". Like "verdolagas" this plant is also a wild plant that was plentiful along the irrigation ditches.

The word "quelites" is pronounced as in "che-lit-es" with the letters "che" pronounced similarly to first three letters in the word "chemical". The word "quelites" is a Mexican word used to denote "wild greens". The wild green that comes closest to what I learned was "quelite" is a pigweed plant commonly referred to as Palmer's amaranth. It is native to most of the southern half of North America. As in the case of "verdolagas", my mother would remove the "quelite" leaves from the stems and then add them to the stew broth to cook.

The following excerpt taken from a Wikipedia article indicates that Palmer amaranth is nutritious:

"The leaves, stems and seeds of Palmer amaranth, like those of other amaranths, are edible and highly nutritious. Palmer amaranth was once widely cultivated and eaten by Native Americans across North America, both for its abundant seeds and as a cooked or dried green vegetable."

Another internet article relating to Palmer amaranth is as follows:

"Amaranth leaves contain a wide range of minerals, including a high concentration of calcium. There are very few leafy vegetables that contain higher levels [5] of calcium, making it a veritable superfood in terms of boosting bone strength and preventing osteoporosis. Calcium is a crucial mineral for preventing demineralization of the bones, extending your "active life" well into your old age."

The article can be accessed using the following web link: https://www.organicfacts.net/health-benefits/vegetable/amaranth. html

Yes, "verdolagas" or purslane as well as "quelites" or Palmer amaranth were readily available and by the way, they were free for the taking. I am not sure that my mother knew the outstanding benefits that these wild plants contained but she sure cooked good stews using these plants.

The Cure For Cancer – Good Memories

When we lived in the home near the sand hills on the Ryan farm, we used to play in and around the desert vegetation. Mesquite bushes were plentiful in the desert. Mesquite is a spiny tree or shrub of the pea family, that is native to arid regions of southwestern US and Mexico. Every year during the summer, the mesquite bushes would produce slender, thin pods that we called "mesquite".

When the pods turned a reddish color, we would pick the "mesquite" pods off the shrub and then eat the juicy contents of the pods. Well, we wouldn't really eat it, we would just bite into it, mash it with our teeth and suck the sweet tasting juice out of the pods. The taste was a distinctive sweet taste. I guess the sweet taste resulted from sugars in the "mesquite" pods. After having sucked the sweetness from the pods, we would then spit out the remaining pulp onto the ground.

As a young boy, I used imagine how it might feel to be the first one to discover something new that had not been discovered before. At the same time, it seemed odd to me that nobody made a big to do about the sweet tasting "mesquite" pods. I am not sure how it happened but I used to wonder if perhaps the "mesquite" pods might have curative properties that somehow everyone had overlooked. New medical discoveries from vegetation in the rain forests had been known to have happened so why couldn't it be the same with "mesquite" pods. Heck, perhaps the "mesquite" fruit had some something in it that might even cure cancer.

Fast forward to when I started working at Continental Water Conditioning Corporation after college. I learned about analyses techniques that could be used to determine the presence of organic constituents in materials. From time to time, I would remember the "mesquite" pods back at the Ryan farm and thought about perhaps investing money to have a laboratory perform an analysis of the "mesquite" pod. However, I was so busy with my work at Continental Water in the 70s and 80s that I never actually pursued the matter.

I recently searched the internet for information on mesquite pods and found that indeed "mesquite" pods do have curative properties. I found that mesquite contains lots of calcium for bone health, magnesium for enzyme production, relaxation and mental health, copper and iron for controlling anemia and potassium for water regulation and muscle recovery. Mesquite powder may even have the potential to prevent or improve a migraine and headache pain.

Now as I am writing this memoir at my mature age, I remember all those thoughts about the cure for cancer that I used to have when I was a young boy. I had a vivid imagination. Perhaps the chemical components in mesquite pods do not cure cancer. That's not important now. What is important now are all of those good memories I had as a young boy and as a young man when I used to dream of being the first to find something new that hadn't been found before. As for finding the cure for cancer; I'll leave that to the experts.

Caseta – My Parent's Lifeblood

The Rio Grande River marks the boundary between the United States and Mexico. The small town of Caseta is situated next to the Rio Grande River on the Mexican side. For some reason everybody knows the town by the name of Caseta; however, I found a reference on the web that indicates that the formal name of the small town is really Doctor Porfirio Parra.

The Fabens-Caseta International Bridge

The Fabens-Caseta International Bridge connects Caseta to the town of Tornillo and Fabens across the border on the U.S. side. The driving distance from the international bridge to Tornillo is about 4 miles whereas the driving distance to Fabens is about 7 miles. The original bridge was built in 1938 and was designed as a two-lane bridge. A new, modern multi-lane border crossing bridge was constructed and was inaugurated in 2015.

The old two lane bridge still exists; however, it is blocked off to prevent its further use as a border crossing bridge. The photograph on the left shows the two-lane bridge as well as the immigration station, as viewed

from the Mexican side; that was used up until the year 2015. If you were driving a large, full sized vehicle and there was oncoming traffic coming from the opposite direction, you would have to inch along slowly and carefully watch so that the external mirrors mounted on the driver's side of the two opposing vehicles wouldn't make contact. The bridge width was that narrow. Needless to say, driving an 18 wheel semi truck tractor across the old border crossing bridge was impossible.

The picture shown above brings back many memories. I remember that the bridge would be opened for border crossing traffic at 6:00 am each morning and would be closed at 9:00 pm each night. It was not a 24 hour bridge like the border crossing bridges in nearby El Paso. I remember many times when my father would somehow end up being delayed past the 9:00 o'clock hour at night in Caseta. He would be forced to travel the 25 miles all the way to Zaragoza, Mexico to cross into the United States. From there, he still had to travel another 21 miles back past Fabens to the Ryan Farm.

My Parent's Acquaintances in Caseta

The little town of Caseta, Mexico was very important to my parents both because my father's family lived there as well as because it afforded an opportunity to make extra money. More about the extra money will be described later on. Anyway, Caseta was the place my grandfather Jose and his family lived. My parents seemed to gravitate to that little Mexican town. It seemed to be their lifeblood.

Another reason why Caseta was important to my parents is that groceries were less expensive in Caseta in comparison to groceries in Fabens. I specifically remember that meat products were especially inexpensive in comparison to meat products purchased in Fabens. A couple by the name of Pedro and Quirina Garcia owned a grocery store in Caseta and that is where my father and mother used to go to purchase groceries. My parents became good friends with the Garcia's that owned the grocery store.

Pedro and Quirina Garcia were the parents of a Berta Valenzuela who was married to Cruz Valenzuela. The reason the Valenzuela's are important is that they became my parent's "compadres". The word "compadre" does not have an English translation. In Mexico, two married couples become "compadres" with each other when one couple becomes the godparents of the other couple's child. In effect, the couple that sponsors the child in the Catholic Sacrament of Baptism or Confirmation becomes the "padrinos", or in English, godparents of that child. I don't remember which of my siblings was the child receiving the Sacrament under their sponsorship or whether one of their children was the child receiving the Sacrament.

At any rate, later in life when I was perhaps 13 or 14 years of age, the Valenzuelas asked me to sponsor their son Jose Valenzuela to be confirmed with the Sacrament of Confirmation. His nickname is Willy. He was probably about 9 years of age at the time. Willy and I were always good friends even in our later years.

The Extended Family

As I indicated before, Caseta represented a comfort zone to my parents especially to my father. It was as if they found comfort there more so than  in the new world; the United States. They were never able to divorce themselves completely from Mexico. The reason they were not able to separate themselves from Mexico, specifically Caseta, is that my father's extended family headed by my grandfather Jose lived there. The family consisted of the following siblings: Socorro, Esteban, Sara, Marcos, Reyes, Manuel, Maria, Velia, Lorenzo, Guadalupe and Angelica and of course, Ester, my grandfather Jose's wife.

The siblings were half-brothers and half-sisters of my father due to my grandfather Jose marrying Ester after my grandmother Espedita passed away in San Lucas. My grandmother Maria too was related to Ester and her children. Ester was my grandmother María's sister. So in fact, Ester was my mother's aunt and her children were my mother's cousins.

Los Gueros Cantina

Caseta was the location of a bar that operated under the establishment name of "Los Gueros". My father would refer to it as "la cantina". The Spanish word "cantina" denotes an establishment that serves alcoholic drinks, in other words, a bar. My father became good friends with the two owners who were brothers, although I never knew their names.

I remember many a time when we would wait outside in the parking area of the establishment in the farm's pickup truck while my father spent time with his friends inside the "cantina". My mother, Chuy and I would sometimes spend up to 3 hours waiting for my father to finally exit from the "cantina". Sometimes my mother would become so impatient just sitting in the truck that she would instruct Chuy or I to enter the "cantina" to let my father know that it was time to leave. Well, sometimes it worked and sometimes it didn't.

At times, he would exit from the establishment pretty close to the magic hour of 9:00 o'clock when the Caseta crossing bridge was about to close. He would exit and tell us to quickly get inside the pickup truck so he could quickly drive off to the crossing bridge before it was closed off for the night. Most times we made it across the bridge and sometimes we didn't.

One might ask why we had to wait so long outside the establishment. The answer is "Mexican machismo". The Spanish word "machismo" means having a sense of being manly and self-reliant. A macho man has a strong sense of masculine pride or better said; an exaggerated masculinity. It is associated with a man's responsibility to provide for, protect, and defend his family. It wasn't just my father. It seemed to be an inherent characteristic of strong willed Mexican men at that time. That was my father and I have to admit that I too sometimes can be accused of having that characteristic. But that's not all bad; it may be what motivates Mexican men to achieve.

Fast forward to about 1971 when I was 20 years of age when Chuy returned for a few days to visit us in Fabens when he was about 22 years of age. Chuy wanted to go to Caseta to see our old stomping grounds. We crossed the bridge and drove around the town of Caseta kind of like sight-seeing the old stomping grounds. When we were driving back on the way to the Caseta crossing bridge on the way back to Fabens, Chuy told me that he wanted to have a beer at the "Los Gueros cantina". It seemed odd to me because neither Chuy nor I were beer drinkers and furthermore, he nor I had ever entered that specific "cantina". Nonetheless, I agreed.

We walked into the "cantina" for the first time now as grown men and we were greeted by the two brothers who owned the establishment. It was an awkward moment for us because never before had we entered that establishment as grownups. I guess the owners were surprised as well because they seemed at a loss for words when we entered. They both greeted us and Chuy then indicated to them that we had come to drink beer. One of the owners asked what we would like to drink. Out of the blue, Chuy blurted out "what flavors do you have?". The owner smiled. I felt like crawling into a hole; I was so embarrassed. I thought to myself "a real man doesn't do that". Anyway, the owner rattled off some assorted beer names and then Chuy responded by rattling-off the name of one of the beers.

Shortly thereafter, the owner served us our beers. We acted nonchalantly in hopes that we didn't stick out like sore thumbs in this place that my father frequented. We managed to finish our beers and then we thanked the owners and departed from the premises. When we were about to step into my car, I told Chuy in a humorous way "why did you say; what flavors do you have?". He smiled sheepishly and said "Yea, I guess I should have used different words". Yes, we entered my father's hallowed halls and we wound up embarrassing ourselves (chuckle).

"El Arbolito"

When Chuy was in high school in Fabens, Chuy began to travel to Caseta frequently. I have to admit, Chuy was a good looking dude. I was a book worm and perhaps not as good looking as Chuy. Caseta was important to Chuy because he was a good dancer. He would go and meet with Marcos or Esteban, my father's half brothers. They would take him to a "cantina" by the name of "El Arbolito".

I joined them a few times. In addition to being a beer joint, that establishment had a dance hall as well and the place seemed to be the center of the nightlife in Caseta. As a result of his frequent visits to that establishment, he befriended several girls and would meet up with them there.

I was the book-worm type and while I did join them a few times, I never really felt at home in that type of environment. I am reminded of some words in the lyrics to a song titled "Waterfalls" by a group known as TLC. Some specific lyrics in that song apply to me during those "Arbolito" days; "*don't go chasing waterfalls. Please stick to the rivers and the lakes that you're used to . . .*".

Swimming in the Rio Grande River

From time to time when we were growing up, we would visit my grandfather Jose's family in Caseta. We would wind up staying there because my mother and father had errands to do in Caseta or the nearby town of Guadalupe which was about 3 miles away from Caseta. During those extended stays with my father's family, we would group-up with some of my father's half brothers and we would proceed to the Mexico side of the Rio Grande River and swim in the river. The water was murky and muddy but that didn't matter; we had a lot of fun swimming in the river water. Those were the days when the international boundary was not patrolled by the U.S. Border Patrol as intensely as it is now.

When we finished swimming, we would walk back to my grandfather's home. Having dipped in the muddy, murky waters of the river, we were all covered in mud when we arrived back to my grandfather's home. A few pails of water from the outdoor faucet and wah-lah the mud came right-off our skin. Nowadays, kids swim in swimming pools and lifeguards attend to the safety of the kids swimming in the pool. In those days, we didn't know that swimming pools existed. We also didn't think about the danger of drowning. Somehow nobody ever drowned; we were none the wiser.

Wrestling

One of several events that made Caseta important to my parents is that Caseta used have an open-air wrestling arena. My parents would drag Chuy and I along with them to wrestling matches in Caseta during the weekends. I remember that my mother, probably more than my father, used to love to see the wrestling matches; although my father enjoyed them as well. The wrestling matches were held during the weekends in the late afternoons and also during the evenings.

I remember that in every wrestling match there was typically one wrestler that was the popular wrestler and was cheered on by the spectators while the opposing wrestler was not; although he still had a small following. The opposing wrestler was almost always booed and hissed-at by the crowd. The crowds were always animated and each spectator seemed to pick a side; the popular wrester or the unpopular wrestler.

The popular wrestler behaved properly in the wrestling ring while the unpopular wrestler cheated and behaved badly. Many times the opposing unpopular wrestler wore a mask to disguise his face; one never knew who the unpopular wrestler was unless the popular wrestler managed to forcefully remove the unpopular wrestler's mask during the match. The unpopular wrestler was always referred to as "el rúdo" which means "the rude one" in English. The unpopular wrestler indeed usually was rude and discourteous. By the way, the letter ú in the word "rúdo" is pronounced similarly to the letter u in the name Ruth; remember accents matter in Spanish.

During the wrestling matches the spectators would get so excited and into the fight that they would begin booing and egging-on their respective chosen wrestler. I remember my mother getting so into it and becoming so animated that she even threw rolled up balls of newspaper at the unpopular wrestler. She would clench her fists and yell to the popular wrestler the word "pégale" which in English means "hit him". Again, accents matter in Spanish. Anyway, everyone picked sides. It was quite a sight. I am sure my father did the same; however, I don't remember him being as animated as my mother.

I remember that several times my parents dragged us to the wrestling matches in nearby Cd. Juarez. These matches were held in huge enclosed wrestling arenas. The same thing happened. My mother would quickly pick sides, clench her fist and then began booing the unpopular wrestler. Having berated the unpopular wrestler, she would then begin cheering-on the popular wrestler.

By the way, watching wrestling matches on the television set was a past time of my mother in those days as well. I remember she used to cheer-on a popular wrestler on the television by the name of Gory Guerrero. He was the good wrestler and not the "rúdo" wrestler. My mother always sided with the popular wrestler and heaven forbid, never the "rúdo" wrestler. She always seemed to follow the crowd.

I did some research on the reasons why some wrestlers wear masks. It turns out that wrestlers wearing masks is more a Mexican phenomena than a U.S. occurrence. I further learned the reason why many professional wrestlers traditionally wear masks. The reason is that after they wrestle in an area or a "territory", their popularity and drawing ability eventually diminishes. Wearing a mask enables an easy way for a wrestler to begin working in a new area as a "fresh face". Sometimes wrestlers wear masks in one territory and then unmask themselves in another territory in order to keep their two identities separate.

Yes, we went with our parents to wrestling matches in Caseta and Cd. Juarez and yes, my mother sure had fun watching those matches. Some might think that telling stories of my mother and her antics might sound disrespectful. I just hope she doesn't mind me telling these stories from up above. In some ways, this is a story of my mother (chuckle).

Automobile Racing

One event that my parents always looked forward when I was a young boy were the car races in Mexico. Both my father my mother enjoyed the car races. My parents always seemed to be informed ahead of time about major events that occurred across the border in Caseta and the neighboring towns; especially the annual Porvenir-Guadalupe car race.

The races started in the small town of Porvenir which is located across the Rio Grande River from Fort Hancock on the U.S. side. The race then progressed through San Ignacio and finally ended in the little town of Guadalupe for a total run of 18 miles. By the way, the formal name of the town of San Ignacio is "Praxedis G. Guerrro". Anyway, the larger town on the way to the finish line near the town of Guadalupe was San Ignacio. The race cars raced down the middle of the town at lower speeds compared to the higher racing speeds on the open road.

Most of the route consisted of straight road sprinkled with moderate  twisting curves here and there. However, there was one curve that I remember was especially dangerous because it was a very tight curve. Out of curiosity, I measured the angle of the curve using the map shown on the left. The angle was about 125 degrees. By the way, I happen to know a person that used to live in the town of San Ignacio. She was the care giver of my mother-in-law, Ildefonsa, as well as my wife, Socorro, when Socorro was recovering from a stroke. Her name was Leticia. I asked her whether she remembered the Porvenir-Guadalupe races and she did. She remembered the dangerous curve and told me that the curve is known as "la curva de San Miguel".

The reason I am describing this curve is because as a result of the curve being so tight, several race cars that sped along too fast on the curve wound up rolling-over. My parents and many people preferred to park close to that specific curve to observe the race car roll-overs. When a car rolled-over, one could see a huge dust cloud that would signal that a roll-over had occurred. All along the roadway were people watching the car races. The "curva de San Miguel" area was peppered with vendors selling food, snow cones, balloons and other festive wares. It was a carnival-like atmosphere; it was a big event and it was fun.

The yearly car race was an event my parents especially looked forward to because of a particular race car driver that was so expert at racing and so revered that one might say he was considered a legend. That specific car racer always seemed to win the car race year after year. He was a very popular man and was held in high regard. The event was prestigious because of his presence in the event.

Now as a grown up, the man's popularity as a car racer reminds me of the non-human character that had incredible skills at piloting a high-speed vehicle known as a Podracer in the Star Wars movie episode "Phantom Menance". That non-human character's name was Sebulba. Sebulba was the Podracer arch-rival of the young boy by the name of Anakin Skywalker. I took the following from the web: "Sebulba became the star racer of the Galactic Podracing Circuit, based not only on his formidable racing skills but also his penchant for violence. Many fellow Podracers were killed or injured by Sebulba's reckless steering or out-and-out cheating, but Sebulba was far too popular to be blamed or penalized.".

Except for the violence, cheating and killing cited in the description of the Sebulba character, the popular race car driver of the Porvenir-Guadalupe race was every bit as popular as Sebulba. The race car driver was that good. I'm sure my parents knew the name of the popular race car driver but I didn't. Leticia who is the person that used to live in the town of San Ignacio told me that the person's name was Vidal Varela. She even told me that in later years he owned a mechanic shop in Fabens . . . another missing piece of the puzzle found.

The Porous Border

Fast forward to the year 1962 when I was 11 years of age. My father purchased a horse in Caseta or in Guadalupe when we were now living in Fabens. In order to get the horse across the U.S.-Mexico border, he arranged for one of his half-brothers to illegally cross the horse across the river from the Mexico side to the U.S. side at a location 5 miles south from the Caseta-Fabens international bridge.

My father waited on the U.S. side for his half-brother to meet him with the horse. Upon meeting up with him, my father loaded the horse onto a horse trailer and then proceeded to take the horse to our property in Fabens. It was that easy.

Do it today, and the U.S. Customs detection capability will insure that you get caught. In those days, the border was that porous. These are different times now.

Farming Corn and Cotton in Caseta

I remember that my father began a farming business in Caseta during the time when I was about 7 or 8 years of age. The farming business lasted about 3 or 4 years. He leased 20 hectares of land from a person by the name of Aguilera. The small piece of land was equivalent to about 50 acres. The land was situated somewhere between Caseta and the town of Guadalupe on the Mexico side of the border. My grandfather Jose supervised the day to day activities of the farm for him.

The first year that my father leased the land, he planted corn on the land. Of course I was a young boy and really didn't think about it at the time, but it now seems to me that growing corn might have been counterproductive. Looking back, I am not sure that corn was a profitable commodity to grow mainly because I don't feel there was a large enough market for corn at that time. I could be wrong. Anyway, I never knew if growing corn was profitable to him.

During the next succeeding two years, my father switched from growing corn to growing cotton. My father again leased the same amount of land in the same area as before. Having grown up on a farm, I am familiar with the different types of equipment that are required to grow cotton. Tractors, cultivators, plows and the like are required. My father didn't own this type of equipment so it may be that he rented the equipment he needed to grow cotton. The cotton was picked by hand at the time; a mechanical cotton picker machine was not used.

I remember that when harvest time arrived, the cotton had to be transported in cotton trailers to the cotton gin where the cotton could be processed. All I knew about a cotton gin in those days was that the large cotton ginning facility would process the cotton and the result were bales of cotton. A cotton gin is a facility equipped with machines that separates the cotton fibers from their seeds and then processes the cotton so that the end result is a compressed bale of cotton. A bale is bundle of cotton tightly wrapped and bound with metal hoops. In those days, I didn't know these details.

At any rate, I remember accompanying my father on his trips to Caseta after work at the Ryan farm. Several times, my father needed to transport a trailer full of cotton to the cotton gin. I remember that the cotton gin was located toward the direction of Cd. Juarez but not actually in Cd. Juarez. It must have been located on the road somewhere prior to the location of what is now known as Zaragoza. At any rate, it seemed like a long trip to the gin. We would start out from the farm in Caseta and travel slowly along the way to the gin. We must have traveled at about 30 miles per hour. It took hours to arrive at the gin.

When we arrived at the cotton gin, my father would proceed to park the trailer on the large weigh scale and then he would enter the office adjacent to the weigh scale of the cotton gin. I didn't really think about it at the time, but now I know that the trailer together with the cotton had to be weighed prior to having the cotton removed from the trailer. Although I don't remember, the empty trailer had to have been weighed again so that the weight of the trailer could be subtracted from the gross weight of the cotton/trailer combination to obtain the net weight of the cotton.

Anyway, after the initial cotton/trailer weighing, my father would then pull the trailer to a specific place on the gin property underneath a large metal tube. A gin worker would then board the trailer and would begin to use the large metal tube to vacuum the cotton from the trailer to then transfer it to the gin facility. Once that process was completed, the empty trailer would be weighed and the weight of the trailer would be subtracted from the cotton/trailer weight to obtain the net weight of the cotton. Somehow, my father got paid for the cotton on the basis of the net weight of the cotton.

We now traveled back to Caseta to return the empty trailer to the farm. When we arrived at Caseta, the trailer was unhitched from the pickup truck. It was now about 11:00 pm at night and the Fabens- Caseta crossing bridge was now closed. Remember, the closing time for the bridge was 9:00 p.m. nightly. There now was no choice but to make the trip to Zaragoza, cross to Ysleta on the U.S. side and then return back to the Ryan farm past Fabens. We would arrive at the farm somewhere about 12:00 midnight or 1:00 am in the morning.

These were long days. The cotton was harvested during the fall season so these trips took place during school days. I can't remember how I managed school during the succeeding school day after those trips, but somehow I did manage.

My father had enough work to do on the Ryan farm but he still devoted his evening hours each day to the farm in Caseta. Sometimes my father was lucky enough to work only half days on Saturdays. He would proceed to Caseta in the afternoons to tend to the farm in Caseta. My father made more money than the average farm worker on the Ryan farm but I don't think it was much more. I make that statement because of the information I found in the labor time booklets that show he earned $.60 per hour in 1952. The men he supervised in 1952 earned $.50 per hour.

In order to understand how much money my father earned on the Ryan farm later on in 1958 when he was farming in Caseta, I assumed a 5 percent salary increase per year. I calculated the amount of his hourly wage in 1958 from the 1952 information. It calculated out to be about $.77 per hour. It wasn't much. In addition to the fact that he earned a small amount of money, there always seemed to be family strife between my father and my mother as a result of my father providing money from his salary to my grandfather Jose's family.

My father's extended family lived in Caseta and the family was very poor. My father certainly earned a wage at the Ryan farm and indeed may have been able to financially help out his extended family as best he could with that farm wage. But somehow I think that what he earned wasn't enough to help. That may be the reason why my father created the farm in Caseta. I think he created the farm in Caseta so that his extended family could make a living. That worked but only for 3 or 4 years.

One Foot in Mexico, the Other in the U.S.

As I indicated before, Caseta represented a comfort zone to my parents especially to my father. They were drawn to Caseta for a variety of reasons; extended family, good friends, compadres and even farming. It's as if they kept one foot in Mexico while venturing to plant the other foot in the United States.

The Farm and Airplanes

Life on the Ryan farm when I was 7 or 8 years old; was a life full of adventures. While living on the Ryan farm, we were fortunate to be exposed to equipment and machinery. In a twist of fate, Chuy and I were even exposed to airplanes. This piece describes how we came to know about the exciting field of airplanes.

I remember that when we lived in the home adjacent to the sand hills, my father drove a small, red, farm-owned pickup truck. The pickup truck was the type that had rear external wheel wells that protruded on each side of the open cargo bay. The cab doors on each side bore the Ryan farm markings but it also had a logo that showed a black silhouette of the head of an eagle. I remember that around the eagle head silhouette was wording that contained the name of a chemical company. I don't remember for sure but I think the name was "Ortho". Jimmy Ryan drove a car that also bore the same eagle's head silhouette and markings but no Ryan farm markings.

I searched the web to find that specific Ortho eagle's head silhouette emblem that appeared on my father's truck and on Jim Ryan's car but I was unsuccessful. So I drew up the emblem from memory. The emblem is shown here on the left.

Today it seems to me that in addition to the farm and the lumber company in Fabens, Jimmy Ryan either owned or was a sales representative of an agricultural chemical distributing company whose name, I think, was "Ortho". It could have been Ortho Chemical Company.

There was a period of time when my father would work during specific days in the mornings at the Fabens airport. That work consisted of loading powdered pesticide products onto crop dusting airplanes. There was probably a business arrangement between Jimmy Ryan's agricultural chemical company and the owner of the crop dusting airplane such that the labor to load the airplane with pesticide was part of the chemical sale.

When we lived on the Ryan farm, from time to time, an airplane would appear on the horizon and fly in a circular pattern above the area of the Ryan farm. The airplane was easily distinguishable because of its bright yellow color.

After having circled above, the airplane would swoop down and fly just above the cotton plants in the fields. As the airplane was traveling in close proximity to the cotton plants, a powdery substance would begin to exit from underneath the airplane. The powdery substance would form swirls at each end of the wings as the airplane flew along its path. When it neared the end of the cotton field, the powdery substance would stop exiting from the airplane's underside and the airplane would quickly ascend into the air. The airplane would then circle around high in the air and then re-align itself with the cotton field and proceed to swoop down again toward the cotton field to repeat the process but now in the opposite direction.

After each pass, the next succeeding pass over the cotton field took place a distance of a little more than one wingspan over to one side from the previous pass. In this way, little by little, the entire field would ultimately be dusted. The airplane kept repeating theses passes until it seemed to run out of the powdery substance and then the airplane would disappear over the horizon, flying back toward the direction it had come from initially.

About an hour later, the airplane would return and resume its back and forth passes across the cotton field. At times, the airplane would swoop down close enough that we could even see the person inside the airplane. If we were lucky, the person in the airplane would wave at us and we would wave our arms to make sure he could see us.

The powdery substance that the airplane was placing on the farm field had an odd smell. One couldn't help but breathe in some of the powder that temporarily hung in the air. The powdery substance had a funny weird taste. We knew the powdery substance was some sort of poison but that didn't matter to us. We didn't pay attention to it; it was exciting just see the airplane flying back and forth. As I indicated before, I was perhaps 7 or 8 years of age when I first saw these airplanes. My wife, Socorro, as a child, also lived on a farm near Fabens and she too has similar memories of watching crop dusting airplanes.

I remember that during the summer seasons, my father would go to work very early in the morning. He would start to get ready for work at about 4:00 am in the mornings when it was still dark outside. I remember that this occurred only during certain days of the week. It didn't seem normal to me to see my father go to work at that early hour of the morning.

One evening during dinner, he told Chuy and I to make sure to wake up early during the next morning because we were going to go with him to work. He told us to get our clothes and hats ready before we went to bed. I remember that my father would always insist that Chuy and I wear our hats.

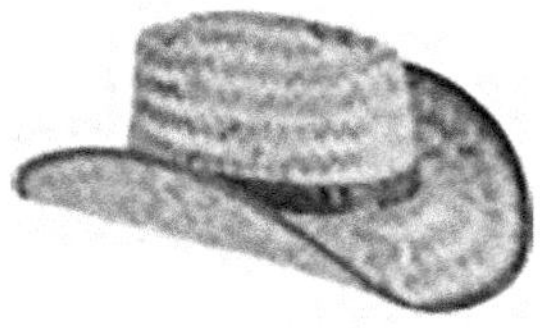

I don't exactly remember what prompted my father to take us with him. It might have been that we asked him previously why he went to work so early or maybe he just decided on his own to take us with him on that following morning.

As to the hats that we wore, my father would purchase our hats from a store in the little Mexican border town of "Caseta". The hats were made of woven straw fitted with a fabric binding sewn all around the entire edge of the brim. The type of hat that my father purchased for us is shown on the left. My father always wore more rugged cowboy hats during working hours. He was used to them and maybe that's why he always insisted that we wear our "cheapie" straw hats.

Very early the next morning we heard my father rustling around the kitchen and we quickly woke up. With great anticipation, Chuy and I quickly began to dress ourselves. When we finished dressing, we followed my father outside to the pickup truck. The sun hadn't yet risen and therefore it was still dark when we left our house.

My father drove the pickup truck to Fabens and then made his way to the small airport located on the outskirts of Fabens. He parked the truck about 100 feet from where many small airplanes were parked. They were all tied down either with ropes or chains to the ground. There was a variety of different airplanes all parked in a row, side by side. Most of them were parked underneath a huge "tejaban" that was used to afford the airplanes protection from the sun. "Tejaban" is a word my father used when referring to a protective structure consisting of a corrugated sheet metal roof supported by metal columns.

As soon as my father turned off the pickup truck's engine, he told us to stay in the truck and to stay out of the way. After admonishing us, he exited from the truck and proceeded toward the parked airplane that was painted an all yellow color. The airplane looked similarly to the airplane we had previously seen flying over the cotton fields at the Ryan farm. The airplane was the type of airplane that had the main wings mounted above the location where the pilot sat. The airplane had two wheels located

toward the front of the airplane under the pilot's compartment. A smaller wheel was located at the tail underneath the rudder and tail wing. We didn't know it then but that type of airplane is called a "tail-dragger" airplane. And of course, we also didn't know all of the terms being used here in this narrative to describe the components of the airplanes.

My father began to un-tie the tie-down ropes that held the airplane in place while in the parked position. Both the right and left wings were each tied-down to metal anchors on the ground. The small wheel at the rear of the airplane was also tied-down to an anchor.

Shortly thereafter he was joined by another man that had also parked his vehicle close by. In the darkness, both the man and my father pushed the airplane from the parking area out to an open area of the airport. Once the airplane was in a stationary position, they proceeded to open a rectangular lid on top of the airplane's fuselage. The rectangular lid was located just behind the intersection of the fuselage and the main wing. The lid served as the cover to a storage hopper inside the fuselage.

They began to open pesticide bags and then proceeded to pour the contents of the bags into the hopper within the fuselage. I don't remember how we came to know that the large paper bags contained pesticides. I do remember my father saying the word "veneno" when referring to those bags. The word "venéno" means "posion" in English. As before, accents matter in Spanish.

In addition to the large propeller connected to the engine up front, a small propeller that measured about 4 to 6 inches in length was located underneath the fuselage just below where the pilot sat. I never knew the reason for that small propeller. Now as I am writing this piece, it occurs to me that the small propeller might have been interconnected to a small auger inside the pesticide hopper that acted to move the powdered pesticide at the hopper bottom to the hopper exit port. About the time that my father and the other man finished filling the compartment with pesticide powder, the sun was coming up on the horizon.

Another man arrived; he was of Anglo descent. He spoke with my father and then proceeded to board the airplane. The man sat in the airplane's seat compartment. The man then positioned his aviator hat fitted with goggles onto his head. The aviator hat seemed to be constructed of a type of heavy canvas cloth in the form of a round cap with large earflaps, a chin strap and again goggles. The man then positioned the seat belt over his shoulders and around his torso.

We observed that my father then walked to the front of the airplane towards where the propeller was located. The man inside the airplane motioned to my father a thumbs-up signal. Then with both hands, my father grasped the propeller blade that was positioned over his head and using a combination of his body weight and arm strength, he pulled the blade down in one quick, swift motion. He immediately moved away and to the right side of the airplane. Now as a grownup I know that manually starting an aircraft engine in this manner is known as "hand propping". Although it didn't seem so at the time, "hand propping" is a dangerous way to start an aircraft engine.

After having "hand propped" the propeller, the airplane engine then started to sputter and the propeller blade began to rotate in a somewhat jerking manner. After a few seconds, the propeller began to spin smoothly of its own accord with the engine noise now clearly audible. The airplane sat there with the propeller turning while at the same time blowing gusts of air towards its rear.

After about 5 minutes of warm up time, the engine noise suddenly increased and the propeller began to turn even faster. All of a sudden, the airplane began to lunge forward. As it made its way forward, it suddenly turned away from us and proceeded toward the runway. A huge gust of wind blew towards us as we sat inside the pickup truck. Even today in my mind's eye, I can still see the rear of the airplane as it moved further and further away from us. I remember my father glancing toward us probably to make sure that we hadn't been blown away by the wind generated by the airplane.

From our vantage point inside the truck cab, we were watching everything. The airplane proceeded to a location on the runway approximately 100 to 150 feet away. It turned to align itself along the direction of the runway and as the engine noise increased even more, the airplane began to slowly move forward. Then it began to speed-up faster and faster. As it traveled down the runway, it became smaller and smaller in the distance and when it reached the far end of the runway we could see the airplane rising into the air.

After having confirmed that the airplane was airborne, my father and the other man returned to the business of the pesticide bags. They began to carry more pesticide powder bags to the location where the airplane had previously been parked.

About an hour from the time the airplane took off, the yellow airplane re-appeared in the distance, high in the sky. It flew to the far end of the runway and began to descend until the wheels touched the runway. Little by little the airplane seemed to grow larger and larger as it came nearer and nearer to our location. Once at the end of the runway, it made its way toward our location and it then came to a complete stop at the same location it had previously been parked.

After the propeller stopped, my father and the man helping my father began to again fill the airplane's pesticide hopper. This repeating cycle of the airplane being loaded, then flying off went on until about 9:00 or 10:00 am in the morning and then all three of us would ride back to our home on the farm.

I was about 7 or 8 years of age when my father used to take Chuy and I to the airport to watch him load pesticide onto the airplanes. In subsequent trips to the airport, my father allowed Chuy and I to exit from the pickup truck to see and touch the airplane. To my surprise, the airplane seemed to be made of a type of rigid fabric and its construction seemed rather flimsy to me. When the airplane was not operating, my father would even allow us to sit in the pilot's seat but with strict warnings not to touch any of the controls. In retrospect, even had we accidentally messed with the controls, the engine would never have started because the propeller had to be "hand propped" in order for the engine to start. Anyway, as soon as the pilot arrived, we would then be told to go back to the truck and watch from within the pickup truck cab.

Chuy and I looked forward to the days when my father would take us with him to the airport. I remember that every night at dinner either Chuy or I would ask my father if we were going to the airport the next morning. Whatever his answer, Chuy and I were always alert in the mornings so that at a moment's notice we would be ready to go to the airport.

Going to the airport to watch the goings on was exciting. All of this occurred during the summer months because I remember that the ambient temperature would begin to increase and the mornings would start to get hotter and hotter. I remember that there wasn't any pressure to get ready for school during those days. We would wear our woven straw hats to keep from getting sun burnt.

By the way, one might ask why the pesticide dusting was performed only in mornings. I don't know for sure but I believe the reason the dusting was done in the mornings was because the morning dew on the leaves of the cotton plants provided more adhesion of the pesticide powder onto the leaves and of course, the cotton bolls.

I remember that during that time, Chuy grew to become an expert at building makeshift toys. As I indicated before, during the airplane days, I was 7 or 8 years of age and Chuy was 9 or 10 years of age. One day after returning from the airport, Chuy somehow located a wooden crate. The crate's longer dimension consisted of flat wooden slats. The width of the slats was about 2 or 3 inches and their thickness was about 1/4 or 3/8 of an inch. The ends of each slat were nailed to two wooden and thicker end pieces of the crate.

With a hammer and a saw, Chuy disassembled the crate. After some sawing and nailing with a hammer, Chuy fashioned an airplane out of wood that was somewhat similar to the airplane we kept seeing at the airport. The 3 inch wide by 24 inch length slat became the main overhead wing. A smaller cut-up slat became the tail wing. The rudder was made from a smaller piece of thin wood. The fuselage had been sawed off from a 1 inch x 2 inch piece of wood. The propeller was a small piece of wood nailed into the end of the fuselage closest to the main overhead wing. The center hole at the middle of the propeller was oversized so that it could spin around the nail that was hammered into the front end of the fuselage. Finally, two larger nails were hammered into the underside of the fuselage at an opposing angle to each other. These two larger nails underneath the fuselage simulated the main strut wheels of the airplane; of course without actual rubber wheels.

The more difficult thing about these makeshift airplanes was keeping the vertical rudder attached to the fuselage. We didn't know about "Elmer's

glue" at the time or about grooving the back part of the fuselage to force-fit the rudder onto the fuselage. So Chuy improvised by nailing four smaller nails vertically in the fuselage section where the rudder was supposed to go. He would then push the wooden rudder downward by applying vertical pressure so that the rudder would fit snuggly in between the two nails on one side and the other two nails on the other side of the rudder. It wasn't pretty but it's all he could do.

While writing this piece I constructed a small wooden airplane as an example of the type of airplane we used to construct when Chuy and I were boys on the farm. The photograph on the left shows that wooden airplane. There you have it. Our first airplane and it was Chuy that did it.

I was never satisfied with the two larger nails that we hammered onto the fuselage to simulate the strut wheels. This just never seemed to be right. I always felt that somehow there had to be a way to make or find rubber wheels that could make the airplane look more like the airplane we saw at the airport. I was always watchful wherever we went in hopes that I could find suitable wheels for our airplanes. I never did find a suitable solution to the wheel problem.

I can't remember whether Chuy told me about his plans to build the first toy airplane prior to doing it or whether he just did it and I just followed along. I do remember that the initial airplane gave rise to the construction of a fleet of airplanes. And I do remember that I too constructed my own airplanes after having watched Chuy do it.

Later on, the airplanes became double wing biplanes. We built airports and airport runways in the sand. It was fun playing with our airplanes. We didn't know the terms used to describe the parts of an airplane such as fuselage, rudder or hand propping; it didn't matter. All we knew about the components of an airplane was that my father would refer to the wing as an "ála" and the propeller as an "élis". Remember accents are important in Spanish. While writing this piece, I checked for the correct spelling of the Spanish word for propeller and it is "hélice". Yes, we were kids that lacked the sophistication of knowing the correct word spellings.

I remember that in later years during my grade school years, I would visit the Fabens County library. Needless to say, I always gravitated to the library section where I could find books about airplanes. I'm pretty sure that very few grade schoolers, if any at the time, knew who Curtis LeMay was; political views aside.

My first experience flying in an airplane was in a Boeing 707 from Los Angeles to El Paso in 1970 when I was 19 years old. As a result of my travels while working in the water treatment business, I've since flown as a passenger in a variety of airliners including Lockheed L-1011s and McDonald Douglas DC10s. I never flew on a McDonald Douglas 747.

When I was 49 years of age, I took flying lessons on small Cessna airplanes. We flew above Fabens and even the Ryan farm during those flying lessons. Even now as a grownup during my later years in life, when I find myself inside a toy store, I still gravitate toward the toy airplane section. I like to see the toy airplanes because today's toy airplanes are so life-like. I've never been a model airplane collector but I do enjoy looking at the toy airplanes in the stores. It brings back memories of the time when Chuy and I made our own toy airplanes. The sophistication of today's toy airplanes make me wonder what it would have been like had Chuy and I been able to play with these airplanes of today instead of the awkward wooden airplanes we used to make.

A lot has changed since I was 7 years of age when those little high-wing tail dragger airplanes were used for crop dusting. Today we still refer to agricultural airplanes as "crop dusters" even though powdered pesticides are no longer used. Instead, agricultural airplanes now spray liquid pesticides.

With a little help from the internet, I found that the Piper Cub model J3 seems to be very similar to the airplane we first saw at the Fabens airport way back then. Its specifications are reported to be 65 HP engine power, 75 mph cruise speed and 1,220 lbs. empty weight. Compare that to today's low-wing airplane specifically designed for agricultural use that is manufactured by a company by the name of Air Tractor. The specifications for the model

AT-502B manufactured by Air Tractor are 750 HP engine power, 154 mph cruise speed and 4,546 lbs. empty weight. What a difference time makes.

Later in 1968 when he was 19 years of age, Chuy graduated from Fabens High School. Soon after graduation, he moved to the Huntington Beach, California area to start his life there. I remember Chuy telling me that he had taken flying lessons in California. Although he attended Golden West College to pursue a professional degree, life's pressures didn't allow it.

Chuy passed away in November of 2014 at 65 years of age. Prior to his passing, he worked at Northrup Grumman Corporation in Hawthorne, California for about 20 years. Northrup Grumman is the company that developed and built the B-2 Stealth Bomber. The B-2 Stealth Bomber was built in Pico Rivera, California only 20 miles away from Hawthorne. As a child, Chuy constructed those awkward little wooden airplanes and at the end, he worked for a giant in the aerospace industry; a bittersweet memory.

The Multitude – Canal Fish

Fast forward to the time when I owned the company by the name of Fluid Process Systems and my father worked for me. One day, I happened to remember something that had to do with the irrigation canal near the town of Tornillo. During that time, my father worked in the fabrication shop at the company I owned. The manufacturing shop was immediately adjacent to my office. As a result of that proximity, I was able to converse with my father frequently; mostly about work but sometimes about matters having to do with family.

One day during his lunch hour, when he was eating his lunch sitting there in the shop, I happened to come by and began to converse with him. I remembered a certain occurrence when we lived on the farm and I proceeded to ask him about it. He refreshed my memory and the following is an account of that conversation.

One day when we lived in the home beside the sand hills, it happened that my father was attempting to find the irrigation canal supervisor which everyone knew as "el canalero". In a previous section, I indicated that the word "canalero" means "irrigation canal supervisor" in English.

The reason that my father was attempting to locate the canal supervisor was to obtain information from him regarding the approximate upcoming scheduled date when the Ryan farm would be allowed to irrigate its cotton fields. The irrigation canal supervisor's responsibility was to keep an eye on the irrigation water that flowed into the canals from the Rio Grande. It was his job to manage the distribution of the irrigation water to each individual farm. His responsibility included informing the farm owners when their turn came to use the irrigation water for irrigation. The irrigation canal supervisor frequently drove up and down along the dirt roadway adjacent to the water distribution canals.

Anyway, as my father was driving down the canal road attempting to locate the canal supervisor, he happened to drive upon a road bridge that crossed over the canal. The road bridge on the canal was on a paved roadway near the town of Tornillo. The canal was not full of water at that time but it did have a depression where non-flowing, stagnant water had puddled. The water was probably left over from the previous irrigation cycle.

As he drove by that area, he noticed movements within the large puddle of water; that caught his eye. He had gone passed the puddled area somewhat so he stopped. He drove the pickup truck in reverse and then came to a stop immediately adjacent to the puddle.

He saw that the movement of the puddled water was due to the presence of numerous fish. He stepped off the truck and walked down the slope to the canal floor. As he neared the puddle, splashing began in earnest; it was a multitude of fish that was causing the vigorous splashing. His immediate thought was to catch as many of the fish as he could. He then realized that he was going to need help catching them; there were just too many fish. He knew that once he caught the fish, he wouldn't have any way to carry them back home so he decided to go back home to obtain several metal tubs in which to place the fish. When he arrived back home, he told us about the fish he had found in the irrigation canal and then told Chuy and I to get several tubs ready to take with us back to the location where he found the fish. My father was hurrying us along because he didn't want to risk somebody else finding them and taking them all. We hurried up as best we could and loaded the tubs into the cargo bay of my father's pickup truck.

Chuy and I climbed aboard into the cab of the pickup truck and my father then began to drive toward where the fish were located. As we drove along, my father began to explain in detail what he found and our excitement grew; we were ready to catch fish. When we arrived, I saw "a ton" of fish swimming in the puddle! Chuy and I immediately rolled up our pant legs in order to avoid getting them wet. We entered the puddle and it soon became apparent that it would be necessary to remove our pants altogether. Both Chuy and I removed our pants and we were left with only our underwear, of course with our shirts on.

We re-entered the puddle and began to grab at the fish. The fish were so numerous that we could even feel them touch the bottom part  of our legs and feet. My father did not wade into the puddle and he remained outside the puddle. He instructed Chuy and I to grab the fish and then throw them toward him so that he could then place the fish in the tubs. Soon thereafter, we began the process of grabbing the fish with our hands. It was tricky because the fish were so slippery that grabbing them with our hands took some care.

Anyway, we grabbed them one by one and began throwing them toward my father. Little by little even our shirts were getting wet but we didn't care. It was a ton of fun placing our hands in the water and slowly sneaking up on the fish, grabbing them and immediately throwing them toward my father. When the first tub was half full, it became apparent that the weight of the fish inside the tub was going to make the tub way too difficult to carry up the slope of the canal levee. So we decided to place the tubs in the cargo bed of my father's pickup truck and then collect the fish in one tub placed next to the puddle.

When the tub next to the puddle was filled halfway, Chuy would then help my father carry the half-filled tube up the slope. They would then empty the half-filled tub's contents into the tubs already in the cargo bed of the truck. This went on until at last all three tubs in the truck's cargo bed were filled. The remaining half-filled tub was then carried up the slope and placed in the cargo bed of the truck. At last we were finished.

Chuy and I were a mess. The activity involved catching the fish with our bare hands. The muddy water had splashed up to our faces and even our hair. My father was laughing at us because of our messy appearance. Upon seeing my father laughing at us, Chuy walked back down the slope of the canal and then to the puddle. He grabbed a tin can that was half floating in the water and then quickly swung the tin can, still in his hand, in such a way that the water inside the tin can flung toward my father. My father was no dummy; he quickly side-stepped to the side in order to avoid the water. Chuy was having fun with my father.

My father then told Chuy to come back up and away from the puddle. Chuy came back up. By then I had already placed my pants back on. Chuy then did the same. We were all done. The mission was accomplished.

When we arrived back to our home on the Ryan Farm, we helped our father remove 2 of the 4 tubs of fish from the cargo bed of the truck. He then told us that he was going to drive over to see if Esteban Gutierrez and Roberto Martinez would like to have the rest of the fish. When he left, we began to de-scale the fish. The next step was to gut and clean the insides of the fish. It took us a long time to do that. By the way, the fish we caught were what are called carp fish.

Carp fish are different from other fish. Carp fish has exterior scales on its body, so the fish is first de-scaled before it is gutted. Carp flesh are also very spiny and bony and can be dangerous to eat due to the fact that the tiny spines and bones when eaten could wind up lodged in a person's esophagus. As a result of the tiny spines and bones, my mother always over-fried the fish to provide some insurance that the many tiny bones could easily be detected and removed. That even wasn't enough. Suffice it to say that one had to just be very careful to pick the flesh from the bones. One might say that carp was a poor man's fish.

To my father, finding the fish and extracting the fish from the water that day was a big thing. My father had to provide for us and I guess the free fish was a break he needed. The fish, although difficult to eat, did provide sustenance for our family. To Chuy and I, pulling the fish out of the water was a lot of fun. I had never seen so many fish at one time. The fish probably numbered in the area of 200 to 300 fish; it was a multitude a fish.

In the end, Chuy and I lent my father a hand because he felt that taking that many fish to our home was important. If it was important to him then it was important to me. This story serves as a small remembrance of my father.

The Honest Truth

About a week prior to Christmas when I was about 8 years old, my parents asked Chuy and I to board the car because we were going on a trip to Fabens. Sara, my father's half sister, remained at our house; taking care of Irma, Gloria, Mario and Graciela. As was customary, we obeyed our parents and boarded the car. We still lived in the home beside the sand hills on the Ryan farm.

Anyway, we traveled along to Fabens. When we arrived in Fabens, I remember that my father parked the car in front of the grocery store known as the Star Food Mart. Chuy and I were seated in the back seat of the car and my parents were seated up front. After parking the car, my father and my mother turned around to look at us while still seated in the front of the car. They both stared at Chuy and I as if needing to tell us something. They kept staring at us for quite a while as if not knowing what to say.

My father hemmed and hawed something about Christmas. My mother also chimed in talking about this and that having to do with Christmas. Very abruptly, my mother said "Chuy y Chava, quiero decirles que no hay Santo Clos". Her words translated to English mean "Chuy and Chava, I want to tell you that there is no Santa Claus". My father also repeated a semblance of the same words while still looking at us.

This revelation hit me by surprise and I believe Chuy was also surprised as well. I remember both he and I remained motionless for quite some time, trying to understand what had just happened. Down deep inside I was shocked. I couldn't believe it. I didn't want to show my true feelings about there not being a Santa Claus; I sat there trying to appear as if what they had just said was not important. In an effort to save face, I responded "si, yo sé" which in English means "yes, I know". Bear in mind, I was 8 and Chuy was 10 years old; we may have been a little too old to still believe in Santa Claus.

Anyway, Chuy then chimed in and said "si, ya sabíamos" which in English means "yes, we already knew". I am positive Chuy felt the same shock that I did. We hadn't asked questions during my parent's explanation about Santa Claus and my parents didn't proceed to explain further. Soon thereafter, they stepped off the car and we followed them inside the store without further comment in relation to Santa Claus.

Now knowing that there was no Santa Claus was hard for me. It took me some time to fully reconcile myself to the fact that Santa Claus wasn't real. I never asked Chuy about how he felt but I'm almost sure he was impacted to the same degree that I was.

I recently asked my wife, Socorro, if she remembered us having told our own kids that there wasn't a Santa Claus. She told me that we didn't have to; our kids just grew up and they just came to know that Santa Claus didn't exist. Socorro and I never had to do the deed that my father and my mother had to do.

Today I still remember the day when my father brought the car to a stop in front of the Star Food Mart in Fabens. While still in the car, both my mother and my father turned around to look at Chuy and I. They proceeded to tell us the honest truth . . . "there is no Santa Claus" (Chuckle). The real Santa Claus is in one's heart.

A Parent's Learning Experience

Fast forward to the year of 2006, when I was 55 years of age and the Christmas season was upon us. It had been a good year and I felt strong and vibrant. I had lots of energy that year.

During that year during the Christmas holiday, I decided to dress up in a Santa Claus costume. I wanted to surprise my grandchildren. I wanted to have them see Santa Claus delivery gifts in real life at their homes. I wasn't sure about the specific year when I did that and so I asked Socorro if she remembered the year when that happened. She reminded me that it occurred two years after the movie "Polar Express" was showing in the movie theaters. I immediately checked the web to see when the movie was showing and yes, I found that the movie indeed was showing in the year 2004. So that confirms that my Santa Claus experience took place during the year 2006.

I had never done this before but I figured I'd do it to reinforce my grandchildren's belief in the goodness of Santa Claus. Every child hears about Santa Claus, but which child actually sees Santa Claus in real life coming to their home to actually leave them their Christmas gifts?

My plan was to show up at my grandchildren's homes between 1:00 a.m. and 2:00 a.m., in the wee hours of the morning. I am the type of person that doesn't like to stay up past 10:00 p.m. and so I was uneasy about staying up so late but in the end, I decided it was for a good cause.

About a week prior to Christmas Eve, I told my children about my Santa Claus plan; they all agreed to the plan. I purchased a Santa Claus outfit. By the way, during that time, Carla my niece, and her two children were living with Gracie, my sister. I told Gracie and Carla about my plans regarding my grandchildren. I offered to do the same with Carla's children; Gracie and Carla accepted.

That Christmas Eve, I reminded Adrian, Amanda, Andy and Carla about my coming to their homes after midnight. I reminded them to leave the doors unlocked so that I could enter without having to ring the door bell or knock on the door. I told them that I would carry muffled jingle bells with me. As soon as I entered their homes, I would un-muffle the jingle bells so that the gentle ringing of the bells would alert them that Santa Claus had entered their homes.

As agreed, just past the midnight hour that Christmas morning, I dressed up in the Santa Claus costume. The first home on the list was Amanda's home which sits across the street from where we live. I had Socorro park our car some distance away so as to enable a quick getaway without being noticed by Amanda's kids. I then instructed her that as soon as I exited from Amanda's home that she and I were to quietly board the car and that she was to drive slowly forward without turning on the car's headlights. Socorro agreed.

Socorro accompanied me to my daughter Amanda's home and she waited just outside the door. Now before going in, I removed my glasses, because after all, Santa Claus doesn't wear glasses. I handed them to Socorro for safe keeping. Anyway, I un-muffled the jingle bells to make sure that upon my moving around, they would jingle. I had previously prepared several empty boxes and had placed them inside a big Santa Claus bag. Prior to entering Amanda's home, I quietly lobed the big bag full of empty boxes over my shoulder and then went in.

I walked toward the location of the decorated Christmas tree making sure that the jingle bells could be easily heard. In fact, I rustled the bells with my hands to insure that they'd ring a little louder. I kept focused on making movements, feigning placing gifts under the tree while all the time trying to look through the corner of my eye to see if Alex, Ana or Ben, my grandchildren, were peeking in. I wasn't wearing my glasses and so it was difficult to see if my grandchildren were peeking in. I proceeded without confirmation that they were there; went through the motions anyway and then slowly walked to the entrance door and then exited.

Socorro and I then made a mad dash down the street toward where Socorro had parked the car. We boarded the car; she started the car and then we slowly drove some distance without turning-on the car's headlights. We finally breathed a sigh of relief. I asked Socorro if she had seen the kids peeking-in and she said she hadn't. So 1 out of 4 done. By the way, Amanda later told me that Ben in particular, had become so scared that he didn't even venture to peek-in to see Santa Claus. He had remained hidden under the bed's covers with fright. I was saddened to hear that Ben had experienced a frightening moment and not a good memorable experience.

After having visited Amanda's home, Socorro and I then proceeded to drive to Andy's home and we repeated the same Santa Claus visit. I recently spoke with Andy about that episode. He reminded me that at the time, he only had Alicia and Aleyna. Abby and Ariana had not yet been born. I needed him to remind me about Alicia's and Aleyna's reaction to having seen Santa Claus in their home during that Christmas.

Andy told me that yes indeed Alicia and Aleyna both saw Santa Claus. He told me that he was holding Alicia in his arms when they both peeked-in to see me around their Christmas tree. When Alicia saw me, she was so shocked that she quickly reached with both hands toward the nearby corner of the wall and then pulled herself toward the corner to escape from seeing Santa Claus. It was a knee-jerk reaction on her part. Aleyna, on the other hand, just stood there motionless, interested in watching Santa Claus.

Then on to Adrian's home and again I went into his home and became Santa Claus. Socorro hung in there by me; I think she too was having fun doing this.

Anyway, Adrian recently told me that Araceli was in the 3rd grade at the time when Santa Claus came a calling; she was 8 years old. I couldn't remember the details of Araceli's reaction to my visit. I asked Adrian if Araceli had in fact seen me when I went to their home dressed as Santa Claus that morning.

Adrian confirmed that she indeed had seen Santa Claus during that visit. He indicated that when he heard the jingle bells jingling, he prompted Araceli to go and see who was making the noise. He and Araceli peeked-in to see me. Araceli was so excited at the sight of now seeing Santa Claus in her house that Adrian feared she might make a noise. Adrian motioned to her by placing his forefinger vertically over his mouth to signal that she should not make any noise. Araceli motioned back to Adrian in the same manner to communicate to Adrian that she understood that she was to remain quiet and was not make any noise. Adrian told me that she could hardly contain herself; he was having trouble keeping her still. When I started to leave from the area where their decorated Christmas tree was located, Adrian told Araceli to quickly return back to her bedroom so as not to be seen by Santa Claus.

Knowing Araceli as a little girl and how animated she used to get when excited about something, I can picture her in my mind just wanting to crawl out of her skin at the sight of Santa Claus in her house. I will never forget that image of her.

During a recent conversation with Araceli, now at 22 years of age, she recalled the time when she saw Santa Claus in her home. She indicated that she told everyone at school that she had seen Santa Claus at her home. She also told me that she felt special because the other kids hadn't seen Santa Claus at their homes; she was the only one that did.

Anyway, after having visited Araceli's home, Socorro and I then drove to Fabens. When we arrived in Fabens, I went into Gracie's home and did the same thing. By then, I was a master at it. This time, while I was feigning placing the gifts under the tree, through the corner of my eye, I saw both Mia and Vince, Carla's little children, peeking-in from the adjoining room. I finished, exited and that was it; another successful venture.

It is our family custom that all our children and grandchildren get together at our home during mid-morning on Christmas day to exchange gifts amongst ourselves. My kids were giving me the high five for having done what I did. They thanked me.

I never did that again; I should have. Parents who read this memoir should consider this as a learning experience and should do the same with their own children or grandchildren. It makes for wonderful memories. Remember, Santa Claus is in one's own heart.

Having masqueraded as Santa Claus brought back good memories of my Santa Claus years when I was a child on the Ryan farm. I remember that my parents would always wind up taking us to visit their friend's families during Christmas Eve. We'd spend Christmas Eve at their friend's homes. It seems strange that we used to spend Christmas Eve at other people's homes because now all our children and grandchildren spend their Christmas Eve's at our home; as it should be.

On another subject, I am reminded of the time when Adrian as a little boy wrote a letter to Santa Claus. Socorro showed me the letter he wrote to Santa Claus asking for this and that. She asked me to write a reply so that Adrian would know that Santa did receive his letter. It turned out that Santa Claus used a red marker to write the letter. Of course it wasn't Santa Claus; it was me. Without thinking, I used a red marker which at that time was my customary way of writing notes that stood out. I learned that my employees paid more attention to notes containing red colored text than notes written in black or blue ink.

Anyway, when Adrian received the letter from Santa Claus, he commented to Socorro that Santa Claus's writing seemed a lot like mine. It never occurred to me that my writing was that detectable. These are the dumb things well-intentioned parents do.

Little League Baseball

In 1961 when I was 10 years of age, I joined a Little League baseball team in Fabens. I had just finished 3rd grade and it was summer time. I don't remember how I ended up joining the baseball team but I did. We still lived on the farm during that time. I played the catcher position for the team and our team was known as the "Gold" team. We all wore yellow, gold colored tee shirts and caps. Little League was played with the standard hard ball. The pitcher pitched the ball toward the batter with an overhand throw.

I remember that our coach was a tall, lanky man of Anglo descent. We referred to him as Coach Patterson. The problem with joining the team was that baseball practice took place during the afternoons which was during the same time that my father had to work on the farm. As a result, he couldn't drive me to daily baseball practice. Baseball practice started at 4:00 p.m. in the afternoon.

I had a bicycle that I would ride from our home on the farm to the baseball field in Fabens each practice day as well as on game days. The path consisted of about .7 miles of dirt farm road from our home to the highway, then about 3.8 miles west on Highway 80 to Fabens and then up Fabens Street to the baseball park. The total distance traveled was about 4.5 miles. I actually never paid much attention to the distance I traveled until now that I am writing this piece. All I knew was that I needed to ride my bicycle to the baseball park to participate on the team.

I remember that the ambient temperature was very warm and that I would work up a sweat on the bicycle ride to Fabens. After work, my father would drive the farm truck to the baseball field to pick me up. When I was finished practicing with the team, he would place my bicycle in the cargo bay of the pickup truck and then we would return to our home on the farm. Living on the farm had its disadvantages. The kids that lived in the town had a head start on me.

It's been many years since that happened but I still remember the 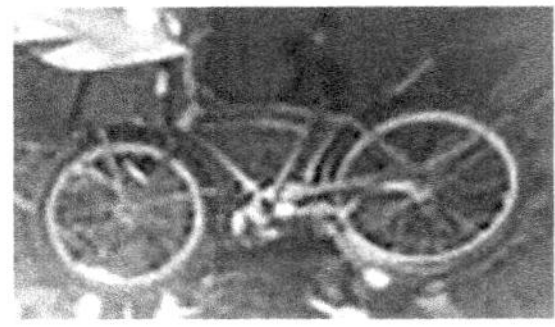 bicycle that I used. Now looking back, I wonder how it was that I wound up with that particular bicycle. I realize now that my bicycle was much heavier than today's modern bicycles. The bicycle had a red sun-worn color and it was not the sleek modern bicycle type that we commonly see nowadays.

My bicycle was fitted with fenders over the tires that added weight to the bicycle. The metal component known as the "top tube" of the bicycle was covered with a metal shroud that made the bike visually more appealing but it also added more weight to the bicycle. I don't have a photograph of my bicycle; however, I found one almost like it being displayed at a local restaurant that Socorro, my wife, and I visited recently. The bicycle photograph is shown on the left.

I remember that I was a very competitive ball player. I absolutely hated to lose. I hated to see my team members make dumb errors that kept us from winning a game. I remember that I used to yell harshly at them whenever they committed what I considered dumb errors. Not catching the ball or not tagging the opposing team's player were errors I just couldn't tolerate. I did not like to lose.

I was the catcher. The catcher crouches just behind the batter when playing baseball. During one game, I remember having been so close to the batter that when the batter swung the bat, the tip of the bat hit the tips of my ungloved fingers of my left hand. It hurt like a "son of a ". I didn't want the umpire to call an error and so I didn't make a big fuss about the pain on my fingers. That is how competitive I used to be. As I said, I did not like to lose.

I remember being very angry during one of the ball games because one of our team members had once again missed catching the ball. The home plate umpire that crouched immediately behind me calling the strikes and balls took notice of my anger. During the brief periods between pitches while the umpire and I were both facing the pitcher's mound, from behind he began to tell me to calm down and not get so angry at my teammates. He was saying the words not in a scolding manner but in a way so as to attempt put me more at ease. I was pretty pliable when it came to discussions with people older and so I did settle down after having heard his calming words. The name of the umpire was Roberto Salcido and we all called him by the name of "Bobby". He was about 20 years of age at the time. Bobby was a Fabens home town boy. Fast forward to when I was older, during chance encounters around town, we would exchange friendly greetings. I would wonder whether he remembered that I was the little boy that used to scold his teammates. Later on at 28 years of age in 1979, I ran as a candidate for election to the School Board of the Fabens Independent School District and was subsequently elected. About 6 months later, I was offered a more attractive professional position in Salt Lake City. I moved my family from Fabens to Salt Lake City. I later learned that Bobby Salcido had been appointed to the School Board position I vacated when I left Fabens.

One of the baseball players on my team was a boy by the name of Frankie Estrada. Frankie was the older brother of Maria Estrada. She was a close friend of my wife, Socorro. I remember that Frankie played first base position on the team. He was very good at catching fast balls. There was never any need to be angry at Frankie because he played baseball very well. In my mind's eye, I can still see him on first base scooping up the baseballs with his glove. He did it effortlessly.

Another person I remember that played baseball when I played for the Gold team was a boy by the name of George Diaz. He played for one of the opposing teams. He was tall and of heavy build but not obese and oddly enough everybody called him by the name of Georgie; as if he was a small statured kid. The reason I remember him is because he was the fastest pitcher I had seen at the time. His pitches were super fast. Unfortunately, he was on an opposing team. The reason I mention him in this piece is that I admired him. He didn't seem to cause baseball errors like the rest of my teammates.

By the way, I often wonder why I became the type of person that could not tolerate defeat. Somehow I became a stickler for perfection at that young age. As I indicated before, I absolutely hated to lose baseball games and at the same time, I admired Frankie and Georgie because they seemed to play perfectly. It took Bobby Salcido to bring me back to earth.

I am the type of person that can remember specific events in the past as well as the approximate time when the event occurred when I hear a specific song that was popular when the event occurred. In short, I can place a date to the specific occurrence of an event by simply hearing a song.

I remember a song titled "Hello Mary Lou" that was very popular during the time when I played on the Little League team. It was sung by an artist named Ricky Nelson. The song was one of several that were played on the loud speaker system used by the announcer during the baseball games. The song was also sometimes played during intermission periods when the announcer wasn't calling the game. Now as a grown up with a little help from the web, I found that the song reached No. 9 position on the Billboard music charts on May 28, 1961. I don't think I heard the song being played on our radio at home because my father and mother always tuned the radio to Mexican music stations so it had to have been at the ball park.

From time to time after our games, my father would get delayed and would arrive late to pick me up to return home. After the Little League game ended the Pony League game would start. During those times, I got to see the older kids play in the Pony League baseball games. The Pony League kids seemed much older to me and the fast balls that the pitcher pitched seemed super fast.

I was 10 years old at the time and during the next baseball season I would be over the permissible age limit to play on a Little League team. I would be 11 years of age and would now have to play in a Pony League team. In comparison to the Pony League kids I was a runt. As a result, I remember deciding not to play in the Pony League teams the following year. That was the end of my baseball career. Later on as a grownup in high school I played football and participated in cross-country running and track but never baseball.

Socorro, my wife, recently asked me if Chuy, my brother, also played baseball when I did. He didn't play baseball and I don't remember why it was that he didn't play. It could have been because he was two years older than I and my father needed him to work on the farm. Prior to having joined the baseball team, Chuy had always been the leader and I had always been the follower. One might say that he hatched the plans and I followed his instructions. Playing baseball on a team at 10 years of age without Chuy was probably the first time I ventured out on my own. Chuy wasn't there to tell me what to do. What I did in baseball was because of me and not because of Chuy. I suppose that is when I started to develop a sense of independence.

A few years ago I told my wife, Socorro, about my having ridden my bicycle from the farm to the Fabens baseball field when I was 10 years of age. Her first reaction was concern that my parents had allowed me to do so at such an early age. She told me that she would never have allowed one of our kids to do the same at that age. It is interesting to note that those yesteryears seemed more innocent than today's times. About the time that I began writing this section of the memoir, the television station NBC reported on a piece titled "How Richard Speck's Rampage 50 Years Ago Changed a Nation". The story was about a person that killed eight student nurses while in their dormitory in Chicago, Illinois. I remember the story because in 1966 when the killings occurred, I was 15 years of age. Prior to that time, one didn't seem to hear about atrocities such as murder or for that matter multiple murders. Ours was a more innocent, safer time.

One more thing about my playing on the gold team; we ended up third place in the league.

The Looming War

Life on the Ryan farm was exciting because it seemed that there was always something to see or do. Even though it was an exciting place for us, I now feel we were somewhat isolated from the rest of the world. I sense that had we lived in Fabens earlier on, we would have been able to better understand the goings-on in the world. It probably would have been better living in El Paso but at that time our universe revolved around Fabens. Many things were going on in the world in 1960 and 1961 that we as kids on the farm were not exposed to.

One of the things that were going on in those years relates to one chance occurrence when we lived in the home adjacent to the sand hills. One day while I was playing outdoors, I remember hearing a strange noise that in a span of perhaps 10 seconds became louder and louder and ultimately became so loud as to become almost unbearable. When the noise was at its loudest, I quickly looked all around to try to determine where the noise was coming from. I looked up and to my surprise I saw the largest airplane I had ever seen fly right over me. The airplane was traveling at high speed from the direction of Tornillo toward the direction of Fabens.

In those fleeting seconds that the airplane was visible in the air right above me, I was able to see that the airplane had swept-back wings sticking out from the main fuselage. The shadow that it cast during those brief seconds when the airplane flew over our house was huge! The airplane was flying so low as to be almost hugging the ground surface.

I remember Chuy and my mother rushing out of the door of our home looking around wondering what had caused that loud noise. They immediately noticed that I had been outdoors during the few seconds when the noise had occurred and they then began to ask me if I had seen where the noise had come from. I remember being so excited at the sight of the "huge airplane" I had just seen and I began to describe the airplane that had just flown over our home. It was one of those moments when you raise your arms and spread them wide apart in the air to demonstrate you experienced something huge and exceptional. I was so excited. It had been the right time and the right place for me but not for Chuy and my mother. Somehow I wasn't able to do justice to the explanation because after having described what I saw, they looked at me for a moment and then they just walked away perhaps even thinking that I was crazy. The sight of that "huge airplane" is burned in my mind.

Sometime later after the "huge airplane" event occurred, I remember that we were all seated at the dinner table having dinner. My father was conversing with my mother while we ate dinner. I began to listen to their conversation because my father was speaking to my mother about something that seemed very serious. I remember that my father was going through considerable effort to explain something to my mother and toward the end of the discussion, he then said the following words to my mother "va haber guerra". The Spanish phrase "va haber guerra" translates to English as "there will be war". I remember that when my mother heard those words, the expression in her in face all of sudden grew somber. My father was everything to me. If he said that we would be engaged in a war, then we would soon be at war. No doubt about it.

As much as I had tried, I hadn't understood the entirety of what my father had said to my mother during that dinner but I did understand the phrase "va haber guerra". I was 10 years of age in 1961 and a year prior to that my father had bought us a black and white television set equipped with a V-shaped rabbit ear antenna. We used to watch a show titled "The Twentieth Century" narrated by Walter Cronkite. The program presented filmed reports on news and cultural events that were important in the 20th century. The show did not just present the events but it also provided commentary that better described those events. Subjects such as World War I and World War II were presented and thoroughly explained.

Based on what we knew about wars from television programs like those and now my father saying "va haber guerra", I knew it meant guns, soldiers and maybe even death. I remember clutching my BB gun rifle knowing full well that my gun would surely help to protect us from the bad, enemy soldiers. Pretty innocent, wasn't it? I knew my father had a 22 caliber rifle and in my mind, that would also protect us.

As a side note, I've always been hesitant to use real live rifles because of an eye accident my father had with a rifle. I was very young when it happened. I didn't witness it but my mother told me that when he pulled the trigger, the gun fired but the barrel came loose from the gunstock. The barrel moved backwards and hit my father near or on the eye. I remember that my father wore an eye patch for a long time. The eye injury probably was not permanent because my father never wore an eye patch in his later years.

As I indicated before, the "huge airplane" event is burned in my mind. Now as a grown up, I am convinced that what I heard and saw during those fleeting seconds as a child on the farm was a low flying B-52 jet bomber. The airplane I saw had swept-back wings and was enormous. That's the reason I think it was a B-52 military jet.

I now know that international relations between Cuba and the United States were very tense during the years of 1960 and 1961. The failed Bay of Pigs invasion into Cuba occurred in April of 1961. The first attempt to hijack an airliner to Cuba occurred in El Paso, Texas on August 3, 1961. I remember watching the hijack drama as it unfolded on the black and white television set that my father had purchased for us. Later on in October 1962, Russia would be at odds with the U.S. during the Cuban Missile Crises.

Based on all that international tension that was occurring between Cuba, Russia and the United States at that time, I believe the B-52 flight  over our house on the Ryan farm must have been part of a military exercise arising from that international tension. Today, with a little help from the web, I know that B-52 jet bombers were indeed in service at the time I saw that "huge airplane" flying low over our house on the Ryan farm. I now also know that B-52s were sometimes flown very near to the ground to the point of almost hugging the ground surface. By flying under 500 feet of altitude, the B-52 could evade radar radio waves and therefore could have reached targets without being detected.

The following is taken from a June 21, 1964 article on the web titled "Early B-52's Get Low-Level Radar" that shows the ground- hugging capabilities of a B-52: "Most early model B-52 bombers of the Strategic Air Command have now been equipped with a radar system that can pick out changing land features ahead of the plane in the same way an automobile's headlights illuminate the road. The system, known as terrain avoidance radar, is one of several modifications used to give the long-range bombers lowlevel attack capability. The B-52 was designed as a high-altitude weapon.". The article can be accessed using the following web link: https://www.nytimes.com/1964/06/21/early-b52s-get-lowlevel-radar. html

The world situation was very tense at the time. As a kid on the farm, I didn't know all these details but I knew something was up because I had heard my father express concern. I don't remember the year when my "huge airplane" experience took place. But based on what I know now regarding the world situation at that time, I am guessing that it must have occurred sometime in 1960 or 1961 when I was 9 or 10 years of age.

Fabens Independent School District

All my siblings and I attended school at the Fabens Independent School District. As indicated before, the Ryan farm was located between Fabens, Texas and Tornillo, Texas. The two towns are about 5.5 miles apart. The size of the township of Tornillo is about 10 percent that of the Fabens township. The Ryan farm was located within the jurisdiction of the Tornillo Independent School District and not in the Fabens district. By all rights, the Ryan and Renteria children should have attended school in the Tornillo Independent School District; however, we actually attended school in the Fabens Independent School District.

During story times with my mother, she told me that Mr. and Mrs. Ryan had somehow arranged for us to attend the schools in the larger Fabens School District. She told me that the Ryans felt that the larger Fabens schools were more beneficial for their kids as well as the Renteria kids. As a result of the Ryans' insistence, we ended up attending what my mother understood at that time to be the "better" school system.

Camp School

As I indicated before, both my parents were non-English speaking and so the Spanish language was our first language as children. I don't remember having learned any of the English words that Joe or Pat Ryan might have spoken to us even though we managed to play together. We lived on the farm and we were isolated from other Mexican people that might have known how to speak English.

It wasn't until I started elementary school that, little by little, I began to learn the English language. I can still remember how hard it was to learn English in the school environment. Some teachers even spanked the students with wooden paddles if a student was caught speaking Spanish in the classroom or out on the school grounds during recess periods. It also didn't help that at the end of the school day, we would return to our home environment where only Spanish was spoken by our parents. Thinking in Spanish and then speaking in English wasn't a piece of cake.

My brother, Chuy, was 2 years ahead of me when I started first grade at 6 years of age. Students like Chuy and I that were Spanish language dominant had to first attend what at that time was known as Camp School. Camp School consisted of a collection of adobe, stuccoed buildings located at the outskirts of the town near the small airport. The airport was used by crop duster airplanes.

Students that were English language dominant went directly to Risinger Elementary School without having to start at Camp School. When she was a little girl, Socorro, who later became my wife after graduating from high school, also grew up on a farm near Fabens. She grew up on the Grijalva farm. Like my parents, her parents did not speak English. However, as a little girl, she had the good fortune to grow up with two older brothers who started school before her. One of her brothers, Salvador Martinez, was 6 years older while the oldest brother, Antonio Martinez, was 10 years older.

Both of her older brothers had also attended Camp School. Through that interaction with her older brothers, she knew how to speak and write English when she entered first grade. As I indicated before, she grew up on a farm. The farm belonged to a person by the name of Frank Grijalva. His family was English dominant and that helped Socorro learn English as a little girl as well. She started school at Risinger Elementary school and didn't have to go to Camp School like I did.

I spent my first year at Camp School in the grade that was referred to as "first low". "First low" grade came to be known to Hispanics as "primero burro" or loosely translated to English; "donkey first grade".

After one year in "first low" grade at Camp School, I then advanced to "first high" grade. Camp School became known as the school that Mexicans go to. After one more year in second grade at Camp School, I was then transferred to third grade at Risinger Elementary School. At the time, the three buildings comprising Risinger Elementary School were much nicer and more modern than those at Camp School. The buildings at Risinger Elementary School were of brick construction while those at  Camp School were of stuccoed adobe construction. The photographs on the left show several of the buildings at the Camp school as they exist today.

I have to admit that as a child, I used to be embarrassed about having to attend school for Mexicans. The fact that I was in "primero burro" grade didn't help my self-esteem. I don't remember exactly how we came to know of the existence of Risinger Elementary School, but we knew. We knew that it was the school reserved for kids of Anglo descent. I remember that my father would make light fun of me for being in that grade. As a result, I grew shy about having attended that school and, in particular, that specific "primero burro" grade. I suppose that nowadays, the "primero burro" grade could be considered kindergarten grade.

As a grown up, I never felt a need to remind my father about him having poked fun at us during the Camp School days. Later on as a grown up, I was comfortable in my skin and I didn't feel it necessary to bring up an old wound. Besides, I respected my father too much to remind him about such things. Now as a grown up, I suppose I can point to one thing that makes up for having to attend Camp School; I made honor roll during each of the three years I attended Camp School. Gloria, my younger sister, was the last of the Renteria children to attend Camp School. She was the fourth child of the Renteria clan.

The next youngest was Mario. He entered Risinger Elementary school directly without having to attend Camp School.

In later years as a grownup, I sometimes wondered why the school was called Camp School. I had often heard that it had been a "CCC camp". After a little work on the internet, I found out that the collection of buildings then known as Camp School were built under a program authorized in 1933 by President Franklin Roosevelt. Those were the depression years. The program was called the Civilian Conservation Corps and the buildings were sometimes referred to as "CCC camps". The program was a New Deal public work relief program meant to provide jobs and housing for unemployed and unmarried men. The program continued until 1942.

There's one more thing about Camp School. While writing this piece, my wife, Socorro, told me that she remembered that the older people in Fabens used to say that the Camp School buildings were used during World War II to house German and Italian prisoners of war. I found an article on the internet that confirms that German and Italian prisoners were indeed kept in Fabens during World War II. Although the article doesn't specifically state that the prisoners of war were kept at the buildings that were then known as the Camp School buildings, it does at least support the stories told about prisoners of war in Fabens. The following quote was obtained from the internet article: "In World War II, the Americans took prisoners, and they brought them into places like El Paso and many other places I'm sure. They set up camps. There was one in Fabens, in particular. I think they had about fifty people there.". The internet link is as follows: http://braceroarchive.org/items/show/47?view=full

While I was writing this piece, I drove by the location where the old Camp School is located. The three buildings comprising the old Camp School are still present. The grounds are a bit more kept up in comparison to the old days. It is now being used as a "Head Start" facility for pre-kindergarten education for low-income children. Martin, the youngest of my siblings, attended Camp School after it had been converted to a "Head Start" school. Martin was born in April of 1965 so he was probably 5 years of age in 1970 when he attended "Head Start" school.

All in all, this facility probably yielded a pretty good financial return. There's one last thing about Camp School as it relates to my brother, Martin. As indicated before, Martin started his first school year at the "Head Start" school that was formerly known as the Camp School. During family get-togethers, we often joke around with Martin about him having been my mother's favorite child. We call him my mother's "chiple". "Chiple" is a Spanish slang word that means "to be pampered, spoiled or much loved as by a parent, sibling or friend".

During the old days prior to my mother's death, we would sometimes playfully joke with Martin and call him "chiple". My mother would come to his aid and tell us to leave him alone. In a joking but playful manner we would then remind my mother of a story she had once told us about Martin when he first started to attend "Head Start" school back in 1970.

And the story goes like this. A pre-school child is normally accompanied to the child's first day of school by the parents or, as a minimum, by the mother. Once the child becomes acclimated to the other school kids and the school room, the parent then leaves the premises knowing that the child won't feel abandoned and will probably do well during the rest of the first day at school. In some cases, the child may require repeated accompaniment for a few more days. In Martin's case, my mother said that it took about 3 weeks of her having to stay in the classroom during the entire length of the school days to keep Martin from crying. Although it may have been three weeks, we tend to forget that fact and embellish things a little. So the slightly more embellished story goes like this: "it took my mother 6 months of taking Martin to "Head Start" to get him to stay in school without him crying for his Mommie" (chuckle).

School for African American Students

All through my school years from 1st grade through the 8th grade in 1966, I never saw a black African American student in our classes. It's not that there weren't black people in Fabens; it's just that they didn't go to the schools in the Fabens Independent School District. The black people that lived in Fabens were economically very poor. They were poorer than our family. It wasn't until I was in high school in 1966 that I noticed black African American students now attending school at the high school.

Back in the Camp School days, I remember noticing numerous black children congregating at a house building structure across the street from where the Camp School buildings were located. I don't remember how I came to know, but the dilapidated building across the street was the school for the black children. It wasn't even a school building; it seemed to be just a run-down house.

Now as a grown up, I know about the Civil Rights Act of 1964. I was 13 years of age in 1964 and had no clue about what was going on in relation to segregation. The Civil Rights Act of 1964 enacted on July 2, 1964, was civil rights legislation in the United States that outlawed discrimination based on race, color, religion, sex, or national origin. But for President Lyndon Baines Johnson who pushed for the civil rights legislation, the black children would not have been able to attend the Fabens Independent School District.

Later on during my high school days, 2 black African American boys and a Black African American girl began attending our school. The name of one of the black boys was Paul Williams. He was in Chuy's class; two years ahead of me. I remember he was tall and lanky and was a very friendly person. At that time, Chuy and I were in the high school band and so was Paul. Paul played percussion the instruments and was very good at it. I never asked him if he attended the "dilapidated house" school near the airport but I'm sure he has his own story to tell about those difficult times when segregation was the norm. By the way, the other black boy's name was David Milner. He too was a very kind and gentle person. The girl's name was Jessie Milner; however I never interacted with her. She seemed quiet and reserved as well.

I can remember that as a child, I had the feeling that relegating the black children to the "dilapidated school" seemed wrong but at the same time, nobody in Fabens seemed to care. I didn't understand it then but I do now as a grown up. Again, but for President Lyndon Baines Johnson who pushed for civil rights legislation in 1964, Paul probably would not have been able to attend school in the Fabens Independent School District.

There's one "more" thing about the schooling of the black students at Fabens. While reviewing the content of the website titled "History of Fabens, Texas", I noticed the following statement "Fabens also had a school for Black students located at CC Camp.". The quote can be viewed using the following website:

http://www.fabensisd.net/apps/pages/index.jsp?uREC_ID =337295&type=d&pREC_ID=744789

I disagree with this statement because during 1957 to 1960 when I was a student at Camp School, the black students did not attend our school. They did attend the "dilapidated house" school across the street from the Camp School facilities. So while the "dilapidated house" school for the black students was near the Camp School facility, the black students didn't actually attend school at the Camp School facilities at least during the years from 1957 to 1960 when I attended school there.

There's one "last" thing about the schooling of the black students at Fabens. The above mentioned website also contains the following statement: "In the fall of 1961 all the Black students were transferred to the various other buildings of our school district.". I take issue again with this statement because as I indicated above, it wasn't until I was in high school in 1966 that I noticed black students now attending school at Fabens High School. I suspect that it wasn't in 1961 that black students were transferred to the Fabens School District. Instead, I suspect that the Civil Rights Act of 1964 had a lot to do in bringing about the transfer of the black students to the Fabens Independent School District.

The Poll Tax

I remember that during the time when we lived in our home adjacent to the sand hills on the Ryan farm, my mother would from time to time be consumed with paying what she termed "el pol tax". Those were just words to us at the time because we were so young.

As I grew older, I noticed that the subject of the tax would arise only during voting time. That's when I learned that what my mother was referring to what was known as the "poll tax". I put two and two together. My mother was a U.S. citizen and she was entitled to vote and that's why paying the "poll tax" was so important to her. By the way, my father never seemed to be worried about paying the "poll tax". That's because at that time, he was a permanent resident alien and not a U.S. citizen.

My recollection of my mother's preoccupation recently led me to want to learn more about the subject of the "poll tax". Prior to now, I thought that the "poll tax" had been a U.S. government requirement; I found it to be not so. I found that the "poll tax" was a tax levied by some states as a means of raising revenue; at least that was what most people were led to believe. In reality, the "poll" tax was levied as a means of keeping "black people" from voting; especially in the former southern slave states of the United States. The "poll tax" was part of what is known as Jim

Crow laws. The Jim Crow Laws were state and local laws that enforced racial segregation.

I obtained the following quote from an internet article titled "What Was Jim Crow":

"Jim Crow was the name of the racial caste system which operated primarily, but not exclusively in southern and border states, between 1877 and the mid-1960s. Jim Crow was more than a series of rigid anti-black laws. It was a way of life. Under Jim Crow, African Americans were relegated to the status of second class citizens. Jim Crow represented the legitimization of anti-black racism."

The article can be found using the following link: https://ferris.edu/jimcrow/what.htm

I also found that the following on the internet:

"The Twenty-fourth Amendment (Amendment XXIV) of the United States Constitution prohibits both Congress and the states from conditioning the right to vote in federal elections on payment of a poll tax or other types of tax. The amendment was proposed by Congress to the states on August 27, 1962, and was ratified by the states on January 23, 1964."

The article can be found using the following link:

https://en.wikipedia.org/wiki/

Twenty-fourth_Amendment_to_

the_United_States_Constitutionhttps://en.wikipedia.org/

wiki/ Twenty-fourth_Amendment_to_the_United_States_Constitution

So in the end, had my mother not paid the "poll tax" she would not have been able to vote. I knew that fact at the time but I didn't know how the "poll tax" came to be. Both the "poll tax" and the Jim Crow laws were an injustice to black people. The "poll tax" was an injustice to poor Hispanics. The "poll tax" was like a rock that killed two birds with one throw.

Risinger Primary School – 3rd Grade

From Camp School, I was transferred to Risinger Primary School when I was 9 years of age. I attended third and fourth grade at Risinger Primary

School. The grades at Risinger Primary School were divided into letter class designations.

For example, grade 3 was subdivided into four classes that were designated as 3A, 3B, 3C and 3D. When I entered the third grade at Risinger Primary School, I was placed in the 3C class. I didn't know it at time but Socorro, who would later be my wife, was placed in the class designated as 3A. I don't remember whether the classes at Camp School were subdivided in similar manner to that of Risinger Primary School. The photograph on the left shows the current day building at Risinger Primary School.

I was 9 and then 10 years old during third grade. I remember that the Anglo children tended to be placed in the classes that were designated 3A and 3B. On the other hand, the Hispanic children tended to be placed in the classes that were designated 3C and 3D. There were exceptions like Socorro and several others who was Hispanic that ended up in class 3A. I remember there were no Anglo children in my class. Not knowing any better at the time, it did seem normal to me that the Anglo children belonged in the A and B classes. Today I don't feel that should have been so. My take now is that keeping the English speaking children apart from the non-English speaking children resulted in the dumbing-down of the classes having only non-English speaking children.

The most significant thing I remember about being in the 3rd grade was the Maypole dance. Once a year, on or about May 1, the school  would put on a student presentation known as the May Day presentation. I remember the yearly May Day presentations were held during the evening hours around 5 or 6 pm so that the student's families could attend. Starting several weeks prior to the date of the presentations, the students in each class would practice their respective class presentations. Each class was assigned a specific presentation and it so happened that the students in my class were assigned the Maypole dance.

The Maypole dance involved the use of a high vertical wooden pole anchored to the floor. The ends of several long brightly colored ribbons were attached to the top of the pole and the opposite ends of the ribbons were allowed to hang until touching the floor. Each student would grasp the end of a ribbon and when the music began to play, the students would skip around the pole with the girls going one way and the boys going the opposite way. The students continued skipping in an interweaving manner until the entire pole was wrapped with the ribbons.

I never really knew why those presentations were held on or about May 1 of each year. I also never knew the origins of the Maypole dance; it certainly wasn't something my parents knew about. Now as a grown up with a little help from the internet, I found that Maypole dancing is a form of folk dance that originates from Germany, England and Sweden. Little by little we were being immersed into the Anglo culture.

My third grade teacher was Mrs. Dorothy Murray. She was very kind but at the same time, somewhat strick. If by chance she caught one of us speaking Spanish, she would bring out the flat wooden paddle and paddle the offending student. The flat wooden paddle was similar in size and shape to the wooden paddle used in the game called "paddle ball". Paddle ball is played with a flat wooden paddle that has a small rubber ball attached to the paddle's center with an elastic string. Paddling a student when caught speaking Spanish now seems unfair to me. Perhaps it was part of the Anglo immersion process as well.

The Anglo immersion process did affect me in subtle ways. For example, prior to entering school, I spoke Spanish entirely. During that time we used to have a pet dog whose name was "Tumbalo". The Spanish word "Tumbalo" means "knock it down" or "knock him down" in English. I agree it was a dumb name for a dog but that was definitely his name. Much later when I entered school, our family acquired another dog and I remember that I myself named him "Taffy". I remember having picked the name from a book I read which was about a boy that happened to have a pet dog named Taffy. Yes, slowly but surely the Anglo immersion process was taking its hold on me.

By the way, a dedication plaque outside the Principal's office at Risinger Primary School contains my name along with 6 other school board members. I was a member of the school board in 1978 when Risinger Primary School was renovated. It was at that time that the dedication plaque was placed at the school. The full story of how I came to be a school board member at the Fabens Independent School District will be presented in a later chapter.

The Contract Labor Business

I remember that during the summer of 1960 Chuy and I worked on the Ryan farm "chopping cotton". We did that work during the times when we weren't irrigating the cotton fields. We were paid $.50 per hour. Our day started at 8:00 a.m. in the morning and we worked until 12:00 noon, took an hour for lunch and then we resumed chopping cotton from 1:00 p.m. to 5:00 p.m. They were long 8 hour days.

By the way, the phrase "chopping cotton" is a misnomer. "Chopping cotton" really means chopping or cutting the weeds surrounding the cotton plants; not chopping or cutting the cotton plants.

Chopping cotton or cutting the weeds is done by using an implement known as a hoe. However, there was one exception. Once during the growing season when the cotton plants were about 4 to 5 inches high, it was necessary to thin-out the cotton plants. This was done by cutting a swath of cotton plants with one stroke of the hoe, skipping about 3 or 4 plants and then repeating the same process over and over again. The entire length of each earthen furrow was chopped in this manner. The objective was to allow the remaining thinned- out plants sufficient nutrients from the soil so that the plants could then grow as high as possible and therefore produce the maximum amount of cotton.

Chopping cotton wasn't that easy. It had to be done during the summer cotton growing season; from the beginning of June through the end of August. The morning temperatures in the El Paso area in June were about 80 degrees Fahrenheit and the highest temperature could sometimes increase as high as 107 degrees Fahrenheit by 3:00

p.m. in the afternoon. Drinking water was essential when chopping cotton in the fields.

I happened to be fair skinned and light complected and had problems as a result of that fact. We would wear hats to ward off the sunlight. We would even wear long sleeved shirts to keep our arms from getting sun burned. During those long, hot summer days chopping cotton, my lips would get so dry and chapped that they would sometimes even bleed.

This would happen even if I wetted my lips with water. Chuy, my brother, never seemed to have that problem. It just seemed that I was the only one that constantly had to be careful with my lips. Nowadays people use a product known as ChapStick® which contains many different ingredients including petrolatum which helps in avoiding chapped lips. Who knew about these products in those early days when I worked in the cotton fields chopping cotton?

By the way every impact of the hoe against the dirt to cut the weeds resulted in a jolt on the hands, especially when the field had just been irrigated and the dirt was compacted. Hoeing 8 hours a day eventually resulted in bruising of the cupped part of the hands. Eventually, the constant bruising would cause calluses to form on the hands that sometimes even contained puss. Those wounds were painful. One had to bear the pain until actual hard calluses formed on the inner part of the hands. When the hard calluses formed, handling the hoe 8 hours a day was not as painful.

I don't remember exactly how it happened but my father started a contract labor business. Somehow he figured out that other farms had the same requirement that the Ryan farm had. Laborers were needed to chop cotton on the other farms.

While we still lived in the home beside the sand hills, I remember that my father owned a station wagon. He assigned my mother to drive the station wagon to pickup other women at various neighboring farms early in

the morning. She would take them to the specific farm that had contracted with my father for cotton chopping laborers. At the end of each week, the farmer that contracted with my father would pay my father a lump sum of money proportional to the number of laborers that worked during that week. My father in turn, would pay each individual woman laborer for that week. I am not sure what kind of profit margin my father built into the amounts that the farmer paid. It had to be profitable or else my father wouldn't have continued doing this for several years.

I remember riding in the station wagon every morning during the summer as my mother drove from location to location picking up the women. I remember it was only women and not men. I don't remember Chuy having accompanied us on the station wagon. Chuy was 2 years older than I and he must have remained behind to help my father with the work on the Ryan farm. When I was 9 years old in the year 1960, Irma, Gloria, Mario and Gracie were still babies. I remember that Sara, my father's half sister, would take care of the babies at home during the days when my mother was working in the fields. There was a lot a coordination going on; it became a well-oiled machine.

By the way, when the women were picked up in my mother's station wagon they would always bring along large, straw "Charro" hats. As indicated in previous chapters, "Charro" is a word that is used to refer to a traditional horseman from México, who wears a type of wide-brimmed hat that is broad enough  to cast a shadow over the head, neck and shoulders. These hats are known as "charro hats".

The women wore these hats because they offered maximum protection from the sun. Remember, this work was done during the summer months and the sun's rays could easily burn exposed skin. In addition to the wide-brimmed hats, they would also wear inexpensive cotton gloves to protect their hands; again from the sun's rays. I chose to wear the normal straw hat for fear of being ridiculed and of course "a man" doesn't wear gloves so I didn't either. In retrospect, I should have worn those items to protect myself from the sun as well.

Several years later, farmers began to use herbicides to prevent weeds from growing in the fields. These herbicides were engineered to kill only the weeds but not the cotton. Eventually the contract labor business came to halt as a result of the herbicide usage.

As far as thinning-out the cotton plants was concerned; that too ended when the farmers began to use a farm implement known as a rotary chopper. The rotary chopper rotated in similar fashion as the cooling fan on an engine but at a much slower rate. The rotary farm implement was attached to the rear 3 point standard connection on a farm tractor. The ends of the metal arms connected to the center of the rotary chopper were fitted with triangular shaped, sharp edged spades. As the tractor moved along, the sharp edged spades would dig into the dirt to chop swaths of cotton plants leaving behind equally spaced clumps of cotton plants. The rotary chopper worked so well that laborers for thinning out the cotton plants were no longer needed. There is one final item that I remember. One of those farmers that contracted with my father to provide contract laborers was a person by the name of Grijalva. I remember that the Grijalva farm was located between the town of Fabens and the small village of Cuadrilla north of Fabens.

As part of the contract labor group, we all happened to be working thinning-out the cotton plants at the Grijalva farm. While we were working, Mr. Grijalva began to focus on my work and he walked closer to where I was working to observe my work in more detail. He followed me as I chopped cotton for quite a while and eventually he instructed me to stop. He then told me that I was not thinning- out the plants properly. He then took the hoe from my hands and then he chopped a few swaths of cotton plants to demonstrate how he wanted me to do the work. I began to thin-out the plants in the same way he had done and after a while, again he stopped me. He was now somewhat upset with me because he felt I hadn't followed his instructions properly. He showed me again. Again I attempted to mimic his work.

He finally called my mother and told my mother that he was not happy with my work and that I should not continue to work. My mother had no choice but to tell me to wait in the station wagon for the rest of the day.

By the way, after I married my wife, Socorro, I told her the story of the time when I was told not to continue working on the farm owned by the Grijalva person. From the way I described Mr. Grijalva, Socorro immediately knew who the man was. She told me that it was Efrain Grijalva who had told me not to continue working. It turned out that Efrain Grijalva was Socorro's baptismal godfather. She was very familiar with Efrain Grijalva's manner and told me that her godfather was very meticulous and headstrong. She told me that he would frequently fire people on the spot without question if he didn't approve of their work. She was sure it was her godfather, Efrain Grijalva.

I was 10 or 11 years of age when that happened. I have a sense that my young age was his problem. Anyway, what a coincidence?

Risinger Primary School – 4th Grade

I started fourth grade at Risinger Primary School when I was 10 years of age in 1961. I was in class 4C. My fourth grade teacher was Mrs. Mary Jane Ryan. I don't remember ever having known that Mrs. Ryan was a school teacher prior to entering fourth grade. I don't think that my parents knew that she taught school in Fabens because they never made mention of that fact.

Mrs. Ryan was a very kind teacher. She always had a smile on her face. I don't remember her ever being cross with a student. I don't remember Mrs. Ryan ever using a paddle on a student or for that matter, ever punishing a student. All during that school year, she would call me by my formal name of "Salvador" and not "Chava". Several times prior to that time, during chance encounters between her and my parents while I was present, she would address me as Chava but now it was different.

Fast forward to the future, her husband, Mr. Jimmy Ryan passed away in 2003. He was buried at Fort Bliss National Cemetery. Unbeknownst to me, he had been a World War II veteran. I attended Mr. Ryan's funeral and while there, paid my respects to Mrs. Ryan. When I walked up to her to give her my condolences, she knew who I was. I remember speaking with her at the cemetery after the funeral service. Mrs. Ryan was in good spirits in spite of the fact that her husband had passed away. She told me that Mr. Ryan had died in her arms. They had been expecting his death. I remember hugging her and telling her "you are my life-long friend and you were my fourth grade teacher". She looked around and responded to everyone "and I take credit for Chava's success". She then proceeded to say "and I take credit for the success of everyone that came through my class room". Hearing her address me by the name of "Chava" made my day because that meant that we were indeed good friends.

The Ryan boys were also at their father's funeral. I met all the Ryan brothers: Joe, Pat, Mark, Paul, Michael and David. I reminisced a little with Joe and Pat about our days at the farm when we were kids. As I indicated before, Chuy and I used to play with Joe and Pat when we lived on the farm. The rest of the Ryan children were either too young or hadn't been born yet. With the exception of Paul and Mark, the Ryan family had moved away to east Texas sometime around 1966. I think they moved to Victoria, Texas. I was 52 years of age now. It had been about 40 years since

Chuy and I had played with Joe and Pat on the farm. Joe asked that I say hello to Chuy. He told me that he had been keeping tabs on Chuy through his dad, Mr. Ryan.

Mrs. Ryan passed away in 2014 as well. Upon reading her obituary I learned that she graduated from North Texas State University. As a child at the Ryan farm and even when she was my fourth grade teacher, it never occurred to me that she was an educated woman. I don't remember her as an arrogant person. She always had a smile on her face. We always knew that her name was Jane Ryan but the obituary shows her first name was Mary Jane. She was a very good person. Her funeral service was in Fabens and she too was interred at Fort Bliss National Cemetery. One of my regrets in life is that I didn't go to Mrs. Ryan's funeral. I can't remember why, I just didn't go.

Mrs. Ryan was and still is important to me. In a precious section, I included Mr. Jimmy Ryan's obituary. Out of respect for her, I decided to include her obituary in this memoir.

"Mary Jane Ryan of Fabens, Texas passed away peacefully on Saturday, March 8th, 2014 at the age of 88. She was born to Seth and Dorothy Duren, on October 6, 1925, in Archer City, Texas where she was raised with her two sisters Adele and Francis Mae. After completing her bachelor's degree at North Texas State University, she moved to "Fabulous Fabens", Texas where she met James "Jim" Ryan who would be the love of her life. During her 40+ year tenure in the Fabens Independent School District, Jane taught many subjects and grade levels including art, music, reading and her favorite, the 5th grade. She was always eager to hear news of the children she taught over the years as they grew up and became pillars of the community. After retiring from a rewarding teaching career, she turned her attention to her other passions. She was a long time member and former president of the Paso Del Norte Porcelain Arts Club as well as a member of the El Paso Lower Valley Retired Teachers Association and the Rio Valley Woman's Club. She was known by family and friends as always dignified but with just the right amount of sassiness. She found joy attending church services on Sundays, attending the opera and theatre with friends, and watching Tiger play golf on television. An avid gardener, she would often be found tending to her rose bushes and ensuring the hummingbirds were well fed. Mary Jane is preceded in passing by her parents Seth and Dorothy as well as her beloved husband Jim, her siblings Sonny, Adele and Francis Mae, her son Paul and granddaughter Carley Ann. She is survived by her sons and their spouses Joe, Denise, Seth, Mark, Sherry, Michael, Patti, David and Paul's wife Kit. Jane had 12 grandchildren and 5 great grandchildren. A devoted wife, mother, grandmother and friend, Mary Jane Ryan will always be remembered, loved and missed by the family and community that she leaves behind. Funeral Service will be held at First United Methodist Church of Fabens located at 201 Camp St. Fabens, TX at 10:30AM on March 21st to be followed by a committal service at Fort Bliss National Cemetery West Shelter located at 5200 Fred Wilson Ave. El Paso, TX at 1:00PM. In lieu of flowers, the family asks that contributions be made to the First United Methodist Church of Fabens, P.O. Box 416, Fabens, TX 79838. Services directed by San Jose Funeral Home-Fabens (915) 764-2254. Published in El Paso Times from Mar. 18 to Mar. 26, 2014" Grade School – 5th Grade I started fifth grade

in Grade School when I was 11 years of age in 1962. Having graduated to 5th grade from 4th grade felt like a giant step forward. Going to school in the two- story building that was Grade School a few hundred yards away from Risinger Primary School felt like I wasn't in "kiddie" school anymore. There was a feeling of stature that went along with going to school at the Grade School. Even the girls now seemed grown up to me.

A new significant fact was that my teacher was now a man. Prior to this grade, all my teachers had been women. My teacher's name was Mr. Batton; I don't remember his first name. There wasn't anything special about Mr. Batton; only that he seemed to be an older man possibly in his 60s. His wife, Mrs. Batton, also worked as a teacher at the Grade School.

I remember that my 5th grade experience was relatively uneventful. However, I am sorry to say that 5th grade was the only grade where I didn't receive "honor roll" at the conclusion of the school year. Prior to this grade and after this grade, even in high school, I was awarded "honor roll" at the end of my school years.

Not having been selected for "honor roll" by Mr. Batton was unexpected and disappointing. I felt I had performed well in my studies as I had done in all of my other grades prior to 5th grade. I recall that my grades in my report card were always up to par and compared well to grades I received in my prior school years. Looking back, I should have asked Mr. Batton for a reason why I wasn't selected for "honor roll". I should have at least asked him to review my grades to see if possibly this had been and oversight or an unintentional error.

So now that I am a mature man still wondering why I wasn't awarded "honor roll" at the conclusion of my 5th grade class troubles me. Will I ever get over it? Probably not. In my mind, I did do good work in 5th grade. My parents never knew that I didn't receive "honor roll" in 5th grade or for that matter that I received "honor roll" in any of my other school years; at least they never made a big when I did. They were just too busy trying to cope with making a living. It's funny how a grown man in his 60s never reconciled himself to not having received the award. So in the end, 5th grade to me is like a door that never wound up closing completely . . . unfinished business.

The Construction of Our First Home

Sometime during my school year in the 5th grade, my family moved from the Ryan farm to Fabens. Our street address in Fabens was 208 I. Avenue. The home still exists. I definitely remember that the move occurred when I was 11 years of age. This was in 1962. In those days, our new Fabens home was on the outskirts of the town of Fabens. The town has grown significantly and now it is in the middle of Fabens.

About two years prior, my father purchased two lots of land on "I" street. I still remember the elderly couple that sold the property to my father. The elderly couple's name was Mr. and Mrs. Mims. The Mims' lived in a mobile home located near the existing convenience store located at the corner of Fabens Street and G Avenue. The reason I know about the Mims couple is that from time to time my father would send me to their residence to deliver the monthly payment of $50 dollars.

The family by the name of Ochoa also purchased land from the Mims. Their single lot was adjacent to the two lots my father purchased in

Fabens. When we lived on the Ryan farm on the bracero housing quarters adjacent to the railroad tracks, the Ochoa family lived about half a mile walking distance east toward Tornillo from where we lived. They lived on the Marshbank farm. Jose Ochoa and Maria Elena were the heads of that household and our family used to visit them from time to time. They were an older couple and their older children were much older than Chuy and I. The only three children that were about our age were Jesus, Juana and Jose. In an earlier story about spooky things that my mother experienced at the farm, Jesus, or Ruly as we grew to call him, was supposedly the little boy that my mother saw in the window that frightened her. Anyway those 3 children were our close friends.

Back to the subject at hand; I don't know how I know this but I think the Mims owned a large part of the land that was later sold in and around the area where we ended up living in Fabens. In fact, now as I am writing this piece, I often see the Mims name on property advertisements in and around El Paso and the lower valley including Fabens. I often wonder if the elderly couple I knew to be the Mims couple are the same people that gave rise to the Mims that appear in property advertisements here and there in the El Paso valley area.

By the way, the property my father purchased from the Mims was near an area of the town that was known as "Yucca Heights". The homes in the "Yucca Heights" area were where the upper middle class people of Anglo descent lived. The homes in that area were modern cinder block homes with very manicured yards. In contrast, the homes outside but near that subdivision were constructed of adobe block just like our home. "Yucca Heights" was the in-thing in those days but not anymore. Slowly but surely, the families of Anglo descent moved out of the area.

Returning to the subject of our home; we constructed our Fabens home by ourselves. Fabens wasn't and still isn't incorporated as a municipality so there were never any building codes that dictated how and where the homes should be constructed. Over the years, there have been at least 2 attempts to incorporate Fabens into a township but those efforts were unsuccessful. Fabens still continues to exist without a town government. The town relies on the County of El Paso for paving, signage, policing and the like.

As I indicated before, about 2 years prior to my being in 5th grade when I was 11, my father began to construct our home in Fabens. The construction was done during Saturdays and Sundays. Those were the only days that my father didn't have to work at his regular job on the Ryan farm. Chuy, my brother, and I helped my father during the construction. Somehow my father knew how the home needed to be constructed. I don't remember ever having seen another person taking charge of the construction and I don't remember seeing any drawings, plans or sketches that showed how our home was going to be constructed. My father managed every step of the construction.

I often wonder about my father's boldness. How did he learn how to construct a house? As I indicated before, there were no drawings or sketches that I was aware of. The answer might lie in the fact that he purchased property in Caseta. In a previous section, I indicated that records show that he purchased the Caseta property in 1959 but the paperwork doesn't show that the property had building structures on it. It's very possible that he helped build the two-room adobe structure where my grandfather Jose's family lived in for many years. How he learned to construct our home in Fabens . . . I'll never truly know. The fact is, my father took on the challenge of building our home in Fabens.

Anyway, my father's home project was done over a two year period of time. My father's half brothers from Caseta would help out from time to time. Chuy and I were there for every step of the construction. We were the gophers . . . go for this, go for that.

We helped my father construct the foundation out of home-made concrete. I say home-made because the concrete wasn't purchased from a concrete company like it is done today. I remember that my father took us somewhere to the desert to load the pickup truck with a type of gravel-laden granular sand that was unlike the sand that one sees in and on the sand hills. Nothing came easy. With shovels in hand, we loaded up the pickup truck with gravel as best we could. Back on the property, my father constructed a sieve apparatus from wire mesh material that he purchased from the local Ryan Lumber Company. Once the sand was brought to the property where the home was to be constructed, we would then shovel the sand up against the sieve apparatus that was placed at about a 45 degree angle from the ground. The sieve apparatus enabled the separation of the larger gravel rocks from the smaller granules of sand. The resulting sand was then mixed with cement in a large metal trough that my father called a "canoa". "Canoa" simply means "canoe" in English. I was unable to find a more accurate translation for the trough so for purposes of this piece, I'll call it a large metal trough. By the way, it wasn't easy lugging around the heavy bags of cement.

Anyway, the cement was added to the sand already in the trough. Water was then added to the mixture while at the same time, Chuy or I, with a hoe, would move the mixture back and forth. Once the entire mixture was mixed into a watery concrete mixture, the mixture was poured within the wooden forms to become the foundation of the home. The metal wheel barrow  we used to move the concrete mixture from the trough to the place where the material was to be used became our friend.

My father purchased the adobe blocks from someone in Caseta and they were delivered on a large flat bed truck to our property. By the way, in a previous section, I described how adobe blocks were made. They were basically made by mixing earthen clay with water. Anyway, the adobe blocks weren't brought in all on one load. Judging from the small deliveries of adobe blocks that were delivered over an extended period time, I believe that my father was purchasing adobe blocks only when he could spare the money. It was a poor man's construction project after all.

When the foundation was sufficiently dry, my father and his helpers began to lay the adobe blocks on top of the finished concrete foundation.  One by one, Chuy and I would carry the adobe blocks from the area where they were stored to the location where my father was laying the adobe blocks. The adobe blocks were set in place with cement mortar. The cement mortar was made from a mixture of sand, cement binder and water; unlike the mud mortar that was typically used in adobe structures in Mexico. In addition to carrying the adobe blocks to the location where my father was laying the blocks, we also had to mix and carry the cement mortar in a pail so that my father could use it. Remember that Chuy and I were the gophers.

As the adobe was being laid, the next row of adobe blocks on top of the previous layer would then be laid. They were laid in such a way that the top adobe block was offset by half a block laterally from the adobe block underneath. My father knew that this interlocking pattern would provide for strong walls.

The adobe blocks were about 12 inches wide. The resulting thickness of the walls was therefore 12 inches. As the adobe blocks were being laid, the door frames were also placed in position. The door frames were constructed out of, I believe, 2" x 8" wood lumber. When the adobe block wall height was at the appropriate level, the window frames were set in place. Again 2" x 8" wood lumber was used for this purpose.

Eventually, the adobe blocks were all set in place to form the walls of the structure. A wooden form was constructed all around the top of the adobe walls. Concrete was poured all around the top of the walls within the wooden forms. This concrete atop the adobe walls was called the concrete ring.

I didn't know it at the time but I now believe that the concrete ring served to stabilize the adobe walls so as to prevent them from swaying out or in and thereby collapsing. In addition, the concrete ring on top of the walls served as an anchor for the roof that would come next in the construction. Vertical threaded bolts were placed into the concrete ring when the concrete was being poured. The threaded part of the bolts stuck vertically upwards above the concrete ring. The vertical threaded part of the bolts in the cement ring would later serve to anchor the wooden rafters that would then support the roof. The roof was then installed. My father hired two persons to assist him with the roof installation. I still remember their names. Their names were Andy and Mercy. Their day jobs were at the Ryan Lumber Company. Andy and Mercy were experts at carpentry work. The roof was finally installed.

The finishing touch was the stucco mortar that was applied onto the interior and exterior walls. Remember that the walls were constructed of adobe block and stucco by itself wouldn't have adhered to the adobe wall. As a result, prior to applying the stucco, wire mesh was first affixed to the adobe walls with long nails. The wire mesh served to anchor the stucco mortar onto the walls. Both the exterior walls as well as the interior walls were covered with stucco. Of course the exterior and interior painting of the house was done but without lime whitewash as was done on the old bracero housing facilities back at the Ryan farm. Our home was painted with real exterior and interior paint. We were moving up in the world.

About 2 to 2-1/2 years later, which seemed like an eternity, we now had a home of our own. Ever since my father and mother arrived to the United States during the bracero program, they had lived in a home that didn't belong to them. Now they had a home of their own that we all built. There was a feeling of security at last.

Recall that the work was all done on the weekends and yes, Chuy and I were the gophers . . . go for this, go for that. That's how I learned what it took to construct the Renteria home. Later in time, my father expanded the home and added 3 more rooms to the home. This probably occurred during my high school years between 1966 and 1970. To this date, the home still stands and Gracie, my sister, lives in the home.

Grade School - 6th Grade

After 5th grade, I moved forward to 6th grade. I was now 12 years of age at the start of 6th grade in 1963. My teacher was a woman by the name of Mrs. McCullough. Mrs. McCullough was an elderly more mature woman of thin stature.

I remember that Mrs. McCullough struggled to keep order in the classroom. She always had a paddle handy on top of her desk. That didn't help because by now the boys and some of the girls were the same height or perhaps even taller than Mrs. McCullough. She definitely did struggle keeping order in the classroom.

I remember that I developed a bond with Mrs. McCullough. The bond occurred as a result of my being at very good at penmanship. Penmanship is the art or skill of writing by hand. As a result, the work that I handed in to her was always very neat. By the way, proper penmanship is no longer a requirement in today's public schools because of the advent of personal computers. Having the ability to type is everything now.

Anyway, Mrs. McCullough pressed me to enter the UIL penmanship competition. The University Interscholastic League (UIL) is an organization that administers almost all athletic, music, and academic contests for primary and secondary schools in the State of Texas. I initially wasn't all that thrilled with the thought of competing against other students, but my interest grew as Mrs. McCullough persisted for several more weeks. I wound up competing and I did quite well. I wound up losing to some girl. I earned Mrs. McCullough's respect as a result of being awarded 2nd place.

One fall day in November, as usual my classmates and I were participating in Mrs. McCullough's classroom. The class was proceeding like any other day in Grade School. I went home for lunch and then returned to school to resume class in the afternoon. Shortly after returning back from lunch while now seated at our desks, we heard an intercom announcement from the principal. The principal called all the teachers for a brief meeting at his office. Before she exited the classroom to attend the teacher's meeting, Mrs. McCullough asked us to stay seated at our desks and of course to behave. She returned back to the classroom about 15 minutes later. While she was walking in, she told us told to take our seats and to quiet down. It took a while for the students to finally quiet down.

I noticed her somber face and I could also see that her eyes were tearing up.

Once everyone was now sitting still at their desks, she began to tell us that she had just been informed that the President of the United States had just passed away a few hours ago. We all just sat there at our desks wondering what that meant; we were young and immature. For a while, Mrs. McCullough just sat there without speaking further. She then started to explain more about the office of the President of the United States. She was having trouble speaking; it was as if she was having trouble reconciling herself to the fact that the President had died. Her speech was slow and measured. As she continued speaking, we could now see that she was indeed tearing up and her voice was unsteady. After another long pause, she began to explain a little more about the subject of the Presidency.

About an hour later, we heard another intercom announcement instructing the teachers to again assemble at the principal's office. Again, Mrs. McCullough warned us to behave just as she was walking out the classroom door. About 15 minutes later, she again returned; now she seemed very upset. She again told us to quiet down and to refrain from talking. She then proceeded to tell us that she had just learned that the President had passed away. She indicated that the President had died from having been assassinated. She explained something about foreign governments having been involved in the assassination of President Kennedy. She conveyed the information in an even more serious tone.

During much of the afternoon, Mrs. McCullough now conducted the class in a much more deliberate and slow manner. We as students now understood the seriousness of the situation. Everything now seemed difficult. There was no longer student chatter going on as the afternoon wore on. Things seemed different in the classroom. The class ended for the day and we all went home.

All this happened on a Friday so there was obviously no school during the weekend. I don't remember how we learned that school classes were canceled starting the following Monday. I do however remember that indeed classes were cancelled for a few days during the following week after the President was shot. There was no such thing as cable news channels in those days. There was only the ABC, CBS and NBC networks as well as a Mexican channel that aired from Cd. Juarez. All the channels canceled their regular programming and there was nothing but news about the assassination of President Kennedy.

During the week after the assassination, the person that was alleged to  have assassinated President Kennedy was himself assassinated by a person by the name of Jack Ruby. The person that was accused of the President's assassination was a person by the name of Lee Harvey Oswald. This added to more national intrigue and uncertainty. For weeks, everything on the television was about the assassination of President Kennedy. It was a frightful time for me. Even my parents seemed nervous; they loved President Kennedy. It seemed that the entire country was consumed with the assassination of President Kennedy during the ensuing year. Countless books were written about the subject of the assassination. Countless assassination scenarios were presented. Conspiracy theories abounded. I remember that the Warren Commission was created to investigate the assassination.

A year or 2 later I became interested in learning more about the subject. I thoroughly read a book having to do with the assassination. Although the book was helpful, the scenarios presented in the book just added to more confusion. In the end, the motive for the assassination was never really established. A cloud hung over everybody for quite a while. Those days, especially the 2 weeks after that event, were very stressful to me. I'll never forget; it was a time of doom and gloom.

The Boy Scouts

During the time that I was in 5th grade in Grade School, I joined the Boy Scouts. That was when I was 11 years of age in 1962. The formal name of the organization was Boy Scouts of America. The Boy Scout designation for our troop in Fabens was Troop 52.

The Scout Masters were Roberto Olivas and Hector Flores. They were both young men; probably 25 to 30 years of age at the time. We used to call Mr. Olivas by the name of Beto.

These two men were the leaders of our Boy Scout troop. I respect them highly because they devoted their time in developing boys into responsible young men. I doubt they were paid for their service.

I don't remember who prompted me into joining the Boy Scouts but somehow I did. I do remember that one of the things that initially interested me greatly about joining the Boy Scouts was that the scouts wore a green uniform that included a neckerchief and a military style folded cap known as a garrison cap. The uniforms have changed since I was a boy scout when I was young. For one, scouts don't wear garrison caps anymore and also the uniforms have changed.

The photograph on the left shows the old style uniform that we used to wear. By the way, during the first year of my being a boy scout, I didn't wear a uniform because my parents just couldn't afford the expense. Eventually, they did purchase the shirt, the neckerchief and the garrison cap for me.

By the way, my penchant for things having to do with the military was strong in those early years. Yes, the Boy Scouts did seem to be the military for young boys and that appealed to me. In a subject not directly related to being a boy scout, I remember having seen students my age assigned to assist other students cross the busy pedestrian crosswalk located on Highway 80 just south and across the railroad tracks from the Grade School. I remember riding along in father's farm truck one day while he was driving along Highway 80 near that specific crosswalk. When we drove past that particular pedestrian crossing I noticed that the crossing guards were students my age and the most interesting thing about them was that they were wearing military helmets like those that soldiers wore during World War II. The thought of wearing that Army helmet and doing that work immediately excited me . . . what could be better than that?

Later at home, I told my father that I wanted to be a crossing guard just like those kids. He responded by telling me that the only problem was that we lived on the Ryan farm and that we had to ride the school bus to and from school every day. I told my father that I still wanted to be a crossing guard. Participating as a crossing guard meant that I would not be able to ride the bus back home in the afternoons. I somehow convinced him to pick me up every day at the specific hour after the crossing guard duty ended. Yes, I became a crossing guard and yes I wore the coveted Army helmet which is really what I wanted. This lasted for a few weeks. This short lived adventure ended because my father told me that this was taking too much time away from his work at the farm. For a while, I got to wear the Army helmet and man I thought I looked good in it.

Anyway, the Boy Scout organization, like the military, used a ranking system. When I joined the Boy Scouts, I was automatically assigned the rank of "Tenderfoot". Through a series of training sessions in various subjects and earning what were called merit badges, one could then be promoted up. Eventually I was promoted to Second Class scout and that was my rank for the rest of my days as a boy scout. Every promotion in the scout program was done by way of small ritual ceremonies. The  next rank upward was First Class and the ultimate rank was Eagle Scout. I didn't know it at the time but with a little help from the web, I found that the ranks are actually as follows: Scout, Tenderfoot, Second Class, First Class, Star, Life and Eagle.

Another interesting thing about being in the Boy Scout organization was the Boy Scout Oath and the Boy Scout hand sign. One had to memorize the Scout Oath. It was analogous to the Pledge of Allegiance that one had to recite everyday at the start of every school day. The Boy Scout hand sign was also a requirement. It was made with the right arm held straight out from the shoulder in a horizontal position. The elbow was then bent 90 degrees, with the hand in an upward vertical position. The three middle fingers were placed vertically straight upward with the thumb holding down the pinky finger.

Anyway, when we attended weekly Boy Scout meetings just before we began our meetings we would all recite the Scout Oath in unison while holding up the right hand with the Boy Scout hand sign. The Scout Oath was then recited as follows: ***"On my honor I will do my best to do my duty to God and my country and to obey the Scout Law; to help other people at all times; to keep myself physically strong, mentally awake, and morally straight."***.

One other thing about the Boy Scouts; the Scout Oath was important but the Scout Law was doubly important. I obtained the following from the web:

"The Scout Law has 12 points. Each is a goal for every Scout. A Scout tries to live up to the Scout Law every day. It is not always easy to do, but a Scout always tries. A Scout is:

- ***TRUSTWORTHY. Tell the truth and keep promises. People can depend on you.***
- ***LOYAL. Show that you care about your family, friends, Scout leaders, school, and country.***
- ***HELPFUL. Volunteer to help others without expecting a reward.***
- ***FRIENDLY. Be a friend to everyone, even people who are very different from you.***
- ***COURTEOUS. Be polite to everyone and always use good manners.***
- ***KIND. Treat others as you want to be treated . Never harm or kill any living thing without good reason.***
- ***OBEDIENT. Follow the rules of your family, school, and pack. Obey the laws of your community and country.***

- ***CHEERFUL. Look for the bright side of life. Cheerfully do tasks that come your way. Try to help others be happy.***
- ***THRIFTY. Work to pay your own way. Try not to be wasteful. Use time, food, supplies, and natural resources wisely.***
- ***BRAVE. Face difficult situations even when you feel afraid. Do what you think is right despite what others might be doing or saying.***
- ***CLEAN. Keep your body and mind fit . Help keep your home and community clean.***
- ***REVERENT. Be reverent toward God. Be faithful in your religious duties. Respect the beliefs of others."***

From time to time our Scout Masters arranged camp outings to various locations away from Fabens. The objective of the camp outings was always to teach something; camping technique, knot tying, starting a fire without using matches and the like. During the camp outings the Scout Masters would emphasize respect for people and respect for nature.

I specifically remember three camping trips. There were several but I only remember these three. One camping trip was to a location beside a river known as the Black River. The site of the camp was located about 7 miles northeast from the small town of Whites City, New Mexico. Now as a grownup, every time we travel from El Paso toward Carlsbad, I'll look for the intersection of route 720 from the main highway; look to the right and remember that specific scout camp site. The location can be viewed using Google Maps with the lat-long coordinates of 32.203110 latitude and -104.255948 longitude.

Another camping trip we made was to a place called Little Box Canyon that was located close to the Rio Grande south of Esperanza, Texas. An unfortunate accident happened while we were camped beside the Rio Grande River at that location. More on that accident will be described later in his chapter. The approximate location of the camp site can be viewed again using Google Maps at the lat-long coordinates of 31.111784 latitude and -105.632353 longitude.

Yet another camp outing was a 2 week summer camp at a Boy Scout facility known as Camp Dale Resler located very near Cloudcroft, New

Mexico. The location of that camp site can be found at 32.947166 latitude and -105.731188 longitude.

During the summer of 1963, my Boy Scout troop spent 2 weeks of summer camp at Camp Dale Resler. Camp Dale Resler was and I think still is the property of the Boy Scouts of America. It was a sprawling camp area located deep in the Lincoln National Forest. The camp was so extensive that at the time we attended summer camp, it hosted about 18 perhaps 20 different Boy Scout troops. Looks can be deceiving; at that time it seemed that we were out in the deep wilderness but in fact the camp facility turned out to be only about a mile from the Cloudcroft town center.

By the way, I remember that the fee to attend Boy Scout camp was I believe $125.00. For some reason, that amount is stuck in my mind. When I approached my father about the fee, he wasn't too excited about it. A few weeks of prodding changed that.

Anyway, the typical day at summer camp consisted of hiking as well as classes provided by the staff personnel on topics such as knot tying, pitching tents, wood carving and the like. Each troop would carry its troop flag on a small pole when moving as a group from here and there. The troops would meet for breakfast and supper at the main mess hall. Yes, it was called a mess hall; not because it was a messy hall but because that's what the military calls a room or building where soldiers eat together. Every troop would normally cook their own lunch and in fact cooking was a subject that was emphasized as part of our scout training.

During the night, we would sleep inside tents; two to a tent. It was our responsibility to keep the interior clean. In fact, the camp site staff would sometimes make random inspections of tents to ascertain that the living quarters were up to their standards. If it rained and it did rain several days, we had to stay inside our tents until the rain subsided. The photograph on the left shows the old style military tents we used at summer camp.

Living in what we thought was the wilderness was new to us. Spending two weeks away from home when I was 12 years old was new and at the same time sad for me. It was the first time in my life that I had been away from my parents for an extended period of time. Especially during those sad days, I would hike away by myself from our camp site toward a location nearby a highway. I'd have my crying bouts there. I don't mind saying it now, but I missed my mother.

Sometimes I'd stare toward the direction where I thought Fabens was from the camp and imagine my mother and father going about their business; of course without me. I was young and very, very homesick. I remember a song that was playing on the radio in those days.

The song's name was "Sukiyaki" and was sung by a Japanese vocalist in Japanese. While writing this piece, I searched the web to see when the song debuted; it was originally aired in Japan in 1961 and it debuted in the United States in 1963. That's how I remembered the date when I spent summer camp at Camp Dale Resler. Even today, when I happen to hear the song on the radio while driving along in my car, it brings back memories of those days when I missed my mother so much.

Another song that reminds me of summer camp that year was a song titled "Camp Granada" which also started airing in Autumn of 1963. The song is a hilarious spoof about a kid that is writing a letter to his mother from summer camp. In that letter, he is telling his mother that he misses home and that if allowed to go home he will behave and be a good boy. Near the end of the song, the kid indicates that it stopped raining and that all of a sudden he's started having fun. In the end, the kid tells his mother to disregard the letter. The song hit home with me because I too was homesick. Look it up on the web; the video contains the lyrics shown along as the song plays. The song title is "Camp Granada" and was sung by Allan Sherman.

Anyway, all the troops were ordered to attend a ceremony at the center of the camp compound the night before our last day at summer camp. The ceremony was held sometime around 8:00 p.m. at night. It seemed strange to me that we were ordered to meet at such a late hour but that's what we all did. We witnessed an induction ceremony of about 10 or 12 young men into what was known as the "Order of the Arrow". The young men were of Anglo descent and they were all dressed in North American Indian attire and of course with headbands fitted with feathers.

The young men were seated around the main campfire and all the scouts sat cross-legged in a large ring around the young men. As part of the ceremony, the master of ceremonies approached each of the inductees individually and recited several passages involving honor and trust. One could hear a pin drop; everyone was so quiet trying to listen in. After the ceremony which took about an hour, each of the young men were dispatched to different locations in the forest and that is where they spent the entire night alone by themselves. It seemed so mysterious that they were dispatched to be alone the entire night in the forest. We came away awestruck because there was a feeling of honor being bestowed on these young men.

I never really fully understood what the Order of the Arrow was. While writing this piece, I found the following on the web: "The Order of the Arrow serves as Scouting's National Honor Society. More than 176,000 members strong, the Order recognizes Scouts and Scouters who best exemplify the Scout Oath and Law in their daily lives.". So what we witnessed were young men who were the best of the best . . . so glad to finally know.

I previously made a reference to an accident having occurred during our camp outing to Little Box Canyon near Esperanza, Texas. When we arrived to the location, we set up camp about 500 feet away from the Rio Grande River. During the first day, we hiked in single file to the top of a nearby mountain. I remember that view from atop the mountain; it was spectacular. I can almost see it in my mind's eye even today.

During the next day, we pressed our Scout Masters to let us go swimming in the Rio Grande River. I remember the river had water in it and it didn't appear to be flowing swiftly; so it didn't appear to be dangerous. Anyway, we were given permission. We were excited that we were about to go swimming. It's possible that the Scout Masters hadn't really planned on the trip to include swimming because I remember that nobody brought swimming shorts with them.

Anyway, we all stripped down to our underwear and then we proceeded to enter the water. All of us had been playing in the water for perhaps 5 minutes when all of a sudden, one of the boys nearby began to yell something while pointing upstream in the river toward someone that was splashing in the water about 50 yards away. The boy suddenly yelled out "it's Pepino . . . he doesn't know how to swim!". The boy kept yelling out the same phrase several more times. We all stopped playing around in an attempt to listen to what the boy was screaming. We then realized what was happening . . . one of our scouts whose name was Pepino Hernandez was flailing his arms perhaps because he was drowning. We realized that we had to get to him as soon as possible.

I remember some of us quickly swam to the shore and then began to run towards Pepino through the brush along the bank of the river. Somehow I wound up being the first to reach the place where we had seen Pepino flailing his arms but now there was no sign of Pepino; the water was still and undisturbed. It was obvious to me that Pepino had sunk.

I looked behind to see if the other boys were coming and yes, they were but they were still far off. There was no time to wait . . . I made a decision to dive into the water to try to rescue Pepino. I was able to dive deep into the river but I was not able to touch the bottom. I swam up for air and again I dove back down into the murky water. I was still unable to touch bottom and worse yet I was unable to touch any part of Pepino's body. By that time, two other boys had caught up and they too began to search for Pepino in the water. One of the boys had run back to the campground and told Beto, our Scout Master, about what was happening. By now, it was 10 or 15 minutes since I first dove into the river in search of Pepino.

Beto arrived and quickly did the same without success. One of the boys all of sudden mentioned that perhaps Pepino had exited the river and had walked back to the camp site so we all ran back to the camp site and we found that Pepino was not there. We all knew now that Pepino had drowned. Eventually Beto and the assistant Scout Master, Hector Flores, told us to stay at the camp site and not to go near the water. We all just waited at the camp site during the better part of the day while either Beto or Hector went to the town of Esperanza to call for emergency help. This was the time when cell phones didn't exist. An ambulance arrived about an hour later and about 2 hours after that, two men arrived equipped with Scuba diving gear. At about 5:00 p.m. that afternoon, the two divers along with Beto and Hector returned to the location of the ambulance carrying Pepino totally covered with a blanket on a stretcher.

My father appeared about that time along with several other parents in their individual vehicles. My father told me to get into his truck because he would be taking me home. So that was the unfortunate accident that happened at Little Box Canyon. Sadly, I don't remember Pepino's funeral.

Another defining event occurred during the time when I was a boy scout. As I said earlier, boy scout meetings were held weekly. The meetings were held in an adobe-stuccoed building located along Main Street a few blocks away from the Fabens town center. At the conclusion of each meeting, sometime around 8 p.m. at night, we would disband and proceed to walk to our respective homes. Some kids would get picked up by their parents and others would just walk home.

From time to time while walking home, a group of street boys would follow me. These were not boys from the troop mind you; they were street boys who got their kicks from harassing boys like me. The number of street boys varied; they were a gang of 4 or 5 boys. As I walked along, they would make taunting remarks at me and I acted as if I didn't notice. During several of those walks home they would even kick me on my behind. It hurt but I continued walking forward acting as if nothing had happened.

One of those street boys was a boy who was known by the name of "el sopas" which in English means "the stew". I don't remember his real name. I do remember he was dark complected and a little shorter than I. I am not sure why he was called by that name but that's the way it was. It was demeaning for me to have to walk the gauntlet, so to speak, every time I walked home after the scout meetings.

I remember one specific time when our Boy Scout troop met early in the afternoon. After the meeting at about 4:00 p.m. that afternoon, I began my walk home. Again, there they were; the street boys waiting to taunt me. I can't remember if they actually struck me or just taunted me during that walk home.

Anyway, after having taunted me, the street boys desisted and left me alone. As I continued walking, my father was driving down the street and happened to notice me walking home. He stopped for me and when I boarded the pickup truck, he must have noticed something about me; possibly my being upset or perhaps with tears in my eyes. Anyway, he noticed that I was upset and he then questioned me about what was going on. I responded by telling him that the street boys had harassed me again. He quickly asked me who the boys were that had harassed me. I told him it had been several boys and I also mentioned the name of "el sopas". He then asked me where I had last seen the boys and I conveyed to him their approximate whereabouts.

My father immediately turned the pickup truck around and proceeded to drive to the general area. He finally located a group of boys that were walking along together. He asked me if those were the boys that had bothered me and I told him that yes, they were. He stopped the truck as near as possible to them, stepped off the truck and then asked for the boy known as "el sopas". "El sopas" identified himself to my father.

My father then told him "I understand you want to fight my son"; of course in Spanish. My father then ordered me to step off the pickup truck and I did so. My father then told the boy "here he is. I want you and him to fight it out without anyone else getting involved; one on one . . . it will be a fair fight". I shuddered with fear when I heard his words but somehow I succeeded in not showing fright. I couldn't believe that my father was actually encouraging the boys to fight me. The boy didn't move; I suppose that he hadn't expected my father's taunting words. After a few seconds of silence, the boy said something to the effect that he didn't want to fight me. My father gave him one last opportunity and the boy continued saying that he was not interested in fighting me. My father turned toward me and told me to get into the truck and we then drove off leaving the boys behind. From that day forward, "el sopas" and the rest of his street buddies never bothered me. I think this occurred in 1963 when I was 12 years of age.

Fast forward to 1966 when I would be 15 years old and I would have to fight the final battle with yet another hoodlum. My sense is that I became a target because I was light complected and in the minds of that street gang, they might have thought that I was of Anglo descent. Far from it; I was Hispanic just like them.

In the end, I proudly belonged to Boy Scout Troop 52. I learned to comport myself properly and to face difficult situations even when I felt fear.

Grade School - 7th Grade

After graduating from 6th grade in Grade School, I moved on to 7th grade. I was now 13 years of age in 1964. My 7th grade teacher was Mrs. Covington. Mrs. Covington was somewhat younger than Mrs. McCullough. She was very mild mannered and easy to get along with. This year I was assigned to class 7A and not to class 7C. In a previous section, I indicated that that children of Anglo descent tended to be placed in the classes that were designated A and B while Hispanic children tended to be placed in the classes that were designated C and D. Being now in class 7A meant that at least half of my classmates were students of Anglo descent. This was different. In all of my previous grades I had been placed in C classes where all of the students in those classes were Hispanic.

Now in grade 7A, I noticed that all the students spoke English without resorting to speaking Spanish. In a previous section I spoke about the "Anglo immersion process" as it related to 3rd grade teachers paddling students when they were caught speaking Spanish. Well now I was immersed into a new environment where speaking in English all day long was the new normal. I knew and felt that being placed in 7A was different. Now as I am writing this memoir, I wonder who it was that made the decision to place me in 7A class instead of continuing on to class 7C. Was it my having done well in the UIL completion during my previous year or did Mrs. Jane Ryan have something to do with it; I'll never know.

Another difference was that we no longer attended classes in one classroom for the entire school year. Now, we were assigned to a home room which in my case was Mrs. Covington's classroom. What was different was that now we spent the first hour of the school day in our home room being taught by our home room teacher. After that hour, the bell would ring to signal a classroom change. We would then pick up our classroom materials such as books, pencils and the like and walk to another classroom where another teacher would teach a different subject during that hour. When that hour ended, again we would walk to another classroom and yet another teacher would assume the teaching role. This went on the entire day during the morning and the afternoon.

It was different and it was chaotic during the first week or so because the students sometimes wound up in the wrong classroom. Eventually, all the students settled in to this new way of switching classrooms. Prior to writing this memoir, I never gave much thought to the reason for this new merry-go-round way of teaching 7th grade. It dawned on me that in previous grades only one teacher taught all the subjects. I can only guess that the course material was now getting more specific and perhaps more difficult that the teachers now needed to specialize in specific subjects.

As an aside, about the time when I was attending 7th grade in Grade School, I remember that Esteban Renteria, my father's half brother, used to play the acoustic guitar. He would sing along as he strummed various chords on his guitar. I asked him to show me how to play the guitar and he did. He showed me three basic chords; the C, F and G chords. The Mexican songs he played only required those 3 chords. That was my first introduction to playing the guitar. By the way, fast forward to when my granddaughter Abigail was about 6 or 7 years of age. She used to refer to the guitar as the "contar" . . . close enough for our baby Abigail. Anyway, during the fall of that year, I joined the football team. I don't remember the position I played but I was on the starting team.

Our coach's name was Mr. McMains. I remember he was a pretty gruff but fair man.

One day while we were dressing up for practice, all the boys were acting up in the dressing room. I don't remember exactly what we were  doing but we must have been doing something extremely horrible because when Coach McMains stepped into the dressing room he told us all to line up because we were going to get paddled. Well we had no choice; we all lined up and prepared ourselves to be punished. He told us to strip completely naked and we all did so.

He took out a 3/4 inch thick wooden board that had been fashioned into a paddle. The paddle width was about 4 inches and the length of the paddle was about the same length as that of a baseball bat. He started with the first boy. Coach McMains then told the boy to stand erect and then said to him "hold your balls". The boy grabbed his testicles with both hands, assumed the position as instructed, and then Coach McMains then swung back and bam; struck the boy once on his buttocks.

The pain was so great that the boy began to jump up and down holding his buttocks. After a while his pain began to subside because eventually he began to settle down. Yes, it was going to be a bad day for me judging from what I had just seen. The next boy followed and then the next, always resulting in the same outcome; the boys jumping up and down from the sheer pain. My turn came. I felt the hit. Wow! I could feel the blood rushing to my head, the pain was so great. And yes, I couldn't help but jump around the same as the other boys. This went on until the very last boy was done. Needless to say, we learned to respect Coach McMains. I can assure you that whatever we did that day that warranted the paddling never occurred again.

In the area of school subjects, a new concept was presented to us starting in 7th grade. It was the subject referred to as "new math". Prior to 7th grade, mathematics encompassed the traditional subject matter of addition, division, multiplication and division. During those pre-7th grade years the numbers kept getting larger and more complex but it basically boiled down to basic arithmetic. In new math, the traditional subject matter was no longer emphasized. The new normal was set theory, different base numbering systems other than base 10, symbolic logic and many other new mathematical concepts.

It seemed that controversy existed in relation to this new method of teaching math. I don't remember where the controversy originated; it could have been from the teachers grumbling here and there. I do remember that it was viewed as a stressful change at the time.

The following web article titled "What Ever Happened To New Math?" shows in more detail what "new math" was:

"In practice, this meant learning how different number systems worked, that the number 9 in the decimal, or base ten, system would be the number 100 in base three. It meant learning about the set, a grouping of things: a beach as a "set" of grains of sand, for example. It meant learning the difference between a number like 7 and its representation the numeral, which could be expressed many different ways—21 minus 14, 7 times 1, VII. It meant learning to draw ruler like number lines and divide them into sections to discover fractional multiplication. It meant learning about frames—boxlike symbols used as substitutes for the x, y, z's of algebra. It meant learning a new language with terms like open sentence, complementation, and truth set. It meant, in essence, learning to discover the hidden patterns in mathematics before knowing what they were called and reasoning out solutions before knowing rules—all at an earlier age than had ever been attempted before."

The article can be viewed by using the following web link: https://www.americanheritage.com /content/whatever-happened- new-math-0

Now while writing this memoir, I began to wonder how "new math" became a reality. Back in those days, I knew it was a big thing. Based on information from a Wikipedia article it appears that "new math" was the result of fears that resulted from the Soviet Union having launched the "Sputnik" satellite in 1957. There was widespread fear that Soviet Union engineers were more mathematically advanced than engineers in the United States.

I found the following Wikipedia article on the web that describes how "new math" originated:

"New Mathematics or New Math was a brief, dramatic change in the way mathematics was taught in American grade schools, and to a lesser extent in European countries, during the 1960s. The change involved new curriculum topics and teaching practices introduced in the U.S. shortly after the Sputnik crisis, in order to boost science education and mathematical skill in the population, so that the technological threat of Soviet engineers, reputedly highly skilled mathematicians, could be met."

The article can be view using the following web link: https://en.wikipedia.org/wiki/New_Math

I didn't know it at the time but to some extent, my 7th grade was the start of my technical career. I began to learn new mathematical concepts that in addition, augmented the math subject matter in High School. I feel this was one reason why I ultimately proceeded on to college after High School.

By the way, during my school years, I came to know a variety of people that were schooled in Mexico in their early years. Based on observation, students schooled in Mexico seemed to be very adept at working math problems in their head without having to use pencil and paper. While they were strong in basic arithmetic, they seemed to have a lack of knowledge of more advanced conceptual mathematics. In several conversations with those students, I found out that arithmetic in Mexican schools was taught by memorization and habitual repetition and I concluded that problem solving and logical deduction in mathematics was not. That's why I now believe that the new manner of learning math in the United States was more effective.

I suppose that the 7th grade students that year were exceptional well behaved because at the end of the school year we were bussed to an outing at a place known as Hueco Tanks. Hueco Tanks is a scenic rocky area located east of El Paso. To get there, one drives about 22 miles east from downtown El Paso on Highway 62. One then turns left on Route 2775 which intersects with Highway 62 and then drives another 2 or 3 miles toward the rocky-looking mountain to arrive at Hueco Tanks.

Hueco Tanks is an important historic site to the local Tigua Indians because it is the home of many rock pictographs painted by the Indians in the past. In those days, Hueco Tanks was easily accessible by visitors. It is now a Texas State Park and is fenced in.

It's a nice place to experience nature at its best.

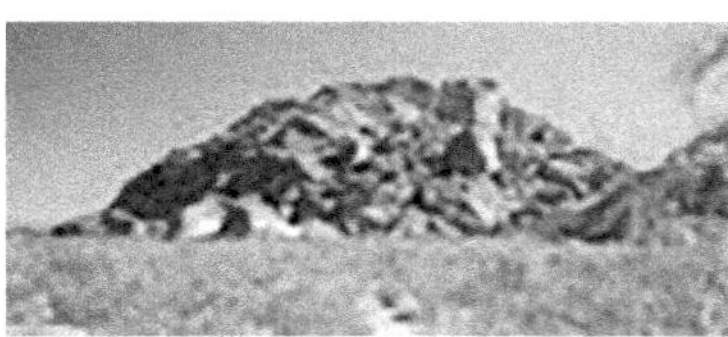

By the way the words "Hueco" means "hollow" in English. So Hueco Tanks really means "Hollow Tanks". The place has many depressions on the large rock formations that serve to catch rainwater during rain storms; that's probably why it is called Hueco Tanks. Anyway, it was a fun outing.

One other thing; 7th grade is when I became aware of a pretty girl. She was attractive, beautiful and very talkative. She had a great smile, dimples on her cheeks and spoke English well. I don't remember ever having conversed with her during 7th grade but I did take notice of her. Her name was Socorro Martinez.

Grade School - 8th Grade

After 7th grade then came 8th grade. It was now 1965 and I was 14 years of age. My 8th grade home room teacher's name was Mrs. Suggs. Mrs. Suggs had a reputation of being a very stern teacher. I felt she was a fair teacher; at least I felt she was to me.

As in the 7th grade I played football during the 8th grade. I don't remember the position I played that year but it wasn't in the backfield. I was on the offensive and defensive line. I played both first string offense and first string defense. During one specific practice session, Coach McMains asked me if I'd like to try my hand at the fullback position; I accepted. The team then ran about 5 plays with me in the fullback position. I must have not done well because after those plays, he instructed me to resume the original position on the offensive line. Yes, I wasn't made to be on the backfield and I knew it.

Somehow I wound up in a music class during the 8th grade. Music class was held at the High School band hall and not at the Grade School building. I remember we were taught to play a small plastic musical 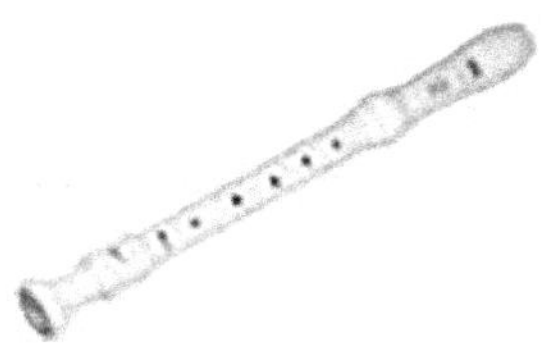 instrument known as a "recorder". It was a very simple plastic instrument that only required one to blow into the mouthpiece. The fingering of the instrument involved placing fingers over specific holes along the length of the instrument. In this way, different sounds or notes, as they were called, could be made. The name of the instrument seemed odd to me but that's what it was called. That was my first introduction to reading musical notes.

I don't remember anything extraordinarily special that happened when I was in the 8th grade. As usual I received "honor roll" for that year as in other years, except of course during my 5th grade.

I remember that toward the end of the school year, all students in the 8th grade classes were bussed to an outing to a place in the sand hills known as San Felipe Park. San Felipe Park was and is located on the road leading east from Fabens, crossing Interstate 10 and forward about 4 miles further; on the road known as San Felipe Road.

For some strange reason, the outing was known as a hayride. Literally, a hayride is a ride taken for pleasure in a wagon carrying hay; there was no such thing as a wagon filled with hay that day. While on the hayride outing, the students ate hotdogs and hamburgers provided by the school and the students had a nice time with each other playing volleyball and strolling around the hills. Anyway, I don't really know why the school provided the hayride outing except that perhaps it was the school's reward to the students for a good fruitful year at school. I did take notice of a young girl that caught my eye. She was short and very attractive. Her name was Socorro Martinez.

The end of the year also brought with it graduation day from Grade School. I was class salutatorian having succeeded in earning the second highest grade in the 8th grade. While writing this memoir, I struggled to remember the name of the valedictorian but alas I was unable to recall who that was. I was asked by Mrs. Suggs to prepare my speech that was to be delivered during the graduation ceremony. She also told me that the entire class would be assembled at the High School auditorium for a practice run prior to the actual ceremony that was to take place a few days later. I prepared my speech and readied myself for the student practice session.

The graduation practice day arrived. The student procession began and all the students including myself took our seats. One of the teachers then directed the valedictorian to proceed with the speech; he or she finished and then it was my turn.

While I was speaking, a student by the name of Freddy Vasquez began to taunt me. He was seated where the rest of the students were seated in the auditorium. I took notice of him because he wouldn't desist. As I continued with the speech, he continued making smart- alecky remarks as if trying to confuse me. After a while, I stopped in the middle of my speech; I had reached my boiling point. I looked directly toward where he was sitting and I then motioned with the open palm of my right hand toward him as if to signal him "wait till we get outside". It was my threat to him; I was that angry.

When the rest of the students saw my response, some to them made a sound as if taunting Freddy. I continued and finished my speech and then I took my seat. The rest of the practice session proceeded without event. When the practice session concluded, we exited row by row in an orderly fashion. Since I was seated closer to the auditorium stage, I was one of the last to exit the auditorium. I was still heated and angry.

When I exited the auditorium, I walked down the few steps of stairs, went to where Freddy Vasquez was standing and I immediately started a fist fight with him. It didn't matter to me that I was going to get into trouble with my teachers; all that mattered was that Freddy Vasquez taunted me in front of everybody in the 8th grade and I needed to get even with him.

We wound up wrestling on the grass and somehow I gained the advantage. I wound up on top of him holding him down with my legs straddled on each side of his body. Once in that position, I began to punch him on the face over and over again as hard as I could. This continued for a while until finally the teachers arrived and they pulled me off of him. I remember I was still angry after being pulled off from him but I made no attempt to continue.

That's how the fight ended against the class bully, Freddy Vasquez. From then on and for the rest of the time prior to and during our 8th graduation, Freddy kept his distance from me. After graduating, I never saw him again in school. In retrospect, I should have defended myself prior to that fight outside the school but I have to admit that I always tried to avoid physical fights.

In later years, situations would come up where I would be tasked in management positions both as an employee as well as at my own company. When confronted with a difficult management situation, I would always remember the lesson I learned long ago involving Freddy Vasquez. The lesson is this: "Never place a person in a corner without providing the person a small dignified exit because absent that dignified exit, that person who you thought was weak will muster enough courage to fight back with all its might and may even beat you." I was the weak person that ultimately mustered enough courage to fight back hard.

In my case, it didn't matter what trouble I might have gotten into by attacking Freddy Vasquez. He left me no choice; I had to do it. As a result of this fight, I never had to fight again all through my remaining school years in Fabens. Respect is not given; it is earned.

By the way, the pretty girl I kept watching in 7th grade continued to be ever present in my 8th grade classes. She became a cheerleader on the cheerleading organization that 8th grade year. She rooted for our football team. Man, she was good looking and very talkative.

California: The First Venture Out

Fabens in 1966, when I was 15 years of age, was a small town of about 3200 persons. While writing this memoir, I was unsure of the population in Fabens at that time so I reviewed the U.S. Census records on the web and found the following information: 1960, 3134 inhabitants; 1970, 3241 inhabitants.

Anyway, by the summer of 1966 my family had grown to 8 kids so finances were very tight. The last of my siblings, Martin my youngest brother, was previously born in April of 1965.

During the school months just prior to graduating from the 8th grade, there was no part time work to be had; the town was too small. I remember that the hourly pay for "chopping cotton" was still $.50 per hour. An 8 hour day in the hot sun would pay $4.00. For about a 2 or 3 week period of time right after school ended that summer, Chuy and I worked chopping cotton at a nearby farm.

At that time, across the street from our home in Fabens lived the De La O family; the head of the family was a person by the name of Francisco De La O. We knew him as Don Panchito. His two sons were Refugio and Luis. Cuco is the Spanish nickname for Refugio. Cuco was about 19 years of age while Luis was probably 17 or 18 years old. Anyway, somehow Cuco learned that the labor wage rate in California was $1.50 per hour. At the time, that wage rate represented a 3-fold increase compared to the local wage rate in the Fabens area. Somehow Cuco and Chuy hatched a plan to borrow my father's personal pickup truck to travel and work in California. Indeed, Cuco and Chuy approached my father about borrowing his truck. They told my father about the higher wage rate in California. In addition, they told him that their plan was for Cuco, Luis, Chuy and I to travel to California in my father's truck in search of higher paying jobs. We didn't have to convince my father; he wound up lending us his pickup truck.

Shortly thereafter, we began our travel to California by way of New Mexico along the towns of Las Cruces, then Deming and then Lordsburg. By the way, the pickup truck was equipped with a camper enclosure that covered the rear cargo bay of the pickup truck. I remember very well that Luis and I rode inside the camper enclosure while Cuco and Chuy did all of the driving.

The driving distance from El Paso to Bakersfield, California seemed to take forever. Based on a Google search, the driving time today between those two cities is 13 hours and 10 minutes but remember, the speed limits in those days was perhaps 60 miles an hour. Anyway, that first night was spent sleeping in the pickup truck somewhere in Bakersfield; probably because we couldn't afford to stay at a motel. Poor people don't have many options and that was us. I remember that the next day we began to travel northward toward the town of Delano, California. Along the way, we stopped at various farms here and there. Cuco and Chuy would take the lead in asking the farm owners if they needed laborers but they kept getting rejected. We arrived in the town of Delano during the late afternoon and we spent that night again in the pickup truck. Trying to sleep in the back of a pickup truck was not like sleeping at home.

The next morning, we proceeded northward again. The majority of the farms were grape farms. Again Cuco and Chuy took the lead in soliciting work along the way. Again and again they would come back empty handed to the truck where Luis and I were waiting.

Toward the end of the day, we arrived at a little town known as Goshen, California. I don't remember how it happened but that evening  we ended up renting a very small trailer to sleep in. I remember that the trailer was very small and had a silver-aluminum sheet metal exterior similar to the photograph shown on the left. I remember that two others including myself slept in the trailer. I don't remember exactly but either Chuy or Cuco slept in the cab of the pickup truck. It was a hot miserable night with mosquitoes flying all around.

Morning finally came. The small trailer was equipped with a small stove so Cuco and Chuy decided to go buy eggs, baloney and soft drinks for breakfast. When they returned from the grocery store, Luis and I hurriedly cooked breakfast and at last we all ate a hot meal. It was our first hot meal since we left Fabens 3 days prior. All during the trip we had eaten nothing but baloney and mayonnaise sandwiches. By the way, I wasn't in charge of the money but I'm almost sure that by then we were scraping the bottom of the barrel. During the rest of the day, we again drove to the local farms in search of employment. The Goshen area was full of grape farms. Some of the farms that we visited had large, extensive fruit orchards. As usual Cuco and Chuy took the lead in asking for employment. I remember Luis was a timid person and like myself was comfortable with Cuco and Chuy taking the lead. The day progressed toward the afternoon and we still had no luck finding employment at any of the local farms. We all returned back to the small trailer during that late afternoon. Again as before, we slept in the tiny trailer; another miserable night.

When morning arrived, Cuco drove off to the store to purchase milk and other foodstuffs. He returned about an hour later; he seemed excited as he stepped off the truck. He proceeded tell Luis, Chuy and I that somebody at the store had told him about a farm in Delano that was hiring workers to work in the grape fields. We began to feel a sense of excitement and most importantly hope. Maybe this was our opportunity to finally find what we came for in the first place; work. We quickly ate our cold sandwiches and began to drive, retracing our way back to Delano which was about 43 miles south.

We arrived at Delano. Cuco drove in to a local gasoline station to refuel the pickup truck. Chuy asked the gasoline station attendant for the location of the specific farm that he was told was hiring workers. As luck would have it, the attendant provided directions to that specific farm location. We hurriedly boarded the pickup truck and took off toward the location of the farm.

When we arrived at the farm, Cuco and Chuy immediately stepped off the truck and proceeded into a small office building on the farm to speak with the person in charge. Luis and I waited at the truck while Cuco and Chuy were inside the office. About 30 minutes later, they returned back to the truck with good news; well perhaps so-so news. They told Luis and I that indeed the company foreman had indicated that there was work available in the grape fields and that they did have room in the labor camp housing quarters for us. The only problem was that the minimum working age to be allowed to work on the farm and live in the farm's labor camp was 16 years of age. Since I was 15 years old, I wouldn't be able to work there. My heart sank upon hearing this news. How about me? What was I going to do?

Soon thereafter, Chuy turned to me and began to tell me that the farm foreman had also informed them that there was another farm in the area that might want to hire me even at my age of 15 years; my heart sank even further. Chuy tried to soothe my fears. The thought of Chuy, Cuco and Luis working together on that farm while I would be working on a separate farm seemed really impossible to me. Chuy continued telling me that it would only be for a short time because perhaps some other employment opportunity would come up where all four of us could work together. I grudgingly accepted.

There are many things that I can't remember about what happened next but I do remember that we did visit that other farm and in fact, I was hired to work on that farm. I remember that one of the supervisors led me to the labor camp's housing quarters and pointed toward the bunk bed I was going to sleep in. I was assigned the bottom bunk bed. The photograph on the left shows the bunk bed I slept in.

The next morning at about 5:00 a.m., I heard the loudspeaker begin to loudly play Mexican music. It was the labor camp's morning wake-up alarm system. It was time to wake up and get ready for the work day ahead. Everybody in the barrack where I slept began to get up from their beds and they slowly began to dress. Some of the men proceeded to the showers although most of the men just got dressed and then proceeded to walk to the cafeteria hall for  breakfast. I did the same. I was the youngest of all the workers. I didn't know how to get around or what to do so I just followed the men as they lined up with trays along a serving line. The food was served to the men in similar fashion as that of a cafeteria serving line.

After eating breakfast, we began to walk to the door to exit the cafeteria. As each man exited, he was given a lunch bag. I too was given a lunch bag. I followed them stepping up and onto the cargo bed of a large  truck. The photograph on the left shows a semblance of the men sitting in the cargo bed of the large truck. It was one of several large trucks that stood parked in a row, side by side. Once on the bed of the truck, everyone took their seats on the benches anchored to the truck's cargo bed. I did the same. After a while, the drivers started the engines and a few minutes later, each truck began to move out and away from the camp site.

A few miles later, the trucks arrived to an area covered entirely with rows of trees. As we stepped off the truck cargo beds, each person was given  a wooden ladder and two metal pails. I could see each man approach a tree, set up the ladder and then climb the ladder with a pail in hand. They began picking the fruit from the trees. One of the men took notice of me probably because he saw that I was hesitating getting started. He promptly showed me how to set the ladder and then he showed me which fruit was ripe enough to pick from the tree. They referred to the fruit on the trees as "ciruelas". I'd never seen this purple colored fruit before. Later on I would learn that the fruit was what's known as "plums".

We worked from 7:00 am until 12:00 noon lugging around the ladder from tree to tree, picking the plums, placing them in the two pails. We then took the pails to a truck were the plums were placed in wooden boxes. The boxes were then placed onboard the bed of a cargo truck.

We took an hour for lunch sitting on the ground underneath the trees. We all ate the sandwiches and the apple that were packed inside the lunch bag that was provided to us when we left the cafeteria previously that morning.

After eating their lunch most of the men would lie down on the ground, place their hats over their face and they would then fall asleep. When 1:00 p.m. rolled around, the foreman would shout out several times and everyone would awaken. They would then ready themselves for work again. We would work until 5:00 p.m. in the afternoon.

At quitting time, we would board the trucks that would take us back to the labor camp where the barracks were located. Once at the labor camp, some would proceed to the cafeteria to eat dinner and others would shower before eating dinner. After eating dinner, I would go to the barracks where my bed was located to lie down. A quick shower and I would be back at my bed. At 9:00 p.m. it was lights out; nobody was allowed out of the barracks. The next day was a repeat of the previous day. By the way, nobody spoke English; not even the foreman.

The first work week at the labor camp went by. I don't remember if we worked on Saturday but I am certain that we didn't work on Sundays. Chuy would come over from the labor camp where he worked to visit me during Sundays. I don't remember him ever taking me to visit the labor camp where Cuco, Luis and he worked. During a couple of Sundays, he didn't show up to visit me. Weekends were very hard and lonely for me.

There was nothing to do and worse yet I didn't have anything in common with the rest of the men in the labor camp. I was 15 years of age and the youngest of the men might have been 19 or 20 years old. The laborers at the labor camp numbered about 50 to 75 people. From time to time, I would overhear their conversations and that's how I found out that they were all from Mexico; they would refer to places like Michoacan and Jalisco.

During the lonely times over the weekend, I would walk to one of the irrigation ponds nearby the labor camp and just sit there by myself for hours just to think. I would wonder what my father and mother were doing back in Fabens; I missed home so much. It wasn't like today when you can just call someone on your cell phone and talk with that person. We didn't have a telephone at our home in Fabens anyway. This was a change from just having graduated from the 8th grade as a salutatorian. Now I was being immersed with people that didn't speak English at all. It was like being on a deserted island with no way out. Saturday nights were something that I dreaded. During Saturday nights, most of the men would go to the nearby city of Delano to drink at the local bars. It was their night off. I'm not sure how they managed to get to Delano from the labor camp but somehow they did. At about midnight on Saturday, the men that had gone to town to drink at the bars started trickling back to the labor camp.

During one specific Saturday, as usual, I went to bed at the same hour as I normally did during the weekdays. As I indicated before, I had been assigned the bottom bunk bed and another man had been assigned the top bunk bed. I remember that the man assigned to the upper bunk bed was heavy set. That man returned to the labor camp at about midnight after having been drinking in Delano; he was drunk. I woke up when he began to climb into the top bunk bed. He finally settled into the bed and I sensed that he fell asleep because he wasn't making any noise.

About 15 minutes later, he began to make what appeared to be choking sounds. I listened but tried to fall back to sleep. The choking sounds continued until finally I heard a loud noise and then bam; he vomited over the side of the bed. The vomit fell to the floor like a water fall. Remember, I was on the bottom bunk bed. When this happened, I crawled out the bed as best I could without stepping on the vomit on the floor. I stood motionless a few yards away.

Ultimately, the man climbed down from the top bunk bed, walked to the bathroom and retrieved a pail and a mop. When he returned, he cleaned up the mess he had created. The memory of this awful occurrence is fixed in my mind; I've never been able to forget it. Anyway, we worked in the two labor camps for about a month.

For some reason, either Chuy, Cuco or Luis came up with the idea that there were better paying jobs in the town of Stockton, California north of

Delano. I remember them mentioning something about picking a thing called "betabel". I'm not certain how they found out but from thereon, Stockton became our destination. I never knew what "betabel" was until now that I am writing this memoir. The English word for "betabel" is beets or sugar beets.

I don't remember the details of having left my employment from the labor camp but I did. We began our trip to Stockton and it took us about half a day to travel the 218 miles from Delano to Stockton. As in the past, we were stopping along the way to inquire about employment. I don't remember the details about our drive to Stockton or about being in Stockton. All I remember is that we spent a week or two trying to find work in the Stockton area. In the end, we exhausted our money supply and now we were in dire straits. I remember Chuy mentioning something about my aunt Anita and my uncle Tomas; they lived in Huntington Beach, California. We ultimately traveled from Stockton to Huntington Beach where my aunt and uncle lived; it was a 376 mile journey down south toward the Los Angeles area.

We were down to our last few dollars when we arrived at Huntington Beach. It was nice to visit with my relatives. I finally felt a sense of security. We were all very skinny because we hadn't been eating well. I remember my aunt Anita fixed dinner for all of us and it was delicious.

We told our uncle Tomas the story about where we had been and the efforts we had made at finding employment. My uncle quickly volunteered to find us employment with a friend of his. His friend's name was Timoteo and he was the foreman of a farm owned by a Japanese man. The owner's name was Tad Fujita.

Sure enough, the next day my uncle Tomas spoke with his friend and wah-lah we all had a job. The job was that of picking tomatoes. I guess my being 15 years of age wasn't a problem in this case. For the following 3 weeks, Chuy and I stayed at my uncle Tomas' home while Cuco and Luis stayed at a nearby labor camp.

For the following 3 weeks we all worked on the tomato farm picking tomatoes. This was the first time we experienced picking tomatoes. The foreman provided us small metal carts each equipped with four wheels. We loaded empty wooden boxes on the cart and then pushed the cart along the rows of tomato plants. We picked the ripe red fruit from the tomato plant vines located on either side of the cart. When the boxes were full, we would mark the spot where we left off and then proceed to a large truck stationed at the end of the rows. We would off-load the boxes full of tomatoes onto the cargo bay of the truck. We would then return back to the spot we had previously marked and then resume picking the tomatoes.

It was now mid-August. During the last part of August, my uncle Tomas, my aunt Anita and their family would leave for vacation back to the El Paso area and then proceed to Delicias where my uncle would visit his mother. We agreed with my uncle Tomas that Chuy and I would follow my uncle Tomas back to Fabens when it came time for them to leave on the vacation trip back to El Paso.

During the third week in August, we started driving back from Huntington Beach all the way back to Fabens. We followed my uncle in our pickup truck. Cuco and Luis stayed behind and continued to work on the tomato farm. I'm not sure how they got around since the vehicle we all used to get around in was my father's pickup truck; somehow they managed. We arrived safely back home. It was a wonderful feeling being back home secure with my parents; it was home sweet home at last.

During the last 3 weeks that we worked on the tomato farm, Chuy and I managed to save some money. We used that money to purchase school clothes both for ourselves as well as fir our younger brothers and sisters.

In retrospect, stepping out on had been risky. We always seemed to be broke during the trip. I stayed at a labor camp all by myself at the age of 15 years of age. I am not sure I would have allowed my children to do same. Bad things could have happened.

Later on at the completion of my junior year which would be the 11th grade, I would be making several key decisions regarding my future. In many ways, this experience contributed toward paving the road to my future. This chapter is one of the most important chapters in my life and it's been a life-long dream of mine to finally write it.

Growing Up On Welfare

As I indicated in a previous chapter, my mother always managed the meager family resources so that our family could sustain itself well. Because of my father's low income and a family of 8 kids, my family relied heavily on a welfare program provided by the U.S. government. I didn't know it back in those days, but now I know that the welfare program that we participated in started in 1961 when I was 10 years of age. I remember that all through my grade school and high school years, our family relied on this program. This was during the years of 1962 through 1970.

A few weeks before writing this part of the memoir, I met my sister Norma for lunch. She had traveled to the Fabens area for a short vacation trip. During that lunch meeting, we spoke about subjects relating to our family's early history. Our discussion led to the subject of the welfare program that was so crucial to our family when we were growing up.

While discussing the subject of my mother, Norma made a comment about my mother that caught my attention. She indicated that our mother was a "go getter". It hadn't dawned on me that my mother was indeed "a go getter" but she was. I responded to her by telling her "you know that we were raised on welfare" and she agreed that we had. She then commented "yes we were poor but at the time we didn't feel like poor people. We had plenty to eat; maybe not like rich people but we had enough". Well it did seem like we did have enough, but it was because my mother tried her best to feed our family well.

In the 60's when I was growing up, food stamps were dispensed to assist low income families. Nowadays that program is referred to as the SNAP program which stands for Supplemental Nutritional Assistance Program but in those days we knew the program as the Food Stamp program. The Food Stamp program, and now the SNAP program, was and is now administered by the government agency known as the United States Department of Agriculture or better known as the USDA. My family was one of those low income families that needed that extra help.

As a young boy I never knew what it took to procure food stamps but my mother sure seemed to know. Based on personal experience in dealing with governmental agencies, I can only imagine that she probably filled out a ton of paperwork that was necessary to prove that my father's income warranted food stamp assistance. In the end, she somehow managed to acquire sufficient food stamps to fill-in the gaps that resulted from my father's relatively low income.

The following internet article presents a brief description of the Food Stamp program and how it came to be enacted. The internet article is titled "Farming in the 50's and 60's – Food Stamps".

"In 1961, the Congress enacted a pilot program designed to help both poor people and farmers – the Food Stamp Program. The program was actually a revival of an idea that had been tried during the Great Depression. In both the 30s and the early 60s, farmers were producing more food than the nation could consume or export, and there was a large group of people who were going to bed hungry. On the one hand, food stamps were and are a sincere attempt to alleviate hunger, but on the other hand, the program is designed to help farmers as well."

The article can be viewed using the following web link: https://livinghistoryfarm.org/farminginthe50s/money_09.html

I am thankful for the existence of the Food Stamp program because we actually did need it. When I married my wife, Socorro, and left my parent's home, I never again needed assistance from the Food Stamp program. During my lifetime, I have paid my taxes and have done it gladly. In my thinking, it was my way of saying thank you for the help that my parents needed at the time.

In recent years, there has been much debate concerning these assistance programs. Some say that the assistance program encourages laziness. Others use the phrase "on the dole" to imply that people receiving assistance should feel shame for accepting the hand-outs from the Food Stamp or the SNAP assistance programs. Despite a general feeling that these programs are helpful, a few naysayers try to cast doom and gloom on the subject. In their minds, these assistance programs are a waste of taxpayer's money.

What most people don't know is that the Food Stamp and the SNAP programs are part of the farm bill that the United States Department of Agriculture administers. The key phrase here is "farm bill".

The following internet article describes the nature of the budget for the farm bill. It presents the funding in the farm bill that provides for assistance to poor people as well as to farmers. The title of the article is "Which costs more: Food stamps or farm subsidies?" It was written by Dave Helling on July 13, 2013. I modified the article to appear as a bulleted list to enable ease of review.

- ***Okay, the math is rough...but let's take a look at what splitting the farm bill into an ag [sic] subsidy title and a food stamps title might actually mean.***
- ***The House farm bill shot down in June would have cost $939 billion over ten years. For easy math, let's round up to $1 trillion, or about $100 billion annually.***
- ***Of that, 80 percent — $80 billion — goes for food stamps. The rest, broadly, goes for ag [sic] help, about $20 billion a year.***
- ***In 2013, 47.6 million people received food stamps. That means recipients get about $1,680 in benefits, on average, each year.***
- ***There are roughly 3.1 million farmers who split the remaining $20 billion in the farm bill. That works out to $6,451 per farmer.***
- ***So overall spending on food stamps is much higher than farm subsidies. But on a per-person basis, farmers come out ahead.***

The article can be found using the following link: http://www.kansascity.com/news/local/news-columns-blogs/the-buzz/ article322811/Which -costs-more-Food-stamps-or-farm-subsidies.html

The doom and gloom naysayers possibly don't know that the farmers come out ahead. They don't know that $1,680 on average is paid to each SNAP recipient while $6,451 on average is paid to each farmer.

Yes, my family needed financial assistance and yes, my family survived on welfare. For a time, I felt badly and maybe embarrassed that indeed we received this free benefit from the government.

As I indicated before, after leaving my family and then beginning a new life as a married person, I never again needed that benefit from the government. After graduating from High School, I started paying my dues to society in the form of income taxes.

Knowing what I know now, I feel justified in saying that the naysayers were wrong. Yes, the poor people needed help but the more well-to-do farmers also benefited as a result of that government help.

High School Freshman Year

A few days after arriving back to Fabens from our first venture working in California, I started school in the 9th grade or better said, my freshman year in high school. Being a freshman was a new experience; I felt like a small fish being thrust into a huge pond.

High School Band

During the previous year in 8th grade, I had attended band class at the high school band hall. Mr. Rex Carnes, the band teacher, had introduced us to the "recorder" while still in the 8th grade. Now as a freshman, we again had Mr. Carnes as the band teacher. Chuy, my brother, was a junior and I was now in the same band class as he.

The new freshman students were given a choice as to which instrument they wanted to play. I was one of several students that chose the trumpet. Nowadays, the band student rents the instrument he or she plays in high school. In those days, the school loaned the instruments to the students and that was the case with my trumpet.

Playing the "recorder" was easy compared to playing the trumpet. All you had to do was blow into the plastic mouthpiece of the "recorder" and a sound was made by the instrument itself. Playing the trumpet, on the other hand, was totally different. For one thing, the instrument was constructed of metal and the mouthpiece seemed too small for my mouth. Simply blowing into the mouthpiece only produced a sound of flowing air and not a musical note. To produce a note on the trumpet, I now had to squeeze my lips together against the metal mouthpiece. Then I had to blow into the mouthpiece; making my lips vibrate as I blew the air into the mouthpiece. The first few sounds coming out of the trumpet must have sounded like that of a cow mooing awkwardly. Little by little we began to get the hang of it. As time progressed, we started to learn how to finger the valves on the trumpet to produce different pitches of sound.

Starting school in September meant that football season was in full swing. In addition to having to learn how to play the trumpet for the first time, I now had to march on the football field while at the same time trying to play half-decent sounding notes. I remember a girl by the name of Lydia Quezada that was the drum major. She just wasn't convinced that I was marching in step with the rest and I became her personal project. She kept correcting me over and over again as I tried to march in unison with the others. She's a good friend now, but in those days, I dreaded having to march on the football field for fear of having her notice my miss-steps.

In the end, being in band instilled in me a sense of determination and dedication that I didn't have before. Not every student was in band and those of us that were, felt a sense of pride belonging to the school band. It was as if we shared a common loyalty to Mr. Carnes.

A Terrific Mathematics Teacher

Another teacher that was important in my development during high school was a math teacher whose name was Robert Herzing. He was a tall,  heavy set man. I thought he was a genius at mathematics. During my freshman year he taught algebra I. I especially remember him because of his prowess in algebra. I had two years of algebra with him. He taught the second part of algebra; algebra II, during the second year in my sophomore year. Unlike other courses such as English and history where one had to think in more abstract terms, mathematics with Mr. Herzing was more done by rote and rules. I could understand algebra; it came easy to me.

The Pretty Girl

From the very start of my freshman year, the pretty girl that I began to notice during the 7th grade and that was a cheerleader during the 8th grade continued to attract me. She too played the "recorder" back in the 8th grade band class. Now she was in high school band class as well. It was the month of October and I just couldn't figure out how to approach this pretty girl to let her know that I liked her. I finally decided to take the coward's way out.

One of the students in band class was Norbert Grijalva. Norbert's father was the owner of the farm where this pretty girl grew up; so Norbert was familiar with the pretty girl. I asked Norbert to do me the favor of telling the pretty girl that I liked her. Like a true friend, Norbert did as I asked. What a relief, but now the pressure was on. The day would come when I would have to say hello to her but for the time being at least she knew I liked her.

I kept avoiding her for about two weeks in band class until one day as I was about to take my seat, she happened to be walking-by facing toward the direction I was sitting in. I had no choice; I said hello and she cheerfully returned the greeting as she kept walking past me. I had succeeded in not losing my nerve. From that point forward, I knew I would have to force myself to say hello and be as charming as I could possibly be; I was a nerd after all. Every morning at the start of band class I would make sure to greet her with a cheerful "good morning" and then say "goodbye" to her at the conclusion of band class.

The band hall was a separate building from the main high school building. They were separated by about 300 feet. Typically after band class was over, all the students would walk from the band hall to the main high school building.

One day after band class, I purposefully feigned being busy doing something with my trumpet; waiting for the pretty girl to pass by. When she passed by, I immediately closed up my trumpet case and walked quickly to catch up to her. I caught up to her as she exited from the door. As soon as she exited through the door, I said hello to her. She always seemed to be in a good mood and today was no different; she responded with a kind "hello". I remember introducing myself to her and then chitchatting with her as we walked toward the high school building. When we reached the building, I said goodbye to her and we then proceeded to our respective separate classes. That's how I finally broke the ice. We began dating in early December of 1966. Fast forward to February 1971; I wound up marrying her.

The First Rock Band

During the second semester of my freshman year, now 1967, a few of my friends and I began to experiment with the idea of forming a musical band. A rock band known as "The Monkees" was becoming well known at that time and we began to notice their success. The group known as "The Beatles" was also very popular at that time.

I remember a few of us got together at Bobby Estrada's home who was in the 8th grade at the time. Bobby owned a nice drum set and he knew how to play it well.

I remember another person having attended the meeting. His name was Kenny; I can't remember his last name. He brought his electric guitar and a small amplifier with him. I remember he played and sang the song titled "House of the Rising Sun" which was authored by a group known as the "The Animals". Wow, this was exciting; I loved how he strummed and fingered the chords on the guitar. The general feeling was that we could couple this with what we were learning in high school band to create a viable band. One thing I haven't mentioned thus far is that at the time, all I had was a trumpet and even that was loaned to me by the school for use in the school band class.

We met several more times again at Bobby's home. Eventually Kenny dropped out. He told us that his parents had decided that it was best that he not continue with us because they feared he wouldn't concentrate on his school studies. That slowed down the process a bit. Eventually, the group morphed into a group that was called "The Skeptics". It included Bobby and me and in addition, Henry Ramirez, Ernest Nuñez and Michael Contreras. We practiced at a run-down building near the center of town in Fabens. I borrowed an electric guitar and an amplifier from someone. I know we played at a dance during that spring but I don't remember exactly when and where we played. I do know that we were far from having the sound of the popular bands of those days.

All of my rock band buddies were far from being well-to-do as well. We lived in a farming community and not in a large city. Our futures were tied to the farms; our futures seemed bleak and uncertain. College for poor kids wasn't even an option. Somehow the rock band appeared to us as a vehicle to achieve success; at least it did to me. So I began to believe that being successful in a rock band was my way out of Fabens.

That's how my freshman year in high school ended. At least I had a glimmer of hope now.

Summer Work in California – 1967

As indicated in a prior section, during the previous summer, Chuy, Cuco, Luis and I traveled to California to work. In retrospect, that initial trip turned out to be the motivating factor that enabled us to venture out from Fabens. That trip opened our eyes to the that fact that working in California during the summers was beneficial to our family. As a result of that initial trip, our family wound up traveling to California for the next four succeeding summers. These were the summers from 1967 to 1970.

About two weeks prior to the end of my freshman school year and while we were still in school, my father traveled to California. The purpose of his trip was to find a suitable place for our family to stay during the upcoming summer months that were to follow immediately after the end of school in Fabens. The plan was that once having found a suitable place for our family to stay, he would then return back to Fabens to make arrangements so that our entire family could travel from Fabens to California.

During that brief trip to California, he stayed with my uncle Tomas and my aunt Anita in Huntington Beach, California. The school years during that time usually concluded just before the Memorial Day holiday weekend and that's when my father returned to Fabens from his trip to California.

During that holiday weekend, we packed our clothes, some pots and pans and other things that my father and mother deemed necessary. My father saw to it that the pickup truck was properly lubed and oiled. He installed the truck bed camper. The truck bed camper was an enclosure that was fitted to the rear cargo bay of the pickup truck. The final step was to load everything into the pickup truck and then board-up the house windows with plywood sheets. This was done in order to deter potential thieves from entering the house while we were away for the three month time period.

We all boarded the pickup truck. My father, mother and Chuy rode in the cab of the pickup truck while the rest of my siblings and I rode in the rear mounted camper. There were a total of ten family members riding in the pickup truck.

By the way, the phrase "migrant workers" applied to our family. This is because the phrase "migrant workers" means "workers who move from place to place to do seasonal work". That's what we did.

Chuy was 16 years of age when he and I, along with Cuco and Luis, first traveled to California the previous year. He had his driver's license. Now he was 17 years of age and he drove most of the way to California. The approximate total distance from Fabens to the rental house where we ultimately wound up staying was 832 miles. We didn't stay at motels along the way. With bathroom stops along the way, as well as driving at 60 to 65 miles an hour, the trip took close to about 20 hours.

We finally arrived at the place that was to be our home for the next three months. The place was a somewhat dilapidated wooden structure. Another home was situated nearby and the family that lived there was a family by the name of Hinojosa. They had lived there for several years. By the way, I remember the approximate location of the home where we stayed. It was located somewhere close to the intersection of Edinger Avenue and Brookhurst Street. I also remember the name of the town; Fountain Valley.

The next day was work day; there was no time to waste. We got up very early. We readied ourselves and my father drove Chuy and I to a tomato  field owned by the same person that owned the tomato fields we had worked on during the previous summer. We wound up with a foreman whose name was Agustin; I can't remember his last name. Getting hired was no problem since we told Agustin that we had worked on a Fujita tomato field during the previous summer. After answering a few questions and providing our social security numbers, Chuy and I began to work. My father left and we worked picking tomatoes during the entire day. My father returned at 5:00 p.m. that afternoon. He picked us up and we returned back to the rented house. By the way, the photograph on the left shows a tomato field and the manner in which the tomato plants were supported upright, tied to wooden poles with string.

I remember that washing up after having worked in the tomato fields was a chore. When picking tomatoes, the hands and wrists come in contact with the green pigment of the leaves and stems of the tomato plant. This contact causes the green pigment to build up into a thick green crust on the hands and wrists. Washing the substance off our hands and wrists with soap and water took a long time. In addition, the dust that came loose after rustling the leaves while picking the tomatoes became airborne. It ultimately found its way in between our clothes and skin. Coupled with the heat of the day, the result was an itchy-scratchy sensation all over our bodies.

By the way, the reason my father didn't work at the Fujita tomato field was that he had arranged employment at another farm where beans were farmed. He was a tractor operator at that other farm. My uncle Tomas probably helped my father find work at that farm because later on, I somehow found out that my uncle Tomas was a good friend of the foreman on that farm. The foreman's first name was Alvino; I don't remember his surname.

We worked all summer long picking tomatoes. We worked Monday through Friday, Saturday, Sunday and then again started the new week on Monday. For the entire three months or so, we did not have one day off. The only way we were able to visit the beach areas in nearby Huntington Beach was to drive there after working hours during the evenings. Our cousin, Jose Bejarano, would drive us to the beach.

During that summer, I began to learn about human nature. In a previous section, I indicated that our foreman's name was Agustin. Agustin was a young man of Mexican descent; probably about 25 to 30 years of age. He spoke Spanish well but spoke very broken English; he was Spanish language dominant.

Agustin was a ruthless, authoritarian foreman. When instructing the Mexican workers in Spanish, he would speak to them in a very harsh, un-caring tone; almost dictatorial. Somehow, Chuy and I always seemed to stay on his good side probably because we were the only English speaking workers there. When the owner, Tad Fujita, would show up, Agustin would assume a different, very positive posture; almost to the point of being artificial. In my opinion, there wasn't anything wrong with being firm but he didn't need to be ruthless to the point of demeaning the workers. It seemed that the power given him to direct the operations on the tomato field simply went to his head.

Fast forward to the future when I was thinking about starting-up my own company, I remembered Agustin's approach to managing the workers he supervised. During the start of 1983, I made a decision to start-up my own water treatment company. The company's name was

Fluid Separations Corporation. One of several reasons for starting-up that new company was to provide employment for my father and members of my family. Especially with my father but also with my extended family, I didn't want them to work under ruthless foremen like the one I observed when we worked on the Fugita farm.

Anyway, I previously indicated that the neighboring family was the Hinojosa family. During our stay that summer, I noticed that the Hinojosa boys, who were about our age, did not work. They just spent their time idling at home during the summer days; needless to say, I was envious because we, on the other hand, worked every single day. I was curious as to why the Hinojosa boys didn't work. During an evening after work, I asked one of them why it was that they never asked their father to find them a job or even come to work where we worked. His response surprised me. He flatly responded by telling me that it wasn't his responsibility to work. He said it was his father's and his mother's responsibility to work. He further told me that he never asked to be born in the first place and that's why he felt it was not his responsibility to work. That put me in my place. I suppose we were raised differently. Neither I, nor any of my siblings were ever that disrespectful to our parents.

In the end, working for a little more than three months did have its advantages. We were able to save money for the family. My parents were able to purchase school clothing for my siblings that were of school age as well as for myself.

As far as working in the tomato fields was concerned, we gained the respect of the foreman, Agustin, and the owner, Tad Fugita. That respect would later benefit Chuy and I during subsequent summer work at the Fugita farm.

One final item; while working in the tomato fields that year; we became friends with several workers. One specific person was a man by the name of Felipe Guardiola. The reason he stuck out from the rest is that he was originally from a town in Mexico south of Eagle Pass, Texas. Somehow he found out that we were from the El Paso area. During conversations with him, he indicated that every year he would pass through El Paso when traveling to and from California. His mentioning El Paso especially heightened our interest in him because we were happy to hear references to El Paso; we were homesick for El Paso. Felipe and his family would later become very important to our own family.

One other final item; during the previous freshman school year, I began dating my girlfriend. It was difficult saying good-bye to her for the summer, to say the least. We had been so close during the school year. We did correspond by letter a few times while I was away.

I was so in love with her that I decided to send her flowers when I was in California. I wound up purchasing an arrangement of roses to send to her. I didn't know about UPS or FedEx delivery services in those days and possibly they didn't exist at the time. I was only familiar with the U.S. Postal Service. I packaged up the flowers in a box, enclosed a love letter in the box and then mailed it to my girlfriend.

I don't remember having received a reply from her indicating that she received the roses although I was told recently that she did reply. When I returned from California at the end of that summer, I asked her if she liked the flowers I had sent her and I remember she responded that she did and then thanked me for having sent the flowers.

Fast forward to sometime after I married her. We happened to be discussing the subject of our having to travel to California during those summers to work. During the discussion, she remembered my having sent her flowers during one of those summer trips to California. She smiled and then told me that the flowers did arrive but that the flower arrangement had dried up and that most of the flower petals had separated from the flower bulbs. She indicated to me that I should have called a local florist so that the roses could have been delivered by the florist. I never thought about taking that approach when I sent her the flowers. It would have been difficult for me given that I never took a day off from work. In the end, the flowers although they arrived in a dry condition, did come from the heart.

I'm the type of person that remembers past events when I hear specific songs being played on the radio. One specific example that brings back memories of having to leave my girlfriend behind for the summer is a song titled "Sealed With A Kiss" sung by a vocalist by the name of Brian Hyland. The song actually debuted years earlier in 1962. One specific verse in the lyrics that illustrates how I felt about leaving my girlfriend is as follows:

"I don't want to say goodbye for the summer Knowing the love we'll miss Oh let us make a pledge to meet in September And seal it with a kiss"

During those summers, I was a love sick puppy; I missed my girlfriend.

High School Sophomore Year

The new school year started. I was now 16 years old in 1967 and in my sophomore year in high school.

The Delay

School resumed at the beginning of September but my siblings and I started school two to three weeks after school began. The reason for starting so late was that my father delayed our return back to our home from California. Although my father was the main bread- winner of the family, our work in California contributed substantially to the family's overall financial well-being. Although we prompted him constantly about returning back home in time to begin school on the first day of school, he nonetheless delayed our return on purpose. He never really provided us an exact reason for delaying the return. However, I believe he wanted us to work those extra weeks so that we could earn additional income prior to finally leaving California and returning back to Fabens.

By the way, on the trip back we stopped at a farm near Eloy, Arizona where my mother's uncle, Jesus Gonzalez, and his family lived. In spite of the urgency that I felt to return back to Fabens, my parents insisted on us staying with our relatives for a few days. We stayed with them about 3 or 4 days. I suppose my parents just needed to spend some leisure time with their relatives before resuming our return back to Fabens.

I have to say that although I did understand my father's need to delay our return, my resuming school later than usual made me feel like a new kid on the block at school. By the time we returned back to school, class officer elections had been completed and chair assignments in band had already been made. More on chair assignments will be presented in the next few sections. Anyway, being a new kid on the block meant that it was catch-up time for me.

The End of "The Skeptics Band"

We arrived back to Fabens from California on a Friday. I went over to see my friend, Ernest Nuñez, to let him know that I had returned. I showed him the new guitar and amplifier that I had purchased in California. At last I had my own instrument and amplifier.

He had previously written me to let me know that the Skeptics band was going to perform at a "gig"; the day of the gig happened to be the next day which would be Saturday. The "gig" would be held at a local dance hall known as Lara's Hall. The word "gig" is slang and is used to denote in our case a live musical performance. As planned, we did the "gig" that Saturday night.

Ultimately "The Skeptics" band failed because two of the band members dropped out. Their parents didn't want them involved in the band because they feared their sons were not going to be able to concentrate on their school work. An additional member began to lose interest and this finally led to the band being no more. This all happened a few months after my having returned back to Fabens.

The New Band Teacher

Back at school, the band teacher during my sophomore year was no longer Mr. Carnes. The new band teacher was Mr. Ronald Maneth. Mr. Maneth had a different teaching style. Whereas Mr. Carnes' teaching method was more deliberate and perhaps very precise, Mr. Maneth's style was more brash and louder.

Chuy, my brother, was assigned first-chair trumpet. He was very good at playing the trumpet and was an expert at reading music. The seating arrangement was such that they were made based on how well one played the instrument. All the trumpet players sat in the seat corresponding to their ability to play their instrument. It was a ranking order and as a freshman, I was by no means close to Chuy's coveted first-chair.

The Band Class Clowns

By the way, I remember two seniors that always seemed to partner up during band activities. Their names were Rojelio Castillo and Reymundo

Garza. I don't know why but Rojelio used to go by the name of Roy. Reymundo was known as simply Rey. I guess the reason why I remember them was because of their antics; they were the band class clowns; but in a good way. They were very likable upper classmen.

I especially remember them because of a specific conversation I had with them that occurred as we were nearing the end of football season. They expressed sadness because the marching band's activities would be slowing down soon after the last football game. The band would now transition into playing orchestra music rather than the more bouncy, marching music that we played when marching during half-time at the games or rallying during the games. Band trips out of town would come to an end at the end of football season as well.

During that specific exchange, they indicated that the rest of the year would be boring because band class would just consist of practicing for the Christmas concert and the end of the year concert in the spring. It was as if two wise men were preparing me for a boring future; at least in the immediate future. As strange as it sounds, I remember them for that reason. However, the rest of the year in band actually didn't turn out to be boring for me; I enjoyed it.

Joining the Football Team

As I indicated before, football was the thing during the start of school in September. I had settled in well into school after returning back from California. I had my girlfriend, Socorro, and like all good boyfriends, I carried her books around as we moved from class to class during the school days. I would walk her home at the end of the school day.

I had one nagging problem, however. After each class, my girlfriend and I would try to meet at her locker. Each student was assigned a locker in which to store books and personal belongings. As my girlfriend and I moved together between classes, we would sometimes happen to cross paths with the football coach. The coach's name was Wayne Mains.

From time to time during those encounters in the hall, he would make snide remarks and he made them so that I could hear them. I can't remember his exact words but it had something to do with me preferring to be with a girl rather than doing a real man's job; that of football. I was of thin build but of tall stature. I knew the game he was up to. He was trying to shame me into joining the football team. He kept at it constantly until I finally succumbed to the pressure.

I joined the football team and was placed on the B-team. The B-team played on Saturday mornings as opposed to the coveted A-team that played on Friday nights. The pressure was off for now; I felt that the coach now respected me. I don't remember that I played spectacularly well; I was just a good teammate. Now in retrospect, I feel I really did need that extra push from Coach Mains.

The Start of "The Night Flames"

About a month after the end of "The Skeptics" band, Chuy took me aside and began to tell me about a plan he had about starting a new band. He wanted a band with trumpets and saxophones in addition to the normal guitars and, of course, the drum set.

As an aside, Chuy was greatly influenced by the success of a band from El Paso known as "Bobby and the Premiers". Somehow Chuy managed to borrow a record disc that contained songs played by that group. We had a record player at home. I distinctly remember that he used the record player to play a song by "Bobby and the Premiers" titled "This is the Beginning". One could easily tell from listening to that song, as well as to the rest of the songs on the disc, that the group used trumpets and saxophones extensively in their work. That's probably the reason why Chuy wanted a horn section in the new band he was contemplating. I didn't know it at the time but the type of music he demonstrated was a type of music we now know as "rhythm and blues".

Chuy's plan was that he would take care of leading the horn section. I, on the other hand, would play the guitar and in addition, would take care of instructing the bass guitarist and the drummer.

Anyway, we managed to recruit various friends we knew at school that shared the same interest. We all met at our small garage located at the rear of our home in Fabens. That was our "practice hall". I remember it was very cramped; we could hardly move around inside the practice room but somehow we managed.

Little by little we began the process of developing the group into a musical band. Chuy was a master at developing the music just from listening to the tunes on the record player. He developed the written music to aid the other horn musicians. We ultimately became a pretty good band. We had a good sound.

A professional group known as "James Brown and the Famous Flames" was also very popular in those days as well. They played a type of rhythm and blues that appealed to the black population. We needed a "catchy" name for the band. As a result of the James Brown influence, Chuy and I came up with the name for our band: "The Night Flames". During the school year, we were contracted to perform at several local venues but primarily at the Fabens Catholic Community Center.

I am not certain how it happened but we wound up with a friend that took care of the business side of the band. His job was to identify and arrange engagements for our band to play at specific venues. He took care of negotiating the price for the engagements. His name was Refugio Sierra. We called him by his nickname of Cuco.

By coincidence while writing this piece, I happened to meet up with Cuco Sierra at a local gasoline station while he was filling-up his vehicle. He initially looked at me; staring intently at me. I was initially baffled as to why this man kept staring and then he asked "is it you?". Not knowing what to say, I responded "well I'm a Renteria". He then said "don't you remember me? I'm Cuco Sierra". All of a sudden, I remembered. We both shook hands warmly. It was a great feeling seeing an old friend. Among other things, he told me that his wife, Rosa, passed away less than a year ago. I gave him my sincere condolences.

During our brief meeting, he reminded me about the good old days when he arranged for all of the band members to be fitted with bright red glittery evening coats. Unlike today, in those days, rock band members always dressed alike during their presentations. We wore those classy evening coats when we played at our gigs. Yes, we were a rhythm and blues band and yes Cuco made sure we got paid for our gigs. I remember it wasn't much; it was more a labor of love.

What was more important at the time was that we had found a way to become famous and potentially to make big money. It also seemed that we had found a way to become successful and perhaps even finally found a way out of Fabens.

By the way, during our brief meeting, Cuco asked me if I had photographs of the band and I responded by telling him that I was about to ask him the same question. It seems nobody back then remembered to take photographs of the band. I suppose when one is young, photographs just don't seem important; they do now at my late age.

Typewriting

One of the surprises I experienced during my sophomore year had to do with the subject of typewriting. Typewriting was on the school curriculum and like it or not, one had to take typewriting class. Who would have thought that boys needed a skill "that only women needed to have"? I grew up believing that secretaries were always female. I suppose this was a chauvinistic attitude in those days; not so today.

Anyway, I attended typewriting class during the first semester of my sophomore year. The typewriters that were used in typewriting class were  ancient and kludgy. Remember, this was in 1967 when dinosaurs still roamed the earth . . . ha-ha. Like the standard computer keyboards of today, the keys were also positioned in the same QWERTY keyboard layout fashion. The acronym QWERTY refers to the keyboard layout having q, w, e, r, t, and y as the first keys from the left on the top row of letters. So from that standpoint, the layout of the keys on those old typewriters was the same as the modern keyboards of today; but that's where the similarity ended.

The basic idea was simple with those old kludgy typewriters in high school: a key is pressed and a lever attached to it swings another lever called a type hammer. The head of the type hammer then moves up toward the paper and strikes the inked ribbon creating an image of a specific letter on the paper. This was all mechanical and one had to press hard enough on the keys to get the type hammer head to strike sufficiently hard to end up with an intelligible letter on the paper. If the finger presses on the keys weren't exactly the identical, the end result would be faded letters and perhaps uneven rows of letters. Even worse, if one accidentally pressed a finger in-between the keys; the finger would slip through and get caught between the keys.

Fast forward to the time when I started working as a technical professional in 1974, the typewriters were now modern IBM Selectric style machines. A simple press of the key would electrically activate a "typeball" that popped up toward the paper and then struck the inked ribbon to result in a specific letter being printed. This type of typewriter was used was when I started working for Continental Water Conditioning Corporation in El Paso.

When I was employed at Continental Water Conditioning Corporation, in order to generate a piece of correspondence, and in some cases to prepare an instruction manual, I had to dictate the words into a handset known as a "Dictaphone". The "Dictaphone" was similar to a normal telephone handset. The "Dictaphone" handsets were connected to a central dictation system. The women in the secretarial pool then listened to the recorded words and they then typed the correspondence or the document using IBM Selectric typewriters. The persons dictating the words never touched the typewriters.

That was then; this is now. Today, knowing how to type is essential in the business world. The advent of modern word processors, and now more recently laptop computers, makes producing correspondence and technical documents relatively easy.

In the end, my resistance to learning to type back in my sophomore year in high school was counterproductive. Starting in 1983 when I purchased our first Osborne computer equipped with word processing capability, at least for me, the process of document production has been a breeze. I am now a good typist thanks to the sophomore high school curriculum that required that even boys had to take typewriting class. Voice recognition software now makes it possible to speak into a microphone and the words just appear on the computer screen. We've come a long way from typing class in 1967. By the way, my chauvinistic belief that women and not men needed to be typewriter savvy went out the window a long time ago . . . ha-ha.

Track

During my sophomore year in high school, I participated both in cross-country running as well as in track. A teacher by the name of

R.J. Coers was our track coach. I ran the 880 yard dash in track that year. I remember two seniors that were also on the track team. Their names were Jesus Ochoa and Manuel Rodriguez.

Jesus Ochoa was the neighbor boy that grew up on the farm with us when we were very young. That's the time when we lived in the white stuccoed building that used to be located adjacent to the railroad tracks on the Ryan farm back in the 1950s. He was the person we used to call Ruly but now we called him by his Spanish nickname of Chuy. He was an expert runner. I remember he had very muscular thighs that helped him excel in the 880 yard dash.

Manuel Hernandez, on the other hand, ran the mile run. I remember that he was short statured but he had a lot of stamina. That's what it took to excel in the mile run. I don't remember he ran sufficiently well to finish in the first, second or third place but I do remember he was always present during the track meets.

These two persons are important to me because they were seniors and I considered them mature and wise upperclassmen; they were my friends.

By the way, Manuel joined the Marines after graduating in May of 1968 and ultimately passed away a year later in the Vietnam War on June 2, 1969. I'll always remember him for being a good friend and for having served his country with honor.

Mexican Mother's Day

By the way, there is one final item that happened that school year. Mother's Day was always celebrated in Mexico on May 10 of each year regardless of the day of the week it fell on. The members of the "The Night Flames" including myself were, and of course are, of Hispanic origin. We all agreed to do something special for our mothers for Mother's Day. Being musicians, we decided to serenade our mothers on that day.

I am not sure who came up the idea; but we decided that we would play a song titled "Las Mañanitas" to our mothers during the serenade and in addition, we would serenade them at dawn before sunrise on Mother's Day. The phrase "Las Mañanitas" is loosely translates into English as "The Little Morning". The reason for serenading during the early hours of the morning was because of the lyrics contained in the song.

The song's lyrics contain several stanzas that lead one to believe that the person who is about to be serenaded, in this case our mothers, is initially asleep during the early hours of the morning. One specific stanza, among several others, that demonstrates this fact is shown below along with its accompanying loose English translation:

Ya viene amaneciendo	The dawn is gradually coming
Ya la luz del día nos dio	And the light of day is upon us
Levántate de mañana	et up in the morning
Mira que ya amaneció	And see that the sunlight is upon us

We decided that during the dawn of that day we would perform the serenades. However, we ran into a problem. The problem was that there were not one but several mothers that were to be serenaded and they all couldn't be serenaded at 5:00 a.m. in the morning. After all, they all lived in their homes scattered around town.

It quickly became obvious that the serenades would need to begin early-on; perhaps at 2:00 or 3:00 a.m. in the morning. This would allow us sufficient time to perform a serenade, then quickly leave and then drive to a different location to repeat the serenade at another location and son on. So we decided to start with the first serenade at about 2:00 a.m. in the morning. Three of us were tasked with playing the acoustic guitars during the serenades.

Typically, we would all arrive at the home of the mother to be serenaded; making sure to keep from making too much noise as we positioned ourselves next to the main door of the mother's home. It was difficult because we kept bumping into each other in the dark as we walked toward the front door of the homes; it was hard to see. We didn't want to wake up or alarm the mother's neighbors; after all, we were doing this during the wee hours of the morning.

We would then begin to play and sing the song. A few minutes later, the mother inside the home would open the door and stand there while we played and finished the serenade. We made certain that the band member whose mother we were serenading was standing at the front of the band so that the mother would recognize her son. When we finished the song, the mother would thank us and in unison we would all say "happy mother's day". We would then proceed to walk back to our cars to drive to the next mother's home.

We did this for each mother. Nearing the end, my fingers were raw after having played the guitar over and over again. Couple that with the fact that we hadn't slept at all, we were dead tired when we finally finished.

By the way, some band members including myself decided to push the other band members into agreeing to serenade our girlfriends' mothers. Yes, we convinced them even though they weren't band member's mothers; those mothers got serenaded as well. I made points with my girlfriend that day. Of course, my girlfriend was Socorro.

The end of the 1967-1968 school year brought about Chuy's graduation from High School. I was not able to attend his graduation because at that time, the graduation ceremonies were always held in the high school auditorium. Because of the small seating capacity of the auditorium, only the parents of the graduates were allowed to attend the graduation ceremony. A total of 63 seniors graduated that year; our school was a small school.

Summer Work In California - 1968

In a previous section, I indicated that during the middle of May of 1967, my father traveled to California a few weeks prior to the end of the school year to find temporary housing for our family in California. He was successful and that resulted in our working in California during the entire summer of 1967. We returned back from California after having worked there during the entire summer.

A few months after having returned from California in 1967, my father purchased a semi-tractor truck. It was an old semi-tractor truck that was used to pull a 60 foot flat bed trailer. He worked as an independent contractor hauling cotton from the cotton farms in Dell City, Texas to the cotton gins in the El Paso area. He worked transporting cotton during the fall season of 1967 when the cotton was being harvested. The cotton hauling business temporarily ceased during the beginning of the winter months in early 1968. My father's semi-tractor trailer truck sat idle for the rest of the winter and spring. Sometime in March of 1968, my father left Fabens to travel to California to work on the farm he had worked on during the previous summer. As previously indicated, the name of the farm foreman was a man by the name of Alvino. Toward the end of the school year in May of 1968, my father returned back to Fabens to begin preparations to again take the family back to California to work during the upcoming summer months.

As in the previous year, we again traveled to California during the day of the Memorial Day holiday. We arrived in California the following day and settled into the rental home that we were to live in for the rest of the summer. The home was located in the city of Santa Ana, about eight miles from the location of the rental home that my father had rented the year before. I remember that this rental home was located on 4th Street in the city of Santa Ana.

We arrived in California on June 1st or June 2nd. We started working on Monday, June 3rd. A few days after having started working, we heard by way of television newscasts that Robert F. Kennedy had been shot during the wee hours of the morning on June 5, 1968. That came as a shock because John F. Kennedy, Robert Kennedy's brother, had been assassinated back in 1963. In a previous section of this memoir, I indicated that the John F. Kennedy assassination occurred during the time when I was in the 6th grade.

At the time, I remembered that the assassination of President John Kennedy in 1963 brought the entire nation to its knees. Now in 1968, the assassination of Robert F. Kennedy happened while he was campaigning for a good cause; President of the United States. As in the case of his brother John Kennedy, Robert Kennedy was also held in high regard in the United States; especially with the black community. It seemed a shame that good intentions were being rewarded with such vile actions.

In the grand scheme of things, I was a "nobody". But even a "nobody" like me felt the weight of the assassination. Thank God conspiracy theories didn't abound. It might have been because unlike John Kennedy's assassination, Robert Kennedy's assassin was caught red-handed immediately after he fired the shots at him.

Anyway, back to the subject at hand. As in previous years, we showed up to work at the Tad Fugita farm. Mr. Fugita welcomed us back and we started to work immediately; however, this time we began working in the strawberry fields; we picked strawberries. The strawberry field was located alongside Bolsa Avenue near a cemetery. The location of the field was at the intersection of Bolsa Avenue and Hoover Street in Westminster, California. By the way, we met up with Felipe Guardiola. Chuy and I greeted him; he remembered us from the previous summer when we worked together in the Fugita tomato fields.

Chuy and I worked picking strawberries during the first few days. Picking strawberries was new to us. Unlike the tomato plants that were supported upright on wooden poles tied with string, the height of the strawberry plants was only about a 6 to 10 inches from the top of the furrows. Because of the relative low height of the strawberry plants, one had to bend over at the waist to pick the strawberries.

The strawberries were picked and placed into a cardboard box that was mounted on a small movable cart fitted with a single small wheel up front. The photograph on the left shows an example of the movable cart. The cart was similar in construction to a small wheel barrel but was fashioned out of small diameter metal rods to minimize its weight.

One had to be careful to pick the strawberries so that the leaf cap part of the strawberry remained attached to the top of the berry. The leaf cap is the leafy part at the top of the berry that has a crown-like appearance. At the time, I never really understood why the berries had to be picked with the leaf cap attached. I can only surmise that the attached leaf cap extended the shelf life of the berry.

Anyway, after an hour or so of picking strawberries, my back started to hurt. There was no option; I had to kneel on one leg to keep from having to bend over. After a while, even kneeling on one leg was uncomfortable. Eventually, the only

option was to kneel on two knees and walk along the furrow on my knees.

Looking around, we discovered that the rest of the workers were wearing knee pads tied to their knees with straps. They didn't seem to have any trouble walking on their knees along the strawberry furrows. As I indicated before, strawberry picking was new to us and we were unprepared; we worked without knee pads the entire day. Needless to say, my father purchased knee pads for us and we used them from there on.

I might add; although knee pads helped, they weren't the total solution. There really was no solution. One had to deal with sharp, throbbing pain in the knees every night when trying to fall sleep.

Another interesting thing about working in the strawberry fields was that no longer were we working on an hourly basis; now we were being paid according to the number of strawberry boxes that we picked. This was called "piecework".

Every time we filled-up a box of strawberries, we would take the box filled with strawberries to the flat-bed truck located nearby. The person tending the truck would take the box, perform a cursory inspection to make sure that the strawberries in the box were ripe and that the strawberries had their leaf caps attached. He then loaded the box onto the truck.

We would then hand him a punch card marked with our name at the top of the card. He would use a hand-punch to punch the card to account for the box having been delivered. In this way, the number of holes on the punch card represented the number of boxes that we picked. At the end of the day, we would turn in the punch card to the foreman and he would then record in his log book the total number of filled boxes turned in.

During that first day, we noticed that many of the strawberry pickers were women and not just men. When my father came to pick us up just before quitting time in the afternoon of the first day, he too noticed that not only men but women were also picking strawberries. By the way, the foreman's name was Timoteo; he was the foreman we met during the previous summer working at the Fugita farm.

My father spoke with the foreman about bringing my younger sisters to work alongside Chuy and I. The foreman indicated that there was no problem with bringing them to work. Irma and Gloria were younger than Chuy and I. I suppose they were allowed to work in spite of their age because the pay was based on piecework and not on hourly work.

During the next day, both Irma and Gloria joined us. We started to work at the strawberry field at 7:00 a.m. in the morning. Chuy took Irma as his helper and I took Gloria as my helper. Chuy and I took four carts and four empty boxes from the flat bed truck. We handed a cart and a box to Irma and another cart and box to Gloria. We then +walked toward two furrows that weren't occupied by other pickers. We selected two furrows that lay side by side. Irma took her position about 10 feet ahead of Chuy while Gloria positioned herself about 10 feet ahead of me. We all began to pick the strawberries.

Because they were younger, Irma and Gloria were much slower at picking strawberries and as a result, Chuy and I would quickly catch up to them. Once having caught up to them, they would then move up along the furrow another 10 or 15 feet to begin picking again. Irma and Gloria never really filled the boxes with strawberries; after picking a few strawberries, they would dump them into Chuy's box or my box.

From time to time Irma and Gloria would slow down or stand up and just look around as if day dreaming. I was very aware that we weren't going to make any money if we didn't fill the boxes with strawberries. It became a constant struggle trying to keep Irma and Gloria focused on picking strawberries. They were very young and I felt for them but we were there to earn money; not to day dream.

The hourly wage rate at the time was about $1.70 per hour. This amounted to a wage of $13.60 for an 8 hour day. However, picking strawberries was more rewarding. There were days when Gloria and I would pick 90 boxes and even up to 120 boxes of strawberries. At $1.00 per box, this meant $90.00 and sometimes $120.00 per day. The piece-rate of $1.00 per box picked was indeed a motivating factor for me. As a result, I remember pushing Irma and Gloria to pick faster. As a result, there were some days when they were not very pleased with me.

I remember noticing a few men picking up to 250 boxes. We later found out that some of these men were from a city in Mexico known as Michocan. They were masters at picking strawberries. The rest of us looked up at these men as champions. Yes, this was our little world.

Anyway, I previously mentioned that Chuy and I knew Felipe Guardiola after having met him during the previous summer while working in the tomato fields. Now in the strawberry fields, we met Felipe's wife who also worked as a picker in the strawberry fields. In addition, we met several of his sisters who also worked in the fields. One specific person we met while working there was Berta Guardiola, Felipe's sister. Fast forward to about 2 years in the future; Chuy and Berta would become husband and wife.

The strawberry season ended about a month and a half after we arrived in California; sometime during the middle of July. After the strawberry season, we then began to work on the Fugita tomato fields.

Chuy and I spent the first few weeks picking tomatoes in the tomato fields. Sometime during the third week, Mr. Fujita approached Chuy and I about taking on the responsibility of irrigating the tomato fields. We didn't hesitate; we immediately accepted the offer to do the irrigation work. We were provided with a $.20 cent per hour increase. We felt good about having been selected to do what we considered an important job. There is saying that goes like this "in the land of the blind, the mythical one-eyed cyclops is king". To us, having been selected to irrigate the fields was equivalent to being promoted to a high position.

For the rest of the summer, Chuy and I took care of the irrigation of the tomato fields. We learned how to start and stop the large engine-driven pumps that were used to pump water from the wells through 8 inch diameter aluminum pipes. The pipes distributed the water to the earthen furrows in the tomato fields. No longer did we have to start work at 7:00 a.m. in the morning but we did sometimes have to monitor the irrigation of the fields way into the evening hours; sometimes until 10:00 p.m. at night.

We operated independently from the tomato pickers. Tad Fugita, the owner, was our supervisor. He really didn't supervise us because we knew what needed to be done. During the times when the fields didn't need to be irrigated, we would work picking tomatoes at the higher hourly rate we were paid when irrigating the fields. This was a plus for us.

It bears noting that the majority of the tomato and strawberry pickers on the Fugita farm were brought in from a labor camp located in the nearby city of Huntington Beach. The labor camp served as a source of migrant workers for several other farms in the area as well. To my knowledge all of the men housed in the labor camp were from Mexico; there were no women living in the labor camp. It also bears noting that there were no persons of Anglo descent housed in the labor camp. All of the workers that were housed in the labor camp were poor Mexicans.

Anyway, in a previous section, I indicated that we worked during the three months or so of our stay in California without taking a day off from work. However, I do recall that during the succeeding summers we did take one day off from work. It could have been during this summer of 1968; I can't remember for sure.

We finished up the summer, said our good-byes to the foreman and the owner, Tad Fugita, as well as to the Guardiolas. We then traveled back to Fabens. My parents never told us how much money we earned in total but I imagine it was quite a bit. That money had to last us until the beginning of the following summer.

High School Junior Year

It was September of 1968 and I was 17 years of age. It was the start of my 11th grade or better said my high school junior year.

Being Alone

As usual, we arrived back to Fabens from having worked in California during the summer months and as usual we arrived about 2 to 3 weeks after the start of the school year. As before, my father had placed more importance in having us work the extra few weeks even if it meant delaying our return to school. I didn't agree with him at the time but now in the role of bread-winner, I do agree that those sacrifices had to be made in order to properly finance our family's well-being.

One big change was that Chuy did not return back to Fabens with us from California. He remained in California to continue working. He had graduated at the end of the previous school year.

As a result of this absence, I sensed a peculiar feeling during the start of the school year. I felt a sensation of being alone. Chuy was no longer present. Chuy had always been 2 years ahead of me in school. Therefore, during my first 2 years in high school, Chuy was also in high school. Although Chuy and I weren't in the same classes, I always felt his presence. Prior to this time, it was as if I always had a lifeline available to me in case I got into trouble.

Chuy, at least to me, was always the risk taker and in a sense my leader. In a previous chapter, I indicated a phrase that Chuy used when we were about to embark on an adventure when we were young boys. Chuy's typical phrase was "no le digas a mi Amá" which in English meant "don't tell my mother". Having said those words, he would then proceed to tell me the plan that "we" were about to embark on. It was like planning a mission. Another factor that contributed to that feeling of being alone was that Chuy had previously been the leader of "The Night Flames". The responsibility of leading the band was going to now fall upon me and nobody else. The sensation of my being alone persisted for that entire school year.

The Football Team

Immediately upon my return back to Fabens, as in the previous year, I joined the football team. Coach Mains continued to be the head coach. The prior year I had played on the B-team. He promoted me to the coveted A-team which played on Friday nights. The intensity of the game went up not a few notches but a whole bunch. The games were for keeps now. Every play resulted in crunching blows. The opposing teams wanted to win as badly as we did. I played the right tackle position while on offense and defensive end when we were on defense. I remember that my jersey number was always 76.

I remember that the Saturdays after the football games were the physical recuperation days. I could barely get out of bed during those Saturday mornings; my entire body hurt. In some ways, the physical pain was worth it because belonging to the A-team meant that I was popular in school. I felt a new-found sense of importance and belonging, now being a member of the football team.

High School Band

As in the previous school years, I was in high school band class. Mr. Maneth was still the band teacher. Being on the A-team of the football team meant that a conflict now existed with my being a student in band. The role of the high school band during the fall months was to play and march during the Friday night half-time shows when the football team played. Obviously, I couldn't participate in the band during the Friday night football games. Although he never outright told me, I could tell this didn't sit well with Mr. Maneth.

By the way, in spite of my not fully participating in the high school band's activities, I progressed sufficiently enough in my music abilities that I now earned the second-chair trumpet player position.

After the football season ended, I resumed my full time role in the high school band.

"The Night Flames"

From the start of that school year, several members of the "The Night Flames" group kept pushing me toward restarting the band. I remember my good friends Ernest Nuñez and Cuco Sierra being those band members. I resisted because I had my hands full with football and school. Football was unforgiving; one had to practice every afternoon during the school days, of course play during Friday nights.

About midway through the football season, the band members of "The Night Flames" band and I resumed practicing in spite of still participating on the football team. Little by little we began to re-ignite the fire. Chuy was no longer present, so Norbert Grijalva took over some of the duties of leading the horn section. We managed to do a "gig" once or twice during the football season. After football season we resumed our activities anywhere Cuco Sierra was able to arrange "gigs" for us.

The Complimentary Remark

Three of us that were members of "The Night Flames" band were also classmates in the high school band class. In high school band class, Norbert Grijalva played the trumpet, Ricky Hernandez played the trombone and I played the trumpet.

I remember one specific day during band class when a classmate in band class happened to make a very complimentary remark about "The Night Flames" band. Although I remember the classmate having made the complimentary comment, I don't remember the specific classmate that made the remark. The classmate made the remark sufficiently loud that I'm sure many in the band class including Mr. Maneth, our band teacher, heard it.

Oddly enough Mr. Maneth acted as if he hadn't heard the remark. I half-expected that he would have made some complimentary response to Norbert, Ricky or myself but that didn't happen. I am certain he heard the comment and it seemed strange to me at the time that he didn't respond with a comment, positive or negative. Truthfully, my feeling was that he should have commented positively because the success in our rock band could have been considered the fruits of his labor. In other words, we were successful because he taught us well. But that didn't happen.

Yes, I didn't understand why he didn't jump up to give us an "atta boy". It's a little thing but I guess it's important because I still remember that episode.

Merging the Bands

During the spring semester of that school year, we started thinking about improving the band so that we could improve our chances of perhaps evening recording our own music. There was another band in Fabens that played Mexican music as opposed to rhythm and blues or rock. They concentrated on playing Mexican music at dance events but their tone and musical style were awesome; they played very well.

Anyway, I brought up to idea to our band members that maybe both bands could team up to develop a new more appealing sound. My thought was that this merger could have potentially increased our popularity and might have even brought about a recording contract with some record producer. The band "Bobby and the Premiers" did it; why couldn't we.

I don't remember how or who did it but somehow we contacted them and the idea was proposed to them. They accepted to at least make an effort. We assembled the two bands at our home in Fabens. It resulted in a mess of equipment in our living room; all the way from saxophones, trumpets, trombones, guitars and of course guitar amplifiers. We now had two drummers. It was a hodgepodge of people inside our living room during that evening.

We began by playing two music pieces that were typical of the type of music that we intended for the new combined band to play. We asked them to play music pieces that they might consider to be akin to the type of music that we had just played. They played one of their musical pieces but it was clearly still Mexican music.

We decided to have the two bands practice playing a music piece by the name of "Tell Mama" authored by an artist known as Etta James. I played the record on the record player several times so that each musician could begin to learn their part in the musical arrangement. We spent several hours coaching each other and making notes of the various parts of the music. We then slowly began to intertwine all the parts into one score.

In the end, we sounded horribly. It was obvious that they were used to their style of Mexican music and they just weren't flexible enough to learn the style of music that I thought would get us a quantum leap higher. Although they didn't come right out and said it, it was obvious that our type of music wasn't their cup of tea. In the end, we all agreed that it wasn't a good idea to combine the bands; what could have been a great band resulted in nothing. Playing polka style Mexican music was their style but it was far from the modern American music being played in those days.

I remember the names of two of their band members and the instruments they played: Gabby Quezada on saxophone and Mario Trujillo on guitar. I respected them highly then and I still do today.

"Existentialism"

An English literature teacher of mine in high school frequently used the word "existentialism". Every time I think about that teacher, the word "existentialism" creeps into my mind.

The teacher's name was Ronald Caples; he was my junior and senior English teacher. While I was writing this piece it became important to me to find out what this word really meant. It turns out that "existentialism" is defined as ***"a philosophical theory or approach that emphasizes the existence of the individual person as a free and responsible agent determining its own development through acts of the will."***

An internet article titled "Philosophy" refers to "existentialism" in the following manner: ***"Most importantly, it is the arbitrary act that existentialism finds most objectionable-that is, when someone or society tries to impose or demand that their beliefs, values, or rules be faithfully accepted and obeyed. Existentialists believe this destroys*** *individualism and makes a person become whatever the people in power desire thus they are dehumanized and reduced to being an object. Existentialism then stresses that a person's judgment is the determining factor for what is to be believed rather than by arbitrary religious or secular world values."*

In my view, "existentialism" can simply be expressed as *"It is better to lead than to be led".* At this late age, I finally understand why English  classes during my junior and senior years with Mr. Caples didn't seem planned or deliberate. He did send us home with reading assignments but the discussions in class consisted of having the students present individual thought; of course with some degree guidance from him. No wonder he allowed us to speak freely about the assigned subject matter. It didn't matter to him how trivial or how serious our commentary was about the assigned reading matter. I now know that his approach was to allow the students to take the lead. He was actually pushing us to think on our own rather than to be told what to think or know. I respected him highly.

There was another teacher in high school that taught English literature. Her name was Mrs. Wynnel Witaker. I was never assigned to her English literature classes. My wife, Socorro, who had English literature classes with Mrs. Whitaker thinks that Mr. Caples' method in comparison to Mrs. Whitaker's seemed unorthodox. Yes, I agree that it might have been contrary to traditional or accepted methods but his approach was indeed suited to free thinking. I thought and still do that Mr. Caples was a brilliant thinker; I felt he was very intelligent.

I came to know Mr. Caples very well. He introduced me to his girlfriend, Minerva. She was a professor at the University of Texas at El Paso. We all became close friends. From time to time he would invite me over to his apartment in Fabens for sandwiches in the evenings. By the way, I always addressed him by the name of Mr. Caples rather than Ron or Ronald as a sign of respect. Some might say that my friendship with him involved the ulterior motive of gaining a higher grade but that wasn't so. We never discussed grades; we were just good friends.

A New Awareness

All through my previous school years, the teachers at our high school were of Anglo descent. Yet, the majority of the students were of Hispanic descent.

During my junior year, I started noticing the presence of a few Hispanic teachers. One specific teacher that comes to mind was a teacher by the name of Mr. Raul Rodriguez. I never had him as a teacher and I never knew the subject or subjects he taught in high school. I never spoke to him; I would just see him standing there beside the entrance door to his classroom as we walked along the hallway when we moved from one class to another. 

Seeing a teacher of Hispanic descent in high school seemed odd to me. Prior to him, I had never given any thought to the fact that all the teachers prior to that time were of Anglo descent. I guess I, as well as the students, became accustomed to the fact that teachers were all of Anglo descent. In addition, to demonstrate how uninformed I was prior to that observation, it never dawned on me that first, teachers had to have gone to college and second, that they had to have earned a bachelor's degree from a college.

While writing this piece I remembered that the majority of the students in Fabens were of Hispanic descent yet the teachers, at least up until my high school years, were of Anglo descent. I dug into a few school yearbooks that I had and found that Mr. Rodriguez wasn't the only Hispanic teacher present at that time. Based on the school yearbook information, I confirmed that indeed teachers of Hispanic descent were in the minority.

The table below shows that the percent of Hispanic teachers ranged from only 5% to 12% of the total teachers in high school at that time. In a later section of this memoir, a more complete review of percent representation will be presented that includes not only percentages of Hispanic teachers but also percentages of Hispanic school board members as well as percentages of Hispanic students.

School Year	Teachers Total	Teachers Anglo	Teachers Hispanic	Percent Hispanic
1966	20	18	2	10.0%
1967	20	19	1	5.0%
1968	25	23	2	8.0%
1969	25	22	3	12.0%

Many factors in life end up contributing to certain outcomes. In the end, noticing Mr. Rodriguez as a high school teacher during my junior year woke me up to the fact that persons of Hispanic descent could indeed be teachers.

Plotting a New Direction

During my junior year, I attended chemistry and the teacher was a man by the name of Cecil Kirchner. Chemistry to me was a fascinating subject. In a previous section, I stated that algebra was easy for me. Now chemistry in addition to algebra was an interesting challenge to me.

I especially remember Mr. Kirchner because he fully expected that I was going to go to college after graduating from high school; he took that for granted. Whenever I would walk up to his desk to ask him a question relating to the subject matter of the class, he would answer the question and then grin and say something like "but you'll learn more about that when you're in college" or at other times he would say "you'll do well in college".

In my mind, I was going to work as a farm hand after graduating from high school. My father worked on a farm all his life and I too was destined to do the same type of work. College to me at that time was something only the kids of Anglo descent did. Mr. Kirchner's pushy manner continued during the major part of the school year. I did very well in Mr. Kirchner's chemistry class. Toward the end of the school year I began to take his comments about college more seriously.

Although I knew that college was something that kids of Anglos descent did, little by little I began to believe that there might be a place for me in college as well. I did well in math and the sciences and so I began to think that perhaps that might be enough for me to succeed. At the same time, I wondered how I would go about paying for the tuition to attend college.

Something else that began to influence my thinking about college was a mechanical drafting class in high school. The building that housed the school band room also housed a mechanical drafting classroom; the right side of the building housed the school band room while the left side of the building housed the mechanical drafting classroom.

From time to time, I would notice boys walking to and from that classroom with wooden drawing boards and T-squares. A T-square is an instrument used to draw straight horizontal lines. The boys carrying those boards and T-squares looked cool and intelligent. Somehow I found out that mechanical drafting was something that engineers were required to do and that interested me greatly.

During the final one or two months of my junior year I really began to feel and believe that somehow I might be able to make it to college. I don't exactly remember the step by step process I took, but during my junior year, I managed to enroll in the following year's mechanical drafting class. Enrolling in the mechanical drafting class was the first step.

Step two was to drop out of high school band. Now being enrolled in the mechanical drafting class meant that there was no room left in my subject schedule to fit in high school band class. The decision to drop high school band was difficult but there was no other way; I dropped high school band. I told my girlfriend, Socorro, about having dropped high school band for the upcoming senior year. She couldn't believe it. Nobody ever dropped band class. My band classmates attempted to discourage me from dropping band class. It was sad leaving high school band but I had no choice.

Step three was to reconsider my participation in "The Night Flames" group. I knew that to make it to college I would have to devote almost all my time toward my final year's studies. Somehow I would have to concentrate all my efforts toward that goal. That meant that I would also have to drop out of "The Night Flames" band. It was a hard decision but again I felt I had no choice; I dropped out of the group. The group ultimately disbanded.

The Only Way Out

Prior to music, my only future was that of being a farm hand. Through "The Night Flames" group, music was to be my successful way out of Fabens. Leaving farming and now music behind, college now seemed my only way out. My future would now lie in my ability to prove that I had sufficient talent to make superior grades during my senior year in order to make it to college.

Summer Work In California - 1969

We finished up the 1968 to 1969 school year and there we were back in California ready to go to work. We were confident that we would be welcomed back to the Fugita strawberry fields.

Returning Back to California

At the end of the summer of 1968 when we previously returned back to Fabens, Chuy, my brother, had remained in California. He lived in the labor camp in Huntington Beach all during the 1968 to 1969 school year. Now when we returned back to California during the summer of 1969, we lived in a rental home on Bolsa Avenue in the city of Santa Ana. Chuy joined us and lived with us during that summer. I still remember the little Corvair that my father purchased for him to drive around. He used that car all through his stay at the labor camp.

As before, we went to work in the strawberry fields. Irma and Gloria were now a year older and helped pick strawberries more willingly. We were now seasoned veterans and knew how to make money picking strawberries. It was easier now. The pain in the knees was still there from having to walk on our knees but it was a necessary evil. As in the past, my father continued working on the bean farm while we worked in the strawberry fields.

The Tomato "Packing Shed"

As in previous years, the strawberry season ended around mid-July and we transitioned to working in the tomato fields. A few days after beginning to work in the tomato fields, the foreman took me aside and told me to hop in his pickup truck. He took me to a large corrugated metal warehouse that was located near the area of Edinger Avenue and Gothard Street in Huntington Beach.

The warehouse had an extensive concrete loading dock and it was being used to process tomatoes that were harvested from the tomato fields. I met up with Tad Fugita there. He indicated that he needed someone to supervise the operation of the tomato processing plant. He offered me the job of supervisor and I accepted.

The processing plant was staffed with about 10 women and 6 men. My role was to supervise only the men that worked in the plant. The women were in charge of packing the tomatoes and they were supervised by a woman. The tomato processing plant was known as the "packing shed". Mr. Fujita took the time to show me how the various areas of the plant operated. The plant was in full operation at the time of my visit.

When I arrived home after that day, I told my parents about having been transferred to the "packing shed". My father asked me to ask Tad Fugita about the possibility of having Irma, my sister, work alongside the women at the "packing shed". The following day, I asked Mr. Fujita about the possibility of hiring Irma and he responded in the affirmative. Irma joined me the following day.

If I Could Just Remember

By the way, I also remember Olivia Valenzuela as one of the women that worked at the "packing shed" during the summer of 1969. In a previous section of this memoir, I mentioned that Cruz and Berta Valenzuela were my parent's "compadres". Olivia Valenzuela was Cruz and Berta's daughter. She was a year or two younger than I was. Olivia's other siblings that were about my age. Their names were Cruz and Willy Valenzuela. It stands to reason that if I remember Oliva Valenzuela being present as a worker at the "packing shed", then I would remember Cruz and Willy having been there somewhere in the mix. I know they were there; however, they were probably working in the Tad Fugita tomato fields. The story would be more complete if I could just remember.

Processing the Tomatoes

Anyway, back to the subject of the "packing shed". One area of the loading dock was used by the incoming tomato transport truck. The  tomato transport truck was used to transport the tomato-filled field boxes after the tomatoes were harvested in the tomato fields. The wooden field boxes were heavy duty reusable boxes that could stand the wear and tear. When the workers loaded the field boxes onto the truck in the field, they were stacked right on top of each other to a height of about 6 feet. When the transport truck arrived at the "packing shed", the stacks of wooden field boxes, now filled with tomatoes, were off- loaded with the use of foot activated hand trucks.

The foot activated hand trucks were constructed similarly to that of an 'L' shaped platform with two wheels at the bottom. However, instead of the 'L' shaped platform at the bottom, the foot activated hand truck was equipped with clamps on each side but at the bottom, that closed to grab the stack of boxes when the operator pressed on the foot pedal located in the middle rear of the hand truck. When the foot pedal was lifted with the foot, the clamps would open, allowing the stack of boxes to be released from the hand truck. After the clamps of the hand truck were closed, the man operating the hand truck would then tilt it backwards at an angle in order to move the stack of boxes around, with the wheels bearing the weight of the stacked boxes. The use of the foot activated hand truck made the task of moving the stacks of boxes easier.

Anyway, the off-loaded stack of boxes would then be placed in a temporary holding area. One of the men would move a stack of tomato-filled boxes from the holding area and then place the stack near the roller conveyor. A photograph of the roller conveyer is shown on the left. Another man would then gently dump the tomatoes from the boxes onto a cylindrical roller conveyor. The roller conveyor slowly carried the tomatoes into a spray washer. As the tomatoes moved along, rolling inside the spray washer, they were spray washed with a series of strong water spray nozzles. By means of the roller conveyor, the tomatoes were then slowly transported into an air dryer to remove residual water that clung to the surface of the tomatoes.

The roller conveyor continued slowly moving the tomatoes to a waxing machine. As they moved through the waxing machine, the machine applied a thin wax film on the tomatoes to provide them a glossy, shiny surface. The roller conveyor was configured to make a right 90 degree turn. After slowly moving through the 90 degree turn, the tomatoes continued to move to the tomato packing area.

When the tomatoes arrived at the tomato packing area, a group of eight or ten women would begin to sort the tomatoes by size as they moved along the roller conveyor. The women's role was to pack the tomatoes in attractive wooden boxes. The photograph on the left shows an example of the packed tomato box.

The finished packed boxes were then stacked one on top of another until the stack was about six or seven feet in height. One of the men would then move the finished packed boxes into the finished product area using a manual foot activated lift-truck. The final step was to load the stacked boxes of tomatoes into the semi- truck trailer. Manual foot activated lift-trucks were used to load the semi-truck trailer.

That was the work performed at the "packing shed". The rest was up to the truck driver. His role was to transport the load of tomatoes to the city market located 40 miles away in Los Angeles.

An Interesting Man

By the way, the person that drove the truck-tractor was a middle-aged person by the name of Bill. He stood out because he was the only person of Anglo descent that worked at the packing shed. I don't remember his last name. He was an interesting person. I admired him because he seemed so knowledgeable. It seemed he knew everything about everything and to boot, he was the driver of the massive large truck-tractor rig.

The shiny modern truck-tractor had the Fugita farm markings on each side. It looked very professional. Later on when we got to know each other a little more, he would allow me to sit in the passenger's seat of the truck-tractor as he maneuvered it around the plant. This was my first introduction to a modern transport truck-tractor. To an 18 year old like me, the complex gadgetry inside the truck-tractor cab was super interesting.

Anyway, Bill would come in each day at about 1:00 p.m. or 2 p.m. in the afternoon. He would start up the truck-tractor and move the trailer forward a bit. He would open the rear trailer doors and then move the truck trailer back so as to position the rear of the trailer as close as possible to the edge of the loading dock. Along with one of the men I supervised, he would begin to load the stacks of finished tomato boxes into the trailer.

The Typical Workday at the "Packing Shed"

The workday for the men at the "packing shed" began at 8:00 a.m. in the morning. The first 2 hours of the day was spent on maintenance of the equipment and cleaning up of the facility. The first tomato transport truck bringing in the tomatoes from the field would begin arriving at about 10:00 a.m. in the morning. Two of us would off- load the tomato boxes and would begin placing the stacked boxes of tomatoes in the temporary holding area.

The women would start to trickle in at about a quarter before 11:00 a.m. They would take their places along the roller conveyor and at 11:00 a.m., we would begin gradually dumping tomatoes onto the roller conveyor that slowly moved the tomatoes into the washer. About 5 minutes later the washed and polished tomatoes would arrive via the roller conveyor at the women's packing stations and the tomato packing process would begin in earnest for the day.

Throughout the day, the tomato transport truck would periodically arrive from the tomato field. We would off-load the tomato-filled stacked boxes from the transport truck while at the same time, feeding the tomato processing machines. The packing process would grind to a halt at 1:00 p.m. for a 30 minute lunch and it would begin again soon thereafter. We would then stop the packing process again at 6:00 p.m. to eat supper during the next half hour.

The tomato pickers in the field ended their day at 5:00 p.m. but by then, the quantity of tomato boxes in the packing shed had increased to cover almost the entire space allotted to hold the harvested tomatoes. The tomato packing process had to continue until all the day's picked tomatoes were processed. We worked processing the day's remaining stock of harvested tomatoes and would wind up finishing at about 9:00 p.m. at night. Everybody went home except for three of us; Bill, the semi-truck trailer driver, another man and myself. Together with the other man, we assisted Bill with the loading of the packed tomato boxes into the semi-truck trailer. That was the end of our day.

The Day the "Packing Shed" Stopped

As an aside, those of us that lived through the Kennedy assassination in 1963 remember where we were and what we were doing at the time of that event. Like the Kennedy assassination, I remember where I was and what I was doing during the first manned moon landing on July 20, 1969.

The day of July 20, 1969 fell on a Sunday. The tomato picking operation in the fields continued during the weekends and the "packing shed" operated 7 days a week as well. As I indicated before, we never took a day off, even during weekends or holidays. I can't remember who it was but someone brought in a television set to the "packing shed" that day to be able to follow the goings on of the Apollo 11 moon landing.

At about 7:30 p.m. during that day, the "packing shed" operations came to a standstill. I don't remember for sure, but I think it was Tad Fujita that gave the order to temporarily stop the operations. Everybody including the women gathered around the television set to witness the astronaut step onto the moon's surface. The astronaut's name was Neil Armstrong. On that date at about 8:00 p.m. in the evening, we witnessed the astronaut's first step on the moon's surface. We heard the now famous words from Neil Armstrong: "That's one small step for a man, one giant leap for mankind."

We looked at each other smiling in amazement and satisfaction. Those were pioneering days and yes, we as a team witnessed that moment. For a brief moment following that event, we felt good about ourselves. About ten minutes later, the "packing shed" operations resumed.

Was It Worth It?

In the end, we earned a nice sum of money during that summer. We were paid based on "piecework" in the strawberry fields. The pay for "piecework" was much better than the pay on an hourly basis. Between Irma, Gloria and myself, we were able to earn nice paychecks every week. Now, working long hours at the "packing shed" meant that I was getting paid plenty of overtime. My days started at 8:00 a.m. in the morning and ended at 10:00 p.m. at night. That was 14 hours per day less two 30 minute breaks for lunch. During each week, I worked 91 hours; 51 of those hours were paid at time and a half.

Some Left Overs

While I was busy in my little world trying to make money for my family during that summer, little did I know that a significant event was occurring back home in Fabens. Back in Fabens, a group of researchers from the University of Notre Dame were working on a study which would later become colloquially known as the "Notre Dame Study". The study created controversy because the local farmers would come to view the work as counterproductive to their efforts. The entire explanation will be provided in a later chapter titled: "Fabens, Texas: A Community Study". By the way, I found out about this effort about 10 years later.

As usual toward the end of the summer of 1969, we left California to return back to Fabens. As in the previous summer, Chuy remained behind in California. I don't remember whether he resumed staying at the labor camp or whether he rented an apartment to live in.

As an aside, Chuy never worked at the "packing shed". When I was transferred from working in the tomato fields to now working in the "packing shed", he remained working in the Fugita tomato fields. Today, I wonder why I never pressed Mr. Fugita about transferring Chuy to the "packing shed". It's strange but I don't remember Chuy ever prompting me to put in a good word for him so that he could work in the "packing shed" along with me. He would have made more money working at the "packing shed" than in the tomato fields. Today, I could kick myself for that.

Finally, I remember that while traveling back to Fabens from California, a song by the name of "Black is Black" sung by a group known as "Los Bravos" was playing on the radio. I remember a conversation with my mother while the song was playing. She indicated that the song always reminded her of Esteban Gutierrez, her brother. It seemed odd to me at the time because an American pop song instead of a Mexican song reminded her of her brother. To this day, whenever the song is played on the radio, I remember my mother's comment about my uncle Esteban and that trip back to Fabens.

High School Senior Year - 1969

I started my senior year in the fall of 1969; I was 18 years of age at the time. As in previous years, my family and I spent the summer months in California working as migrant workers.

The Greyhound Bus Ride

After having worked during the summer months in California, we started back from California when the school year had already begun in Fabens.

This time we left from California a week after school started. As before, on the way back, we arrived at my mother's uncle Jesus Gonzalez's home near Eloy, Arizona.

No sooner had we arrived, I started to pressure my father and mother about staying only a night or two so that we could proceed home as soon possible thereafter. Both my father and my mother kept ignoring me; their intention was to stay a week with our relatives before proceeding to leave back to Fabens. The reason I needed to return back as soon as possible was because I wanted to start school early enough to still be able to participate in the class officer elections. The other reason was that I missed my girlfriend and I wanted to see her again. Anyway, I continued pushing my parents but they kept resisting.

Finally, I told them to take me to the Greyhound bus station in nearby Eloy so that I could purchase a ticket for a bus ride back to Fabens. After another day of insisting, my father finally succumbed.

I remember my father and my mother's uncle Jesus driving me to the bus station. My father bought me the bus ticket; I boarded the bus and left Eloy. Luckily, the Greyhound bus route went through Fabens. When I arrived in Fabens I walked to our home. Previously, when we left for California 3 month prior, we had boarded the windows and of course locked the doors. When I arrived, I removed the boards from the windows and settled-in.

The next day, I started my first day at school. I was lucky enough to have returned in time to participate in the class officer elections. I was elected class treasurer which was one of four class officer positions. Needless to say, I met up with my sweetheart, Socorro, as well.

As I indicated before, toward the end of my junior year I had enrolled in this year's mechanical drafting class. Mr. Mains was the teacher of this class but was also the coach of the football team. Of course, I rejoined the football team. Everything was falling back into place.

Breaking Up

Prior to finishing up my junior year, I had decided that my senior year was going to be all about preparing to go on to college. I still didn't know how I was going to afford college tuition and other expenses that came with it. All I knew was that now I was going to have to concentrate very hard in obtaining the highest possible grades in every school subject in my senior year.

My pre-planning was complete, except for one thing. I needed to tell my girlfriend, Socorro, that she and I wouldn't be able to continue being her boyfriend during our senior year.

I felt I had to separate myself from her because I had to concentrate only on things that would insure my having the highest possible grades in all my school subjects. For about a week I kept thinking about how to tell her that we would not be able to be boyfriend and girlfriend during that year. I didn't want to hurt her feelings and so I needed to be careful in my presentation to her. I finally mustered up enough courage and told her. She couldn't understand my reasons for doing it. It broke my heart. For that entire school year, she and I didn't date. Passing each other while walking in opposite directions along the school halls was awkward but somehow we both managed.

My Good Friends

In a previous section of this memoir, I spoke about Mr. Robert Herzing having been my Algebra teacher during my freshman and sophomore years. In addition, I spoke about Mr. Ronald Caples having been my English literature teacher during my junior year. Mr. Caples continued being my English teacher during my senior year.

Mr. Herzing was Mr. Caples' good friend. As a result of my friendship with Mr. Caples, Mr. Herzing and I also became good friends. Mr. Caples used to call Mr. Herzing by his nickname, Bob. I always addressed him as Mr. Herzing as a sign of respect.

I remember Mr. Herzing was an archer. He was an expert marksman with a bow and arrow. During a conversation with Mr. Herzing, he asked about fishing areas in the local area. I told him that the only fish we had in the area was carp fish and that was in the irrigation canals and the drainage canals located throughout the local rural area. To my surprise, Mr. Herzing was very interested in doing some fishing in the canals. I wound up taking both Mr. Caples and Mr. Herzing to the nearby canals. I was under the impression he was going to bring along a fishing pole with lures. However, his idea of fishing was shooting the fish with a bow and arrow. He was very accurate. Mr. Caples wasn't so much into fishing; he would just come along for the rides.

Fast forward to 1974 when I graduated from college and I now lived with my new family in our new home in Fabens; Mr. Herzing visited us. Socorro and I hosted Mr. Herzing and his new wife at our home. By the way, one day while I was walking to my car at the UTEP parking lot, by sheer coincidence, I happened to run into Mr. Caples. We hugged and greeted each other. It was good to see him again.

Mathematics During My Senior Year

My mathematics teacher during my senior year was a person by the name of David Cazares. Mr. Cazares was my first Hispanic teacher. Prior to Mr. Cazares all my teachers had been of Anglo descent.

Mr. Cazares was an exceptional trigonometry teacher. I remember that he took time to provide us with an introduction to a mathematics subject known as calculus. His calculus presentation was not presented as an in- depth course but it did provide us a good initial view of some new mathematical concepts. For some reason, I don't think the calculus introduction was part of the class because we were never tested after those calculus classes.

We were all seniors. From time to time, he would remind us that we would have to know such and such when we got to college. It was as if he was sure that the students in my class would be going on to college. Looking back, I now have a sense that he was purposefully nudging us forward. I now fully appreciate his efforts.

During my senior year, Mr. Cazares assigned our class a senior project. He left it up to each student to come up with a topic involving mathematics. I remember that I just couldn't think of a subject for my project and it was due about a month prior to our high school graduation. Like any other student, I wanted my project to be exceptional and I wanted the topic of my project to somehow involve calculus; to show off a little. I took it upon myself to study a calculus book that he owned. Nothing in the book made sense to me and the deadline was looming near. I finally lucked out. I read a section in the book that described the operation of "integration".

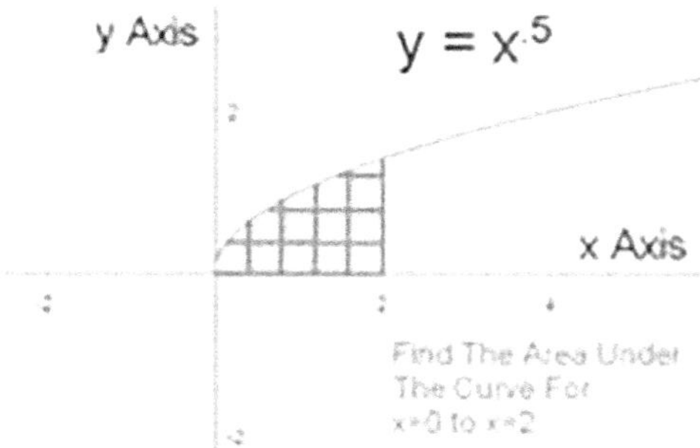

Without going too much into detail, one basic premise of "integration" in calculus is that the "integration" operation yields the area underneath a curve between two "x values". I chose a very simple curve.

In the graph shown on the left, the graph of the equation y=x.5, which is the same as y=√x is shown. The objective was to determine the area underneath the curve between the x value of 0 and the x value of 2. By the way, the area under the curve can be manually calculated by simply counting the squares and partial squares shown in the red grid in the pictorial above; this yields an approximate value.

The beauty of the "integration" operation in calculus is that an exact value can be determined instead of just an approximate value.

Equation   y = x.5
Integrate F(x) = x.5

$$\int_{a}^{b} F(x)\,dx = \int_{0}^{2} x.5\,dx = \frac{2}{3}x^{1.5} = 1.8856 = Area$$

The "integration" operation is shown in the pictorial on the left. For the sake of brevity, I won't go into the details of showing the actual step by step process used to determine the final result. However, the exact value of the area between the x values of 0 and 2, at least to the 4th decimal point, is 1.8856. To a mathematician, this stuff is old hat but to a high schooler at Fabens High School in those days, this stuff was simply awesome. I don't remember if we were graded on this senior project but I do remember that my project did draw most everyone's attention in that class.

Mr. Cazares was also the sponsor of the "Slide Rule Club" in school. The club membership was open to anyone but it wound up consisting mainly of students in my math class. The objective of the club was to learn how to use a ruler-like device known as a "slide rule". The picture on the left shows my "slide rule" that I still keep as a memento of both my high school years and my college years. My slide rule measures 1-1/2" width by 12" in length and is stored in a black, leather carrying case.

During my high school years, hand-held calculators had not yet been developed. "Slide rules" were basically hand-held calculators. "Slide rules" in those days were used to facilitate quick multiplication and division without having to resort to pencil and paper. They were also used for functions involving exponents and logarithms, but not for addition or subtraction. 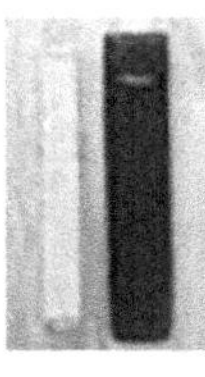

By the way, the first lunar landing occurred on July 20, 1969 which was a few months prior to my being a senior in school. I've seen videos of mission control engineers filmed during that specific moon mission showing them using "slide rules". I was lucky to have had Mr. Cazares as my math teacher.

Mr. Kirchner, My Mentor

Mathematics and the sciences were relatively easy for me. During my junior year, Mr. Cecil Kirchner had been my chemistry teacher. Now he was my physics teacher during my senior year.

He was a good mentor to me. As I indicated before, he would from time to time mention to me that I should consider going to college after I graduated from high school. I was and still am grateful to him for his encouragement. He was one of several important factors that finally made me believe that I could go on to college.

I remember listening to his encouraging remarks but I also remember that I would brush off the remarks because I didn't think I would be able to afford the tuition to go to college. In those days only the kids of Anglo descent went to college. Mr. Rex Carnes was the high school counselor during my senior year but he never once counseled me or provided me literature about colleges and universities. I hate to say it but I sense that Hispanics weren't important to him. I really don't know if he counseled the students of Anglo descent; he must have because after all, he was the counselor during my senior year. I just know I never received any guidance from him.

Even without Mr. Carnes's counseling, Mr. Kirchner's moral support was one of the major reasons why I was now pointed toward college. Mr. Kirchner was the person that provided me information about applying for a scholarship from a company by the name of Farah, Incorporated.

Interacting with him as a student during my senior year would not be the last time that I would speak with him.

The Ultimate Price to Pay

During one specific Friday night football game, we were playing against Cathedral High School on our home field in Fabens. They were known as the Fighting Irish and we were the Wildcats. They were not a pushover during the game; they held their ground well.

One of our half-backs on offense was a student by the name of Amador Villalobos. He was a junior in high school. He was short statured but was very fast. He played the half-back position. During the game, while we were on offense, he sustained an injury and wasn't able to get up after being tackled. Getting physically hurt in football was normal. After some rest on the sidelines, one would recover and was then ready to get back into the game.

Anyway, after seeing an injured player on the field that night, the referees called a time out and then the coaches ran toward where Amador was laying on the field. The coaches began the normal procedures that are performed to coax an injured player back on his feet. We were huddled on our knees about 20 yards away. Several minutes passed and the coaches were still working on Amador. It was now about 10 or 15 minutes and an ambulance stretcher was finally brought onto the field. Amador was placed on the stretcher and was then taken off the field. Needless to say, having an ambulance arrive to take an injured player off the field in a stretcher was not normal. Once Amador was taken off the field, the game resumed. We played the rest of the game to its completion. Amador was probably injured during the second half of the game. This is because I don't remember the coaches having discussed Amador's injury during the half-time session that the coaches had with us. I don't remember who won that game but I do remember the presence of a more somber mood among the team members.

Anyway, we all went home after the game. The next day, word around town was that Amador was in the hospital in El Paso and that he hadn't woken up after having been injured. Sunday rolled around and someone arranged a prayer vigil ceremony in Fabens. I remember attending the vigil.

Amador passed away from head trauma while in the hospital the following Monday. I don't remember having attended his funeral. It's odd that I just can't remember it.

It's been almost 50 years since that event occurred. The ambulance attendants taking him away on the stretcher is still vivid in my mind. There was a somber mood at school during the following week.  It was as if a dark cloud hung over the community. The rest of the football season was a wash; I don't remember having won any of the succeeding games. Although some might differ, I could tell that the members of the football team lost their will to fight on the football field for the rest of the season.

The tragedy occurred during the fall of 1969 in the 1969-1970 school year. The 1970 Fabens High School yearbook contains a page that shows the yearbook being dedicated to Amador Villalobos; a fitting tribute for the ultimate price to pay.

The Price One Pays

After Amador's death, we continued with the rest of the football season. Back during my sophomore year, Coach Mains had shamed me into playing football. Now playing football as a senior was important to me. I was a jock and an important contributor to the team.

During one specific game after Amador's death, I sustained an injury to my left knee. During that specific play prior to sustaining the injury, I was so totally fixated on the opposing team's ball carrier moving toward the right side of the field that I failed to see one of his blockers coming toward me from my left side. The blocker hit me squarely on the left side of my left knee; I felt the awful pain. I fell to the ground and after the play ended, I couldn't stand up. Coach Mains came toward where I had fallen. I also saw my father's face as I lay on the grass turf. He had run down from the bleachers to where I laid to see what had happened to me. Ultimately, I was helped to limp off the field.

I spent the rest of the game sidelined with an ice pack on my knee. When the game was over, my father came down once more from the bleachers and assisted me to our pickup truck. I spent that night at home in pain. The next day, my left knee had completely swollen up. I hobbled around our home as best I could. Monday, came and my knee was still extremely swollen. My father took me to the local medical clinic. The doctor used a large syringe to extract fluid that had collected inside my knee joint. Needless to say, the liquid extraction was painful. At last my knee looked somewhat normal.

The following week during the daily football practice sessions, I spent my time in the dressing room immersed in a cold water whirlpool machine. I didn't play during that Friday night's game. The next week, I could run although I still had to be careful so as not to re-injure my knee. We traveled to Alpine, Texas to play against the Alpine Bucks. I was on the side lines during the first part of the game and our team was taking a beating.

Coach Mains asked me if I was ready to play and I responded to him that yes I was ready. I went in on defense. The play began, I started to run without watching my knee and my knee gave out; I was limping again. The coach gave the signal and I limped off the field. That was the last game of the season and we lost the game.

To this day, I can still remember seeing the opposing team's blocker from the corner of my eye coming at me and the severe pain that resulted. My knee never really healed properly. All during my life I've had to be careful with my left leg due to the knee injury in high school. Fast forward to when I was about 45 years of age. I went to see an orthopedic doctor about finally fixing my knee. I remember the doctor's name; Dr. Licon. After reviewing the X-rays, he told me that there was nothing he could do with my knee since it had somehow deformed to a point where surgery wouldn't help. One other thing, my father had to foot the medical bills. The school didn't pay for any of the medical expenses. So being a proud jock had a price. That price was an injured knee that lasted for years.

I went on earn my letter jacket and I still have it in my possession. It reminds me of my warrior days. Since I didn't participate in sports during my freshman year, my letter jacket has 3 bars instead of the 4 bars. I did participate in track and cross country running during my four years of high school.

Farah Manufacturing

In a previous section of this memoir, I indicated that during my senior year, Mr. Kirchner provided me the information that led to my applying for a scholarship from Farah, Incorporated. Farah, Incorporated in 1970 was the largest men's pant manufacturer in the El Paso area. It hard a huge manufacturing facility near the intersection of the I-10 Freeway and Hawkins Blvd.

A short history of Farah, Incorporated is available on the web.

The article can be viewed using the following web link: https://tshaonline.org/handbook/online/articles/dlf02

The following excerpt was taken from that web article: "The Farah, Incorporated, of 1970 had seven domestic manufacturing facilities, five in El Paso and one each in San Antonio and Las Cruces, New Mexico. Combined, they comprised 1,837,000 square feet of manufacturing space and employed 9,500 workers." Farah was an important industry to El Paso because of the number of people it employed.

Anyway, I don't remember how I obtained the application but the fact is that I completed the application and mailed it to Farah, Incorporated. About a month later I received a letter from a Mr. Gordon Foster who was then an executive at Farah, Incorporated. In his letter, he indicated that I had been chosen to receive the award of a four year scholarship to the University of Texas at El Paso. He further indicated in his letter that he wanted me to visit their business offices and provided a specific date and hour in his letter so that he and I could meet.

As requested, I proceeded to the address he indicated in the letter. I showed Mr. Foster's invitation letter to the guard that monitored the plant entrance. I was then directed to proceed to the office entrance. When I entered the office door, I walked to the receptionist and introduced myself. It was as if the receptionist knew who I was.

She immediately called Mr. Foster and about five minutes later, Mr. Foster came to the receptionist area to meet with me. He was a tall, grey haired man dressed in a business suit. He showed me to his office and we had a very nice conversation. He told me that he wanted me to see the manufacturing facility and we walked to several locations within the facility. Yes, he was a very kind host. We finally returned to the receptionist area and we said our good-byes. Prior to exiting, I thanked him profusely and I promised to do my best at college. That was the last time I saw him.

By the way, the amount of the scholarship was $4,000 dollars for four years or $500 dollars per semester. In 1970 the amount of

$4,000 dollars had the same buying power as $26,156.39 in 2018. The latter value was calculated using an "inflation calculator" that can be accessed using the following web link:

https://www.dollartimes.com/inflation/inflation.php?amount= 4000&year=1970

Somehow word got out at school that I received the scholarship from Farah, Incorporated. All of a sudden, my classmates were congratulating me. I've never been the boastful type but I did feel a new sense of importance in school. I had finally solved my problem; I now had the ability to finance my college career. 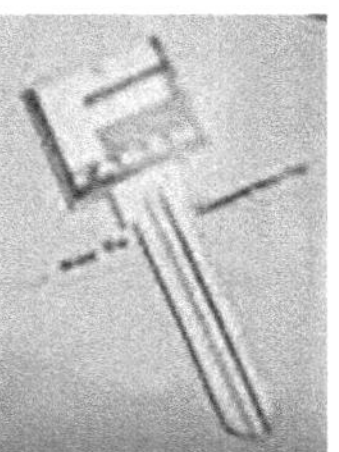

I owe Farah, Incorporated at debt of gratitude for having believed that I could succeed at the University of Texas at El Paso. Fabens High School too benefitted from Farah, Incorporated as it purchased a full page ad in the 1970 yearbook.

Senior Ditch Day

The school year was coming to a close and the members of the senior class were suffering from "senioritis". "Senioritis" is a term used to denote a malady that almost all seniors had. "Senioritis" is defined as "a supposed affliction of students in their final year of high school or college, characterized by a decline in motivation or performance.".

An informal tradition at Fabens in those days was what was known as "senior ditch day". "Senior ditch day" was a term used to denote a specific school day during which seniors actually ditch school and don't attend regular classes for the entire day. I don't remember who determined the day of the ditch day but somehow everyone knew of the day. I've always been curious to know if "senior ditch day" was actually sanctioned by the school because the school administrators didn't make a big fuss about the seniors being absent during that day.

Anyway, the tradition was that the senior students all showed up to their first class in the morning and after roll call, they would exit and leave the school for the entire day. Almost all the senior students left except for a few students and I. At that point in time, I knew I was going on to the University of Texas at El Paso and I just didn't want to cause a problem and risk my future. Well truthfully, I couldn't see myself skipping school; I was a nerd after all.

Uncle Sam's Invitation

Sometime during the last month of my senior year I received a letter from an organization known as the Selective Service Board. The letter indicated that I was to report for a physical and written examination at the Mills Building in El Paso. The "Selective Service Board" was the organization that administered entry of young men into military service during that time. Things have changed since my senior year in 1970; now the military is an all volunteer military.

As required by law, I registered with the Selective Service Board when I was 18 years of age. After a young man registered, the Selective Service Board would then assign a military status designation to the young man that registered. If the young man was in high school or college, the military status assigned to that young man was 1-S which meant deferment from the military due to attending school. Those that weren't in school and had no valid reason to be deferred were deemed ready for military service and were assigned the 1-A military status. There were other designations but these two designations to me were the most important.

During the last month that I was in high school when I received the notice to report for the military examination, my military designation was still 1-S. I had already received my acceptance letter from the University of Texas at El Paso. I remember being concerned at having received the notice to report to the Mills Building for the examination since I was still designated 1-S and was still in high school. Further, I was going to proceed on to college.

The day of the examination arrived. I traveled to El Paso and proceeded to one of the upper floors of the Mills building. I found a large room filled with young men who were there for the same reason. A large burly man dressed in military uniform was barking orders instructing the young men to get in line. I joined them. Little by little we were processed in. We each filled out personal information forms. When I handed in my paperwork, I indicated to the officer in charge that I was in possession of a student deferment and that I was going on to college. I showed him my 1-S card and even showed him my University of Texas at El Paso acceptance letter. He took the documentation and without comment told me to get in line for processing; he didn't seem interested in discussing the matter with me.

Once everybody was processed, we were separated into groups of about 30. Each group of 30 was taken to a physical examination area. We were told to disrobe completely and to stand in line. Several persons dressed in medical attire wearing stethoscopes began to examine each person, one by one. They thoroughly examined each person's sexual parts. At one point, they instructed us to lean forward while holding our butt cheeks apart with our hands. They inspected our behinds. The normal lung and heart testing with stethoscopes was also conducted.

The groups of 30 were being herded here and there as if herding cattle. We would be instructed to move from one testing area to another and then still another. It was kind of funny watching the other naked young men moving from one area to another while at the same trying to cover their private parts with their hands as best they could.

The physical examination part of the evaluation was completed by noon. Everyone was instructed to dress. Every person was then given a sack lunch to eat. During the following hour we ate our lunch and then we waited for the next session to begin.

During the afternoon, we were all herded over to a huge room filled with desks. We were ordered to take our seats at the desks. The desks were similar to those used in school. We were each provided pencils and exam booklets. This was the written part of the examination. We were allowed about 2 hours to complete the written part of the test.

When everyone finally turned in the completed booklets, we were told to wait at our desks. About an hour later, the officer in charge announced that he would begin calling out the names of those persons that were selected to join the military. The officer then informed us that the persons whose names were to be called out would then have to report back to the Mills Building the following day to begin the induction process for military service. The officer then provided information as to what to pack such as specific clothing and toiletries. All of a sudden it got interesting. Almost every young man began to look around eyeing each other as if to attempt to determine ahead of time who was going and who was staying.

The roll call began and everyone sat up straight to listen. One could hear a pin drop; it was so silent. The officer began to slowly call out the names. As the names were called, the young man whose name was called would get up from his seat and proceed to leave. Little by little the huge room started to empty out.

The officer finally finished calling out the names. My name had not been called. I made it; I wasn't called. I estimate there were about 5 to 10 percent of the original young men remaining. We were then told that in all probability we would receive notices to report back in the near future. We were then allowed to leave.

Some might say it was unpatriotic to wish not to be called for duty in the military. In those days, the United States was at war with the country of Viet Nam. I remember the nightly television news broadcasts at the time. It seemed that every day there were multiple stories about something or other related to the Viet Nam war. It was a daily reality. Yes, like all wars, this was a dangerous war. Yes, like any human being at the time I was afraid of joining the military and like any person summoned to serve, I would have served. In my view, a courageous person performs because he has to. By the way, based on information taken from an internet article, I found that the reported U.S. soldier total death count in that war was 58,220.

The Senior Trip

In a previous section, I indicated that at the start of my senior school year my girlfriend and I discontinued dating. The first couple of weeks after starting my senior year, I indicated to her that I had to concentrate on my studies and that it was best that we discontinue dating for the rest of the school year. I indicated to her that I felt it was necessary because I needed to dedicate my full efforts at my studies in order to improve my chances of going to college. She didn't like it and I didn't like it either but it was my only recourse.

My senior school year progressed and toward the end of the school year our school took all the members of the senior class on what was known as "the senior trip". The senior trip was and probably still is a tradition for all senior classes. The senior trip was, in a sense, an award to the seniors for having done well during the school year.

That year's trip was to Ruidoso, New Mexico. Ruidoso, New Mexico is situated in a forested area of New Mexico. It is covered with pine trees. The weather is more temperate there compared to the weather in the El Paso area. The seniors all rode in Greyhound style buses on that trip to Ruidoso. We had fun that day. Horses were rented for the students to ride. A picnic was held for the seniors in Ruidoso. Overall, everyone enjoyed the outing.

When I climbed onto the bus on the return trip back to Fabens, I noticed that Socorro was seated by herself. The bus seats were wide enough for two persons to sit on. I asked her if it was alright if I sat beside her and she replied that she didn't mind. It was good to sit with her after having been apart for so long. We made up during that ride home. I've been with that pretty girl ever since. That pretty girl is now my wife.

Graduation

High school graduation was approaching. The total number of students that were to graduate that year was 84. I remember that the school's administration was concerned about the lack of seating capacity in the high school auditorium. The thought was that perhaps the seating capacity of the auditorium might not be sufficient to accommodate the students, parents and well-wishers during the commencement ceremonies. As a result, the school administrators decided that the commencement ceremonies would be held at the football field to accommodate the crowd. From there on every graduation ceremony has now been held at the football field.

About two weeks prior to the commencement date, the top 10 students were advised of their class ranking based on their overall grade point average. I was 5th in the class of 84 students. The valedictorian was Stan Hernandez and the salutatorian was Johnny Little. I don't exactly remember who was 3rd and 4th. I was one of several students that were asked to prepare commencement speeches to deliver at the graduation ceremonies. I prepared mine.

By the way, I still have a copy of my speech. It turns out that somehow Irma, my sister, remained in possession of the paper version of my speech for many years. By sheer coincidence, while I was writing this memoir, she happened to be visiting in the El Paso area from her home in the Dallas, Texas area. During a get-together she happened to mention that she had a copy of my graduation speech. A few weeks later she mailed me the manuscript.

The three page manuscript was worn around the edges but was still legible. The graphic on the left shows an excerpt of the beginning of the manuscript.

My speech was titled "Gratitude". In the speech, I acknowledged the presence of the community and expressed gratitude for the support they provided to the graduating class of 1970. The old manuscript was provided to me by my sister, Irma, 48 years later after I used it in our commencement ceremonies. I was glad to see an "old friend"; the manuscript of my speech.

I remember how nervous I was when I delivered my speech. Although I wasn't first, second, third or fourth in the student rankings, I was fifth. Through my speech, I was allowed to express our gratitude to those well-wishers that came to our commencement ceremonies that year.

My having been awarded a four year scholarship from Farah, Incorporated was announced in the graduation ceremony for the Fabens community to hear. Prior to having been awarded that scholarship, my road upward was blocked. Short of that scholarship, my only other choice was that of becoming a farm hand. My scholarship changed that. There was still no guarantee that I would finish successfully at the University of Texas at El Paso. The scholarship was a big push in the right direction, however. Finishing college would be up to me.

Summer Work In California - 1970

A few days after my graduation from Fabens High School, we started to prepare for the trip to California. My immediate future was cast in stone. I would proceed to California, work during the summer and return back to Fabens at the end of the summer. I would then start college at the University of Texas at El Paso.

Being Welcomed Back

As before, my family traveled to California. And as before, prior to my father returning for us from California, he had rented a rental home in California for us to stay in during the summer months. The rental home was located in Huntington Beach, about a quarter of a mile walking distance from the Huntington Beach pier.

Chuy was now married to Berta Guardiola; she was now my sister-in-law. When we arrived and moved into the rental home, both Chuy and Berta also moved in with us. I am not sure where they lived prior to our arrival at Huntington Beach. Chuy and Berta probably moved in with us in order to conserve their money. I remember that the rental home wasn't very large. Our nuclear family consisted of nine members. With Chuy and Berta, eleven people in total now lived in the rental home. I can't remember the exact sleeping arrangements, but it must have been a tight squeeze in that small rental home.

The day after our arrival in California, Irma, Gloria and I showed up at the Fugita strawberry fields. I don't remember if Chuy was already working in the strawberry fields or if he was working somewhere else; however, I do remember that Berta did in fact work in the strawberry fields.

As in the past, we were welcomed by the foreman and the owner, Tad Fugita, at the strawberry field. We were seasoned veterans and again as in the past, we promptly began earning our money.

The Mid-July Transition

By mid-July, the strawberry season was waning. Again, we all transitioned to working in the "packing shed". Irma, Olivia Valenzuela and now Berta, Chuy's wife, worked as packers in the "packing shed".

We worked the same long hours as before, working every day even during Saturdays and Sundays.

The Exciting Ride

Bill, the truck driver, was still transporting the packed finished tomato boxes to the city market in Los Angeles. As I indicated before, Bill would allow me to sit in the passenger's seat of the tractor-trailer rig as he maneuvered the semi-trailer attached to the tractor around the "packing shed" yard.

I was curious to know where Bill took the finished boxed tomatoes after we loaded them into the semi-trailer. I asked him and he told me all about the city market in Los Angeles.

One day while working in the "packing shed", Bill asked me if I wanted to ride along with him in the tractor-trailer rig to the city market after we finished at the "packing shed". I responded in the affirmative right away. He then warned me that we would return back to the "packing shed" from the city market at around 1:00 a.m. or 2:00 a.m. in the early morning. I told him that was not a problem.

We pulled out of the "packing shed" at about 10:00 a.m. that night with the semi-trailer fully loaded. I rode in the passenger's seat while Bill was expertly maneuvering the trailer from lane to lane as we traveled along the freeway. It's been a while since those days so I don't remember if the truck was equipped with a 10 gear transmission or an 18 gear transmission. It was, however, interesting watching him change from one gear to another while at the same time keeping his eyes glued to the road.

We arrived at the city market about an hour later. The facility was huge. It had many tractor-trailer rigs parked at its docks. The market handled every kind of produce one could think of. One could see row after row of boxes with plums, carrots, lettuce, and other fruits and vegetables; and of course tomatoes.

Bill maneuvered the truck so that the rear of the semi-trailer bumped against the loading dock at the city market. We waited for about fifteen to twenty minutes while the paperwork was being processed. A group of workers finally appeared and they began to off-load the stacked boxes of tomatoes from the semi-trailer. The last stacks of tomato boxes were finally off-loaded.

Bill and I boarded the tractor-trailer rig and he started the engine. As soon as he started the engine, he looked up and then looked toward me. He asked me if I wanted to drive the tractor-trailer rig back to the "packing shed". For a second I thought he was kidding and then suddenly I realized he was serious; I said yes right away.

We both stepped off from our respective seats, walked around the front of the tractor in opposite directions and then we re-boarded the rig. The cluster of dials and gadgets on the panel boggled the mind but I knew that the speedometer and the tachometer were  the main instruments that needed to be managed during the drive. I knew the layout of the gear shift pattern because I had observed Bill managing the gears on the way in to the city market.

I placed the tractor's gear shift in first gear and then slowly began to let out the clutch; the tractor-trailer rig began to move. I was in heaven. Following Bill's directions as we moved along, I drove the tractor-trailer rig to the freeway. Finally on the freeway, I drove the tractor-trailer rig for about an hour along the freeway. Bill never once corrected me while I was driving. We finally arrived to the freeway exit that led to the "packing shed". Having exited from the freeway, I now drove the tractor-trailer rig along the streets until we finally arrived at the "packing shed" parking lot.

Now at the parking lot, Bill asked that I bring the tractor-trailer rig to a halt. He then told me to exit from the driver's seat because he needed to park the trailer. He maneuvered the tractor-trailer rig so that the rear of trailer could be placed squarely against the dock. He did so expertly.

I was in heaven. Bill had placed his confidence in me and had allowed me to drive his tractor-trailer rig. I had driven from Los Angeles to Huntington Beach without a hitch. Chuy was waiting for me in the parking lot inside his Corvair and we both rode home. I'll never forget the opportunity that Bill provided me that night.

The Blissful Vacation

Mario, Graciela, Norma and Martin spent that summer at the beach in Huntington Beach. On the other hand, Chuy, Irma, Gloria and I worked day in and day out. The beach from our rental home was only a quarter of a mile walking distance. My younger siblings all developed nice bronze sun tans on their skin while lying on the beach. With their surf boards, they surfed the waves and partied all day with the rest of the beach crowd.

At least that's what I now tell them jokingly at our family get-togethers, now that we are all grown up.

In all seriousness, my younger siblings actually didn't work during the summers when we lived in California during those summers. They were just too young. I joke with them now because Chuy, Irma and Gloria and I did have to work non-stop to help out with the family finances. In the end, we all did our part; even the little ones.

The United Farm Workers Union

From 1966 to now 1970, our family had traveled to California to work in the strawberry fields and the tomato fields during the summer months. Our family was a migrant worker family because we moved seasonally from our home to where we could find employment.

Little did we know that during that same time frame, when we were working on the Fujita farms, a serious labor conflict was in progress between the grape farm workers and the grape farm owners during those years. The conflict occurred during the years from 1965 to 1970 which I now know coincided with the years we traveled back and forth to California. At the time, we were oblivious to the fact that the labor conflict was occurring in Delano, California just 180 miles driving distance north from Huntington Beach.

Later on when I was in college after 1970, I would hear about the grape boycott but it didn't really register in our mind as something significant. To me, it was just some distant squabble involving some farm workers and farm owners.

Even during my life as an adult, I never paid much attention to the stories I would hear about Cesar Chavez who was the leader of the farm workers. By the way, the highway that runs alongside the international border between El Paso and Cd. Juarez is named after Cesar Chavez. The name of the highway is the Cesar Chavez Border Highway.

It wasn't until I was writing this part of the memoir having to do with our working during the summers in California that I became interested in learning more about the farm workers strike back in the 1960s. By sheer coincidence, I recently happened to see a television movie titled "Cesar Chavez". The movie was released in March of 2014. An actor by the name of Michael Peña starred as Cesar Chavez. The movie was about Cesar Chavez and the events that led to the successful outcome of the farm workers strike in Delano, California. I recently dug into the internet to find out more of the details involving that conflict. It turns out that the farm workers union began a labor strike in an attempt to gain wages equivalent to the federal minimum wage. The strike began in September 1965 and ended successfully five years later in July of 1970. The United Farm Workers union was able to come to a collective bargaining agreement with the grape growers that affected 10,000 farm workers.

I obtained the following excerpt from the internet using the following link: https://en.wikipedia.org/wiki/Delano_grape_strike.

"The Delano grape strike was a labor strike by the Agricultural Workers Organizing Committee and the United Farm Workers against grape growers in California. The strike began on September 8, 1965, and lasted more than five years. Due largely to a consumer boycott of non-union grapes, the strike ended with a significant victory for the United Farm Workers as well as its first contract with the growers.

The strike began when the Agricultural Workers Organizing Committee, mostly Filipino farm workers in Delano, California, led by Philip Vera Cruz, Larry Itliong, Benjamin Gines and Pete Velasco, walked off the farms of area table-grape growers, demanding wages equal to the federal minimum wage. One week after the strike began, the predominantly Mexican-American National Farmworkers Association, led by Cesar Chavez, Dolores Huerta and Richard Chavez, joined the strike, and eventually the two groups merged, forming the United Farm Workers of America in August 1966. The strike rapidly spread to more than 2,000 workers."

The phrase "so near yet so far" is sometimes used to infer that someone almost achieved what they wanted, but in the end just failed. With a slight twist, the phrase "so near yet so far" can be used to describe our ignorance of that conflict. The farm workers and grape growers conflict was so near in proximity to us but yet so far from our minds that we didn't realize that poor migrant workers were being affected. I highly recommend watching the movie "Cesar Chavez".

My First Ride on an Airplane

Anyway, back to the subject relating to working in California during the summer of 1970. When I applied for admission to the University of Texas at El Paso prior to leaving for California, I also applied for a week-long college orientation session that was to be held at university. The orientation session was to start at the beginning of September just prior to the start of the college school year.

I knew full well that my father would delay our departure from California until mid-September as in prior years. At about mid- summer now in California, I told my father about my having to leave at the end of August to attend the orientation session at the university back in El Paso. My father responded that we wouldn't be able to return early because of his commitments to his employer at the bean farm. We however, agreed that I would return back by myself and the rest of the family would remain behind for another two weeks.

I can't remember how my father and I decided how I was going to travel back to El Paso, but I wound up returning to El Paso traveling on an airline. My father and Chuy took me to the Los Angeles International Airport and I returned on an American Airlines Boeing 707 to El Paso. That was the first time that I flew on an airplane. A lot had transpired from the days on the farm when Chuy and I used to construct toy airplanes out of wood from wooden crates.

Life Choices

About a week prior to leaving my job at the "packing shed", I told Mr. Fujita about my having received a scholarship to go to college starting in September. He congratulated me and wished me well. The last day came and I bid everyone farewell; they too wished me well.

I had done well in the position of supervisor at the "packing shed" and Tad Fujita saw me as a responsible person. I had every intention of returning back the next summer. Life has its twists and turns and ultimately those twists and turns result in changes in one's path as life progresses. Although I fully intended to return, my life choices in the ensuing months would change all of that.

Ethnic Minorities Were the Student Majorities

The memories of my school years are important to me. As I progressed though elementary school, grade school and then high school, little by little, my path became clearer to me. My school years were the launching pad that I needed. Had it not been for certain specific life changing events during the latter years, I would have wound up working on a farm somewhere in the Fabens area. That was my destiny; at least, I thought it was at the time. This is not to say that being a farm hand was not honorable work. Music became important to me during my high school years because, for a time, it seemed the only way to succeed and make it out of Fabens. Important events occurred; however, that ended up opening the door to my being able to attend college.

Luck Was Everything

Not many Hispanic students were lucky enough to go to college at the time. The high school system, at least in Fabens, wasn't geared to produce college bound Hispanic students. Those Hispanic students that did go to college did so without being nudged along; they did it of their own accord. To my knowledge, Hispanic students were not formally counseled to nudge them along to high school to college. Although I was an A-student, I was never counseled by Mr. Rex Carnes who at that time was the school counselor.

Was I not counseled because I was Hispanic or did I just get forgotten along the way? I'll never know for sure. I did however succeed in making it out of Fabens; that is, not becoming a ranch hand or a farm worker. My first step in that process was attending college.

Sensing Low Self Esteem

All through my years in High School and now while writing this memoir, I was always curious about why it was that the majority of the teachers in the Fabens School District were other than teachers of Hispanic descent. It is fair to say that I suffered from an inferiority complex that was brought on by the presence of a majority of non- Hispanic teachers as compared to Hispanic teachers. Although it might sound unfair, I always viewed non-Hispanic teachers as teachers of Anglo Saxon descent. That is to say,

I subconsciously grouped non-Hispanic teachers as Anglo Saxons even though some of them might have been of teachers of Italian descent and others might have been of Polish descent and so on.

Low Rate of Hispanic College Graduates

While writing this memoir I remembered the inferiority complex I felt while in High School back in the 1960's. Now as a grandfather while I am writing this memoir, I have had the opportunity to attend several school presentations in which my grandchildren have participated. It is now common to see more Hispanic teachers as compared to non- Hispanic teachers involved with my grandchildren. As a result of this, I began to feel a need to understand why it was that the majority of teachers now present in the local High Schools were of Hispanic descent.

In May of 2018 while writing this memoir, I visited the Fabens High School library and reviewed several school yearbooks to obtain counts of students, teachers and school board members by race; Hispanic and Anglo descent. Based on a review of the total student population during the 1969-1970 high school year, students of Anglo descent were the minority. The majority of the students were of Hispanic descent. On the other hand, teachers of Anglo descent were the majority while teachers of Hispanic descent were the minority. So as a result, in my day, the percentage of teachers of Hispanic descent to the percentage of students of Hispanic descent was inverted. Was it that not enough Hispanic students graduated from college to then become school teachers or did Hispanic students that did graduate from college not join the teaching profession? I am guessing the former; not enough Hispanic students were graduating from college. Toward the end of my high school years I had a feeling that the few students of Anglo descent were indeed being guided toward college; either by their parents and by the school counselor. I had a feeling that money was not an obstacle for the students of Anglo descent. Mr. Rex Carnes was the counselor; that fact is recorded in the 1970 school yearbook. Did Mr. Carnes guide the students of Anglo descent and not the students of Hispanic descent? He was there and he had to have been performing his job. I was not one of those lucky students being guided by Mr. Carnes.

Hispanic Teacher Under-Representation

During the 1969-1970 school year, the total high school student count was 337 students. This number was taken from the high school yearbook published in 1970. The Hispanic students comprised 88.7% of the total high school student population. Only 11.3 percent were students of Anglo descent. The Hispanic students were the majority and the Hispanic teachers were the minority. In fact, of the total of 29 high school teachers during the 1969-1970 school year, only 5 teachers were of Hispanic descent. Therefore, the faculty was comprised of only 17.2 percent of Hispanic teachers.

The reason for the existence of teachers in the first place, is because of the existence of students; not the other way around. With that logic in mind, the Hispanic teacher presence was under- represented in Fabens High School during the 1969-1970 school year when the percentage of Hispanic students to percentage of Hispanic teachers is considered. To provide for proportional representation, the number of Hispanic school teachers would have had to increase to 25 Hispanic teachers from an actual of 5. With 25 Hispanic teachers, the result would have been 86.2 percent Hispanic teachers along with 88.7 percent Hispanic students. Hispanic teacher-student parity would have been achieved with 25 Hispanic teachers.

As indicated, above, the Hispanic student percentages and the Hispanic teacher percentages were disproportional from each other at least during the 1969-1970 school year. An ethnic disparity existed. Based on this statistic alone, it was obvious that Fabens High School was not producing college bound students. Again, either not enough Hispanic college graduates were choosing teaching as a profession when they graduated from college or not enough Hispanic students were going to college to then become teachers. Either way, a minority of Hispanic high school teachers resulted. These statistics are indicators that point to the presence of a disparity.

School Board Member Under-Representation

The yearbook school information was also a source of information relating to the number of school board members of Anglo descent and Hispanic descent. Here too, a Hispanic disparity was present.

In the majority of cases, school board members act on school policy matters based on State mandated guidelines. However, sometimes they do vote on matters having to do with local issues. How a school board member votes on local issues affect the teachers and the students in the school. Although it shouldn't happen, it is possible that the outcome of the school board vote on specific local issues can be unfavorable to students and teachers of both Hispanic descent and possibly even to students and teachers of Anglo descent. So there are many reasons why the racial makeup of the school board is important; especially in a town that had no formal town government such as Fabens, Texas. Fabens, Texas was, and still is in the year 2020, an unincorporated township.

During my senior year in 1970, the Fabens school board was made up of four members of Anglo descent and three members of Hispanic descent. This meant that during the 1969-1970 school year, 42.6 percent of the board was composed of Hispanic board members. As indicated before, during that same school year, 88.7 percent of the students were of Hispanic origin. As in the case with teachers, the reason for the existence of school board members is because of the existence of students; not the other way around. With that in mind, the Hispanic school board member presence was under-represented in the Fabens school board in the 1969-1970 school year when the percentage of Hispanic students is compared to the percentage of Hispanic school board members. That was in the 1969-1970 school year. To provide for proportional representation, the number of Hispanic school board members would have had to increase to 6 Hispanic members from 3. With 6 Hispanic school board members, the result would have been 85.7 percent Hispanic school board members and 88.7 percent Hispanic students. Hispanic board member-student parity would have been achieved at those levels.

By the way, during the school year prior to the 1969-1970 school year, there was only 1 school board member that was of Hispanic descent out of 7 members. This resulted in a value of 14.3 percent Hispanic school board members. Meanwhile, the percent of Hispanic students during that prior school year was 84 percent. To provide for proportional representation, the number of Hispanic school board members would have had to increase to 6 Hispanic members from the actual number of 1. With six Hispanic school board members, the result would have been 85.7 percent Hispanic school board members and 84 percent Hispanic students. Ethnic Hispanic parity based on school board members would have been achieved at those levels.

A Complete Overview of Hispanic Representation

As a result of the preliminary evaluation performed using the information contained in the 1969 and 1970 yearbooks, I felt a need to determine if ethnic Hispanic parity had ever actually been achieved as far as teachers, school board members and students were concerned. I was in personal possession of 5 school yearbooks from 1966 to 1970. In order to determine if parity had been achieved, I needed additional yearbook information beyond the 1966-1970 school years.

I visited the Fabens High School library to review school yearbooks from later years. I developed a table that covers the school years ranging from the 1965-1966 school year to the 2016- 2017 school year. The "Hispanic Parity Table" below shows the results of that review. Note that the number of teachers shown in the "Hispanic Parity Table" are only those teachers in the High School.

Hispanic Parity Table

School Year	Teachers Total	Teachers Hispanic	Percent Hispanic	Board Total	Board Hispanic	Percent Hispanic	Students Total	Students Hispanic	Percent Hispanic
1966	20	2	10.0%	7	0	0.0%	206	149	72.3%
1967	20	1	5.0%	Note 1	---	---	344	287	83.4%
1968	25	2	8.0%	7	1	14.3%	343	282	82.2%
1969	25	3	12.0%	7	1	14.3%	362	304	84.0%
1970	29	5	17.2%	7	3	42.6%	337	299	88.7%
1975	26	10	38.5%	6	4	66.7%	399	361	90.5%
1980	38	14	36.8%	7	3	42.0%	469	432	92.1%
1985	36	11	30.0%	7	4	57.1%	459	432	94.1%
2017	28	27	96.4%	7	6	85.7%	471	469	99.6%

Note 1 School board information not available in the 1967 yearbook

Hispanic Teacher-Student Parity

Was Hispanic teacher-student parity ever achieved? The answer is yes; based on the limited information in the "Hispanic Parity Table". It was achieved in the year 2017 when the percentage of Hispanic teachers actually rose to 96.4 percent while the percentage of Hispanic students was now at 99.6 percent. For all practical purposes, the percentage values were even.

When did the percentage of Hispanic teachers start to increase to approach the percentage necessary to achieve Hispanic teacher-student parity? From the information in the "Hispanic Parity Table", it appears that the trend upward began soon after the 1969-1970 school year when the percentage of Hispanic teachers jumped from

17.2 percent to now 38.5 percent in the 1975 school year. It could be that starting with 1970 high school graduates, the high school students went on to attend college and some of them actually returned four (4) years later to assume teaching positions in the Fabens Independent School district.

Did it matter that Hispanic teacher-student parity wasn't achieved until the 2017 school year? In the end, the teacher, whether of Hispanic descent or of Anglo descent, was required to teach to a certain state mandated standard. With that point of view, the answer is no, it didn't matter. However, from the point of view that not enough Hispanic teachers were being produced, it did matter.

The lack of Hispanic teacher-student parity meant that not enough Hispanic teachers were being produced. Looking at the statistics that apply to Fabens High School and using it as a model, my supposition is that the increase in the percentage of Hispanic teachers starting in 1970 indicates that more Hispanic students were beginning to go to college to obtain their degrees. In addition, many of those graduates did eventually become teachers. Again, using Fabens as a model, my supposition is that those Hispanic students that graduated from all of the local high schools in the area contributed to increasing the percentage of Hispanic teachers in Fabens High School.

To be clear, a hypothesis is a proposed explanation made on the basis of limited evidence as a starting point for further investigation. My hypothesis is that the increase in Hispanic students going to college starting in the year 1970, was symptomatic of all of the high schools in the area because Hispanic teachers started to show up in the Fabens schools about 5 years later. In the end, this trend proved to be a positive benefit to society because Hispanics started to become social contributors to the local region, at least from a teacher head-count point of view. And starting in 2017, according to the limited data from the Fabens school yearbooks, Hispanics were now contributing equally to society, at least to the same percentage levels as persons of Anglo descent.

Hispanic School Board Member-Student Parity

Was Hispanic school board member-student parity ever achieved? The answer is yes; based on the information in the "Hispanic Parity Table". It was again achieved in the year 2017 when the percentage of Hispanic school board members actually rose to 85.7 percent while the percentage of Hispanic students was now at 99.6 percent. During that year, a total of 6 Hispanic school board members were on the board with 1 school board member being of Anglo descent. The percentage values were as close as they could be since more than 6 Hispanic school board members would have resulted in an under- representation of school board members of Anglo descent.

When did the percentage of Hispanic school board members start to increase to approach the percentage necessary to achieve Hispanic school board member-student parity? It appears from the information in the "Hispanic Parity Table" that the trend upward also began in the 1969-1970 school year when the percentage of Hispanic school board members jumped from 14.3 percent in the 1968-1969 school year to now 42.6 percent in the 1969-1970 school year.

Prior to the 1969-1970 school year, the Hispanic school board member percentage ranged from 0 percent during the 1965-1966 school year to 14.3 percent during the 1967-1968 and 1968-1969 school years. By the way, the 1966-1967 school yearbook did not show photographs or names of the members of the school board.

The following is a condensed version of the "Hispanic Parity Table" that shows only school board and student percentages:

School Year	Board Total	Board Hispanic	Percent Hispanic	Students Total	Students Hispanic	Percent Hispanic
1966	7	0	0.0%	206	149	72.3%
1967	Note 1	---	---	344	287	83.4%
1968	7	1	14.3%	343	282	82.2%
1969	7	1	14.3%	362	304	84.0%

Note 1: School board information not available in the 1967 yearbook

Although school board member information is not present in the 1966-1967 school yearbook, one can make a safe guess that the number of Hispanic school board members in that school year was either 0 or 1. Given the benefit of the doubt, let's assume that the number of Hispanic school board members during that year was 1. Needless to say, the Hispanic school board members were still grossly under-represented during those four school years.

It is also obvious, based on the Hispanic student percentages during those 4 years, that the majority of the population in Fabens was Hispanic. Whereas teacher employment is based on merit and qualification, school board membership is based on the results of the school board elections. Did the Hispanic population during those 4 years vote for persons of Anglo descent to be members of the school board and that is the reason for the high percentage of school board members of Anglo descent or did the Hispanic population simply didn't vote and the Anglo population did?

What is the explanation for the low number of Hispanic school board members during the period from the 1965-1966 school year through the 1968-1969 school year? My supposition is that the Hispanic population was uninformed of the importance of the school board. Remember, as shown in a previous section, most Hispanic graduating students didn't start to go on to obtain a college education until the start of 1970. In addition, I know of several cases where students dropped out of high school to work, especially students from families that were at or close to poverty levels. My wife, Socorro, even knows of a case where a female student from the Ysleta school district earned a full ride scholarship to the Massachusetts Institute of Technology; a prestigious technical college. The Hispanic student's father was so narrow-minded that he refused to let her attend MIT because she was female and he felt it was his daughter's role to help out with the household chores at home rather than go on to college. My supposition is that a sense of provincialism prevailed in Fabens. Educationally, the Hispanic population in Fabens was underdeveloped and that explains the presence of the low number of Hispanic school board members during the 1965-1966 school year through the 1968-1969 school year.

The number of Hispanic school board members increased from 1 to 3 almost overnight from the 1968-1969 school year to the 1969- 1970 school year. Now starting with the 1969-1970 school year, it took 4 or 5 years for Hispanic teachers to start showing up in Fabens High School.

My conclusion is that some politically motivated issue, unknown to me, surfaced during the 1968-1969 school year. This led to the election of 2 additional Hispanic school board members in the 1969- 1970 school year. It could be that this change was the motivating factor that ultimately started Hispanic students to go to college and then 4 to 5 years later, Hispanic teachers started to show up in Fabens High School. In the end, the proper result was ultimately achieved.

Fabens Texas: A Community Study

While I was away in California during the summer of 1969, unbeknownst to me, a community study of the town of Fabens was conducted. The community study was developed by a research group from the Department of Sociology and Anthropology at the University of Notre Dame.

The Notre Dame Study

Since I was away in California during the summer of 1969, I was unaware that this community study was being performed in Fabens. When I returned in September of 1969 after having worked in California, I was none the wiser. It wasn't until about ten years later during a conversation with my wife, Socorro, that I found out about what has come to be known as "the Notre Dame study".

She showed me a loose-leaf typed manuscript that contained 446 pages of typed text. The loose-leaf manuscript was about two and a half inches thick. After asking her about the manuscript, she told me that the University of Notre Dame had conducted a study of the Fabens area. She told me that she had assisted the Notre Dame researchers and that as a result, she was provided a copy of the final written study in return for having helped during the summer of 1969. The manuscript sat in a cardboard box on our bookshelves for many years. In the year 2016, I became curious about the contents of the manuscript. By then the bound manuscript was in tatters. I started reading it and began to learn the depth of the research. It dawned on me that this manuscript was valuable; it contained substantial research information about Fabens as it existed in the year 1969. It was a historical document after all. I repaired the torn and tattered pages most in need of repair using transparent tape. Having repaired the pages, I electronically scanned the entire 446 page manuscript. The manuscript was now safely digitally stored.

After having scanned the entire manuscript, I placed the pages of the manuscript in a 4 inch thick, 3 ring binder.

The title of the manuscript is "Fabens, Texas: A Community Study" by William D'Antonio and Irwin Press. The community study came about when in April of 1969, a person from Fabens by the name of Jess Daffron, Jr. wrote a letter to the Department of Sociology and Anthropology at the University of Notre Dame. Mr. Daffron had previously studied at the University of Notre Dame. In his letter, he requested assistance in evaluating the Fabens area because he was worried that the town of Fabens was stagnating.

One thing led to another and about a month later, a research proposal was drawn up at Notre Dame and a research team was put together. The Catholic Priest at the time was Father Robert Getz.

Through his efforts, the local Catholic Church in Fabens provided $5,000 from the Church's building fund. In addition, the Robert F. Kennedy Institute at Notre Dame funded the project in the amount of $15,000. The University of Notre Dame contributed $10,000 worth of donated in-kind research time. The $30,000 dollars today is worth about $208,330 dollars when adjusted for inflation.

Dr. Irwin Press, an anthropologist from Notre Dame, agreed to head the field group. Together with field researchers from Notre Dame, a total of 602 families were interviewed in the Fabens area during that summer. A 446 page community study was developed. It covered the following topics: town government, education, business,

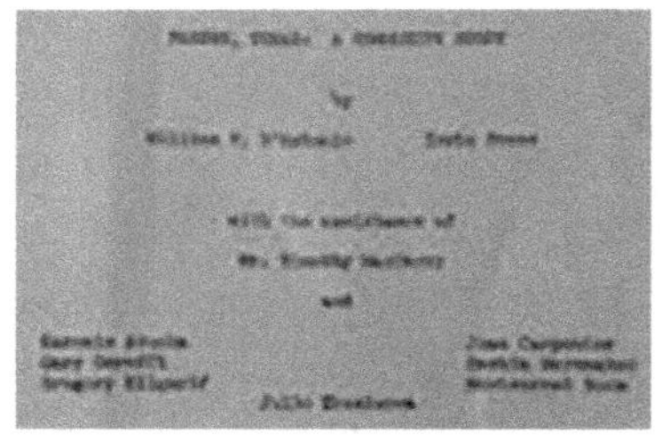

agriculture and in addition, development and self-determination. The community study of Fabens, Texas was concluded and the community study was issued in September of 1970. The photograph on the left shows an actual page from the study. The page shows the persons that contributed in the development of the community study.

The following are two paragraphs contained in the preface of the manuscript. The preface was written by Dr. William D'Antonio, Ph.D. in September of 1970. The two paragraphs describe how the community study was initiated.

"To The People of Fabens

In early April of 1969 W.V. D'Antonio, Chairman of the Department of Sociology and Anthropology of the University of Notre Dame, received a letter from Jess Daffron, Jr., of Fabens inquiring as to the possibility of obtaining professional help for the purpose of conducting a community study in Fabens, Daffron's letter included a specific proposal by the town's priest for establishment of a research project in the community. Many in Fabens— farmers, businessmen, workers—had for some time felt that the community was stagnating. It was Father Getz, however, who first proposed a formal community study for the purpose of pinpointing town problems and potential. Daffron, who had studied at Notre Dame, suggested that the Department of Sociology and Anthropology at the University might be able to offer some specific aid.

The Chairman of the Department, whohadpreviously conducted research into decision-making in both El Paso and Juarez, was able to visit Fabens in mid-April during a lecture tour to UTEP. Professor D'Antonio met with community representatives and determined that the study was both feasible and worthwhile. Furthermore, he was quickly convinced that the Department of Sociology and Anthropology itself would be most interested in direct participation."

In my mind, Father Getz from the Catholic Church and Mr. Jess Daffron, Jr. who attended the University of Notre Dame were visionaries. They could see the future and it wasn't a bright one for Fabens, Texas. They sensed a need for outside assistance for the town of Fabens.

High School Counseling

In June of 2018 when I was writing this section, I carefully read the section titled "B. EDUCATION" contained within the chapter titled "Chapter 10: Conclusions and Recommendations" in the Notre Dame community study. Two paragraphs on page 322 dealing with school counseling caught my eye. The two paragraphs address the subject of high school counseling. These two paragraphs are shown here as follows:

"Experience throughout the country makes it clear that young people are more likely and simply more able to heed the advice and counsel of persons with whom they can identify. It is incredible at this point in history that there would even be any question about the desirability of a counselor of Mexican American background in the Fabens school system.

In fact, we recommend that the present counselor, whose record was reportedly not satisfactory, and whose standing with the community was quite low, be replaced by at least two counselors, and possibly three, two of whom should be Mexican American and well versed in the problems of Mexican Americans."

At this late date in my life, I finally found confirmation of a basic fact; a sense that I always felt. That fact was that Fabens High School was not producing college bound Hispanic students at that time, at least prior to the summer of 1969. Hispanic students were not being counseled during those years. I know it because I can say that I wasn't, at least by the school counselor. In my opinion, the words in those two preceding paragraphs are spot on.

I used to wonder why it was that Fabens High School was not producing college bound students in those days when I was in high school. It could be that the reason for the lack of college bound students was because our parents were not fluent in the English language. The majority of the students in Fabens High School during the 1960s were of parents with little ability to speak English. Teachers at Fabens High School were interviewed by the Notre Dame researchers. Page 248 and 249 of the Notre Dame study contains the following paragraphs that help to explain why Fabens High School was not producing college bound Hispanic students at that time.

"One of the questions asked the teachers concerned the general attitude that the parents had toward education. The majority of the teachers stated that attitudes varied depending upon the groups of parents referred to. Fifty-six percent of teachers said the parents did not care about the education their children were receiving. Due to the cultural background they were not oriented toward a college education. "They see education as a necessary evil," a teacher commented. By contrast, they observed that the Anglo parents desired a college education for their children and as some teachers suggested, "they have the money for it." Some teachers suggested that a program through the school could help change the attitudes of Mexican American parents and in this way the children might be encouraged to seek a college education."

"What they need, a teacher said, referring to the students is "confidence in themselves." As the teacher expressed it, this confidence does not come to them at present through the family; rather it is the teacher who has to give it to them if they are going to get it."

"When the teachers were asked which group of parents they communicated with better, the answers reflected the language handicaps faced by many parents. Some teachers insisted they get on well with "any parent who can speak English.""

I too had parents who were not English speaking, however, I was one of the lucky ones because in my case, the teacher who gave me the confidence was Mr. Cecil Kirchner.

By the way, I later found out that the work done by the Notre Dame researchers created much controversy during and immediately after the study was released. The local area farmers became aware of the work and felt that the study actually provided too much information to the Hispanic community; their fear was that it might open everyone's eyes to unionized farm workers. In fact, page 331 in the Notre Dame study hints at the need to unionize the local farm workers. In that sense, the farmers felt the study was counterproductive to their own efforts. Yes, it seems that the study did open peoples' eyes and could be perceived as detrimental to the farmers.

Racial Stratification

The Notre Dame community study of Fabens, Texas developed during the summer of 1969 would not be the last look at Fabens by outsiders. In 2008, Dr. Richard R. Verdugo, Senior Research Scientist at the National Education Association, published a 27 page case study titled "Racial Stratification, Social Consciousness, and the Education of Mexican Americans in Fabens, Texas: A Socio-Historical Case Study".

In his case study, Dr. Verdugo used the information from the Notre Dame community study to show how race affects inequality in a community. In the second part of his case study, Dr. Verdugo shows "how racial stratification relegated Mexican Americans to the lower rung of society in Fabens, and negatively affected their education."

Ethnic minorities in those days were thought of as inferior and in that racial stratification model, Mexican Americans were not encouraged to move up the education ladder. That was my personal experience. I was never guided to pursue college during my high school years by the school counselor. Again, I was lucky enough to have had a teacher by the name of Mr. Cecil Kirchner as my mentor.

The University of Texas at El Paso

Competing Against Students from the El Paso Schools

For me, competition was a way of life in the Fabens elementary, middle and high school. I competed against fellow students in the same school grade. The students I competed against were real, red-blooded kids. While attending elementary, middle and high school in Fabens, the successful students were visible competitors. I always had a sense of who was succeeding and who was falling behind.

Prior to being awarded my college scholarship from Farah, Incorporated, I knew who my competition was. My competition consisted of my high school friends who had the higher grades.

After my college scholarship award, the competition was no longer my fellow schoolmates in Fabens; now my competition consisted of students from the El Paso schools who were going to attend the University of Texas at El Paso as freshmen along with myself. They were my perceived competition because I hadn't met them face to face yet. How was I going to compete with students from the El Paso schools? For all I knew, the students from the El Paso schools were probably schooled in the use of computers. We didn't have computers in the Fabens schools and therefore my perception was that we were scholastically behind. I perceived that a serious challenge loomed ahead of me once I started college in September of 1970.

Even with the threat of serious competition from the students in the El Paso schools that lay ahead, this was no time to quit. I had promised Mr. Gordon Foster of Farah, Incorporated that I would do my best in college and that made me dig in for the long haul.

Freshman Orientation – Individual Responsibility

In a previous section of this memoir, I indicated that prior to leaving for California to work during the summer of 1970, I applied for a week-long college orientation session that was to be held at the University of Texas at El Paso. The orientation session started at the beginning of September just prior to the start of the college school year.

I returned back to Fabens from California by myself. My parents, brothers and sisters had remained back in California. They continued working for an additional two weeks as usual. I don't remember how I got around in Fabens and I don't remember if I had access to an automobile. Somehow, I got myself to the week-long orientation session at the University.

When I arrived at the University, I was directed to one of the school dormitories. I and another student shared one of the dormitory rooms. All of the students were escorted around the university grounds so as to familiarize ourselves with the campus. We were also escorted to the university cafeteria so that we could again familiarize ourselves with the location of the cafeteria.

During the course of the week, we were introduced to the course curriculums and were provided with study guides. It became very obvious that this wasn't high school anymore. The orientation instructors emphasized individual responsibility. They indicated that it was up to the student to get to the various classes without being prodded by the instructors or professors. During one part of the orientation, the students were assigned to specific department representatives. For example, the engineering majors were directed to 2 or 3 upperclassmen from the engineering department. The liberal arts majors were assigned to another group of upperclassmen corresponding to the liberal arts department and so on.

I finished the week now having a pretty good idea of how I was going to get around the university during the upcoming school year. The key was individual responsibility. We learned that we weren't going to be pushed to attend classes as we were in high school. Attendance was not compulsory. There would be no punishment for not attending class sessions. The only punishment would be self-induced. Being successful at the university meant successfully completing the quizzes and tests. However, to do that, one had to attend classes and study the course material. It was that simple.

Did it help to attend the week-long orientation at the university? Yes, it did. My work was cut-out for me. It was a good running start into adulthood.

Getting There and Back

Living in Fabens and going to school at the University in El Paso was not an ideal situation. The distance between Fabens and the university was about 40 miles. With heavy traffic in the mornings, especially on the off-ramp from the I-10 freeway to the University, the drive from Fabens to the University took about 50 minutes and sometimes an hour. The return trip back to Fabens wasn't as time consuming.

Somewhere along the way, several of the students that attended classes at the university and that lived in Fabens including myself, got together to form a carpool. The carpool was an arrangement we as students made to make the regular journey to El Paso in a single vehicle, with each student taking turns to drive the others. The carpool was a way to save money by sharing the cost among the students. There were some students that didn't own automobiles; those students paid a small fee to defray the expenses that the rest of the students bore when they used their automobiles.

I remember some of the students that traveled back and forth from Fabens to the University in our carpool. Their names were Helen DeAnda, David Corral, Maggie Cruz and Larry Madrid. I am sure they all graduated but somehow we lost touch with each other after we graduated. In the case of David Corral, he and his wife, Juanita, later baptized our daughter, Amanda.

Pre-Calculus and My First Setback

During the first week of the first semester as a freshman, all the freshman engineering students took a required mathematics test. The written test was given to the new freshman students in order to determine if the student was ready to begin with the first calculus course, known as Calculus I. Calculus is the branch of mathematics that deals with the subject of properties of derivatives and integrals of functions, by methods originally based on the summation of infinitesimal differences. The two main types are differential calculus and integral calculus.

Anyway, if the student's mathematics test score was not sufficiently high, then the student would have to take a preliminary course known as pre-calculus. The pre-calculus course was basically a thorough review of algebra, geometry and trigonometry.

After taking the required mathematics test, my score on the test was such that I was required to take the pre-calculus course and could not proceed to take the Calculus I course. I don't remember my exact score. It was a setback for me. Previous to taking the mathematics test, I felt I was ready for the big leagues.

The Real Competition

As indicated previously, my low test score on the first mathematics test required me to take pre-calculus rather than Calculus I. That setback in college made me feel that I was not keeping my end of the bargain with Mr. Gordon Foster of Farah, Incorporated. I had committed to him that I would succeed in college. My competition after having received the scholarship now consisted of students from the El Paso schools that were going to attend college alongside me. Could it be that the Fabens schools in fact didn't prepare me appropriately to compete in the college arena against the students from the El Paso schools?

Anyway, it turned out that many of the students that were required to take the initial required mathematics course wound up having to take the pre-calculus course just as I did. As time went on during that semester, I found that my perceived competition was in fact not real. I found that the students from the El Paso schools were actually at the same scholastic level that I was. I finally felt that I was not at a disadvantage and could stay up with the rest in the more difficult courses that were to come.

By the way, my perception that the students from the El Paso schools were familiar with the use of computers was totally in error. In 1970 when I started college, there was no such thing as PC computers; commonly known as personal computers. PC computers started to appear commercially much later in 1983. The only access we had as engineering students in college to computers was a single mainframe computer known as the CDC 2000 computer. I don't remember the exact number; it could have been CDC 1000. By the way, the acronym CDC stands for Control Data Corporation.

Anyway, the access to the mainframe computer was limited to engineering students enrolled in a Fortran computer programming class.

Fortran was a high-level computer programming language used especially for scientific computation. The extent of access to the computer by students was limited to introduction of programs developed on cardboard punch-cards. The photograph on the left shows a 4" x 8" punch card that represents one line of a computer program. Now knowing of the single mainframe computer at the University, it was obvious to me that the students from the El Paso high schools did not have access to computers as I once thought.

The Most Important Decision of my Life While Attending College

The following may appear to be a digression from the subject of college; however, this part of the memoir chronologically occurred during the second semester of my freshman year in college. This part has to do with the most important occurrence in my life.

In a previous section of this memoir, I made reference to a pretty girl that I noticed during 7th grade in Fabens. She was attractive, beautiful and very talkative. She had a great smile, dimples on her cheeks and spoke English well. She was a cheerleader on the cheerleading organization during my 8th grade year in school. Her name was Socorro Martinez.

Again, as I indicated before, she and I dated for the better part of my high school years except during my senior year. We became very close and shared wonderful moments as we both made our way through high school. We became a twosome at the conclusion of our senior year in high school.

As indicated earlier, after graduation I worked in California during the summer of 1970. Socorro on the other hand, began working as a clothing worker at Farah, Inc. shortly after having graduated from high school. When I returned from California, I began attending college in September of 1970. Socorro continued working as a clothing worker at Farah, Inc. in El Paso.

Sometime during January of 1971 during the time when I was attending college, Socorro told me that she was with child. I knew I was the responsible party. Although we weren't married, I was elated. Having children outside of a marriage was frowned upon then and probably still is now. However, that didn't matter to me; all I knew was that I was going to be a father and was going to raise "my child".

Shortly thereafter, I asked Socorro for her hand in marriage. To my surprise, she didn't immediately accept. I persisted in attempting to persuade her during the ensuing week and she finally accepted my marriage proposal. Both Socorro and I agreed that I should continue to pursue my college degree and that she would continue to work at Farah, Inc. Our plan was that she would work at Farah, Inc. as long as possible up until the expected date of the birth of our child. In addition, I would work during the summer months and attempt to save as much money as possible to make it through the school year. At that time, I had already paid my second semester school expenses and still had scholarship money left over. The only unresolved item was where we were going to live.

We agreed to inform Socorro's mother about our plans. We knew it wasn't necessary to speak with Socorro's father because he and Socorro's mother, Ildefonsa, had been separated for years even prior to Socorro's birth. A few days later, after having proposed marriage to Socorro, I proceeded to Mrs. Martinez's home to ask for her permission to marry her daughter. During the discussion, I told her that my plans were to continue attending school at the University of Texas at El Paso. I was afraid that she might be concerned that I might not have sufficient economic wherewithal to provide for her daughter and the child that was to come later on in the year. I informed her about our plans. I also told her we hadn't decided where we were going to live.

Mrs. Martinez responded by telling me that I should continue with my plans regarding my college studies and that it wasn't necessary that Socorro and I marry. She was confident that she and Socorro could take care of the child without me. I immediately told her that it was my intention to marry Socorro and that Socorro and I would take care of our soon-to-be-born child. Upon listening to my insistence, Socorro's mother finally accepted that Socorro and I were going to marry. She provided us her blessing.

Anyway, Mrs. Martinez then indicated that she was open to the idea of Socorro and I living in their small apartment on Main Street in Fabens. The apartment was sufficiently large and it could indeed accommodate another person. She indicated we could all share living expenses. She then indicated that she could quit her job when our child was born so that she could take care of our child while Socorro continued to work at Farah, Inc. and I could continue my schooling. I was surprised; I hadn't expected that offer. It made sense. I countered by telling her that we would pay her a weekly salary in the same amount as the amount she was currently earning at her existing job. We all agreed and I accepted her offer to move in to their apartment after the date of our marriage. By the way, Mrs. Martinez worked as a maid for the family of a local farmer.

I indicated to Mrs. Martinez that I would inform my parents about our marriage plans and that I would also proceed to speak with the Catholic priest so that we could set the wedding date. The Catholic priest of the local Catholic Church was Father Robert Getz. I didn't expect Father Getz to have a problem with my marrying Socorro; however, I did have a feeling that I was going to have a difficult time with my parents.

In regards to informing my parents, I felt I could speak with my mother about my personal matters; however, I didn't feel at ease confiding with my father about my personal situation. I told my mother about my intention to marry Socorro. I told her that I was concerned that my father would not take the news well. I was afraid he was going to be upset with me. My mother told me that I shouldn't be concerned about upsetting my father; after all, at 20 years of age, I was mature enough to marry. She encouraged me to inform my father and I did. To my surprise, my father was very supportive of my plans to marry Socorro.

After having spoken with Mrs. Martinez and my parents about Socorro's and my decision to get married, I then met with Father Getz to discuss our plans. Father Getz and I were no strangers. He had been the priest at the local Catholic Church during my high school years. During my high school years, I attended Sunday church Mass regularly because I was the guitarist with the church youth choir during the weekly 11:00 a.m. Mass. In addition, sometime during my first semester at college, I was appointed President of a local committee that oversaw a "cooperative grocery store" in Fabens.

The term "cooperative" in "cooperative grocery store" was used because a number of organizations contributed efforts to initiate the grocery store. The grocery store was initially funded with funds provided by the Catholic Church and thereafter, the actual operation of the grocery store was passed on to an organization known as Project Bravo. I volunteered my time as President of the "cooperative grocery store" oversight committee. By the way, the reason for initiating the "cooperative grocery store" in the first place was because there was a general feeling that the grocery prices at the only commercial grocery store in Fabens were too high. The "cooperative grocery store" was an alternative for poor people.

The reason for mentioning my participation in the church youth choir and my volunteering to oversee the "cooperative grocery store" is to reinforce the fact that Father Getz and I were no strangers. We were in fact good friends.

Anyway, I met with Father Getz to tell him about the decision I had made as well as to ask him about marrying us. Father Getz knew that Socorro was my girlfriend. After telling him about the decision I had made about marrying Socorro, Father Getz recommended against my marrying her. I didn't expect his response; I was confused. He indicated that the majority of marriages resulting after a pregnancy were doomed to failure. He indicated that it might be better to wait a year or two to make sure that marriage is what Socorro and I really wanted. I told him that I loved Socorro and that I needed to be present to care for my soon- to-be-born child. Waiting to see if marrying was the correct action to take was not something I wanted. I continued insisting that I wanted to marry Socorro and Father Getz finally agreed with me. He told me that he would be happy to marry Socorro and I. We mutually agreed to the date of February 27, 1971 as the date of our wedding.

Both Socorro's family and my family were poor. I knew it would be impossible for our extended families to contribute economically to assist us with our situation. Our immediate future would have to be financed with our own resources. It was a given that Socorro would have to continue working at Farah, Inc.; at least until I graduated from college. It helped that my school expenses were paid out of my scholarship money. The money left over after paying school expenses seemed to be sufficient; at least for the time being. Working at a part-time job was impossible due to the difficulty of the course work at college; I would have to study constantly to keep up with the requirements at school. The engineering school course work was heavy.

Anyway, the plans for our immediate future were set. I don't remember the exact date when I informed my parents and Mrs. Martinez about our plans to get married. It must have been 2 or 3 weeks prior to the date of the wedding. For now the date of the wedding was set for Saturday, February 27, 1971.

The date of the wedding arrived. I didn't have a dress coat and so I dressed in a white shirt and tie. My extended family and I drove to the church in separate automobiles. I don't remember the exact time of the wedding but it was in the late afternoon; it was probably around 6:00 p.m.

When we arrived, we met up with Socorro's mother, Mrs. Martinez. Socorro's brother, Antonio, also accompanied Socorro's mother. Socorro was wearing a nice white-tan colored dress; she was very pretty. My parents, Mrs. Martinez and Antonio Martinez were the only attendees at our church wedding. Father Getz officiated at the wedding ceremony and about 45 minutes later, Socorro and I were married. My family had planned a get-together at their home to be held right after the wedding ceremony. I invited Father Getz to the get-together but he wasn't able to attend; it was a Saturday and he had other commitments.

After the wedding ceremony, our extended families, Socorro and I proceeded to my parent's home which was now my former home. My mother had previously prepared food for a wedding dinner. That night, we feasted eating the food that my mother had prepared. I remember my father making the wedding toast with wine. After the dinner, Mrs. Martinez and Antonio departed. Socorro and I said our good-byes to my extended family and then we both drove to Mrs. Martinez's and Socorro's apartment. Mrs. Martinez stayed that night at Antonio's home. Our financial situation was very tight; we couldn't afford a wedding night out. Needless to say, Socorro and I didn't have a traditional honeymoon.

The next morning, we woke up and that's when reality hit; Socorro didn't know how to cook. She scurried around the kitchen fumbling with the pots and pans and she finally conjured up what appeared to be a breakfast. I can't remember what she fixed but I do remember she kept apologizing for not knowing how to cook. I say this with tongue in cheek because I know I'll hear from her when she  reads this part of the memoir. She turned out to be a terrific cook and as a result, I never suffered from food poisoning . . . ha, ha.

By the way, Father Getz's words about short marriages as a result of a pre-mature pregnancy never came to pass in our case.

Our first-born son is Adrian. Amanda was born a year later. Andres and Adan came later. Forty seven years later, now in the year 2018, Socorro and I are still happily married. The photograph on the left shows Socorro when she was approximately 19 years of age.

Returning To The Subject Matter
Relating To My College Career

My Chemistry Courses

During the first and second semester of my first year at UTEP, I took two chemistry courses. I earned a B in the first course and an A in the second course. The first course was known as "inorganic chemistry" and the second course was known as "organic chemistry. I wasn't sure why an engineering major like me needed to take chemistry courses but it was a requirement in the curriculum in order to earn an engineering degree.

Both courses consisted of class instruction and as well as a "lab". The "lab" part consisted of attending a 3 hour laboratory session once a week. The laboratory session was spent in an actual chemistry laboratory, fully equipped with laboratory equipment and accessories such as Bunsen burners, test tubes, graduated beakers and other glassware. We performed a variety of experiments in the laboratory using various chemicals and equipment. I suppose the "lab" could be called the applied part of our chemistry training.

I distinctly remember that my second semester chemistry "lab" started at 8:00 p.m. and ended at 11:00 p.m. once a week. That made for a long day at the university every week. Normally, I would carpool with other students from Fabens. However, during the specific day of my chemistry "lab", I would have to make the hour long drive to and from the university from Fabens in my own car without participating in the carpool. After chemistry "lab" ended at 11:00 p.m. during the night, I would drive back to Fabens and arrive home at about 12:00 midnight. I'd go to bed at 12:30 a.m. and wake up at 6:00 a.m. The student whose turn it was to drive his or her car back to the University in the carpool began picking up the rest of the students at about 7:00 a.m. and then again, we were on our way back to the university. Attending classes at the university and driving back and forth from Fabens took its toll both in automobile expenses and driving time. The students in El Paso had it much easier; they didn't drive those long distances.

Something that has stuck in my mind since taking those courses as a young man was what my chemistry professor in my first chemistry course called "colligative properties". I've always associated the phrase with the subject of "osmosis". The subject of osmosis would later be very important, both when writing a technical paper that I presented at Colorado State University during my senior year and then in my first professional position that was to come when I would start working at Continental Water Conditioning Corporation.

Anyway, when I was writing this part of the memoir, I felt a need to revisit the phrase "colligative properties". It turns out that colligative properties of solutions are properties that depend upon the concentration of solute molecules or ions, but not upon the identity of the solute. The solute is the component in the solution that is dissolved in the solution. I now remembered that colligative properties are vapor pressure lowering, boiling point elevation, freezing point depression, and osmotic pressure. The word "osmotic" would later become very important in my professional life after college.

Chemistry was very interesting to me; I was able to understand the course material. It must have been because the chemistry professors were very animated and knowledgeable in the course material they presented. They made the course material interesting. When I finished my second chemistry course I began to think that perhaps I had made a mistake in having chosen to major in engineering instead of chemistry. At that point in time; however, it was too late. I couldn't afford to start all over as a chemistry major and leave the engineering courses behind. It would have resulted in having wasted a year in college to start all over again in the chemistry discipline. The feeling that I was better suited to a career in chemistry became even stronger later on when I graduated from the University. I couldn't help but think that I could have discovered a new product or even a new element with a chemistry background. I know it seems lofty but that's the feeling I had at the time.

Since the time that I graduated, I've had the feeling that I would have done well in one of the chemistry disciplines. In the end, I focused on the engineering discipline and stuck to it during my entire life; no regrets.

The Tau Beta Pi Honor Fraternity

Sometime during my junior year in college, I received correspondence from a person representing the fraternity known as Tau Beta Pi. I was invited to become a member of the fraternity. The fraternity was different from the normal social fraternities commonly present in colleges and universities. Instead, the Tau Beta Pi fraternity was devoted primarily for membership by engineering students and engineering alumni. Not every engineering student was invited to join. Only the students with the higher grade point average were invited to join.

The Tau Beta Pi Association, commonly known as Tau Beta Pi, is the oldest engineering honor society and the second oldest collegiate honor society in the United States. It honors engineering students who have shown a history of academic achievement as well as a commitment to personal and professional integrity. Specifically, the association was founded "to mark in a fitting manner those who have conferred honor upon their Alma Mater by distinguished scholarship and exemplary character as students in engineering, or by their attainments as alumni in the field of engineering, and to foster a spirit of liberal culture in engineering colleges".

I considered it an honor to have been chosen to become a member of the Tau Beta Pi fraternity. I remember having participated in a candle-lit, swearing-in ceremony that was held for several students and myself. Each of the students being sworn-in received a certificate and a medal. For the life of me, I can't remember where I placed my certificate and medal.

My First Calculator – The State of the Art

In a previous section of this memoir, I mentioned that I was introduced to slide rules during my senior year in high school. Now in college, engineering students in the mechanical engineering department was required to carry a slide rule for use in the various engineering classes.

During my high school years and now during my first few years in college, hand-held calculators had not yet been developed. "Slide rules" were used instead of hand-held calculators. "Slide rules" were used to enable quick multiplication and division without having to resort to pen and paper. They were also used for math operations involving exponents and logarithms, but not for addition or subtraction.

It was easy to recognize an engineering student walking around the campus because the long, slender leather case that contained the slide rule could be seen hanging from the student's belt. In those days, it was even common for the engineering students to carry their papers and sometimes books in brief cases. That's probably not so in these more modern times.

Sometime during my junior year, hand-held calculators were now being used by the engineering students. I remember that calculators manufactured by Texas Instruments were being used and were replacing the old slide rules. These units were being sold for $400.00 to $500.00 at the time and could be used for math operations requiring logarithms and exponents. I wasn't able to afford the purchase of a nice, fancy Texas Instruments calculator. However, I do remember that I did purchase a 4-function calculator for about $100.00; it wasn't a Texas Instrument calculator and it wasn't very compact in size like they are now. By the way, based on the rate of inflation, the $100.00 spent on my calculator in 1972 is today about $599.00; quite a difference.

Anyway, the calculator that I purchased could only be used for addition, subtraction, division and multiplication. The calculator didn't come with a nice carrying case. Somehow I found out that Antonio Martinez, my wife's brother, had a brother-in-law that was an expert at constructing leather purses. I paid Antonio's brother-in-law to construct a carrying case for my precious 4–function calculator. Today, a 4-function calculator can be purchased in convenience stores for about $4.00. We've come a long way since my college years when I used a 4-function calculator.

St. Patrick's Day - Kissing the Blarney Stone

I remember having participated in an initiation ceremony that occurred sometime in March during my second semester of my senior year. The engineering students were encouraged to attend an initiation during St. Patrick's day. The initiation was voluntary and as a result only the mechanical, industrial and civil engineering students participated. Noticeably absent were the electrical engineering students.

Anyway, we all gathered that day at a location adjacent to the relatively small rocky mountains near the University campus. We had previously been told to wear casual clothing and not school clothing during the day of the initiation so as a result, we all wore T-shirts and denim pants. When we arrived at the meeting location that day, the students that were to be initiated that day were all blindfolded by the students managing the initiation. We were told to form a line and hold hands. We were then slowly led up a path toward the upper part of the mountain while blindfolded.

Once at a specific location on the mountain, the persons that were managing the initiation positioned each candidate at a specific location. With blindfolds still on, several of the persons leading the initiation recited initiation speeches. At the conclusion of the speeches, we were then told to remove our blindfolds. At that time, the persons managing the initiation began to apply paint with broad paint brushes to our faces, hair and clothing. We had been warned to wear very casual clothing and now I knew why.

At the conclusion of the painting part of the ritual, we were then lead to a large rock that measured about 2 or 3 feet in diameter. Paint was applied on the rock and then the persons being initiated were asked to kiss the stone. The stone was called the "Blarney Stone". After we all kissed the stone, the leader of the ceremony then declared that we were now full-fledged members of the Order of St. Patrick.

While I was writing this part of the memoir, I decided to find out more about the mysterious ceremony that I participated in when I was a senior in college. It turns out that the initiation is celebrated each March in observance of St. Patrick's Day. TCM Day, as it is called, is the longest-running student tradition at The University of Texas at El Paso.

The tradition began in 1920 when UTEP was known as the Texas College of Mines and Metallurgy, or TCM. It is an annual rite of passage to initiate new engineers and geologists into the Order of St. Patrick, the patron saint of engineers. Students, faculty and staff from all disciplines are invited to participate in all the parts of TCM Day. Those who complete every element of TCM Day earn their official TCM Day Green Card and a TCM T-shirt.

I don't remember having received a TCM Day Green Card or a TCM T-shirt although it's possible that I did. I have to admit that it did seem strange participating in what some might consider a silly ceremony but during that day, I did my part and participated with my fellow students. Remember, I was 24 years of age and had a two babies and a wife at the time. However, in the end, if it was important to the University, then it was important for me to participate.

Women Engineers – A Pleasant Surprise

I grew up in the Mexican culture that stressed that men worked outdoors on farms while women worked indoors tending to children.

My father was very much the dominant parent in our family. When my father wanted something done, my mother, I and my siblings would make sure to comply with his wishes. The hierarchy in our family was dominated exclusively by my father.

The line that separated the men from the women began to blur during the year in high school when I was assigned to a typewriting class. At that time, typewriting was something women performed in an office environment; or so I felt. Anyway, typewriting was on the school curriculum and like it or not, I had to take typewriting class. At the time, who would have thought that boys needed a skill "that supposedly only women needed to have"? I grew up believing that secretaries were always female. I suppose this was the chauvinistic attitude in those days; not so today.

During my college career at the University of Texas at El Paso, I noticed two young women that were also engineering students. This was new to me. Heretofore, my thought process was that only men could become engineers. The two young women that were enrolled in the engineering curriculum were Lilia Sanchez and Aida Garcia. They both began college at that same time that I did. To my surprise, they both seemed to easily excel in the difficult course material in the engineering curriculum. Although they were not my close friends I did consider them to be friends. Their capacity to take the challenging course work changed my thinking; women could indeed be capable engineers.

As I indicated previously, during my last semester at the University of Texas at El Paso, I was invited to the Honors Banquet dinner. I was one of the 43 students that was honored in the category of "Who's Who,

1973-1974". Lilia Sanchez was one of the 22 students honored in the category of "Women of Mines". Aida Garcia was present at the Honors Banquet because she was one of 40 Senators honored in the student government. From that standpoint, Lilia Sanchez and Aida Garcia both made their mark as student engineers.

Both Lilia Sanchez's and Aida Garcia's diligence in college showed me that women could in fact become able engineers. They changed my outlook at it relates to women in engineering positions; for the better.

Earning a Living While Attending College

As I indicated previously, I was married and had two children while I was attending college. We lived on a shoestring. The scholarship money that I earned was helpful but it wasn't enough to sustain my young family.

Socorro, my wife, worked at Farah, Inc. all during the time that I attended college. Her working at Farah while I was attending college was invaluable. I wouldn't have been able to finish college had it not been for Socorro's contribution.

I wasn't able to attend summer sessions at the University because I decided to work during the summer months. Working during the summer months allowed me to earn and save money for my family. More on the type of work I did during the summer months during will be provided later in this memoir.

During my junior year and senior year, with the assistance of Dr. Jack Dowdy, who was an engineering Professor, I enrolled in a work study program at the University. I was known as a "Teacher's Assistant" or TA for short. My work involved grading test papers and providing tutoring in the subject of thermodynamics in his engineering classes. Working as a TA was an asset because it enabled me to hone-in on the subject of thermodynamics to a greater extent. The engineering students that I tutored were always grateful and would demonstrate their respect to me for assisting them in their understanding of thermodynamics. I enjoyed the work. Aside from enjoying the work, the work also provided additional income for my small family; that helped a lot.

By the way, during my lifetime, I've had two automobiles stolen from me. The second automobile that was stolen from me was a Chrysler

Concorde that was stolen while parked at a manufacturing plant in Cd. Juarez, Mexico. The approximate year when that happened was in 1994. My automobile insurance company reimbursed me for it so it was no major problem.

My major problem; however, was when my first automobile was stolen. That happened when I was in college when Socorro and I lived in Fabens. I owned a Chevrolet NOVA; it was a small compact car. Prior to it being stolen, the tires were worn and I took it to get new tires installed. Spending money on new tires was no easy task; my family and I were living on a very tight budget.

After having driven back to our apartment, I parked the car in front of the apartment on Main Street which was known as Highway 80 at the time. Socorro then drove off on an errand. When she returned, she again parked the car in front of the apartment but inadvertently left the car keys in the automobile. When we awoke the following day, our car was gone; it had been stolen. Socorro confessed to having left the keys in the car.

I walked to my parent's home and told my father about the theft. We boarded his pickup truck and began to scour the dirt roads nearby to see if we could locate my car but to no avail. This occurrence is worth mentioning in this memoir because that was a time when I felt a deep hatred that I will never forget. The hatred was not toward Socorro, it was a hatred directed toward the strangers that had taken my car. The money situation was tight; the last thing I needed was to lose my automobile that I used to drive to and from college. I'm drawing a blank as to how I managed to get to and from college after my car was stolen because for a while, I couldn't participate in the carpool arrangement with the other students attending college. In the end, one has to overcome unforeseen occurrences and simply move on; that's what I did.

How Backward Things Were

In a previous section, I indicated that I enrolled in a mechanical drafting course in high school during my senior year. I did so in order to earn extra credits to augment my resume and thereby increase the likelihood of being accepted to college. In fact, I found myself having to quit high school band class in order to take the mechanical drafting class. One of the required courses that engineering students in college needed to take was a mechanical drafting course. The course was titled "Graphical Fundamentals of Engineering Design". I took that course during my first semester in college and I did well in it.

The fact that I took a mechanical drafting course in college is only important to demonstrate how backward things were back when I attended college. Drawings were manually prepared using a T-square and a mechanical lead pencil even in college.

Today drawings are prepared using computers. I learned how to draw using the AutoCad® software. In my work, I have often had to develop drawings to demonstrate projects to clients. I have found that "a picture is worth a thousand words" in presentations to clients. We've come a long way since the time of manually drawn drawings.

The Coincidence – My College Senior Project Led to my First Job

During my last year in college, the senior students in my class were divided into groups of 4 students. Each group was required to submit a subject that was designated as the senior project.

Each group was given the opportunity to pick a project subject. I remembered that during my second chemistry course as a freshman in college, my chemistry professor lectured on the "colligative properties of solutions". I am not sure why, but that subject matter in chemistry class stuck with me.

It turns out that the four colligative properties of solutions are vapor pressure lowering, boiling point elevation, freezing point depression, and osmotic pressure. The osmotic pressure property of water stuck in my mind. As a result, I picked a project having to do with the subject of osmosis for our senior project.

The three students in my group and I developed a working apparatus consisting of a piston along with two water chambers separated by a cellulose sheet material. The cellulose sheet material represented the semi-permeable membrane that was necessary to enable water to flow from the chamber containing water with a lower dissolved solids concentration to flow through the membrane into the chamber having water with a higher dissolved solids concentration. Delving into the mechanics of water transport across a semi-permeable membrane is beyond the scope of the memoir. However, the principle of water transport across a semi-permeable membrane is very real.

As a result of the work my group did in the area of osmosis, I was selected by the mechanical engineering department chairman, Dr. John Levosky, to present a technical paper describing the subject of osmosis. During the last semester of my senior year, the College of Engineering rented a Greyhound bus to transport several students and faculty from our senior class to Fort Collins, Colorado. I presented the technical paper on osmosis at Colorado State University in Fort Collins, Colorado. Unfortunately, I didn't keep a copy of the technical paper I presented.

Sometime after graduating from college, I found out about a job opening at a local company by the name of Continental Water Conditioning Corporation. They had an opening for an engineering position. I found out that they were interested in hiring a person to work in the development of reverse osmosis systems. My work on our senior project involving osmosis seemed to mesh with the work that Continental Water Conditioning Corporation was involved in. I ultimately wound up working for them after graduating from the University. It seems I was pre-destined to work for a company involved in the osmosis process. What a coincidence . . . smile-smile.

The Personalities

I wound up spending 4 years at the University of Texas at El Paso. Four years at the University seemed like a lifetime. I was able to rub elbows with very intelligent students and very capable professors. One couldn't help but make friends along the way with fellow students but also with the faculty.

One of the friends I remember most was a student by the name of Roy; I can't remember his last name. He became a good friend of mine. He wasn't from the local area. I believe he was from North Carolina or South Carolina. He wasn't necessarily an intelligent student. What he lacked in intelligence, he made up with drive and effort.

Roy lived in an apartment near the University; along Mesa Street. He showed me how to cook chicken fried rice. I lost track of Roy after we graduated. By chance about 5 or 6 years after we graduated, I happened to meet up with him at the DFW airport while I was changing planes. We reminisced a little during our brief conversation. He told me he was working in the personnel department of some large company. I guess he didn't pursue the engineering route after having graduated from college.

There were many professors that left an impression on me. The most memorable professors are as follows:

- Dr. John Levosky, Mechanical Engineering Department Chairman.
- Dr. Jack Dowdy
- Dr. Lionel Craver
- Dr. Bhaduri
- Dr. Anthony Tarquin
- Mr. Ronald Coleman
- Dr. Leland Blank

The professor that impacted me the most during my college years was a professor by the name of Leland Blank. Professor Blank was in the Mechanical Engineering department but his specialty was Industrial Engineering. One of the required courses in Mechanical Engineering was a statistics course. Professor Blank happened to be the instructor in that statistics course. I was impressed with his grasp of the science of statistics.

During his presentations in the statistics course, he would sometimes interject his views about Industrial Engineering in industry. He explained that Industrial Engineering was a branch of engineering which dealt with the optimization of complex processes, systems and organizations. Industrial engineers worked to eliminate waste of time, money, materials, person-hours, machine time, energy and other resources that did not generate value.

At that time, El Paso was the garment manufacturing center of the United States and Professor Blank felt that the presence of that industry in El Paso meant that Industrial Engineering graduates would have no problem finding employment in El Paso. He explained that the garment manufacturing industry relied heavily on statistics, probabilities and time studies. Farah, Inc. was the major garment manufacturing company in El Paso at the time and that company had provided me with my college scholarship. The more I listened to Professor Blank describing the role of Industrial Engineers, the more interested I became in pursuing an Industrial Engineering degree. In my view at that time, having an

Industrial Engineering degree meant that I could stay in the El Paso area where I was born and raised. As a result, I decided to change from Mechanical Engineering to Industrial Engineering.

Because of the Industrial Engineering course requirements, I had to enroll in an advanced statistics course and in a linear programming course. As a result, I had to forego enrolling in the Mechanical Engineering vibrations course and a heat transfer course. In the end I graduated with a "Bachelor's Degree in Industrial Engineering".

Honors Banquet, April 25, 1974

Toward the end of my senior year at UTEP, I was invited to a dinner known as the Honors Banquet. The Honors Banquet occurred on April 25, 1974 at the Plaza Motor Hotel located in downtown El Paso. The photograph on the left was taken from the front page of a pamphlet that was provided to all the attendees. The dinner was sponsored by the University Student Association.

Five (5) categories of students were honored at the Honors Banquet. The categories were:

- Top Ten Seniors (10 Students)
- Men of Mines (20 Students)
- Women of Mines (22 Students)
- Who's Who, 1973-1974 (43 Students)
- Scholastic Honors, 4.0 GPA, (30 Students)

I was one of the students honored in the category of "Who's Who, 1973-1974". The 4 page Honors Banquet pamphlet I referred to earlier in this section contains the names of all the honorees in the five categories, including my name.

The Pivotal Moment – Mr. Cecil Kirchner

Attending classes at the University of Texas at El Paso became very important to me after receiving the college scholarship from Farah, Inc. At that time, I wasn't thinking about how difficult the college course work might be. All that mattered at the time was that I needed to get started so that I could finish with a college degree.

I started my freshman year full of energy, ready to take on what was to come. As I worked through my first semester, I began to realize that obtaining the professional degree was going to be hard work. The subject matter in most of my classes was difficult. I tried to keep up with the professor's lectures and the homework assignments. I was very fearful of falling behind. Fear was a good motivator for me.

Especially in the engineering courses, the course material was very challenging. El Paso was and is the home of the United States Army post known as Fort Bliss. As a result of its proximity to the University, persons that came from the military enrolled in the classes held at the University. From time to time, students that clearly came from a military background were present in the engineering classes that I attended. Students with a military background tended to be more mature and would typically ask more relevant questions regarding the subject matter during the professor's lectures. In addition, these students seemed to grasp the practical side of the subject matter more than I.

It dawned on me that perhaps the reason they were more attuned to the professor's lectures was because they were familiar with actual equipment. Compared to students with a military background, students fresh out of high school didn't have the benefit of having worked hands-on with equipment. I was one of those students that were fresh out of high school. That meant that I was at a disadvantage compared to students with a military background.

Because I didn't possess the same level of hands-on experience with equipment as compared to students with a military background, my goal became that of striving to earn A's in my course work. New course material kept coming at me every day.

I decided that the way to get through the tough courses was to memorize the course material as much as I could so that I could successfully complete the quizzes and tests. My task then became one of taking the quizzes and tests, "forgetting" the current course material and then moving on to the next wave of course materials so as to be ready for the next quiz or test. That was the only way I could manage to stay up with the course material being presented. So the process became, listen to the professor's lectures, study the assigned chapters in the books, take the quizzes, do a mental download and start all over again with the next onslaught.

I was in college trying to keep up with my studies. My only day off from college work was Saturday. I spent the better part of my Sundays studying the difficult course material. I would study the course material that I felt was going to be covered during the upcoming week so as not to fall behind during the upcoming week. As I indicated before, I was fearful of falling behind. My objective became that of studying and making good grades. I had to keep my eye on the ball, there was no option. My wife, Socorro, spent her time on Sundays tending to our babies, Adrian and Amanda. Andres and Adan had not yet been born. Socorro kept Adrian and Amanda out of my hair while I studied at home. In a certain way, Adrian and Amanda paid the price. This is because for most families, Sundays are family days when the kids are taken out for picnics or just outings. That wasn't so for my kids. Needless to say, I never attended Miner football games while I was a student at the University; my plate was too full.

Some of my former high school friends that hadn't progressed to college were now driving new cars and enjoying life; they had paying jobs. I had a job but my job was a non-paying job, at least for the moment. I was driving a junky car and was living meagerly. My only thought was that someday, I would surpass my friends after graduating from college. My thought process was that maybe someday, I might be able to afford a new car or maybe even a new home. For now, it would have to be a meager existence.

I specifically remember that during my sophomore year in college, I was having a hard time keeping up with the course material. I started thinking about dropping out of college. I remembered how my high school chemistry and physics teacher, Mr. Cecil Kirchner, had pushed me to attend college.

I decided to visit Mr. Kirchner who was still teaching at Fabens high school. During my meeting with Mr. Kirchner, I told him how difficult the course material was in college. He listened intently to me. I thanked him for having encouraged me to pursue my college career and also told him that I was going to drop out of college.

After I finished telling him about my plans, he began by telling me that he had been expecting me and that he had been anticipating that I would someday think about quitting college. He told me that there was one thing that I didn't know about college. He indicated that the hardest courses are the courses that one takes during the freshman and sophomore year. He indicated that the junior and senior year courses were going to be much easier by far. He suggested that I stay in school because the course material was going to get easier. I trusted Mr. Kirchner; he had been my mentor while I was in high school. His words made sense to me. I felt he knew what he was talking about because after all, he himself had succeeded in earning a technical degree when he went to college. His words came from experience. I decided to take his advice. At the end of the discussion with Mr. Kirchner, I thanked him for his encouragement and his kind words and then took my leave.

Based on that meeting with Mr. Kirchner, I decided to abandon any thought of leaving college behind. I finished my sophomore year and then began my junior year. My junior year course work was no different than my two prior years as a freshman and sophomore as far as course difficulty was concerned. The course material was still difficult but somehow I managed to continue. More and more it became apparent to me that Mr. Kirchner's words in reference to the reduced difficulty of the course material in my junior year and senior year were said simply to keep me from abandoning my dream. Although I now knew he had not been truthful with me, I knew he did it for a good reason. I decided to continue plowing through my junior and senior year. To this day, I still have the highest of respect for Mr. Kirchner; he kept me from quitting.

In the end, I finished college in 1974 with a Bachelors of Science Degree in Industrial Engineering. My final grade point average was 3.5. I succeeded in the goal I had laid out for myself after receiving my college scholarship from Farah, Inc.

By the way, the arduous task of progressing through college came with a price. At the end of that experience, I was mentally tired. The course material had been challenging and the quizzes and the tests took their toll on me. My goal was to graduate to begin working to support my young family. Everyone that graduates from a college or university has a photograph showing that they walked in their graduation commencement ceremony, except for me. I didn't participate in my college graduation commencement ceremony. As odd as it may seem, I didn't feel the need to participate anymore; four and a half years was enough.

As for Mr. Cecil Kirchner, my chemistry and physics teacher in high school, I am indebted to him for all eternity. He believed in me and pushed me when I needed to be pushed. I almost quit college. But for him, I would have not been successful in completing my goal; that of obtaining my college degree. He was there for me at the pivotal moment when I needed guidance.

The Issue of Intelligence

Over the years Socorro, my wife, has been my cheerleader. She has been there when I've needed a push. She frequently indicates that I am a smart person. I am generally known as a smart person. To me, saying that a person is smart means that the person is intelligent. In the course of my college career, I have been associated with persons whom I have observed are truly intelligent. This includes some excellent college students and many college professors. I use intelligence as a gage to measure people. To me, intelligence is a high mark. From experience, I can truly say that I am not intelligent; but I am not stupid either. The closest description I can come up with that best describes me is that I am a "hard worker". To me, hard work makes up for not being truly intelligent.

Interesting Tidbits Related to my College Experience

As I indicated in a previous section of this memoir, I'm the type of person that remembers past events when I hear specific songs being played on the radio or on the television. One specific example that brings back memories of my college years was a song titled "Maggie May" sung by a vocalist by the name of Rod Stewart. The song debuted in 1971. Aside from being what I consider to be a very nice song is one specific verse in the lyrics that brings back memories of my college years. The lyric segment is as follows:

*"**Wake up Maggie I think I got something to say to you**
It's late September and I really should be back at school"*

Of course there was no Maggie in my life but the reference to it being late September and being back at school is especially poignant to me.

Socorro and I attended high school during the latter 1960s. We were exposed to the "hippie movement". The latter 1960s was the period in time when the "hippie movement" was in vogue. The term "hippie" was a name given to predominantly white Anglo Saxon members of the counterculture of the 1960s. The youth movement originally began in the United States during the mid-1960s and spread to other countries around the world. Long hair was worn by the men and short skirts were worn by the women. The hippie movement exhibited a sense of anger against the establishment. The "hippie" counterculture opposed the Vietnam War, which was on-going at the time, and its members opposed almost every segment of the status quo in the United States. It was a resistance movement to the prim and proper way of life in the United States. In my opinion the movement was the white Anglo Saxon youth's effort to fit into society.

Another movement in the United States during the 1960s was the civil rights movement. The black culture spawned off what was called the "Black Power" movement. The Black Power movement emphasized racial pride, economic empowerment, and the creation of political and cultural institutions for black people in the United States. During the early 1970's when I attended college, a movement known as the Brown Power movement was started at the University of Texas at El Paso. The Brown Power movement like the Black Power movement sought to empower persons of ethnic descent. In the case of the Brown Power movement, it sought to empower persons of Hispanic descent. An organization known as M.E.Ch.A. was born. The acronym M.E.Ch.A. is short for Movimiento Estudiantil Chicanx de Aztlán which is translated to English as "Chicanx Student Movement of Aztlán"; the x being a gender neutral inflection. As indicated before, the organization sought to promote Chicano unity and empowerment through political action. In my opinion, it too was an effort of the

Hispanic youth to find a way to fit into society at the time.

I never joined the M.E.Ch.A. organization while I was in college; I was too busy tending to my young family and my difficult college studies. The existence of M.E.Ch.A.; however, is worth mentioning because in a small way, the youth of Hispanic descent needed to be recognized and racism needed to be addressed as a problem. In a manner of speaking, M.E.Ch.A. was the start of the assimilation process of the Hispanics into the way of life in the United States.

Job Offers After Having Graduated From the University

As I indicated in a previous section, during the last semester of my senior year in college, I attended several job fairs that were held at the University. During specific days, recruiters representing companies would set up in specific locations at a variety of buildings at the University. I don't remember all the names of the companies that showed up to recruit students; however, the company known as IBM was frequently represented. Another company that I clearly remember that was represented at the job fairs was Exxon. I visited with several of the recruiters. They provided application forms and information on their companies.

As a result of those meetings with the company recruiters I received an offer to work for IBM. The specific IBM division was located in Boulder, Colorado. I can't remember the specific nature of the job so I am unable to describe the work activity I would have been assigned. The other was a company by the name of Exxon. I was pretty sure I would receive an offer from Exxon because during the summer between my junior and senior year in college, I worked for Exxon as an engineering trainee in Andrews, Texas. So receiving an employment offer from Exxon was no surprise.

I also received an offer from a company by the name of Continental Water Conditioning Corporation. They were located in El Paso. I don't remember having become aware of them at the University job fairs. It may have been that I found out about them in the employment section of the newspaper.

In the end, I chose to accept employment with Continental Water Conditioning Corporation. I have to say that I gravitated to Continental Water Conditioning Corporation because it meant not having to leave El Paso. Accepting employment with IBM or Exxon meant having to leave my extended family behind. I just wasn't ready to venture out into the unknown.

The Effect of Extended Families on Hispanics

I have often wondered what it might have been like to have accepted a position with an out-of-town company. Would I have been more successful in my professional career leaving the El Paso area? Hispanics more than those of Anglo descent, tend to be closer to their extended family. During my years at the University, I noticed that students of Hispanic descent tended to be from the local area whereas students of Anglo descent tended to be out-of-towners. It always seemed to be that persons of Anglo descent seemed surer of themselves in far-away places, more so than persons of Hispanic descent.

I have to admit that I found comfort being close to my parents even as a young man. Now at this late age as I am writing this memoir, I have three sons and a daughter that have chosen to live in the same general area where I live in Horizon City, Texas. I do know of a few Hispanics that did venture out of our area.

During the latter part of the year 1979, I chose to accept a position with a company in Salt Lake City, Utah. I moved my family to Salt Lake City and I worked there for about a year and a half. My wife and children were not able to blend into the new environment and we ultimately decided to return to the El Paso area. Could it be that Hispanics tend to be more adverse to risk-taking as compared to persons of Anglo descent? Or, it is possible that Hispanics place more importance in belonging to their extended families than persons of Anglo descent? These are questions that I frequently ponder.

The Launching Pad

I can truly say that college was necessary for me. College in the early 1970's provided me a sure footing into a more modern world. Given that I was raised on a farm and as well as my years as a migrant worker in California, had it not been for college, I probably would have wound up working in agriculture. Absent my college scholarship from Farah Inc., I would have ended up working as a farm hand in Fabens.

Some have said that college is not for everyone. I have even heard some say that college isn't necessary nowadays. Others say that a bachelor's degree nowadays is not enough; a master's degree is what is necessary.

While it is true that some people are more suited to working in the applied trades such as welding, electrical work or building construction, one should not diminish the value of a good college education.

In my opinion, a college degree opens up the world to those that have the tenacity to succeed in college. I have heard of rare cases where some college graduates haven't been able to find a professional job. I can't help but believe that when a college graduate is pitted against a field of non-college graduates that the college graduate will be the one picked for a managerial position.

I graduated with a college degree in engineering. My college diploma gave me a sense of stability and it instilled in me a can-do attitude. As a result, I worked in professional positions during my entire adult life.

In a previous section, I stated that some of my former high school friends that hadn't progressed to college after high school were driving new cars, enjoying life and earning a paycheck; all this while I was stuck in college. I had a job but my job was a non-paying job, at least for the moment. I was driving a junky car and was living a meager life. My thought was that someday, I would surpass my friends after graduating from college. I wound up surpassing my friends and I was able to afford a new car and even a new home. College gave me a sense of self-assurance and the meager existence was no more. College was my launching pad to the modern world.

Summer Work During My College Years

Summer Work During 1971 –
Truck Driver at El Paso Sand Company

Summer arrived after completing my freshman year in college in May of 1971. My father was working with a construction company known as El Paso Sand in El Paso. I can't remember what his job was with El Paso Sand. Anyway, now on summer break, I asked my father if he was aware of any job openings at El Paso Sand where he worked. The following day, he asked his supervisor about job openings and fortunately there was a job opening for a tank truck driver. My father arranged for me to be hired as a truck driver.

When I showed up to work, I found that the truck I was assigned to was a heavy duty, double axle military style truck equipped with a water tank. The photograph on the left shows a typical military style tanker truck similar to the truck that was assigned to me. Several of the construction employees chided me about my job as a tank truck driver. I soon learned why the employees were kidding me about being a truck driver. It turned out that the large tank truck was not equipped with  power steering. The employees that were kidding me about my job knew this and probably figured that as soon as I figured out that the tank truck wasn't equipped with power steering, I would quit.

Not knowing why I was being chided, I boarded the tank truck and began to drive it down the road. Sure enough I quickly found that steering the truck was an arduous task. If not careful, the truck could aptly be called a suicide truck. It took every bit of arm strength to navigate the tank truck along the twists and turns of the road. I didn't give up. At the end of the day, I parked the tank truck and left for home. When I returned the next day, the men no longer chided me. I suppose I earned their respect.

I successfully drove the suicide water truck during the entire summer of 1971. Adrian my first child had been born previously in May of 1971. The money I earned during the summer months came in very handy in supporting my small family.

Summer Work During 1972 – Work At Vowell Construction

The 1971-1972 college school year was difficult for me. The course material had been especially difficult. I was glad that the school year finally ended for the summer.

As in the prior summer, I again asked my father about work that might be available where he worked. He was now working for a construction company by the name of Vowell Construction. Somehow my father was able to pull some strings with his supervisor and I was hired by Vowell Construction. At the time, Vowell Construction was constructing the freeway interchange located between Piedras Street and Raynolds Street.

This freeway interchange is now commonly known in El Paso as the "Spaghetti Bowl".

My work consisted of working with a group of men installing steel reinforcement bar on the roadways and on the concrete aprons located on the sides of the freeway. Steel reinforcement bar is commonly known as "rebar".

Anyway, each man in the crew wore a tool belt equipped with the tools necessary to tie rebar sections together. The work was difficult because tying the rebar sections with steel pliers required that the worker bend down at the waist in order to reach the rebar sections located close to the ground surface. Once the rebar sections were tied together with bailing wire in checker board fashion, the concrete was then poured over the rebar structure and wah-lah, the roadway was constructed.

Eight hours of that work was tough on the back. I was young then; that work was by no means a mature man's work. By the way, the photograph on the left shows steel rebar about to be covered with concrete.

About halfway through the summer that year, our work crew was transferred to the street construction that was in progress on Yarbrough Drive. In those days, Yarbrough Drive only extended from the I-10 Freeway and ended about midway between the I-10 Freeway and Montana Avenue. The street construction consisted of constructing Yarbrough Dirve the rest of the way to Montana Avenue. In those days, Yarbrough Drive was at the outskirts of the City of El Paso.

I was assigned to work with a shovel assisting the operator of a road grader machine. Some refer to the machine as "the blade" or "the maintainer". The road grader is a construction machine equipped with a long blade that is used to create a flat surface during the grading process while  constructing a roadway. The photograph on the left shows a road grader similar to that used during my employment with Vowell Construction.

The operator of the road grader was a mature man of Anglo descent that spoke only English. I became good friends with him probably because

I was one of the few workers that spoke English; almost all the construction workers were non-English speaking. For some reason, he referred to me as "Jasper" even though I would remind him often that my name was Salvador or Sal. It probably was his way of showing humor in order to pass the time away.

Anyway, I finished up the summer with Vowell Construction and then returned by to my college work at the beginning of September 1972. By the way, Amanda, my second child, was born previously in May of 1972.

Summer Work During 1973 - Engineering Trainee at Exxon

Prior to the end of the 1972-1973 college school year, I interviewed with a company by the name of Exxon Oil Company. I don't remember how I happened to find out about Exxon; it could have been that Exxon recruiters visited the college campus at one of the job fairs. I wound up being recruited to work as an engineering trainee for Exxon during the summer of 1973 at a distant town called Andrews, Texas. The town of Andrews was and still is located about 35 miles north of Odessa, Texas. A fellow student of mine, Gilbert Moreno, was also recruited as an engineering trainee at the same time with Exxon. He worked in Midland, Texas during the same summer.

When I received the letter from Exxon confirming my employment with them, I read the letter and found that I would be assigned to work on a project involving the "San Andres reservoir". I was puzzled because the word "reservoir" implied a project involving an expanse of water such as a lake. It seemed odd to me because civil engineers work on projects involving lakes and dams. I was a mechanical/ industrial engineering student and not a civil engineering student. Although it seemed strange to me, I didn't contact the person that wrote the Exxon employment confirmation letter to inquire about the nature of the specific summer job assignment. Who was I to question the intent of Exxon Oil Company.

Anyway, Gilbert Moreno and I decided to live together in an apartment so that we could share living expenses. We chose Odessa, Texas as the apartment location since Andrews was located about 35 miles from Odessa and Midland, where Gilbert was going to work, was about 30 miles from Odessa.

The June day came when I was going to leave for Odessa. I said my goodbyes to my wife and two kids and off I went. The drive to Odessa was about 4 hours. The following day in Odessa, I woke up and got ready to travel to Andrews. Half an hour later, I arrived at the Exxon Oil Company field offices located at the outskirts of the town of Andrews, Texas.

I parked my car in the visitors parking area and then proceeded to walk into the offices. I was greeted by the office receptionist. She immediately called another lady in a nearby office to come for me. The lady that came for me was the executive secretary to the director of the facility. The lady was very kind; she immediately made attempts to make me feel at home. She asked me where I had parked my car and I informed her that I had parked in the visitor's parking lot in the front of the offices. She seemed alarmed and quickly said "Oh no, you need to park in the parking space in the back". In the grand scheme of things I was a "nobody" at Exxon so it seemed normal me to be told to park in the back. I then walked to my car and drove around to the rear of the building. All the parking spaces were taken except for one. I proceeded to the vacant parking space and as I was driving into the parking space, I noticed that the concrete parking barrier was painted with my name; "Sal Renteria – Engineer". Wow, that was me. This was my parking space. The executive secretary's instruction to park in the back was not meant as a dig to a "nobody" like me; it really meant being part of the Exxon team. I was elated.

After parking my car, I walked back to the offices and rejoined the executive secretary. She then walked me to the director's office and she introduced me to him. The director's name was Randy; I can't remember Randy's last name. Randy was a very nice person, he greeted me as if I was a very important person. In truth, I was a "nobody", but Randy made me feel as if I was part of the Exxon team. During the ensuing discussion, I asked Randy about the project involving the "San Andres reservoir" and asked him for the location of the lake which was to be part of my project. He seemed surprised at my question. He looked at me, he pointed downward and said "The San Andres reservoir is located about 5,000 feet down in the ground. It is an oil reservoir and you're going to figure out how to extract the oil from it." It finally made sense to me; Exxon was an oil company and crude oil is found deep underground in rock stratum. I apologized for seeming ignorant and Randy responded in a kind manner by saying it was no big deal.

Randy introduced me to the engineers that were working in the field offices and then ultimately assigned me to an engineer by the name of Jim Hemphill. Jim was a graduate of the University of New Mexico in Albuquerque. He had been working in the Andrews Exxon field offices for about 2 years. His title was "Reservoir Engineer". Jim showed me how to use a computer system used to determine the presence of oil in various deep underground reservoirs.

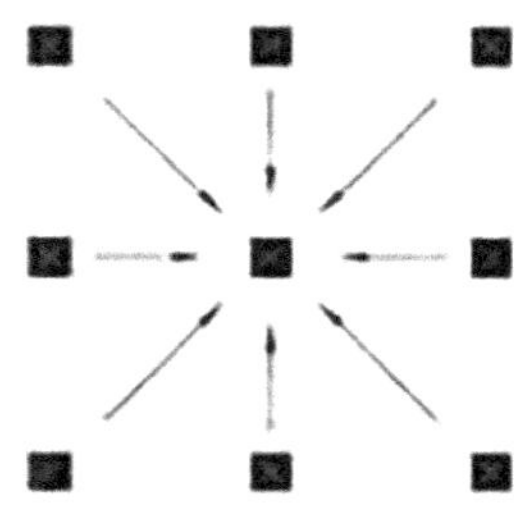

The objective of my work was to evaluate the San Andres reservoir in order to prepare an implementation program designed to extract residual oil from it. The plan was to prepare an implementation program, develop a cost to benefit analysis and then determine if a target rate of financial return could be achieved. The evaluation was done by using what was known then as a "water flood" modeling program that ran in their central computer.

The graphic on the left shows the basics of water flooding. Water flooding was the process of extracting oil from a central well by injecting water into surrounding wells. The concept of "water flooding" was to pump water at high pressure into the surrounding wells so that the oil would be pushed from the surrounding wells toward the extraction well. The oil water mixture produced from the extraction well would then be processed in an oil water separator device to isolate and recover only the oil.

I performed the project work under the supervision of two engineers. One of the engineers was Jim Hemphill; I can't remember the name of the other engineer that provided me direction on the project. In the end, I developed the final project along with costs and an implementation program. The resulting rate of return of the investment was determined to be within the desired corporate guidelines. I submitted the water flooding proposal to Randy at the conclusion of my work contract at the end of August.

Jim Hemphill and I grew to be close friends during the summer of my work at Exxon. He would go out of his way to provide valuable tips that I could use on my project work. He showed interest in my succeeding on the project. I remember him speaking fondly about his alma mater; the University of New Mexico. I remember his eyes tearing up when we said our goodbyes just prior to my leaving Exxon. Living and working away from my small family was difficult for me. In order to minimize expenses I traveled home to Fabens from Odessa once every two weeks instead of every week. I would arrive in Fabens on Friday night and would leave Fabens back to Odessa on Sunday afternoons. I was always homesick for my wife and my two little ones, Adrian and Amanda.

As I indicated previously, I presented my water flooding project to Exxon in August of 1973. In October of 1973 the members of the Organization of Arab Petroleum Exporting Countries proclaimed an oil embargo. The embargo was targeted at nations perceived as supporting Israel. The initial nations targeted were Canada, Japan, the Netherlands, the United Kingdom and the United States with the embargo also later expanded to include Portugal, Rhodesia and South Africa. By the end of the embargo in March of 1974, the price of oil had risen from $3.00 per barrel to nearly $12.00 globally; US prices were significantly higher. The embargo caused an oil crisis, or "shock", with many short and long-term effects on global politics and the global economy.

When I graduated from college in May of 1974, I received an offer of employment from Exxon. In their correspondence, they mentioned that they were very interested in proceeding with the development of the San Andres water flood project. I suppose that the oil embargo during the previous months had made many oil projects on the drawing board worth pursuing. I turned down the employment offer from Exxon.

I opted to begin my career with Continental Water Conditioning Corporation in El Paso even though the salary amount of the Exxon offer was more. My decision was based primarily on the fact that I would have to move my family to Andrews, Texas in order to work for Exxon. Had I not previously received an offer of employment to work in El Paso, I probably would have wound up in Andrews, Texas in the role of reservoir engineer.

One final note on my Exxon experience; in previous sections of this memoir I mentioned that I have a knack for remembering songs that were being played on the radio during important events in my life. One such song was titled "Suavecito" that was played by a group known as Malo that first aired in 1972. I remember the song playing on the radio in the mornings while I drove from Odessa to Andrews to work. Hearing that song play on the radio nowadays brings back good memories of having worked for Exxon as an engineering trainee.

Continental Water Conditioning Corporation

As I indicated previously, prior to graduating from college, I was offered employment with Exxon Oil Company in Andrews, Texas and with IBM in Boulder, Colorado.

After graduating from the University of Texas at El Paso I was lucky to have found employment with a company by the name of Continental Water Conditioning Corporation. The company was located on 1013 Wall Street in El Paso, Texas. By the way, from now on for brevity I will use the name Continental Water instead of the complete name Continental Water Conditioning Corporation. As I indicated previously, I don't remember how I found out about the company. It could have been that they participated in the job fairs at the University and that that's how I became aware of them or I it could be that I became aware of them from reading the newspaper. Remember that in June of 1974 there was no such thing as social media or the internet; there were only newspapers and word of mouth. I remember being interviewed by several persons at Continental Water prior to being employed. Of all the persons that interviewed me, I specifically remember being interviewed by a person of Hispanic descent. I would later find out that his name was Roberto Constantakis. The person who I wound up reporting to was a person by the name of Chuck Jones, he was the head of the technical group. The owner and president of the company was a person by the name of William Burgess while the vice president's name was Donald Hoover. My starting salary was $12,000 dollars per year. In 1974, the amount of $12,000 dollars had the same buying power as $64,032 dollars in 2018. The latter value was calculated using an "inflation calculator" that can be accessed using the following web link: https://www.dollartimes.com/inflation/inflation.php?amount=4000 &year=1970

Continental Water was a small company numbering about 20 perhaps 25 people. As part of the training, I spent about a month working in the various manufacturing departments of the company. By the way, a person by the name of Dominic Aradio was also hired at the same time that I was. Dominic Aradio was an electronics and electrical expert. Prior to his employment at Continental Water, he was employed at a company in Chicago by the name of Barber Colman. Barber Colman manufactured industrial instrumentation products. Continental Water manufactured molded items that were necessary for their product known as "service exchange DI tanks". They also manufactured small to medium size reverse osmosis (RO) systems that used reverse osmosis membranes manufactured by E.I. Dupont Company out of Wilmington, Delaware. The RO membranes were referred to as Permasep RO membranes. I spent some time in the quality control department which tested the RO systems before they were shipped to the company's clients. I spent a week in the company's deionization resin regeneration department. The regeneration department received the exhausted DI resin tanks, regenerated the ion exchange resin with acid and caustic and then loaded the regenerated resin back into the DI resin tanks. The regenerated DI tanks were now ready for distribution to the company's clients. Finally, I spent a week with the service department that distributed the regenerated service DI tanks to the local clients in El Paso. When the DI tanks were exhausted at the client sites, the personnel from the service department would pick up the exhausted tanks from the location of the local clients and return them back to the regeneration department at the company's plant. This business model was present in about 150 distribution Continental Water

branches and dealerships located throughout the country.

Apart from the manufacturing activity in El Paso, the company had about 150 sales and service offices located throughout the United States. About half of the sales and service offices were company-owned branches while the rest were franchised independent dealerships. Being a franchised independent dealer meant that the dealer had to implement the deionization regeneration equipment manufactured by Continental Water as well as pay 10% of the gross sales of deionization equipment products to corporate Continental Water.

After the initial training in the manufacturing facility on Wall Street, I was assigned to the Technical Service department headed by Chuck Jones. Dominic Aradio was also assigned to the department. One of my first assignments was to travel to Amarillo, Texas to assist in the startup of a reverse osmosis system. I flew to Amarillo which was the second time I had flown on a commercial jet airplane. It was the first time I was made responsible for directing the installation of an RO system. The most challenging part of the installation was directing the electrical installation. I knew zero about electronic controllers and pump motor electrical starters. Fortunately with the coaching I received from a person by the name of Eddie Rivera back at the manufacturing facility, I was able to perform the work of directing the overall installation of the system. There was no such thing as cell phones in those days so I burned up a lot of telephone time with Eddie Rivera from the jobsite in Amarillo to the plant in El Paso. When I arrived back in El Paso, the customer's representative had called and had already spoken with Chuck Jones. He had informed Chuck Jones that the installation and startup of the RO system had progressed without a hitch. I was congratulated by Chuck Jones on a job well done when I returned.

After the initial system startup, Chuck Jones began assigning me to more and more startups. I eventually became the "go to" person when it came to RO system installations and startups. About 6 months after starting my employment with Continental Water, I was assigned the responsibility of designing the larger RO systems. Prior to that, the company already had a standard product line of RO systems with flow rate capacities of 200 gallons per day (gpd) up to 9,000 gpd. I was now responsible for the design of RO systems that produced more than 9,000 gallons per day (gpd). Working with the drafting department for about two years, I completed the design of a product line that encompassed flows from 10,000 gpd to 60,000 gpd. Eventually, I developed designs for systems with capacities of 100,000 gpd up to 160,000 gpd.

During those years, I worked with a Continental Water corporate sales person by the name of Jack Jameson. Jack was instrumental in selling a large RO system to a small municipality known as Alta in the state of Iowa. This occurred about 2 years after I started working at Continental Water. I prepared the proposal documents that included mechanical drawings of the proposed system. Jack traveled to Alta, Iowa to hand-carry the proposal to the bid meeting in Alta. I remember Jack telling me about the severe blizzard he had to battle when he was in Alta for the proposal presentation. A few weeks after the proposal was presented Jack received word from the representatives of the township of Alta that Continental Water had been selected as the successful bidder. I remember that all the office personnel and the manufacturing personnel were called to assemble for a meeting in the Continental Water production facilities. Don Hoover, the vice president, made the announcement about the township of Alta, Iowa selecting Continental Water as the successful bidder. Jack Jameson took the accolades and he mentioned me as the person who had supervised the preparation of the proposal. During his presentation, Jack indicated that I was going to be the project engineer for the project. This was a big event in the company's history because at the time, the RO system was going to be the largest system the company had constructed for use by a municipality. About a month later, Jack Jameson and Don Hoover flew the company airplane to Alta, Iowa and picked up Ron Dieber, the municipality's representative. They flew him back to El Paso as a reward for having been instrumental in the selection of Continental Water as the designated company to provide the water treatment system for his municipality. Don Hoover flew the airplane with Jack Jameson and Ron Dieber aboard. I remember that Jack Jameson and Don Hoover wined and dined Ron Dieber during his stay in El Paso.

Eventually, I became the engineering coordinator as the company began hiring more and more engineers. With the additional personnel, we began to design and manufacture on-site regenerable deionization systems. I headed the group of engineering personnel in the design and manufacture of the equipment.

During the spring of 1979, the marketing department at Continental Water began a series of training seminars for the company sales personnel around the country. I assisted the marketing department in presentation of reverse osmosis technology and products to the sales personnel. The sales presentations were held at various strategic locations within the United States. I specifically remember the sales presentation we did in Ridgefield, New Jersey during March of 1979. At the end of the day during March 28, 1979, we started to hear news of a nuclear power plant accident at Three Mile Island near Harrisburg Pennsylvania. A cooling problem had resulted in the discharge of radioactive materials into the atmosphere. At the time, it seemed to me that our location in Ridgefield, New Jersey was far from the Three Mile Island location. Being so far from the location meant minimal effects to us. In reality Harrisburg, Pennsylvania was located east of Ridgefield, New Jersey and it was located only 178 miles away. At the time, I we knew of the severity of the nuclear accident but somehow I felt geographically distant from the location of the nuclear accident. Now as I am writing this memoir, it seems to me that 178 miles from the accident and located east of the accident site, meant that the prevailing easterly winds could have carried the nuclear discharge into the atmosphere toward the direction of Ridgefield, New Jersey. It's interesting that I now know how dangerous the nuclear accident was to us but at the time, we felt insulated from the radioactive material discharge that actually occurred at Three Mile Island.

The acquisition of Texas-based Continental Water Conditioning Corporation allowed Millipore to establish a service base for the Water Systems Division; Continental had a nationwide network of 150 sales and service locations. During the first half of 1980, Millipore's Water Systems Division was consolidated with Continental's operations in El Paso.

During the early part of 1979, I was offered an opportunity by Continental Water Conditioning Corporation to buy company stock. I didn't really understand the significance of the offer and so I didn't pay much attention to the offer. During the first half of 1980, Millipore's Water Systems Division purchased all of the Continental's operations in El Paso as well as all the company owned branches. I later had the opportunity to speak with Don Hoover who was Continental's vice president. This occurred about 10 years after I left Continental Water Conditioning Corporation and started my own company. I happened to meet him at a store and during the discussion, I told him about my having received an offer to purchase Continental stock back in the day. Mr. Hoover told me that I was the only person within the company that was offered company stock. He also commented that he never received a reply from me after having made the offer. He indicated that all of the stock from Continental stock holders was purchased by Millipore Corporation. He indicated that had I purchased the stock that was offered to me, the stock would probably have been purchased at about $250,000.00. I was 28 years old at the time of Millipore's purchase of the stock. Enough said about company stock; a missed opportunity.

While employed with Continental Water, I got the opportunity to visit Washington DC. Continental Water had a branch subsidiary in nearby Maryland. I can't remember the name of the branch manager, however I do remember that he was gracious enough to invite me to stay during the weekend so he could show me around the Washington DC area. I got to visit the Smithsonian Museum; specifically the Air and Space Museum. I'll never forget the visit to Washington DC.

Fabens Independent School District – School Board - 1977

When I was 26 years of age in 1977, I campaigned as a candidate for school board member of the Fabens Independent School District and was subsequently elected. The story of how I decided to run for public office is interesting.

During that time, the school board consisted of two Hispanic members and four Anglo members. The Hispanic members were David Sublasky and Roberto Perez. Roberto Perez, who was known as Bobby Perez, had gradually gained a reputation of always voting the same way as the Anglo members of the board. This was so apparent that I was asked by several community members to run for the Fabens school board against Bobby Perez. I decided to run against him.

I was able to defeat Bobby Perez in spite of his support by the Anglo school board members. I defeated Bobby Perez because the majority of the members of the Fabens Catholic Church supported me. I defeated him by quite a large margin. I remained on the school board until I moved to Salt Lake City, Utah in August of 1979. During my tenure as school board member, the Risinger Elementary School was expanded. A plaque containing my name as board member currently exists outside the  Risinger Elementary School administration building. The photograph on the left shows the plaque that contains my name as a school board member. I am satisfied that my votes on the Fabens school board reflected the needs and wants of the majority of the members of the Fabens Catholic Church.

Community Organizing - 1978

During 1978, local churches in the El Paso County area began to organize into what became the EPISO organization. EPISO is an acronym for El Paso Interreligious Sponsoring Organization. The effort was interdenominational, that is, churches of all faiths participated as members of the organization. EPISO was developed in order to train leaders to be effective community leaders that could educate and inform citizens about pressing community problems and challenges. The organization engaged in public discourse and initiated action guided by conversation, creating opportunities for ordinary people to make real and dramatic change in the community. It encouraged the members to hold elected officials accountable for their public responsibilities.

In 1978, Father James Hall and myself, representing the Fabens Catholic Church in EPISO, attended a one week training session in community organizing. The training was held at a campus facility located in a suburb of Chicago known as Lake Forest, Illinois. The community organizing method was patterned after the method used by Saul David Alinsky who was an American community activist and political theorist. His work through the Chicago-based Industrial Areas Foundation helping poor communities organize to press demands upon landlords, politicians and business leaders won him national recognition and notoriety. Responding to the impatience of a New Left generation of activists in the 1960s, in his widely cited Rules for Radicals: A Pragmatic Primer (1971), Alinsky defended the arts both of confrontation and of compromise involved in community organizing as keys to the struggle for social justice. Father James Hall and I participated in that type of community organizing during a week-long training session.

The biggest takeaway from the training was how to confront landlords, politicians and business leaders and to hold them accountable in completing community projects. It was a kind of guerrilla warfare for the purpose of getting community projects accomplished. The basic method to get a politician to positively act on a given project was to "run an action" on that politician. The action consisted of recruiting as many people as possible to attend some specific pre-announced meeting in which the specific politician was to participate. First, all the people that were to run the EPISO action would flood the meeting room. The leaders "running the action" would make demands of the targeted politician in order to get him or her to agree to take positive action on the project being supported by EPISO. In short, community organizing was a means of effecting public harassment on the politician or politicians to get them to take positive action on the specific project. Father James Hall and I were able to run actions on several targeted persons with some success. The Alinsky method was quite an eye opener for me and Father James Hall.

Fast forward to the year 2008 and it turns out that the newly elected President of the United States was Barack Obama. He too had been a community organizer during his younger years in Chicago.

Assistance From Former U.S. Congressman Richard C. White

Soon after I began to work for Continental Water Conditioning Corporation, I applied to the Farmers Home Administration for a loan to purchase my first home in Fabens, Texas. This occurred in the year of 1975. At that time, Farmers Home Administration offered low interest loans to persons with low income. My application was initially rejected since my gross income was $12,040.00 dollars per year and the maximum permissible gross income amount to qualify for a loan was $12,000.00 dollars per year or less.

I decided to write to Congressman Richard C. White to see if he might be able to assist me since the yearly salary overage was only $40.00 dollars. I can only guess that his office communicated with the personnel at Farmers Home Administration because shortly thereafter, I received confirmation that my loan application was accepted. I was able to purchase my first home with Congressman Richard C. White's assistance. I'll never forget him and will forever be thankful to him. He came through for me when I needed his assistance.

Ever since then, I have always been a home owner. Later on, I accepted employment in Salt Lake City in 1979 and I purchased a home in Salt Lake City. When I moved back to Horizon City, I purchased the home that I have now lived in since 1981.

Mount Olympus Bottled Water – Salt Lake City

During my employment with Continental Water Conditioning Corporation, I had several occasions to assist the dealer franchisee located in Salt Lake City. The dealer franchise was known as Continental Water of Salt Lake City and the parent company was known as Mount Olympus Bottled Water. The Continental dealer franchisee was able to sell a few reverse osmosis systems. I traveled to Salt Lake City several times to assist them in starting up the newly purchased RO systems they had sold to their customers. I was an expert at starting up RO systems and the owner of the Continental franchise dealership took notice of my abilities. His name was William Bailey; I called him Bill for short.

Bill Bailey was so impressed with my knowledge of the water treatment equipment that one day in May of 1979, I received a phone call from him. He offered me a position with his company that would require I move my family to live in Salt Lake City. His offer included an offer of partial ownership of a new company that he wanted to start in Salt Lake City. The ownership offer consisted of a good salary plus owning 5% of the company per year with a maximum ownership of 25% of the company at the end of 5 years of employment. He invited my wife and myself to travel to Phoenix, Arizona to meet with him to discuss the opportunity. Socorro and I met with him in Phoenix. During our meeting, Bill indicated that he didn't want to get in trouble with Don Hoover or Bill Burgess at Continental Water Conditioning Corporation over hiring me away from them. As a result, he cautioned me against letting anyone know about his plan to hire me away from corporate Continental. Bill Bailey suggested that I should resign from corporate Continental and feign resigning to become a water treatment consultant for 2 or 3 months. His plan was that I would work on projects for the Salt Lake City company in the role as a consultant. During the 2 or 3 months as a consultant, I would receive salary payments from the Salt Lake City company to help me along.

Upon my return to El Paso, I submitted my resignation to Don Hoover. He wished me well and 2 weeks later I became a "consultant" with a portfolio of one company. I rented an office in Clint, Texas and worked out of that office for 3 months. By the way, Bill Bailey paid for the rental of the office.

During mid August of 1979, I sold our home in Fabens. My family and I packed up and hired a transport company to carry our furniture from Fabens to Salt Lake City. We traveled from Fabens to Albuquerque, took a left turn at Albuquerque and then on to Gallup, New Mexico. From the four corners area we then proceeded northwest until we arrived in Salt Lake City. It was still mid August and the school year for my children began at the beginning of September. We lived in a rental apartment for a month while waiting for our new home to be finished in Salt Lake City. We lived in the rental apartment for about a month until our new home was finished by a building contractor. The address of our new home was 8239

S. Marion View Circle, Sandy, Utah 84094. I remember that the price of the home was approximately $56,000.00. When corrected for inflation, the value of the home in 2018 is $203,919.00. It was a beautiful home.

Bill Bailey, now my boss, gave me free rein in the development of the new company. The first order of business now in Salt Lake City was to create the new company and its logo. I came up with the new company name for the new company; the name was Water & Power Technologies, Inc. The word "Power" in the name was designed to appeal to large installations of water treatment equipment in power plants. Bill Bailey allowed me to hire a technician to assist me. His name was Butch Weigel.

There was a lot of on-going work required with the RO systems already in place in the Salt Lake City area. Among the largest systems were those installed at the Kennecott Copper mines as well as at a large installation known as N.L. Industries. In addition to the existing work with the installed systems, I sold several new large systems installations. One specific account that I remember was Litton Industries. I sold them a large RO system. I met with Frank Davis who headed power plant development at Utah Power and Light Company but was never successful at convincing him to purchase water treatment equipment.

During my short duration working with Bill Bailey, I assisted Mr. Earl Israelsen from Utah State University in the writing of a technical paper that was later published. My name appears in the acknowledgement section of the technical paper titled "Use of Saline Water in Energy Development" published in June of 1980 by Utah Water Research Laboratory which was affiliated with Utah State University. The paper can still be found on the internet.

I kept busy with my work at Water and Power Technologies, however, my family did not fare well living in Salt Lake City. Salt Lake City was and still is a Mormon community. In 1980, Catholics were a minority in the area. We were Hispanics living in an Anglo Mormon community. My son Adrian who was only 9 years of age at the time, was picked on by the rest of the Anglo Mormon kids. My daughter, Amanda, who was 8 years old was also picked on almost on a daily basis. After living a little more than a year in Salt Lake City, my wife finally said to me "we are going back home to Fabens, are you coming with us?" I had no choice; we were going to have to go back to the El Paso area sooner or later.

Fortunately, at about the same time, I was offered a position with Millipore Corporation back in El Paso. A Mr. Vel Cubrilovich, Chief Executive Officer, made me the offer. By then Millipore had purchased Continental Water Conditioning Corporation. Mr. Cubrilovich offered to pay for moving my furniture back to El Paso in addition to a $5,000.00 stipend as an inducement to return. I took them up on the offer. I explained my predicament relating to my family's problems in Salt Lake City to Bill Bailey and he understood. I then accepted Millipore Corporation's offer to return to El Paso.

Millipore Corporation

I returned to El Paso with my family and we settled in Horizon City, Texas. Millipore Corporation had purchased the Continental Water Conditioning Corporation building in Horizon City. We rented a rental home for about 4 months and then finally purchased my home where we have lived for now 40 years.

I assumed the position of engineering manager at Millipore Corporation. I supervised ten persons that were engineers and service technicians. After about 6 months, I was promoted to sales engineering manager. Along with the regional sales managers I reported to a person by the name of Peter Savas. I was provided with 4 sales engineers and 3 service technicians. The sales engineers were each located in Los Angeles, Boston, Pittsburgh and Miami. Two service technicians were located in El Paso and another one was located in Boston. The objective of the sales engineering group was to sell large RO and DI systems to industrial clients and power plants. In this position, I was able to travel to many locations within the United States in support of the sales effort. I had the opportunity to twice visit the island of Puerto Rico in the Caribbean. I stayed in San Juan, Puerto Rico during those trips.

During my employment with Millipore Corporation, I traveled all over the country. I got to see many areas of the country. I specifically remember taking a trip to Utica, New York. I took a flight from El Paso to Dallas and then a flight from Dallas to Newark, New Jersey. The leg from Newark to Utica meant that I had to take a helicopter ride from Newark, New Jersey to the LaGuardia airport for a flight to Utica. I especially remember that helicopter ride. The helicopter traveled through the city of New York to reach LaGuardia airport. The helicopter ride was awesome. The helicopter didn't fly over the New York skyline; it flew through the high rises as if flying through canyons of buildings. It was something that a farm boy from Fabens could only be awestruck with.

Eventually, the Millipore management in Boston decided to move the manufacturing activity from El Paso to Boston. It was now 1983. I was offered a position in Boston, Massachusetts with Millipore Corporation. The experience that my family had in Salt Lake City, meant that Socorro, my wife, was not willing to leave the El Paso area. I left my employment with Millipore Corporation in November of 1983 to develop my own company, Fluid Resources Corporation.

Fluid Resources Corporation

As part of the employment termination with Millipore Corporation, I was retained by Millipore Corporation to oversee the completion of a contract Millipore Corporation had with McDonald Douglas Aircraft in St. Louis, Missouri. The retainer fee that I was paid was $23,000.00. I used the money to start up my new company. A person by the name of Bill Green and I started up the company. Bill Green was from Los Angeles, California and had been one of the sales engineers that reported to me during my employment with Millipore Corporation. I was president and he was vice-president of Fluid Resources Corporation. A few months later, we renamed the company Fluid Separations Corporation in order to tie in the name of the company to the technologies involved in the separation of dissolved solids from water.

I hired a group of people; two of whom were former employees at Millipore Corporation. Their names were Ed Puga and Joe Padilla. I also recruited my brother, Mario Renteria, and my father, Jesus Renteria, to help out with the manufacturing. Socorro, my wife, helped out as secretary. By the way, we purchased a portable computer in 1983. Prior to 1983, personal computers were not as prevalent as they are today. Anyway, the computer was manufactured by Osbourne Computer Company. It was used primarily as a word processor. Socorro used it to prepare proposals and instruction manuals. I am still in possession of the computer; I can't bear the pain of disposing it as trash.

I remember a person by the name of Marjorie K. Balazs who founded Balazs Analytical Laboratory in northern California. She also founded the Semiconductor Pure Water and Chemicals Conference that was held yearly in San Jose, California. During 1985, I sent in a request to the conference council indicating my interest in presenting a technical paper at the conference. My request included a synopsis of the paper for the council's review. Ms. Balazs wrote back to me and indicated an acceptance of my  request. That year I presented my technical paper titled "Nitrogen Blanket Systems for High Purity Water Tanks" at the 4th Annual Semiconductor Pure Water Conference in San Mateo, California. The presentation was attended by approximately 300 persons involved in pure water consulting, laboratories and equipment manufacturers. The drawing on the left shows a typical nitrogen blanketing system mounted on a water storage tank. As a result of my presentation at the conference, companies such as Dupont, Olin and others purchased nitrogen blanket systems for their manufacturing plants in the ensuing years.

Our first project was the manufacturing of a mixed bed deionization system for the Naval Shipyard in Seattle, Washington. I remember that we took out our first loan from The State National Bank in El Paso in the amount of $24,000.00 to construct the system. One of the larger systems was a $320,000.00 reverse osmosis and deionization system for Advanced Micro Devices, AMD, which was located in Austin, Texas. We worked with a former Continental dealer, Jack Smith, to procure that specific business. We finished it successful within the agreed upon 8 month time period. We also constructed an $80,000.00 two bed deionization system for Lithium Corporation located in South Carolina. I remember that a representative from Lithium Corporation wanted to visit our facilities in El Paso prior to placing the order for the equipment. It turned out that we had one week to turn our offices into professionally equipped offices. We went to a company called Aaron Rents and purchase office partitions along with new office desks and chairs. Everything came together because shortly thereafter, Lithium Corporation sent us the purchase order for the equipment. We were also successful in selling a $580,000.00 ultrapure water system in Carlsbad, California for Hughes Aircraft.

That was the upside of the business.

It was now 1987 and we had been in business for 4 years. Bill Green was spending a lot of business money in California. In early 1987, the company financial reserves began to dwindle. During April of 1987, I traveled to Barstow, California to startup a DI system that we constructed for a solar power company. After I finished the startup, I traveled from Barstow to where Chuy, my brother, lived in Westminster, California. When I arrived, I asked him to take me to Gardena, California where Bill Green lived. I needed to confiscate Bill Green's company car so that I could dispose of it so as not to have a needless car payment to the bank in El Paso. Chuy and I staked out near his residence. When Bill arrived to his residence at about 8:00 pm that night, I approached Bill and told him about having to return the company car. Bill didn't resist and I was able to confiscate the company car without incident. I stayed during the night at Chuy's home. The next morning, I said my good-byes to Chuy and his wife, Berta, and proceeded to drive to El Paso in what used to be Bill's former car. I'll never forget that day since it was Easter Sunday when I drove from Westminster to El Paso. It was a sad trip back.

I'll never forget Sonny Cammack who owned Alamo Water Refiners, Inc. in San Antonio, Texas. We purchased water equipment components from his company. Sonny Cammack believed in me even during the bankruptcy. He continued to sell to us even though my company still owed his company money for previous purchases. Our agreement was that every time we purchased products from his company, we would add 10% to the amount and in this way, we ultimately paid Alamo Water the amount that we owed prior to the bankruptcy. I still have the Alamo Water Refiners catalog.

Shortly thereafter, I placed the company in bankruptcy. We owed the Small Business Administration about $70,000.00. With their assistance, I dissolved Fluid Separations Corporation and initiated a new company by the name of Fluid Process Systems, Inc. The SBA debt was transferred from the now defunct company to the new company. Eventually, I managed to pay off the SBA debt.

Fluid Process Systems, Inc.

The year of 1988 was a fresh new start with the brand new company in the name of Fluid Process Systems, Inc. As indicated before, little by little the entire bankruptcy debt from the former Fluid Separations Corporation was paid off.

We moved the company from the shopping center location at 1500 Horizon Blvd. to smaller offices located at the Land Brokers building located at Horizon Blvd. and Duanesburg Drive. We worked out of that tiny facility for a year or two.

Later on, I was able to purchase a new 20,000 square foot facility located on 998 Peyton Road. In that new facility, we were able to start a new additional product known as service deionization. We constructed a DI resin regeneration facility to regenerate the service DI tanks. This product afforded a steady income into the company. Eventually, we formed an alliance with a water treatment chemical supplier known as Buckman Laboratories. They showed us how to blend their chemicals with local commodity chemicals to result in a complete product line that could be used to treat cooling towers water, close loop water circuits and steam boilers. The water treatment products enabled us to expand our coverage into markets heretofore unknown to us. Adrian, my son, was the person that was responsible for blending the chemicals at our plant facility. We hired additional sales persons to sell the water treatment products along with our standard products such as softeners, reverse osmosis systems and deionization systems. We became a full service water treatment company.

At about the same time that Fluid Process Systems became a water treatment chemical supplier, I opened a subsidiary in Cd. Juarez, Mexico. The name of the company was Procesos de Fluido,

S.A. de C.V. We built a cinder block building at a location known as the Ejido de Sausal. We installed a DI resin regeneration station at that facility as well. The Mexican company is still operating at this date in the year 2020.

The Mangy Dog – A Management Style

Running two businesses with one in the United States and the other in Mexico kept me really busy. One has to deal with employees that sometimes come up with difficult situations that require intervention by the manager; in this case, me.

As an example, on one occasion, a fairly expensive stainless steel pump wound up missing from the manufacturing shop at our El Paso facility. Nobody seemed to know where it went. A few employees privately told me that they suspected that a certain trusted employee had taken the pump. Some of the individuals even came outright and said that they knew the trusted employee had taken the pump even though they didn't actually see the heist occur. I frequently found myself in dilemmas like this one. As a manager one has to make a decision one way or the other.

In a management role, I frequently found it necessary to resort to what I refer to euphemistically as the mangy dog style of management. The mangy dog style of management is a method used to deal with difficult situations where allegations are made when no real proof exists that the allegation is true. In the mangy dog style of management, the manager recognizes that even the rattiest and ugliest mangy dog when taunted sufficiently enough will be driven to respond with so much anger that it will resort to defending itself by biting the insistent accuser without regard for anything else. A good manager must always provide the accused a small pathway out of a difficult situation especially when sufficient doubt exists. When some doubt exists, it is best to provide the benefit of the doubt to the accused to prevent a catastrophic meltdown in the relationship with the accused. Of course if no doubt exists that the accused committed the act, the decision to confront the accused is straight forward.

In the case regarding the expensive missing stainless steel pump, I asked the trusted employee if he knew about the missing pump without outright accusing him of the theft. The response was that he didn't know how the pump went missing. Fortunately, the financial condition of my company was sufficiently strong such that a new pump could be purchased to replace the missing pump.

When there is sufficient doubt in a situation, it is best to provide an escape route so that the accused can exit with dignity. That is the mangy dog style of management.

Saving Fluid Process Systems - Software Development

During the early years of Fluid Process Systems it became apparent that accounting software was necessary to keep track of the sales, invoices and accounts payable. We purchased several software packages but in the end we were unable to implement them to manage our small business. It just so happened that a person by the name of John Blalock officed in the same building that we were in. John and I became good friends. John managed an investment business using software he personally developed using the Clipper software development program. Little by little John began to share some the ways that the Clipper platform might be able to benefit my water treatment business. John taught me the basics of the software development program and little by little I began to use the Clipper software to develop an accounting program for use within our company.

In the end, I became very proficient in developing the software programs that my company needed to operate effectively. I became the on-site software guru at Fluid Process Systems. I developed a sales order program that worked side by side with the invoice system. I also developed a service software application designed to allow our service department to properly track the service exchange DI tanks that were vital to our company's sales.

As time went on, I delved into the development of a Clipper based program that could be used to allow communications from a programmable logic controller manufactured by IDEC Electronics to a desk top computer.

At that time, we used IDEC Electronics programmable logic controllers to control the reverse osmosis systems. The communications link was done by manipulating the RS232 serial ports that connected the IDEC controller to the personal desktop computer. The controller system software was used to connect the RO system controller (IDEC controller) to the personal desktop computers. I used the acronym PMS to signify the Process Monitoring Software. I remember the "eureka moment" when I was first able to get the RO system controller to send data across the cable to the Clipper software on the personal computer desktop. It was an exciting moment when I made that communication link occur. Eventually I developed a statistical process control (SPC) software that was used to analyze in real time, the data that was archived by the process monitoring software. We were far ahead of our competition as far as controller systems were concerned.

Business Recognition

In 1994, the Greater El Paso Chamber of Commerce held an award ceremony to showcase the local businesses in El Paso. They selected 30 small companies as the region's fastest growing businesses in the El Paso area. I was awarded "Outstanding Minority Small Business Entrepreneur" by the "El Paso Small Business Consortium" in 1994 and was recognized as "One of El Paso's Emerging 30 - The Region's Fastest Growing Businesses". It was a proud moment for me to  receive those recognitions. The photograph on the left shows me receiving one of the awards.

Saving The Company – Trade Secret Infringement

In 1997, an employee of mine by the name of Lorenzo Beltran informed me that he was aware of some shenanigans going on with another employee of mine. The employee's name was Ruben Soto. Lorenzo informed me that he had knowledge of Ruben Soto making presentations to several of my clients in hopes of steering them away to his new company that he was in the process of forming. As a result, I visited one of the clients that Lorenzo had indicated that Ruben had contacted and I indeed confirmed that Ruben had solicited that client to join his new company. The following day, when Ruben showed up for work, I confronted him with the information I had learned the day before. He hemmed and hawed but he didn't deny that he had attempted to sway the client toward his new company. I then told him that I was relieving him from his responsibilities with my company and I then escorted him to the exit door. That was the end of Ruben Soto with my company. I later found out that Sergio Perez, another employee of mine, had joined Ruben Soto with his new company.

I contacted an attorney by the name of Mark Osborn with the law offices of Kemp, Smith LLP and briefed him on what had happened with Ruben Soto and now Sergio Perez. Mark Osborn indicated that a charge could be brought against Ruben Soto and Sergio Perez for breach of trade secrets. In essence they had absconded with information from my company and now they were claiming that the information had been generated by their company. I sued them for breach of trade secret infringement.

We fought in court. They kept denying that they used material from Fluid Process Systems in developing their business. This went on for about 8 months. At that point in time, I suddenly had a Eureka moment. I remembered that I had seen some Material Safety Data Sheets (MSDS) that they had printed that applied to their water treatment products. Several of their MSDS documents had this tell- tale sign that appeared on their printed documents. Specifically, the tell-tale sign was a characteristic of printed documents that resulted when the word processor program known as Wordstar® was used to print a document. When that specific word processor program was used to print a document, it characteristically printed an underlined multi-word phrase or an underlined multi-word title in such a way that a second underline symbol was printed in the space between the words to result in what appeared to be a double underline. This was a characteristic of the WordStar® word processor program. This meant that they stole the WordStar® word processor software from my company.

My lawyer, Mark Osborn from Kemp, Smith LLP presented this as evidence to the presiding Judge on the case. The Judge asked Ruben Soto about this. At the same time that Ruben was asked the question, I turned and looked at Sergio Perez. Sergio Perez placed his hands over his face and nodded sideways as if to indicate that they had now been caught red handed. The Judge asked Ruben if indeed his documents had been produced using the WordStar® software program and he responded in the affirmative. My lawyer then told the Judge that the WordStar® software was no longer available in the market because the new Windows software 3.1 had superseded the WordStar® software. The Judge then asked Ruben Soto where he had obtained the software and he responded that he didn't know. He lied. Mark Osborn, my lawyer then recommended that the Judge sanction Ruben Soto and Sergio Perez. The presiding Judge then called a court session recess until the following week. The Judge admonished the defendants that they would be sanctioned and that the amount of the sanction would be discussed during the next scheduled hearing. During the preparations for the next hearing, Mark Osborn convinced me not to follow through with the sanction. He reasoned that Ruben and Sergio would probably fail after their first year of business given that most companies fail after their first year of operation. Instead, Mark Osborn indicated that we could ask the Judge to agree to force Ruben and Sergio to pay a special sanction. He proposed that 10% of each invoice that they issued during a one year period of time be made as payments to my company. I accepted Mark's proposal and that is how the special sanction was applied to Ruben and Sergio.

In retrospect, I should have insisted that the court review their monthly financial statements to insure that 10% of the invoices were indeed being paid without falsifying the invoice amounts. I could kick myself for accepting the sanction without the additional safeguards.

Horizon City Water Treatment Plant

One of the major sales efforts was the sale of a municipal RO system to the El Paso County Water Authority (EPCWA) that provides potable water to the town of Horizon City where we lived and still live. In 1998, I was able to persuade the Horizon Water Authority to consider the use of a reverse osmosis system as a means of eliminating the building moratorium that TNRCC (Texas Natural Resources Conservation Commission) had mandated on Horizon City due to poor city drinking water quality. The effort started in 1998 when I made a presentation to the board of directors of the EPCWA.

Eco Resources was the management company that operated the EPCWA day to day business operations. The general manager's name of Eco Resources was David Goodrum. David Goodrum convinced the board members to visit an existing municipal RO system located in Pascagoula, Mississippi. I accompanied the board members to review the system at Pascagoula. I presented the capital cost for the system as well as the expected on-going operational cost. Shortly thereafter, I participated in developing a joint venture company with a local contractor. The contractor was a person by the name of Benny Davis.

In the year of 1999, we were awarded a contract by the Horizon municipal district to construct the infrastructure buildings as well as the large reverse osmosis system. The system  was designed to produce 4 million gallons a day of reverse osmosis water. The total contract amount for the building infrastructure and the RO system was around $6,000,000.00. The building and the RO system was completed in the summer of the year 2000. It was placed in operation in February of 2000. As a result of this effort, Horizon City is now the fastest growing area in the county of El Paso, Texas. The El Paso Times published an article in September 3, 2000 titled "Brackish water leads to pure success". The photograph on the left was taken from that newspaper article.

The following is an internet link that describes the benefits that the investment brought to Horizon City. http://www.waterworld.com/articles/2003/03/ reverse-osmosis-plant- provides-cost-effective-solution-to -brackish-water-supply-near-el- paso.html

Horizon City Volunteer Fire Department

During 1983 through 1989, I was a volunteer fireman for Horizon City. Horizon City had a population of about 1500. At the time, the City was too small to have a paid fire department so many of us volunteered to make sure that fire protection services were available. I volunteered to be a fireman. I remember an elderly man by the name of Bud Dingy. He served as the trainer that provided fire fighting instructions during our weekly Tuesday meetings.

I participated in extinguishing several fires in the Horizon City area as a fire fighter. During the last two years of my volunteer period starting in 1987, I held the position of Fire Chief of the Fire Department. During my tenure as Fire Chief, I became interested in making sure that our volunteer firemen had the same level of technical expertise as those firemen in a paid fire department like El Paso's. My goal became that of developing a program within our department to certify all of the volunteers in the same way as the firemen for the City of El Paso. We integrated the State of Texas firemen regulations and procedures to train our volunteer fire fighters to those State standards. During my tenure, the Horizon City Fire Department gained a positive reputation. I remember that the fire fighting personnel from Clint, Texas and Socorro, Texas participated in our training sessions in Horizon City.

A while has passed since 1996 when I promoted to the position of Fire Chief but I am happy to say that through those efforts, we now have certified, paid fire fighters in the Horizon City Fire Department. Looking back at that experience sometimes brings shivers up my spine. As unpaid volunteers, we risked our lives without the benefit of having life or health insurance through the fire department. Thank God nobody got hurt during the trainings or the fire fighting episodes. Anyway, after my 2 years of service as Fire Chief, another fire fighter by the name of Allen Keys took over as Fire Chief. My objective has been that the leadership be changed once every two years to allow the fire fighters a chance for promotion. It turned out not to be so. Allen Keys remained in the position of Fire Chief for many years.

An Expensive Mistake In Velardeña Durango - 1990

We all make mistakes once in a while during our lifetimes; I am no exception. In 1990, I spent $23,000 dollars funding a mining operation in a place called Velardeña, Durango near the large city of Torreon, Coahuila in Mexico. The village of Velardeña is located about 90 miles to the south of Torreon. By mining operations I literally mean constructing a hole in the side of a mountain.

About 3 years earlier, I met a person by the name of Gustavo Ramirez. He was a friend of a trusted employee of mine. Gustavo visited my company, Fluid Process Systems, in El Paso. Gustavo was involved in the sales of water softeners in his home town of Torreon, Coahuila. He purchased water softeners from us and always paid cash for the softeners that he purchased. During chit chats he would describe an additional business having to do with the operation of a mine near Torreon. He would invite us to visit him in his hometown of Torreon.

On one occasion, my trusted employee and I made a trip to Chihuahua to visit some of our clients. While in Chihuahua, my trusted employee suggested that we might want to travel south to Torreon to visit Gustavo and some of his clients. It seemed an easy thing to do since we were only 4 or 5 hours drive south from Chihuahua to Torreon. We arrived and we spent some time with Gustavo.

Gustavo took us to meet his brother, Sergio Ramirez, who also lived in Torreon. During our visit with Sergio, he described the mining operation he had south near the small town of Velardeña, Durango. Sergio was very interested in showing us the mine and so we traveled to Velardeña for a one day visit. Sergio showed us a nearby mining operation operated by ASARCO whose formal name was American Smelting and Refining Company. Sergio indicated that he needed investors to fund the on-going operations of his mine. He suggested that I could become a partner in the operations and profitability of the mine along with Gustavo, his brother. They painted a very convincing picture of the operations of the mine. The mine produced zinc, lead, silver and gold.

They convinced me to invest $23,000 dollars and in return, I would get a 1/3 ownership in the mines' profit. By the way, they forecasted about $70,000 dollars in profits in a 3 month time period. I agreed to provide the funds they were asking for and I drafted up a hand written agreement in Spanish that detailed the investment and the payback of the money in a 3 month time period. All 3 of us signed the agreement and my trusted employee and I returned back to El Paso. I was now in the mining business.

A week later, Gustavo showed up in El Paso and true to my word, I withdrew $23,000 dollars from that bank and provided it to him. After having turned over the money to Gustavo, I went about my business of running Fluid Process Systems. Three months later I contacted Gustavo by telephone and he proceeded to tell me that the mine's profitability had been achieved and that he would be traveling to El Paso shortly to pay back the loan.

Weeks went by without Gustavo showing up. I decided that my trusted employee and I should travel to Torreon to meet up with Gustavo and Sergio. We arrived in Torreon and we met with Gustavo and Sergio. They indicated that they had run into some unexpected expenses with the mine and told me that they would be sending me the money in about a month. They again took us to visit the mine. To hear them speak about the mine, one would think that the mine was very productive. We left Torreon and waited about a month for the money.

I resumed calling Gustavo and Sergio and now neither would answer their phones. Gustavo showed up at our El Paso offices about 2 weeks later and this time told me that the money would be forthcoming in a month. A month went by without a call from them. I made more calls to Torreon but failed to connect with them. During the next few years I made more calls to try and reach Gustavo or Sergio but I was ultimately unsuccessful at reaching them.

I visited a Mexican lawyer and discussed the situation with him. The lawyer basically told me that since there was no formal written agreement regarding the loan, it was going to be next to impossible to legally attempt to recover the money. In the lawyer's opinion, the hand written agreement I had drafted and that we all signed wasn't good enough. The lawyer was right; I had no legal formal contract to back up the loan of money I made to Sergio and Gustavo. I never heard from them again. It was a hard pill to swallow. I am not proud of it but I did spend $23,000 dollars foolishly.

Thank God for Corruption - 1999

This story involves my son, Adrian. The events in this story took place during the course of several days starting on Wednesday, November 17, 1999. During that time, Adrian and I had previously agreed that it would be a great idea for our company to be represented at a trade show in Monterrey, Mexico which is about 1,200 miles drive distance south of Cd. Juarez. At the time, I owned a company by the name of Fluid Process

Systems, Inc. in the United States and another company by the name of Procesos de Fluido, S.A. de C.V. in Mexico.

Anyway, the plan was for him to take an airline flight from Cd. Juarez to Monterrey during that specific morning to prepare for the trade show. This story is an account of the events that occurred during several days that started that morning as he was crossing the border from El Paso to Cd. Juarez in his personal vehicle while on his way to the Cd. Juarez airport.

Adrian left the office on his way to the Cd. Juarez airport. As he crossed the Ysleta/Zaragoza international bridge, the Mexican customs agents inspected his pickup truck. They found several boxes of shotgun shells and a pellet hand gun. Public ownership of firearms and ammunition by the public is illegal in Mexico. As a result, Adrian was arrested by the customs agent. He was taken to the Cd. Juarez main customs facility by the arresting agent.

Adrian called me on the cell phone while being transported to the main customs building. He told me where he was being taken. I crossed the Ysleta/Zaragoza international bridge and proceeded to drive to the main customs facility in Cd. Juarez. I caught up with him as he was being processed there.

He was told to sign a statement that was drawn up by the customs agent. The dreaded phrase "levantar el acta" means that the officer prepares a written statement and then has the arrested person sign the statement. The statement indicated that he had been caught in possession of the pellet hand gun and the three boxes of shotgun shells. He signed the statement.

It just so happened that Raul Guerrero, a trusted employee, had called his sister in Cd. Juarez. He had described Adrian's problem to his sister and in turn, his sister called a Mexican attorney that specialized in Mexican customs law. I presumed that Raul's sister briefed the Mexican attorney because he showed up at the Mexican customs facility where Adrian was being processed. That is where I first met the attorney. His name was Alberto Medrano Villareal. The attorney quickly attended to Adrian's problem with the Mexican customs agents. The attorney told me that Adrian would probably be held for 3 days at an interim holding facility called the "PGR" facility and then would be transferred to the Federal prison known as "CERESO". It took me a while to determine the meaning of the acronym "PGR". Everyone took it for granted that we knew what it was. "PGR" stands for "Procuradoria General De La Republica" and is translated to English as "Attorney General's Office". This facility is a temporary holding jail. "CERESO" on the other hand is the Federal prison. Anyway, if found guilty, he would be held for up to 5 years at the "CERESO" facility.

After Adrian was taken from the customs facility on his way to the "PGR" facility, the attorney told me that his services in representing Adrian would be $3,500 dollars. I told him that I would provide him with $2,000 dollars during the afternoon and would pay him the rest the following day on Thursday. He indicated that if everything worked out as planned, he would try to get Adrian released by the next day before he was transferred to the "CERESO" prison.

After meeting with the attorney, I drove to the location of the "PGR" where Adrian had been taken. The guard at the "PGR" facility would only allow attorneys and police to enter into the facility. I was not allowed to enter the facility to meet up with Adrian. I then proceeded to travel to El Paso where I withdrew the $3,500 dollars from the bank.

I returned to Cd. Juarez where I met up with the attorney. I paid him the initial $2,000 dollars. I then proceeded to go to the "PGR" facility to again attempt to see if I would be allowed to meet with Adrian. It was now late in the afternoon. This time I was only allowed to enter through the "PGR" gate but only about 10 feet inside the courtyard. The guard yelled out Adrian Renteria's name and Adrian responded. Adrian was being held in a prison cell with about 15 other men. I then yelled out to Adrian that I was working on his release and Adrian yelled back in acknowledgement. I then took my leave and returned to El Paso.

The next day, I traveled back to the "PGR" facility. I met up with the attorney at the "PGR" gate. I provided him the additional payment of $1,500 dollars. He told me that he had been lucky in that the Judge in the "PGR" facility had been lenient and in fact Adrian was going to be released sometime during the morning. For now , the attorney told me to wait near the "PGR" gate while he went in to see about getting Adrian released.

It was now about 12:30 p.m. Adrian and the attorney finally emerged from the "PGR" jail facility. Adrian was carrying an unfolded red blanket and I noticed that his hair was untidy. Otherwise, he seemed in good condition. I hugged him. The attorney told us to go home and rest. I asked about getting the truck returned. He said that we should meet at this office at 10:00 a.m. the next day so that we could then proceed to the Mexican customs to start the procedure to get the truck returned.

As we walked to the car, I felt a great sense of relief that the worst was behind us. Adrian told me that all during the night he kept seeing a flashing light that appeared a distance away outside from the jail cell. He stared at the light all night long to help him keep from going to sleep. He didn't want to be caught by surprise by a guard or some of the inmates during the night. When morning came, he could now see that the light had been caused by the reflection of a CD that had been twirling in the air while being suspended by a string. That's how I learned that Adrian hadn't slept the entire night.

As we drove away, Adrian asked if I had told everyone that he had been released. I responded by telling him that he should tell everyone himself. He called Socorro and spoke with her. I could sense a sigh of relief in everyone at the office in El Paso. Socorro told Adrian to inform her when we crossed the bridge at the border as she was anxious to have us both leave Mexico. I asked Adrian if he wanted to stop anywhere to eat or drink something. He said he wasn't hungry or thirsty.

Later on I learned why Adrian did not want to eat or drink anything the day prior when he was detained. He told me that he didn't want to have to use the bathroom facilities at the Mexican facilities. In fact, he told me that the bathroom facilities at the "PGR" consisted of nothing more than a large circular hole in the concrete floor of the jail cell. The detainees were forced to defecate and urinate directly into the hole leaving behind a smelly stench. That was the reason Adrian did not accept offers of food and drink at the original detainment facility and now at the "PGR" facility. He also told me that the sleeping beds consisted of nothing more than horizontal concrete slabs sticking out from the walls. The blankets provided to them were thin sheets that actually didn't serve to keep the user warm from the cold of the night. Such was the condition of the jail cells in the "PGR" facility.

Anyway, after we left the "PGR" facility, we proceeded to travel to the office in El Paso. Adrian was very talkative. He was asking many questions about what had happened on the outside to gain his release.

Looking back at the selection of Mr. Medrano Villareal as our attorney, it seems to me that we were very lucky to have employed his services. It is usual courtesy when introduced to an individual to present one's business card. When we first met, he gave me his business card and I provided him my business card as well. I never stopped to look at his business card because everything was progressing at such a fast pace. It wasn't until after we gained Adrian's release that I took the time to read his business card. I found that his business card showed that he was the National Vice President of an organization called "Federacion Nacional De Colegios, Barras Y Asociaciones De Abogados". The English translation of the organization's title is "National Federation of Colleges, Bars and Associations of Attorneys". It appeared to be a very prestigious national position in Mexico. We were lucky.

I don't mind saying that the problem that was presented to me that day was frightening. I know that I have the ability to defend myself when I am confronted with problems of the same gravity here in the United States. Even though I have owned a business in Mexico since 1988, I cannot truly sense that I have the ability to defend myself when confronted with a serious problem in Mexico.

The fact that Adrian was forced to sign an "acta" that was written in Spanish without the benefit of having the ability to fully comprehend what was contained in the document and without an attorney, is proof that things in Mexico are done without a sense of due process. The fact that the Mexican Judge's decision could have sent Adrian to the "CERESO" Federal penitentiary for up to 5 years without the benefit of a jury, is proof that things in Mexico are done again without a sense of due process.

I feared for Adrian during those first two days. A potential 5 year stay at the "CERESO" Federal penitentiary stared Adrian squarely in the face. What turned out to more frightening was that my attorney told me that $1,000 dollars of the amount that I paid him went to personally pay the Mexican Judge that ruled on Adrian's case at the "PGR" facility. That money was the reason for the favorable outcome of Adrian's case. The moral of the story . . . "Thank God for Corruption".

The Passing of My Father - 2000

My father passed away on July 24, 2000. I remember receiving a call from Mario my brother. Mario called me to tell me that my father was very ill and that I should proceed immediately to his home in Fabens. I told Socorro about the problem and then immediately began to travel to Fabens. On our way to Fabens on the I-10 freeway, I noticed an ambulance with emergency lights flashing proceeding in the opposite direction towards El  Paso. I assumed that it was the ambulance carrying my father to a hospital in El Paso. I proceeded to the Fabens exit from the I-10 freeway and turned back around to follow the ambulance. I called Mario to inquire about which hospital my father was being taken. Mario told me that he was being taken to Del Sol Medical Center. I proceeded to drive on the I-10 freeway as fast as possible to Del Sol Medical Center.

When I arrived, I was immediately taken to the emergency room. Mario was already there with my father lying on the emergency bed. My father had passed away. I couldn't believe it. Up to this point, my family had not suffered a death. We all stood beside him with him lying still in the bed. We were all sobbing. I touched his face and forehead. We were all grief stricken. My father had passed away as a result of a profuse head hemorrhage. We spent about an hour with him at the hospital. I can't remember the details about getting in touch with Hampton Valley Mortuary in Fabens. During the ensuing days, we visited with Mr. Hampton, the owner, to select the casket and to take care of the details of the funeral. I selected the very best casket available; my father was that important.

The day of the funeral arrived. I am of the opinion that family members must participate in burying their own. Such an important task can only be done by family members and should not be left up to the cemetery workers. Our family members buried my father that day. At the end of the burial, Mr. Hampton came to me to offer his condolences and at the same time attempted to hand me $100 dollars. He indicated that it was a reimbursement since I had overpaid that amount for the funeral. I told him "you're a good friend of mine, keep the money; you did a superb job, you earned it". Mr. Hampton and I became good friends.

About 6 months after the funeral, I ordered a headstone built for my father's grave. I asked my mother if she minded my ordering the headstone wide enough so that it would cover my father's plot adjacent to my mother's plot where she would be buried in the future. She indicated that she didn't mind and so I ordered the extended headstone that included her name with the date of death blank for the time being.

The following is the text from my father's obituary. *"Renteria, Jesus 72, of Fabens died Monday (July 24, 2000). Visitation will be from 2 to 5 p.m. today in Hampton Valley Mortuary, with rosary at 7 p.m. in Our Lady of Guadalupe Church. Funeral Mass will be at 11:30 a.m. Thursday in the same church. Burial will be in Fabens Catholic Cemetery. Survivors include his wife, Maria; his sons, Jesus Renteria Jr., Salvador Renteria, Mario Renteria and Martin Renteria; his daughters, Irma Golestaneh, Gloria Renteria, Graciela Rodriguez and Norma Lozano; one brother; one sister; 21 grandchildren; and 14 great-grandchildren. He retired from Fluid Process Systems Inc., and lived in Fabens for 51 years."*

Tracing My Father's Foot Steps - El Tizonazo – March 3, 2005

My father, Jesus Renteria, passed away in the year 2000. He was the first in my immediate family to die. His passing left a big hole in my being. As a result of his passing, I became very interested in anything having to do with my dear father. I remembered that for about 5 or 7 years prior to his death, on a yearly basis he would travel to a place in Mexico he referred to as "El Tizonazo". In fact, Graciela, my sister accompanied my father during one of his trips to "El Tizonazo". I remembered my father saying that the festival at "El Tizonazo" was held on the first Friday in March and that year the date of the first Friday in March was March 4, 2005. I decided to trace my father's foot steps by traveling to the place my father called "El Tizonazo". I was curious to see what drew him there every year. The following relates to the trip that I took into the state of Durango where "El Tizonazo" is located.

"El Tizonazo" is located in the state of Durango, Mexico. It is about 388 kilometers south of Delicias, Chihuahua. I left Cd. Juarez to travel southward at about noon on March 3, 2005. I stopped in Chihuahua at the Radison Hotel to send some business emails using my laptop. I arrived at my Tio Fernando Renteria's house at about 6:00 pm that day. The Mexican word Tio translates to Uncle in English. My Tio Fernando was working so I didn't get to say hello to him. I visited his family for about an hour and then left for Jimenez, Mexico which is located south of Delicias. I arrived in Jimenez at about 10:30 pm. I stayed that night at a motel in Jimenez.

I started out the next day (March 4, 2005) to Parral which is located west of Jimenez, Mexico. I asked the lady at the motel front desk for directions to "El Tizonazo". She didn't know exactly, but told me that I should travel to Parral and then take the road south to Durango. She indicated that anyone on the road to Durango would be able to be more specific as to how to get to "El Tizonazo". I left Jimenez at about 7:00 am and arrived in Parral at about 7:45 am. I ate breakfast and asked the waitress at the restaurant for directions to "El Tizonazo". She knew how to get there and gave me detailed directions.

I left Parral at about 8:30 am. Once on the road to Jimenez, I traveled for about 2 hours. Somehow, I missed the turn-off west to "El Tizonazo" from the main road. I had the feeling that the previous turn off was the one I should have taken. I stopped at a lonely home on the side of the road and asked a woman for directions. She told me that I should turn back because I had missed the turn off about 10 kilometers back.

I finally arrived at "El Tizonazo" at about 11:00 am. The site is home to about 15 homes surrounding a Catholic Church. The following is contained in the sign that is placed in the church courtyard:

> Santuario y Parroquia del Señor de Los Guerreros San Jose
> de Tizonazo, Indé

I now knew that my father's reference to "El Tizonazo" was to a place formally known as "San Jose de Tizonazo, Indé".

The location of "El Tizonazo" had 15 homes and Catholic Church surrounded by hundreds of people along with tents and sun shades scattered here and there. There were vendor stands where people were selling food, candies and religious objects. It was a carnival type of atmosphere. I was walking in the place that my father walked when he was alive 6 years ago.

The church courtyard seemed to be the center of the festivities. At the courtyard center were several "matachines" groups. The Spanish word "matachines" is used to describe a troupe of Indian-like dancers that dance to the rhythm of drums. The dancers use simple, make-believe bows and arrows as well as hand rattles called "maracas" to make noise as they dance in rhythm to the beat of the drums being played by others in the troupe. The "Indians" dance in honor of the Mexican version of the Virgin Mary which in Mexico is known as "La Virgen Maria". There were tons of people watching the dancing. The photograph on the left shows the Indians (matachines) dancing.

I made my way to the church entrance which was clogged with people. A throng of people stood at the entrance inching forward to enter the actual church building. The crowd was inching along toward the entrance. After about 30 minutes of inching along with the crowd, I passed through the entrance of the church. I finally saw why the multitudes of people were trying to gain access into the church. Near the altar deep inside the church was a life size statue of Jesus Christ. As the people inched past the statue, each person would kiss the statue and then slowly continue on to exit through the side exit of the church. Before exiting the church, I noticed a large board containing a multitude of pictures attached to it. I asked about the pictures and I was told that the pictures were those of deceased family members whose families chose to place them there. They did so in hopes that their souls would be saved by God. Anyway, as the procession continued, I reminded myself that this is what my father did when he came to pay homage to the Jesus Christ figure inside the church. Stuck in the procession of people, I finally exited from the church.

I continued walking through the crowded outdoors passing by a variety of vendors selling candies, food and religious items. For such a little town, the crowd of people was overwhelming. There were no bathrooms or portable "pottys" in sight. I wondered how the people relieved themselves without the presence of bathrooms.

After about three or four hours, I departed from the place where my father had once walked. I retraced my way back to the main paved road that led back north to Parral and drove the entire way back to El Paso without staying at a motel. Needless to say the ride back was very tiresome. I will always remember the trip I took to "El Tizonazo" to retrace my father's footsteps.

The Passing of My Mother - 2002

My mother passed away about 2 years after my father's death. She passed away on June 13, 2002. She had been sickly for about a year. I spent a good amount of time taking her to her doctors. She was having high blood pressure problems.

Toward the end, her kidneys began to falter so much so that she was placed on kidney dialysis treatments every other day. A doctor by the name of Dr. Gutierrez attended to my mother's medical needs. I remember him say that the heart, lungs and kidneys are tied together. If one of those components degrades, the other two will eventually degrade as well. I saw my mother go from a healthy person to a feeble person during her last year of life.  At the end, it was like seeing a grown person degrade to that of being a baby that needed a lot of care and attention. My mother passed away at Las Palmas Medical Center in El Paso from a heart attack. It had only been 2 years prior that my father had died. My mother's death was not as traumatic for me as my father's death. With my father, death came quickly. With my mother, death came gradually; we were expecting it. The time came when we would need Mr. Hampton's funeral service once again. We buried my mother in the cemetery plot adjacent to my father's grave and shortly thereafter, I hired the headstone company to update the date of death on her side of the headstone.

The following is the text from my mother's obituary:

"RENTERIA, MARIA E. 73, passed away June 13, 2002. A long time Fabens resident. Her husband, Jesus preceded her in death July 2000. She is survived by 4 sons; Jesus Jr., Salvador, Mario, and Martin Renteria. 4 daughters; Irma Golestaneh, Gloria Renteria, Graciela Rodriguez, and Norma Lozano. 21 Grand children and 15 GGC. 1 brother. Visitation Tuesday in Hampton Valley Mortuary Chapel 2 to 5 p.m. Rosary Service 7 p.m. at Our Lady of Guadalupe Catholic Church in Fabens, where the Funeral Mass will be at 9:30 a.m. Wednesday. Interment in Fabens Catholic Cemetery. Directed by Hampton Valley Mortuary, Fabens, Texas."

My Bodybuilding Experience

During 1998, I was suffering from a back problem. I could stand up straight but I had trouble lifting even light items from the floor. I decided that I needed to strengthen my back. I went by Gold's Gym in El Paso and spoke with a representative from Gold's Gym. The representative told me that they could provide training on the equipment at no charge. They were so positive about helping me with my back problem that I signed up for a year. The yearly fee was about $280.00 dollars.

I started working with the exercise machines avoiding the free weights such as dumbbells and barbells. I was told that exercise machines were safer to use especially for "newbies" like myself. I concentrated on one of the machines that was used to exercise the back. I slowly moved on to other machines that were a little more challenging. I made good friends that were also "newbies". I spent 2 years working on exercise machines forever eyeing the young men that were lifting heavier free weights.

Eventually, I mustered the courage to move on to exercising with light free weights. Free weights are more challenging because the weight lifting involves more levels of degrees of freedom. The phrase degrees of freedom means that the weights can move up and down, forward and reverse and finally left and right and therefore muscle development is more uniform and complete. The price of uniform and complete muscle development is more danger when handling the weights. I was still a neophyte but now with the big boys as it related to lifting free weights.

The objective in building muscle is to gradually increase the weight of the free weights over an extended time frame. At a certain point in my development I decided to hire a trainer to assist me in my bodybuilding development. The cost of a trainer was $25.00 dollars per hour. I would hire a trainer twice a week for one hour during each session.

The trainer I remember the most was a young man by the name of Phillip Gonzalez. He was well built from a muscle standpoint and he knew full well the methods in building body muscle. Remember I was 47 years old when I first started exercising and now at 50-53 years of age I was working with free weights. Phillip was about 30 years of age at the time. In the year 2005, Phillip was 34 years of age and I was 54 years of age. Phillip and I decided to compete in a bodybuilding show that was to be held in July of 2006. It was fully a year before the bodybuilding show. I shadowed his exercising during that year. It meant pushing heavier and heavier weights in order to build the muscle as much as possible.

It was now 4 months before the bodybuilding show and Phillip indicated that our diet was now to be only chicken, salads and protein shakes. Fried foods and foods loaded with sugar were to be avoided. The picture on the left shows a typical simple meal consisting of chicken, rice and spinach. In the 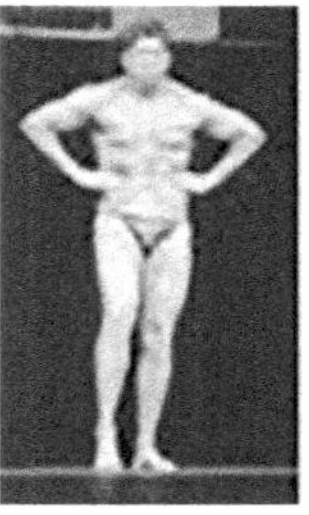 meantime, we continued to exercise with heavier and heavier weights.

It was now 2 weeks before the bodybuilding show and Phillip told me that I should now ration the amount of water I would be drinking. The objective now was to lose as much body weight as possible while at the same time promoting visible muscle. He also told me to purchase a certain type of skimpy show undergarment that I would wear during the bodybuilding show.

The day of the show arrived. It was in July of 2006 when I was 55 years of age. The bodybuilding show was held at the auditorium of the University of Texas at El Paso. There were several age categories in which bodybuilders could compete in. For example, the first category consisted of bodybuilders whose age  was no greater than 29 years of age. The next categories were 30 to 39, 40 to 49 and finally bodybuilders 50 years old and above. Phillip competed in the 30 to 39 age bracket while I competed in the 50 and higher age bracket.

In the end, Phillip earned first place in his age bracket. There were only 4 competitors in my age bracket and I came out 4th in my age bracket. One can say that I came out last.

The photograph on the left shows two of several poses we were required to perform during the show. Needless to say, I was afraid to compete. Who is his right mind dawns skimpy underwear and has a panel of judges judge his body? I felt I needed to compete just to prove to myself that I could . . . if that makes any sense. Had I not competed, I would always have wondered what it felt like. I competed in something that very few people ever experience. In the end, I'm glad I did it all.

The Sale of Fluid Process Systems, Inc. - 1997

During 1997, Culligan International from Northbrook, IL became interested in purchasing Fluid Process Systems, Inc. I interfaced with a person by the name of Evan Lovell who represented Culligan International. They performed a very thorough review of the company to determine if FPS was compatible with their company. They were also interested in purchasing the Mexico operations which was then known as Fluid Process Systems de Mexico. I had no experience in selling my companies so the process of courting Culligan International was an eye opener for me.

After about 4 months of being scrutinized by Culligan International, we finally arrived at a consensus with Culligan International and fixed the price of the sale at an amount of $943,000.00. The signing was supposed to occur at 9:00 am in the morning. Ten minutes before the signing time, Evan Lovell received a call from his corporate headquarters directing him to cancel the purchase. It turned out that Culligan International had cold feet about the acquisition and decided to pull out of the deal. Culligan almost settled on the purchase of my company for $943,000.00 in 1998. I came that close to selling my company.

The End of Fluid Process Systems, Inc.

At the apex of Fluid Process Systems, Inc., the company achieved 2.5 million dollars in sales. I continued with Fluid Process Systems, Inc. until August of 2003. At that time, I was able to sell the cooling tower and boiler treatment segment of the business to Garratt-Callahan Company headquartered in Burlingame, California. Fluid Process Systems, Inc. continued operating by providing service exchange DI and RO systems to its client base in El Paso.

Through a series of mistakes relating to my business, I shut down Fluid Process Systems, Inc. in October of 2006. After shutting down my business, I found that my accounting personnel had not filed and had not paid the IRS Form 940 and 941 taxes owed by my company. I filed for bankruptcy protection in December 2006. My bankruptcy application was accepted by the Bankruptcy Court in May of 2008. I accepted the responsibility for the debts owed as part of the bankruptcy plan. I began making monthly payments of $3,000.00 dollars per month and then $3,600.00 per month until I finally paid back approximately $192,000.00. My bankruptcy attorney was Mr. Bud Kirk and the case number was 06-31379. The bankruptcy was a series of mistakes that shook me to the core.

The Passing of Gloria Renteria - 2011

Gloria, my sister, was the fourth sibling of the entire 8 siblings in the Renteria family. Gloria retired early from working at El Paso Electric as an executive secretary. During the final years of her life she became very forgetful. She frequently spoke the familiar phrase of "I am losing it." By that she meant that she was finding it more and more difficult to remember very basic everyday things. Martin and I took over the responsibility of taking care of the day to day things for Gloria.

At a certain point in Gloria's memory degradation, it became apparent to Martin and I that she was not able to care for herself at her home. Martin and I decided to place her in a nursing home in El Paso. She did better in the nursing home environment although she was prone to falling on the floor. Several times, we were alerted by the nursing staff that Gloria had taken a bad fall and had hurt herself. After about a year in that environment, Gloria started to refuse to eat and she became very frail. After a while she wouldn't eat at all. That is when she began to lose consciousness from time to time. Gloria finally passed away at the nursing home. She was the third family member to pass away.

The following is the obituary for Gloria Renteria, my sister:

> *RENTERIA, GLORIA, 54, Visitation: 2-8:30 p.m. Wed. Jan. 19, 2011 at San Jose Fabens Chapel with Vigil at 7 p.m. Funeral Mass: 10:30 a.m. Thur. Jan. 20 at Our Lady of Guadalupe Catholic Church. Burial: Fabens Catholic Cemetery. Survived by daughter, Maricela Renteria; Son, Robert Thick; sisters, Irma*

Golestaneh, Graciela Rodriguez & Norma Lozano; brothers, Jesus, Salvador, Mario & Martin Renteria. Published in El Paso Times from Jan. 19 to Jan. 21, 2011

The Passing of Jesus Renteria, Jr., My Brother - 2014

Jesus, my brother, was the first sibling of the entire 8 siblings in the Renteria family. The nickname for Jesus is Chuy in Spanish. Chuy passed away on November 20, 2014 in California. He was 65 years of age at the time.

It all started when Martin received a phone call from a Dr. Catherine Van from California. She indicated to Martin that she found Martin's phone number in some papers that Chuy had in his possession. The doctor told Martin that Chuy was very sick and indeed close to passing away. After the phone call, Martin called me and told me about the call he had received from the doctor. The following morning, Martin and I began our trip to California to see Chuy at the hospital.

He was at the Kaiser Permanente hospital in Anaheim, California. Sure enough, Chuy was very sick. Dr. Van indicated that he had brain cancer and that it was slowly spreading to his body. We immediately called his family that lived in California to let them know of Chuy's condition. His family arrived at the hospital. It was good to see them there. That afternoon, Chuy was transferred to a hospice hospital in Orange, California. We spent the next few days at the hospice hospital with him.

I traveled back to El Paso after saying good bye to Chuy while Martin remained. Chuy passed away on November 20, 2014. Martin was with him when Chuy passed.

Martin returned back to El Paso the next day after Chuy's death. Back in El Paso, we gathered a group of family members and then we set out back to California to attended Chuy's funeral service. His funeral service was at St. Bonaventure Church in Huntington Beach, California on Friday, November 28, 2014. Chuy had been cremated and Sylvia, his daughter, kept his ashes. His ashes would later be interred at the Fabens Catholic Cemetery on April 10, 2015.

The following was published in the newspaper in El Paso as an announcement of his internment in the Fabens Catholic Cemetery. Note that the internment was on April 10, 2015.

RENTERIA JR., JESUS "CHUY", 65, Memorial Mass: 11 a.m. Friday, April 10, 2015 at Our Lady of Guadalupe Catholic Church in Fabens, TX. Inurnment: Our Lady of Guadalupe Cemetery. Published in El Paso Times from Apr. 7 to Apr. 14, 2015.

The following is the eulogy I presented during Chuy's service at Our Lady of Guadalupe Catholic Church in Fabens on April 10, 2015:

Good morning. I want to say a few words about my brother Chuy.

Chuy passed away this past November in California. Chuy left Fabens soon after his graduation back in 1968.

He left Fabens and began his life in the Los Angeles area. He lived in California for 46 years. Chuy and his wife Berta created a beautiful family in California. His daughter, Silvia, and Joshua, his grandson, are here today with us. I want to personally thank her and her family for allowing us to bring Chuy back to Fabens to be placed with my parents, Jesus and Maria, here in the Fabens cemetery. I think that Fabens is Chuy's home.

I too don't live in Fabens; however, I live nearby. But I look at Fabens as my home and someday, I too will come home to Fabens as Chuy is doing now.

But enough of that; I wanted to tell you about Chuy.

Chuy was about 2 years older than I. I grew up looking up to my older brother. You might say that I worshipped him because somehow he always seemed to know what to do, especially when we found ourselves in trouble and my mother would threaten to tell my dad about some mischievous thing we did. We dreaded the words that would frequently come out of my mother's mouth "le voy a decir a tú Papa de lo que hicieron cuando él salga del trabajo". Somehow Chuy would find a way to get us out of trouble; although not always.

Chuy and I started up a rock band during our high school years. He and I led the band during those years. Maybe I should say he led the band. I can still remember all of the youthful faces of the friends that were in the rock band with us. Chuy and I were in the Fabens High School band and that experience proved invaluable during our rock band days. Chuy was a master at developing the musical scores on paper. Simply by listening to the tune over and over again on the record player, he would write down the musical score and then would teach every band member his part. I don't think the youngsters of today will know what a record player is but in the stone age when we were kids, they were magical devices.

During the summers we would travel to California to work in the tomato and strawberry fields. When Chuy was 16 years of age and I was 14 years of age, he and I along with two other friends first traveled to California in search of farm work. As a result of that trip, our family became migrant farm workers. This is how he came to know Berta who would later be his wife.

Soon after his graduation in 1968, as usual, our family traveled to California but when time came for us to return to Fabens during the fall to begin the school year, Chuy stayed in California. All during my junior year at Fabens High School I remember feeling a sense of loss because Chuy was no longer nearby. I felt as if I was all alone all of a sudden.

In an effort to keep his spirits up during Chuy's last days when he was still conscious, I asked him about the girlfriends he had while he had been in high school back in Fabens. I can say this because he is my brother but let there be no doubt, Chuy was a lady's man as a young man. And also let there be no doubt, he remembered the names of the girlfriends as well as their ranking from OK to beautiful. We had a good chuckle that day.

I do miss Chuy but he will always be with me in my heart so I can't say farewell to him because I know that he is here close by in Fabens. Thank you for coming and thank you for remembering him.

Garratt-Callahan Company

Sometime in mid-March of 2003, I received a call from a Robbie Hargrove who represented the company known as Garratt-Callahan Company. During the conversation, Robbie indicated that his company was interested in discussing the purchase of my company,

Fluid Process Systems, Incorporated. I indicated that I was interested in discussing the subject. We agreed to meet a week later.

I met with Robbie Hargrove a week later. He indicated that his company was very interested in acquiring the water treatment business portion of my company. He indicated that they were not interested in the reverse osmosis and deionization segment of the business because their core business was in cooling water and boiler water treatment. Purchasing the Fluid Process Systems water treatment business would give Garratt-Callahan a solid foot-hold in the water treatment business in the El Paso area as well as in Cd. Juarez and Chihuahua City in Mexico. We both agreed in principal to continue the dialog with the hopes that the Fluid Process System water treatment business could be incorporated into the overall Garratt-Callahan Company business activity.

During April through August of 2003, I provided information on Fluid Process Systems, Inc. to Matt Colvin of Garratt-Callahan Company. Matt Colvin was the director of finance. At the conclusion, we decided that I should leave Fluid Process Systems, Inc. in August 2003 and then continue to work full time for Garratt-Callahan Company. In return, Garratt-Callahan would pay an amount of about

$400,000.00 in return for the merger of the Fluid Process Systems, Inc. water treatment business. I left Fluid Process Systems, Inc. sometime in August 2003. The remaining Fluid Process Systems, Inc. business was then managed by my son Adrian and daughter Amanda.

Shortly thereafter, Robbie Hargrove started a new Mexican company named Garratt Callahan International, S de R.L. de C.V. The letters after

Garratt Callahan International stand for "Sociedad de Responsabilidad Limitada de Capital Variable" which in English is translated to Society of Limited Responsibility of Variable Capital. Three service technicians were hired in Mexico. The clients on the Mexico side were serviced by Garratt Callahan International while the clients on the U.S. side were absorbed by Garratt-Callahan Company. I began working for Garratt-Callahan Company in August 2003.

I reported to Robbie Hargrove when I began to work for Garratt-Callahan Company. I worked there until the year 2017.

Among some of my achievements was selling a $426,000 dollar system to the Air Force facility located near Las Cruces, New Mexico in the year 2012. Along with the regular business, the system I sold to the Air Force facility placed me as a top sales member of the company. As a result, I was invited to participate in the company ship cruise that was awarded to the top sales persons in the company. Unfortunately, Socorro and I didn't participate in the cruise that year. My supervisor Robbie Hargrove, had a difference of opinion with the National Sales Manager. As a result, Robbie suggested that I not go on the cruise and I am sorry to say that Socorro and I did not participate in the cruise during that year.

Another large system I sold was a water treatment system for a new hospital at Fort Bliss, Texas in the year 2015. The price of the system was $328,000 dollars. At about the same time, I sold a $72,000 dollar system to Mountain View Regional Hospital in Las Cruces. The total of the two systems alone was $400,000 dollars. Along with other smaller ongoing sales, I became the 6th top sales person in the company. As a result, I was again invited to participate in the company cruise. Socorro and I traveled by airline from El Paso to Fort Lauderdale, 
Florida. At Fort Lauderdale we boarded the Royal Caribbean Cruise Line ship named Allure of the Seas. We spent a week on the cruise and traveled to the Bahamas Islands and then to St. Thomas, Virgin Islands finally to St. Maarten, Virgin Islands. We enjoyed the cruise that was fully paid for by Garratt-Callahan Company. The photograph on the left shows Socorro and I standing in front of the ship.

In October of 2017, I resigned from the company. I continued working as a part time contractor for the company until the year 2020 when I finally ended my relationship with Garratt-Callahan Company.

Alicia and Araceli - 2016

My wife and I were invited to an East Lake High School luncheon function at a local restaurant known as Cattleman's Steakhouse. The date of the luncheon function was On May 21, 2016. The luncheon was given in honor of eleven members of the National Technical Honor Society. My Grand Daughter, Araceli Renteria, was soon to be graduating from the East Lake High School and my Grand Daughter was one of the top achievers in the National Technical Honor Society. In fact, another of my Grand Daughters, Alicia Renteria, would be the president of the East Lake Chapter of the National Technical Honor Society during the following school year and she was also present at the luncheon. Ten of the honorees were of Hispanic American origin and one honoree was of African American descent. There was not one honoree of Anglo descent in the honor presentation of that day. I make note of the absence of an Anglo descent honoree not to insinuate negatively but only to call attention to the fact that things have really changed from the time when I graduated from high school to now 46 years later when my Grand Children are graduating from their high school years. I am happy that both Araceli and Alicia are college bound students.

The Legend of Brains Bugito – January 1996

A funny thing happened on January 1996. It was during the time when we only had our first grandson, Alex. He was 3 months old at the time. My family and I took a mini-vacation trip to Ruidoso, New Mexico. More specifically, the funny thing happened on the way driving back home when we arrived at Cloudcroft, New Mexico. We were window shopping at the Cloudcroft curio shops Bund we happened upon a small business that specialized in photographing people dressed in western costumes.

We all dressed up in the business' wild west costumes and sat for two photographs. The first photograph was taken with only the men in the family. The second photograph was taken with only the women in the family. Of course, our family was very young; we only had Elsa, Adrian's wife, and Chris, Amanda's husband, as in-laws. Alex was a tiny, 3 month old baby of Chris and Amanda. Even Alex was dressed up in western attire for the photograph.

The following is a funny, tiny short story of the meanest and baddest baby west of the Pecos River that I named "Brains Bugito". Note "Brains Bugito" is shown in the photograph as the tiny baby in the coon skin hat sitting on Chris' lap. The tiny story follows:

> *"Brains Bugito" was the meanest and baddest baby west of the Pecos River. At three months of age and an awesome stature of 18 inches, Brains Bugito turned the Renteria family from a mild mannered, well meaning family to a bunch that is now known as "The Wild Bunch". Yep, Brains Bugito was the brains of it all. If you've got a few minutes, sit down, rest a spell and let me show you some pictures of the people that "Brains Bugito" turned bad.*
>
> *These are the members of "The Wild Bunch":*

- *Yep, the brains of the gang, "Brains Bugito", formerly known as Alejandro Babcock*
- *Savage Sal, formerly known as Sal Renteria*
- *Crazed Chris, formerly known as Chris Babcock*
- *Awful Adrian, formerly known as Adrian Renteria*
- *Angry Andy, formerly known as Andy Renteria*
- *Gruesome Guy, formerly known as Adan Renteria*

These are the women of questionable repute that belong to "The Wild Bunch":

- *Sadie Socorro, formerly knownas Socorro Renteria*
- *Eccentric Elsa, formerly known as, Elsa Renteria*
- *Aggressive Amanda, formerly known as Amanda Babcock*

A long time has passed since January 1996 when the photographs above were taken in Ruidoso, New Mexico. Now in the year 2020, my family has grown since January 1996.

Adrian and Elsa Dominguez who are shown in the pictures above now have a daughter by the name of Araceli Raquel. Amanda and Christopher Babcock who are in the pictures above are now parents to Ana Victoria and Antonio Benjamin in addition to Alejandro Cristobal who is in the above photograph and is here known as "Brains Bugito". Ana together with Riley Miyashiro are now parents to Akihito, my great grandson. Andy, my son, is now married to Diane Martinez. They are now parents of Alicia Renee, Alyena Marie, Abigail Elizabeth and Ariana Noelle. Adan, my son, is still single and doesn't have any children. I love all of my sons, my daughter, daughters-in- law, my son-in-law, grand children and my great grandson.

The End of the Journey and the Beginning of a New Journey - 2020

Now as I am writing this chapter, as of two weeks ago, I am no longer working for Garratt-Callahan Company. I am now fully retired. I have never been out of a job in my entire life and I have a feeling that this new journey is going to be difficult for me. There will no longer be any work induced timelines or deadlines. The deadlines now will be personal timelines that will result from day to day personal requirements.

The ever present worries that I had while I was in high school have come to a successful conclusion. My life's destiny was that I was going to be a farm hand working in the Fabens area. However, I was one of the lucky ones when in high school. My good grades in high school helped me turn my life around to the point where the road to college opened up. As a result, I was able to earn a college degree in engineering. I will forever remember and be grateful to Farah Manufacturing who provided me with a 4 year scholarship to attend the University of Texas at El Paso. The direction of my life's journey changed with a college degree. During my high school years, Hispanics didn't proceed to college after high school. A few of us lucked out.

A favorite song of mine debuted in 1963 and was sung by the group known as "Jay and the Americans". The name of the song is "Only In

America". The song says it all for me. The following are the lyrics of the song:

Only in America
Can a guy from anywhere
Go to sleep a pauper and wake up a millionaire

Only in America
Can a kid without a cent
Get a break and maybe grow up to be President

Only in America
Land of opportunity, yeah
Would a classy girl like you fall for a poor boy like me

Only in America
Can a kid who's washin' cars
Take a giant step and reach right up and touch the stars

Only in America
Could a dream like this come true
Could a guy like me start with nothing and end up with you

As I said before, the song says it all for me. I was a poor boy from Fabens that succeeded. Indeed America is a land of opportunity and I feel fortunate to have been an American.

I am now close to finishing this memoir which is called "Building Memories". "Building Memories" is a historical account that details where I came from, what I did and now what I will do afterwards. Here's to the start of a new journey and a good life in writing short stories, possibly involving "Brains Bugito".

To the readers of my memoir, I give my heartfelt thanks. Until we meet again.

The Family Tree

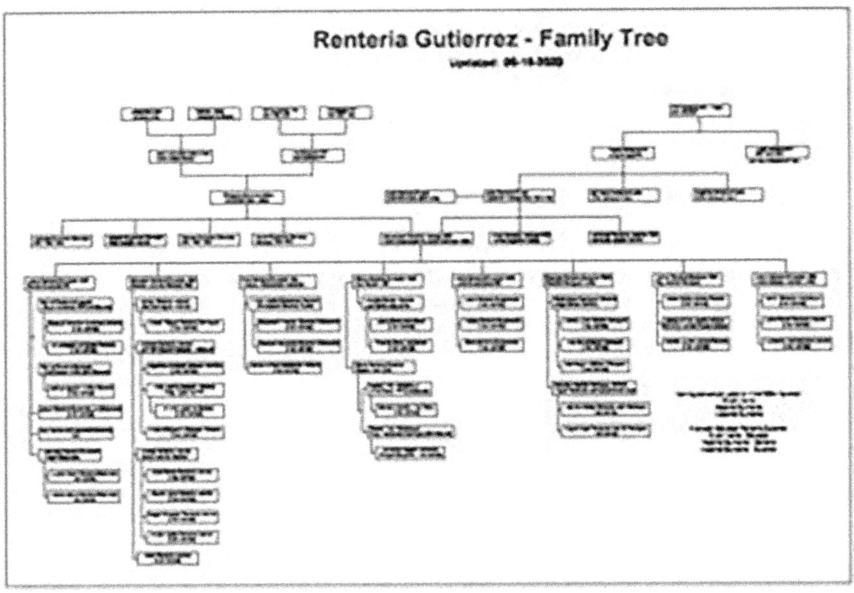